ASIAN LAW SERIES
SCHOOL OF LAW
UNIVERSITY OF WASHINGTON
Number 7

Asian Law Series
School of Law
University of Washington

The Asian Law Series was initiated with the cooperation of the University of Washington Press and the Institute for Comparative and Foreign Area Studies in 1969 in order to publish the results of several projects under way in Japanese, Chinese, and Korean law. The members of the editorial committee are: Herbert J. Ellison, Director of the Institute for Comparative and Foreign Area Studies; John O. Haley; and Dan Fenno Henderson, chairman.

1. *The Constitution of Japan: Its First Twenty Years, 1947–67*, edited by Dan Fenno Henderson
2. *Village "Contracts" in Tokugawa Japan*, by Dan Fenno Henderson
3. *Chinese Family Law and Social Change in Historic and Comparative Perspective*, edited by David C. Buxbaum
4. *Law and Politics in China's Foreign Trade*, edited by Victor H. Li
5. *Patent and Know-how Licensing in Japan and the United States*, edited by Teruo Doi and Warren L. Shattuck
6. *The Constitutional Case Law of Japan: Selected Supreme Court Decisions, 1961–70*, by Hiroshi Itoh and Lawrence Ward Beer
7. *Japan's Commission on the Constitution: The Final Report*, translated and edited by John M. Maki

Japan's Commission on the Constitution:

The Final Report

Translated and edited by

JOHN M. MAKI

UNIVERSITY OF WASHINGTON PRESS

Seattle and London

Library of Congress Cataloging in Publication Data
Japan. Kempō Chōsakai.
  Japan's Commission on the Constitution, the
final report.
  (Asian law series ; no. 7)
  Selected translation of Kempō Chōsakai hōkokusho.
  Bibliography: p.
  Includes index.
  1. Japan—Constitutional law. 2. Japan—
Constitutional history. I. Maki, John McGilvrey,
1909–   II. Title. III. Series.
LAW   342.52'024   80-50869
ISBN 0-295-95767-0

Preface

I FIRST LEARNED of Japan's Commission on the Constitution and its work in 1958–59 when I was in Japan as the fortunate recipient of a Fulbright research professorship. I was engaged in research on the Japanese Supreme Court's constitutional decisions, and that led me automatically in the direction of the commission, which was then in the initial stages of its operations. Early in 1959 I had the opportunity to hear Professor Takayanagi Kenzō,[1] its chairman, deliver a fascinating report on his recent discussion with General Douglas MacArthur on the origins of the Constitution. I concluded that any operation under the guidance of a man with the obvious wisdom and intellectual stature of Takayanagi-sensei was well worth serious attention.

For the next four years I followed the work of the commission, primarily through its published documents, with a mounting sense of excitement as the nature of its contributions became more and more apparent through the breadth of its consideration of virtually all conceivable constitution-related problems and the depth of its analysis of fundamental constitutional issues. In the summer of 1963 I was able to return to Japan when the commission was in the stage of drafting its reports, and to confer with Professor Takayanagi and members of his staff. It was already abundantly clear that the planned final report of the commission would be a major contribution to constitutional studies in Japan.

My reading of the final report after its publication in the early summer of 1964 convinced me that it should be translated and made available to an audience outside Japan broader than the tiny handful of those non-Japanese who are capable of reading the language. Circumstances prevented me from beginning the task, however, until the summer of 1970. After I had virtually completed a rough first draft, a new set of circum-

1. Names are given in the Japanese order: surname first, given name second.

stances forced still another delay of several years, and it was not until 1976 that I was able to complete the first draft.

The most visible problem connected with the translation is the sheer bulk of the original. Obviously a complete translation of the nearly 900 pages was out of the question. In these days of soaring publication costs, there could be no possible economic justification for a complete translation. I concluded that, even so, the first step in the translation should be a complete, though rough, first draft. Such a draft, I believed, would provide a sounder basis for a final version than would a running, selective translation. The rough draft ran to a little more than 900 pages of typescript.

Then followed the process of abbreviation. Fortunately, the original was organized in a fairly rigid mechanical manner, suitable for an objective, factual report, resulting in a fair amount of repetition that could be eliminated without confusing or misleading the reader. I also decided to eliminate some sixty pages of text dealing with the opinions of foreign scholars on the Constitution. Fortunately, the commission had already published a separate volume containing these opinions in the original languages.[2] I also eliminated the brief and repetitive introduction.

Because of their essentially narrative nature, it was impossible to reduce substantially the first three parts of the report. To do so would have eliminated a great deal of essential information. The long fourth part, therefore, amounting to more than 500 pages, became the target of substantial reduction. Part Four contains the opinions of the commissioners which were set forth in considerable detail, frequently verbatim. The reduction was achieved by the following devices: the retention of only those opinions that best exemplified the opposing views on each issue; the condensation of some opinions without attribution by name where it was possible to reduce them to general statements; and the retention of the original statement of opinion verbatim only in those cases where the opinions were apt illustrations of the general arguments put forth or were of intrinsic interest.

It was also possible to reduce by approximately one-half the final chapter of the report, "The Need for Constitutional Revision." The highly mechanical organization of this chapter resulted in a considerable amount of repetition, which made reduction a simple process. The gist of the arguments for and against revision was retained, even though considerable changes were made in the structure of the chapter itself.

Additional reduction in length was achieved through the omission of many hundreds of page references to the other commission reports on

2. *Comments and Observations by Foreign Scholars on Problems concerning the Constitution of Japan, 1946*, plus a seven-page supplement, 1964.

which this report was based. Omission of these references obviously creates no problems for the reader who does not read Japanese. Readers of Japanese can simply refer to the original. The latter will suffer some slight inconvenience in tracking down references because of the omission of some quotations from the original.

The only additions I have made to the original are the Appendix, the thumbnail biographical sketches of the commissioners and a brief bibliography. There was no real need in the original for the biographical material, but it does provide a minimum of information on those commissioners whose opinions might be regarded as particularly thought-provoking. The bibliography contains only a listing of the publications of the commission and of works cited in this translation.

It is a distinct pleasure, not a duty, to acknowledge the role both of individuals and of organizations who provided assistance and encouragement during the translation of the commission's report.

The late Professor Takayanagi stands first and foremost among those to whom I am indebted. As I have written above, my interest in the commission was first awakened when I heard his brilliant report, early in 1959, on the origins of the Constitution. Four years later, in the summer of 1963, he presented me with material and information that were invaluable in providing insights into the commission, its work, and his role in both. The more I delved into the work of the commission the greater became my admiration for his work therein, and the stronger my determination to make available to a non-Japanese audience the results of the commission's work. It was an honor and a privilege to have known this great leader in modern Japanese jurisprudence who was also an eloquent advocate of the rule of law and a staunch defender of Japan's constitutional democracy.

Also in the summer of 1963 Mr. Ohtomo Ichirō, then one of Professor Takayanagi's principal assistants, was most generous with both his time and assistance. He was also most helpful in assisting me in the acquisition of the documents of the commission.

I am especially indebted to Professor Satō Isao, a close associate of Professor Takayanagi, who was a principal consultant to the commission and later the main editor of the commission's report. Professor Satō was extremely helpful in the solution of some problems of translation and also contributed some invaluable advice when I was involved in the difficult task of deciding how and where the translation could be shortened.

I am also grateful to the Japan Foundation for a travel and research grant in the spring of 1973 which enabled me to visit Japan to consult with Professor Satō as I was about to complete the final version of the translation. A timely grant of a sabbatical leave by the Board of Trustees of the University of Massachusetts provided me with valuable time at a critical stage.

JOHN M. MAKI
Amherst, Massachusetts

Contents

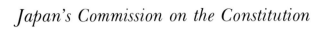

Japan's Commission on the Constitution

Introduction

ON 13 AUGUST 1957 Japan's Commission on the Constitution held its first meeting. Just under seven years later, on 3 July 1964, the commission's work came to an end with the formal submission of its final report to Prime Minister Ikeda Hayato. During the seven years of its life, the commission conducted a massive study of the Constitution of Japan, which had come into effect on 3 May 1947. In its investigations and deliberations the commission explored all matters relating to the Constitution: for example, the circumstances of its abnormal enactment under a military occupation following a lost war; a comprehensive examination of the manner in which the Constitution had actually operated; an analysis of all problems, large and small, relating to each of the document's ninety-nine articles (excluding four supplementary provisions relating to the transition from the Constitution of 1889 to the present one); a thorough examination of broad questions, major and minor, relating to the Constitution; a canvassing of the views of foreign scholars on questions relating to Japan's Constitution; a study of a broad range of foreign constitutions in a search for guidance in confronting Japan's constitutional problems; a compilation of the views of citizens on the Constitution, its operation, and possible shortcomings; and the opinions of all the members of the commission.

An account of the commission's work and its results was left behind in a massive collection of documentary material, primarily the published reports of the meetings of the commission and its committees.[1] The commission held 131 plenary sessions and its committees and subcom-

1. The material in this introduction relating to the documents of the Commission on the Constitution has been adapted from my article, "The Documents of Japan's Commission on the Constitution," 24, no. 3, *J. of Asian Studies*, May 1965, pp. 475–89, later reprinted in Henderson (ed.), *The Constitution of Japan: Its First Twenty Years, 1947–67* (1968), pp. 279–99.

mittees held 325 more. It also sponsored fifty-six public hearings. No less than 418 expert witnesses appeared at the committee sessions, and an additional 487 representatives of the public appeared at the hearings. The minutes of these meetings and a series of committee reports total around 40,000 pages, more than half of which are double-column. These published documents occupy about eight running feet of shelf space.

Even within the context of the total outpouring of the commission's documents, *The Report of Japan's Commission on the Constitution* is itself an impressive volume. Of its 1,161 pages, the main text occupies 882 pages comprising a foreword and four parts (*hen*), which are subdivided into chapters (*shō*) and sections (*setsu*). The remaining 279 pages consist of appended records (*bekki*) and tables (*beppyō*) that contain such valuable factual material relating to the commission and its operations as a list of commissioners giving their terms of service, a detailed chronology of the plenary meetings, bibliographical material, texts of important statements, and lists of members of committees. This translation includes only the main text of the report.

The foreword (not included in this translation) can be described as a general introduction to and a summary of the contents of the report. Part One contains a brief historical sketch of the commission. Part Two deals with the responsibilities, the organization, and the operations of the commission. Part Three concentrates on the investigations and subsequent deliberations of the commission. Part Four, by far the longest, is an exhaustive presentation of the opinions expressed by the commissioners on every issue relating to the Constitution, including the central question of its possible revision.

Released simultaneously with but separate from the report were twelve volumes of appended documents: a long volume containing the opinions of the individual commissioners; a report on the process of the enactment of the Constitution prepared by the special subcommittee created to deal with that fundamentally important question; three committee reports on the actual operations of the Constitution; three division reports on the deliberations on the results of the investigations; a brief report on the possible invalidity of the Constitution, a claim set forth by several commissioners; a report on basic constitutional problems; a report on the fifty-six public hearings held throughout the country by the commission; and a report on the overseas investigations of the commissioners which emphasized the opinions of foreign scholars on Japanese constitutional issues.

The very length of the report might lead the unwary reader to the false assumption that it contains all the material relating to any constitutional issue investigated and deliberated by the commission. While the report does provide a faithful general account of the commission's examination of all the constitutional problems before it, it falls considerably short of providing the full story.

A single example of a major issue, the emperor system, examined by the commission will indicate the size of the task confronting a dedicated researcher interested in seeking out all that the commission unearthed in its investigation of the issue. Such a hypothetical researcher would indeed find a great deal about the emperor system in the final report, but to search out all the material on the issue would involve an examination of the following material: the report of the First Division of the commission, an appended document; the report of the Third Committee, also an appended document; the minutes of the meetings of both the Third Division and the Third Committee; the report on the public hearings, also published as an appended document, as well as the minutes of the local, regional, and central public hearings; the appropriate sections of the final report and the minutes of the meetings of the special subcommittee on the process of the enactment of the Constitution; and finally, the minutes of the plenary meetings of the commission at which the emperor system was discussed. A similar process would be involved in a thorough investigation of any important problem addressed by the commission.

As impressive as the sheer bulk of the commission's work is, a matter of even greater moment is the intrinsic value of the material contained in the work. In the first place, the commission's study must be the most exhaustive ever undertaken of any nation's fundamental law. The report itself, even though only a small fraction of the commission's work, is a treasure house of material on all matters relating to the Constitution. Not only are major lines of constitutional theory and interpretation traced, but there is also a lengthy catalogue of problems relating to the actual operation of the fundamental law itself. Going beyond the matter of the Constitution in the narrow sense, the commission inevitably became involved in a wide range of problems—economic, social, legal, judicial, political, educational and others—created, touched on, or dealt with by the Constitution.

Writing several years after the commission had completed its work, Chairman Takayanagi described the basic policies that governed the commission's work.[2] I shall quote his words at some length because they constitute a useful preliminary guide for the reader to the report itself.

2. Takayanagi Kenzō, "Some Reminiscences of Japan's Commission on the Constitution," in Henderson, *The Constitution of Japan: Its First Twenty Years, 1947–67* (1968), pp. 71–88. The material quoted can be found on pp. 73–76. Several footnotes have been omitted.

The matters Professor Takayanagi writes about are contained in the report but are not readily apparent. He wrote as follows:

The concrete organization of the investigative and deliberative process as well as the basic policies to be followed by the Commission were left entirely to the discretion of the Commission. The basic policies in the conduct of such investigations and deliberations were decided upon as early as the end of the third plenary meeting which was held on October 2, 1957; these were strictly abided by until the Commission's work was completed. The policies were as follows:

1. All Commission meetings, except those of the steering committee, were to be open to the public.

Such a policy was unprecedented in the history of commissions in Japan. All of the Commission's operations thus proceeded in the public eye, not *in camera*. Leading newspapers throughout Japan assigned special reporters to attend and make reports on all Commission meetings—plenary, committee, or subcommittee. Local newspapers sent reporters to the public hearings held in their areas and the opinion of each public speaker was fully reported.

2. The stenographic notes of the Commission's proceedings were to be printed by the Printing Office of the Finance Ministry and adequate steps were to be taken to make them easily accessible to any interested person.

3. Persons who had practical experience with the Constitution, or learned scholars, whether in or out of the government, were to be called as witnesses to report their experiences or to express their opinions.

The aim of this policy was to ensure that investigation and deliberation would not be conducted by the Commission members alone but with the participation of all other qualified persons.

4. Public hearings were to be held.

The aim of this policy was to acquaint the Commission members with the practical experience and opinions of ordinary citizens.

5. In the absence of unanimity after due deliberation, the Commission was not to resort to majority rule. In such a case, the opinions of all members were to be fairly reported with a full statement of their reasons, whether these might be majority or minority opinions, whether favoring or opposing revision.

This policy deviated from the usual practice of commissions in Japan or elsewhere. In the ordinary situation, the opinion of the commission is decided by majority vote or, in the case of a tie, by the chairman. In view of the composition of the Commission, resulting from the nonparticipation of the Socialist Party, it would have been nonsensical to adopt the usual majority rule and thereafter declare that the majority was in favor of constitutional revision. The adoption of a majority technique is certainly necessary for a policy-making body, but the Commission did not consider itself as such. Its function was to furnish materials for policy-making bodies. For such a purpose quality of opinions would be more important than numerical strength.

In declaring this policy, the Commission also had in view the future participation of the Socialist Party, which probably had assumed that the majority rule would be adopted and that their minority opinions would be rejected. As a matter of fact, the Socialist Party did not send members to the Commission and discouraged others from appearing as witnesses. However, eminent jurists who had refused to become commission members, such as Professors Toshiyoshi Miyazawa, Shirō Kiyomiya and Sakae Wagatsuma, appeared before the Commission as witnesses at a later stage.

6. Fact-finding was to precede the policy discussion stage.

As a matter of fact, the fact-finding stage continued for some four years, commencing with fact-finding regarding the making of the Constitution. This mode of procedure was unusual if compared with the history of commissions in Japan. It was suggested by the practice of the British Royal Commissions. I had long felt that commissions in Japan should spend more time in fact-finding prior to the formulation of recommendations. I proposed adoption of this policy in the steering committee which readily agreed. The plenary session adopted the proposal although a minority preferred the usual method.

The British technique seemed to have two beneficial results. If members could agree on relevant facts after joint investigation, there would be a tendency to agree on policy. The fact-finding process would result, moreover, in a wealth of valuable information about actual current practice which could not be found elsewhere.

The Commission failed to fulfill this first function. Its duties covered a wide field and only a few members studied the fact-finding materials with scrupulous care. The Commission, however, amply fulfilled its second function.

The Commission considered it unwise to insist on cross-examination, a procedure which makes the facts found in the British Royal Commissions especially trustworthy. It had no power to compel witnesses to appear. It had to rely on the good will of witnesses who might otherwise have hesitated to appear if subjected to severe cross-examination. Moreover, even Japanese lawyers, who must now employ it in judicial trials, were not yet adequately trained in the art of cross-examination.

Looking back at the commission and its work from the perspective of the late 1970s, it is possible to arrive at a few tentative conclusions as to its significance to constitutionalism in modern Japan. As I have already emphasized, the greatest concrete contribution has been the sheer volume of material that the commission unearthed. For example, it is inconceivable that any future research can produce significant additional information on the critically important problem of the process of the enactment of the Constitution. The same can be said of other fundamentally important constitutional issues, such as the emperor system and the renunciation of war. In addition, factual material on every other constitutional issue also reposes in the commission's documents.

As a perusal of the fourth part of this translation will reveal, the commission also produced a comprehensive collection of constitutional theories, interpretations, and opinions. But these raise the single most important deficiency of the commission, one over which it had no control: the lack of direct involvement of some of Japan's leading constitutional scholars. Their views did not, however, go unrepresented in the commission, particularly by the minority of commissioners who steadfastly opposed constitutional revision.

The minutes of the meetings provide excellent insight into the general processes of deliberation and debate in Japan. Although this report provides glimpses of some of the heat that was generated within the debates in the commission, the minutes are much more lively. Those interested in the social process in Japan where consensus is reputed to reign supreme will undoubtedly be surprised to discover in their reading of this report, that no consensus was reached by the commission. As a matter of fact, no specific recommendation concerning constitutional revision emerged from the commission itself. It is very clear indeed that a solid majority of the commissioners favored revision, both in general and in specific matters, but those views were never converted into a formal recommendation from the commission itself, as Professor Takayanagi pointed out.

It is to the credit of the commission that the views of almost 500 private citizens on constitutional issues were not only heard in public hearings, but were also incorporated into the documentary record of the commission's operations. If nothing else, this testimony demonstrated the degree to which constitutional concerns had penetrated into the fabric of daily life in Japan.

While there can be no denying the fact that the commission did provide a vast store of material for the study of constitutionalism, it is difficult to determine its precise impact on the question of constitutional revision, which was not only the immediate inspiration for the creation of the commission but was also the constant theme of its deliberations. The easy answer is that it had no impact at all.

Legally and practically, the work of the commission was completed when it submitted its report to the late Ikeda Hayato, prime minister at the time. In a brief statement the prime minister declared simply that the report would be studied by the cabinet and duly transmitted to the National Diet. As a matter of fact, the report has never been formally forwarded to the Diet by the cabinet. In addition, there has never been any formal government (that is, cabinet) reaction to the report.

The movement to revise the Constitution has for all intents and purposes come to an end. The only specific issue that regularly comes up for discussion is the renunciation of war in Article 9. As the report of the commission shows, Article 9 has from the beginning been the most controversial provision in the Constitution. Conservative politicians continue to argue the necessity for revision of Article 9 if for no other reason than to remove the cloud of unconstitutionality under which the

Self-Defense Forces continue to exist. But the whole question raised by Article 9—pacifism, the Self-Defense Forces, and the avoidance of war—is one with such high emotional content and such potentially direct political consequences for politicians or for political parties seriously advocating revision of Article 9, that treatment of the issue has never gotten beyond the stage of words. On none of the other issues involving possible constitutional revision that came before the commission has there been any serious discussion of possible revision.

With each passing year two powerful antirevisionist currents flow together: the continued successful operation of the constitutional system demonstrates a decreasing need for possible revision, and the ranks of those calling for revision become more and more depleted as the older conservatives retire from active life. But the real barrier to constitutional revision consists of two related elements, one constitutional and the other political. Under the amendment process constitutional amendments can be initiated only "through a concurring vote of two-thirds or more of all the members of each House" (Art. 96). Because of the nature of Japan's partisan politics, this requirement has meant that amendments could be initiated only if a single party was able to command a two-thirds majority of the seats in both the House of Representatives and the House of Councilors. In addition, the party lines on the question of revision have been very tightly drawn. The dominant Liberal Democratic Party, the right in Japan's political spectrum, has been the party of revision. Consequently, the opposition parties have been solidly against revision. Indeed, antirevisionism has been one of the few issues on which the opposition parties have stood together.

Political trends have also operated to render revision less and less likely. In the general election (for the House of Representatives) of 1958, the first after the Commission on the Constitution came into being, the Liberal Democratic Party won 287 of 467 seats (61.5 percent), or twenty-five less than the two-thirds majority that would have been required for initiating, even in the lower house, a constitutional amendment. In the 1976 election the LDP ended with 256 seats out of 511 (a bare majority), some 74 seats less than two-thirds. This steady erosion of power has dramatically lessened the chances of constitutional revision.

At no time was there the possibility that the LDP would be able to form a coalition with one or more of the minority parties to win the necessary two-thirds majority. The ideological cleavage between the LDP and its progressive opposition has been too great to allow of any accommodation on any issue, let alone the fundamental one of constitutional revision. The LDP has never been close to a two-thirds majority in the House of Councilors.

In the face of the above fundamental constitutional and political considerations, it is clearly impossible to claim for the Commission on the Constitution a decisive role in the struggle over revision. Yet it would be wrong to overlook or to diminish the contributions that the commission made to an understanding of the purely constitutional issues involved in the question of revision. The least that can be said on this important problem is that the commission created a new and special framework within which revision would have to be reviewed. Here I would like to sketch out what appear to me to be the principal components of that framework as they can be ascertained through a careful reading of the commission's report.

First, there is a clear and for all practical purposes unanimous affirmation of what are universally regarded as the three basic principles of the Constitution: popular sovereignty, pacifism (or the renunciation of war), and the guarantee of fundamental human rights. Commissioners, expert witnesses, and citizens supported these principles. Naturally, the antirevisionists were unequivocal in their support of the principles. The revisionists, particularly those on the commission, invariably affirmed their support, even while advocating particular constitutional revisions that would have had the force of undermining them. It is very clear indeed that these three principles, which are regarded as the foundations of Japan's brand of democracy, are firmly embedded in the Japanese consciousness. If that may seem to some to be too optimistic a view, then at least it can be said that in the atmosphere that prevailed during the seven years of the commission's work—and after—it was politically unwise for anyone critical of the Constitution to mount a frontal attack on its fundamental principles.

Second, the long years of investigation, deliberation, and debate failed to disclose a single potentially crippling defect in the Constitution. As the report reveals, many both inside and outside the commission urged strenuously that in their eyes there were such defects, but these were arguments based on special pleading. Again, there was nothing that cried for the remedy of revision because, if left unchanged, it would result in a breakdown of the Constitution or of the order—political, governmental, social, economic, or otherwise—erected on it.

Third, as a statement in reverse of the previous point, the report demonstrates that the Constitution, as is, is functioning effectively in practice as a fundamental law for Japanese society based on general principles of democracy. This consideration alone would seem to cut the ground from under two of the most powerful arguments for revision: that the Constitution was imposed on Japan by a foreign military occupation and consequently was not the result of the freely expressed will of the Japanese people; and that it does not conform with Japanese history, tradition, and values.

Fourth, the work of the commission emphasized the width and depth of the gulf separating the revisionists and antirevisionists. It must be emphasized that the rift between the two camps within the commission simply reflected in miniature the far broader, more significant, and potentially more dangerous confrontation within Japanese society itself. Since it did not happen, any comment on the problem must remain pure speculation, but it is fairly safe to say that any serious attempt to engineer a significant degree of revision of the Constitution would have resulted in a damaging political struggle between the conservative (revisionist) and progressive (antirevisionist) political camps in Japan. No matter what the outcome on the question of revision, one inevitable result would have been a deep scarring of the body politic. In even more specific political terms, the loser in the struggle would have been the Liberal Democratic Party. It should be recalled in this connection that Japan's greatest post-1945 political crisis came in 1960, not quite at the midpoint of the commission's work, over the issue of the revision of the Japanese–American security treaty of 1951 which, among other things, addressed the key constitutional question of the renunciation of war.

Fifth, the vast store of fact and opinion produced by the commission has constituted a resource that could not be ignored if the ruling party and its government ever seriously considered bringing constitutional revision before the people. And the conclusions to be drawn from an examination of that store would scarcely point toward quick and easy revision, whether on a large or small scale.

No review of the commission would be complete without a mention of the remarkable work of its only chairman, the late Professor Takayanagi Kenzō. It is no exaggeration to say that through his leadership the commission became what it was, a broad investigative and deliberative body that, as a group, did not assume a policy-making or a policy-recommending function on the critical issue of revision.[3] Professor Takayanagi was a leading scholar in the field of Anglo–American law, having studied both in Great Britain and in the United States. It was this background that led him to his devotion to the ideal of the rule of law, a philosophical commitment that undoubtedly prepared him for his role within the commission as the defender of the Constitution against revision. In spite of his obviously antirevisionist stand, he presided over the meetings of the commission with admirable fairmindedness. The evidence for this is clear and unequivocal: the degree to which all variations

3. For his role in the commission, his observations on its work, and some of his own views, *see* Takayanagi Kenzō, "Some Reminiscences of Japan's Commission on the Constitution" and "Appendix: Takayanagi Kenzō" both in Henderson, *The Constitution of Japan: Its First Twenty Years, 1947–67* (1968). *See also* Takayanagi Kenzō, "The Conceptual Background of the Constitutional Revision Debate in the Constitution Investigation Commission," in 1 *Law in Japan: An Annual* (1967).

on the themes of revisionism and antirevisionism were expressed in all the work of the commission. Of course, this revealed as much about his skill as chairman as it did about his impartiality.

The Commission on the Constitution has one achievement to its credit that was clearly not anticipated in the law that created it nor present in the minds of its members while they were engaged in their arduous task. It has made a great contribution to constitutional studies in Japan in the last half of the twentieth century. Its fact-finding on such key problems as the process of enactment, its formulation of the wide range of constitutional problems that emerged during the first fifteen years the Constitution was in effect, its item-by-item discussion of each constitutional provision, its weaving of the Constitution into the fabric of society, its laying out of the broad range of constitutional interpretations, and more have all guaranteed a place for it in any serious history or analysis of the Constitution of 1947. It is hoped that this translation will lead others to the same conclusion and will encourage deeper study of modern Japanese constitutionalism.

PART ONE

*The Establishment and Organization
of the Commission*

1. The Establishment

THE CONSTITUTION OF JAPAN was promulgated on 3 November 1946 and went into effect on 3 May 1947. At the time, however, different sectors of the populace had complex attitudes toward the Constitution. The people in general welcomed it, supporting it as a guide for the reconstruction of Japan, but from the outset there was an undercurrent of feeling that some day it should be subjected to review by the freely expressed will of the people because it had been enacted under the special circumstances of the Allied occupation.

In December 1946, immediately after the promulgation of the Constitution, the Committee for the Popularization of the Constitution was established. It was designed to carry out an educational movement that would spread the spirit of the Constitution, allowing it to permeate the lives of the people. The committee forthwith inaugurated the movement throughout the country.

In addition to the above circumstances within the country there were certain complex factors from outside. In October 1946, even before the promulgation of the Constitution, the Far Eastern Commission made the policy decision that between one and two years after the new Constitution went into effect both the National Diet and the commission itself would review it. This decision was transmitted to the Japanese government by General Headquarters, Supreme Commander for the Allied Powers in January 1947. As provided therein Director Suzuki Yoshio of the Office of Justice of the Ashida cabinet received a suggestion from SCAP regarding constitutional review in August 1948, a little over a year after the Constitution had gone into effect. Suzuki transmitted an intention of review to the speakers of both the House of Representatives and the House of Councilors and ordered a study to be made in the Office of Justice. However, the administrative officials of both houses and the justice authorities brought the internal studies to a halt.

In April 1949, before the lapse of the two years provided for in the FEC policy decision, Prime Minister Yoshida Shigeru told the Foreign Affairs Committee of the House of Representatives that the government had no intention of revising the Constitution. The FEC in May 1949 also decided that it would not approve a decision to require a revision of the Constitution.

The international situation arising from the outbreak of the Korean conflict in June 1950 and the resultant establishment of the National Police Reserve in August gave rise to the controversy over the security problem. Since that time the review of the Constitution and the question of the need for its revision, both centering on the security issue, have become quite controversial.

In April 1952 the peace treaty came into effect, and the country regained its independence. Since that time the question of how the Constitution should be treated has become a central issue, and the general review of the Constitution and the necessity for revision have been topics of lively debate.

Between the summers of 1953 and 1954 negotiations involving the Mutual Security Assistance Agreement between Japan and the United States were started. Both inside and outside the Diet, the controversy over the security issue and the related constitutional question has become bitter, particularly because of the statements by Prime Minister Yoshida and President Shigemitsu Mamoru of the Progressive Party at the nineteenth regular session of the Diet relating to the strengthening of self-defense capability, the drafting of a long-range national defense plan and the establishment of the Self-Defense Forces, plus the deliberations at the same session on the ratification of the MSA Agreement, the law establishing the Self-Defense Forces and the Official Secrets Law.

During the above period developments indicated clearly that the constitutional question had suddenly and clearly become a political confrontation. The Liberal Party was revived by Hatoyama Ichirō after a conference between him and Prime Minister Yoshida in November 1953, and in the following March the Liberals set up a Committee on Constitutional Investigation. This committee arrived at the following conclusion at a plenary meeting in September of the same year: "The Constitution of Japan must be completely revised in view of both its content and the process of its enactment." The same party, a month later, in its new policy platform made clear the following intention: "Because the present Constitution must be revised to conform with national conditions, an authoritative public investigative body should be established to prepare for it." The Committee on Constitutional Investigation then released in November "An Outline Revision of the Constitution of Japan" with an appended "Reasons for General Revisions."

The Progressive Party had already set forth constitutional review as part of its policy at the time of its founding, but at its party convention in January 1954 it passed the following resolution: "We recognize the necessity for a thorough review of the Constitution of Japan both because of the circumstances surrounding its enactment and because of experience with it since it came into effect. First, our party will establish its own investigative committee for constitutional review which will carry out a thorough study. At the proper opportunity a Constitutional Revision Commission will be established by law. It should draft a complete plan, which should then be submitted to the constitutionally established procedures for such matters." As a result, in the following April the Progressive Party Constitutional Investigation Committee was established. This committee then announced at a plenary session in September "An Outline of Problems of the Present Constitution" after passing another resolution that had essentially the same wording as the one above.

On the other side, the Left-wing Socialist Party in January 1954 approved its platform on the process of the establishment of socialistic authority which stated among other things: "On the basis of the absolute majority established in the Central Committee we shall revise the Constitution in accordance with the basic principles of socialism, establishing the national or public ownership of basic industries and setting up judicial and administrative organs and the machinery of education, newspapers, publishing, broadcasting, and so forth, in accordance with socialist objectives." Simultaneously they made clear that they would struggle "to prevent rearmament, to dissolve security and defense forces, and to protect the peace Constitution."

In addition, the progressive political parties such as both the Left- and Right-wing Socialists, the Labor-Farmer Party, and such other progressive forces as the labor federations set about creating popular organizations to oppose constitutional revision and to protect the peace Constitution. In January 1954 the Society for the Protection of the Peace Constitution which had started the previous August was dissolved and the People's Federation for the Protection of the Constitution was formed. The federation then approved a platform that stated its practical goals as follows: "In opposition to the plans of the conservative and reactionary forces to weaken the Constitution we shall awaken and organize a broad public opinion to protect the peace Constitution, going beyond faction, ideology, and doctrine. As the first step, we shall turn back by the power of public opinion the plans to weaken the Constitution. We shall then secure the strength in the Diet to defeat any Diet bill for revision. Finally, by means of the final popular vote we shall bury any proposal to weaken the Constitution."

In November 1954 the Left- and Right-wing Socialist parties and the Labor-Farmer Party issued the joint statement "Arguments against Constitutional Revision." This was a declaration of intent to oppose completely the proposals for revision from the Liberal and Progressive parties.

In the same month the Japan Democratic Party was formed through the joining of the Progressive and Japan Liberal parties and the Hatoyama [Ichirō] and Kishi [Nobusuke] factions which had left the Liberal Party. At the time the following item was decided on as a part of the platform: "In view of the circumstances of its enactment and of the results of its operation the Constitution of Japan shall be renovated, after consulting the opinions of all levels of the people, carefully examining its content, and firmly maintaining the principles of pacifism and democracy. To this end the National Diet shall establish by law a deliberative commission on the Constitution."

In December the first Hatoyama cabinet was created on the basis of this party, and in January 1955 Prime Minister Hatoyama in his administrative policy speech before the twenty-first regular session of the Diet made the following statement: "In regard to the Constitution which is the fundamental law of the land, revision is necessary in order to bring it into accord with national conditions because of both the circumstances of its enactment and the results of its operation. To this end I believe that a nonpartisan constitutional investigative and deliberative body should be established in the Diet, involving the participation of men of learning and experience and representatives of other sectors of the nation and that a bill to this effect should be drafted after careful deliberation."

Meanwhile, in December 1954 the Japan Democratic Party had also advocated the establishment of a similar nonpartisan body in the Diet. In the general election of February 1955 the question of constitutional revision was one source of debate between the conservative and progressive groups. In this election the Japan Democratic Party emerged on top. But on the other hand the progressive parties ended in command of more than a third of the seats in the House of Representatives.

In March 1955 the twenty-second special session of the Diet was opened and the second Hatoyama cabinet was appointed. The Japan Democratic Party, the party in power, cooperated with the Liberal Party, which shared its views on the constitutional revision question, and they revised their previous attitudes regarding the establishment of a constitutional investigative and deliberative body in the Diet. In June 1955 they announced their "Outline of a Law for a Commission on the Constitution," which called for the establishment of the proposed body in the cabinet. Then the government party on a motion by Representative Kiyose Ichirō and four colleagues presented also in June to the House of Representatives the "Bill for the Commission on the Constitution" (House Bill No. 31), calling for the establishment of the commission in the cabinet as proposed in the above outline.

This bill was immediately referred to the House of Representatives' Committee on the Cabinet. In view of its importance, Representative Kiyose explained the reasons behind the bill at a plenary session of the House of Councilors on 4 July 1955 and on the following day to a similar session of the House of Representatives. Then on 27 July Representative Furui Yoshimi explained the reasons for the bill to the House of Representatives' Committee on the Cabinet. The following day the bill went through the committee and was sent to the floor of the house. After debate it was passed by a vote of 238 to 129 and sent on to the House of Councilors.

In the upper house it was immediately referred to the Committee on the Cabinet and on the final day of the session, 30 July, Representative Kiyose again explained the reasoning behind it, but it was not considered. At this point Councilor Toyota Masataka of the Ryokufūkai [Green Breeze Society] moved in the committee that in view of the progress of the deliberations on the bill and of its importance it be entrusted to deliberations during the period of adjournment. The motion was approved, but because of confusion in the proceedings of the house's Steering Committee the session came to an end and deliberations on the bill were not completed.

Meanwhile, in May 1955 the League for an Independent Constitution was established with the hope of "achieving as rapidly as possible an independent constitution for Japan based on the new constitutional thought of the post–World War II period." Also, in July 1955 the League of Diet Members for an Independent Constitution was formed with the aim of "creating a great popular movement through an appeal to the people on the necessity for achieving an independent constitution in order to create a new Japan with the pride of an independent people and to contribute to world peace." This organization in August 1955 approved a resolution to pass a law rapidly at the next Diet session for a commission on the Constitution.

Furthermore, the People's Federation for the Protection of the Constitution filed a report to the authorities as a political organization prior to the general election of February 1955 and had started a political movement during the election itself.

In October 1955 the right and left wings of the Socialist Party joined together and formed the Japan Socialist Party (JSP). Then in the next month the Japan Democratic Party and the Liberal Party came together similarly and formed the Liberal Democratic Party (LDP).

When the LDP was established it decided on the following plank in its platform: "We plan an independent revision of the Constitution, firmly maintaining the principles of pacifism, democracy, and respect for fundamental human rights." At the same time it also decided, as both general and urgent policy, that, "in order to revise independently, in accordance with both the free will of the people and national conditions, the present Constitution which was enacted under the occupation, a constitutional commission will be established by law which will prepare a draft of a revised Constitution."

In the same month the twenty-third special session of the Diet was opened and the third Hatoyama cabinet created. In December, Prime Minister Hatoyama before both houses of the Diet in his keynote address asserted that he would like to establish in the cabinet an investigative commission for constitutional revision. The LDP in the same month also established the LDP Constitutional Investigation Committee.

In January 1956 when the twenty-fourth regular session of the Diet was reopened, Prime Minister Hatoyama in his administrative policy speech expressed the intent that "in order to advance the preparations for the creation of an independent constitution by an autonomous Japanese people we shall establish a constitutional commission in the cabinet and carefully examine the constitution." Then on 11 February 1956 sixty LDP members, including Kishi Nobusuke, presented to the House of Representatives "A Bill for a Constitutional Investigative Commission" (House Bill No. 1). This was almost identical with the bill [House Bill No. 31] introduced at the twenty-second session as described above.

On 16 February a plenary session of the House of Representatives heard Representative Yamasaki Iwao explain the bill. After interpellations it was referred on the following day to the House's Committee on the Cabinet. On 21 February Representative Yamasaki again presented the reasons for the bill to the committee. Deliberations continued until 23 March, and on that day the bill was approved as originally drafted, and sent to the floor of the house. On 16 March a public hearing was held, and the opinions of Kamikawa Hikomatsu, Nakamura Akira, and Kaino Michitaka were heard.

Finally on 29 March in plenary session the bill was passed by a vote of 239 to 139 and on the same day was sent on to the House of Councilors.

On 20 February Representative Yamasaki Iwao explained the reasons for the bill in a plenary session of the House of Councilors and after interpellations it was referred to the Committee on the Cabinet for preliminary examination. On 23 February Representative Yamasaki appeared before the committee to discuss the reasons for the bill again. After the same bill had passed the House of Representatives it was deliberated on from 23 April to 9 May. On 7 May Kishi Kuramatsu, Ōnishi Kunitoshi, Tagami Jōji, and Suzuki Yoshio appeared as consultants to express their opinions.

On 10 May the bill was approved in committee but while it was going through committee Councilor Shimamura Gunji proposed that an incidental resolution be attached to the effect that the selection of commission members and the investigations and deliberations of the commission be carried out with care and impartiality. After discussion this was also approved.

This bill was presented to a plenary session on 16 May and passed by a vote of 106 to 65. On 11 June 1956 the Law for the Commission on the Constitution (Law No. 140) was promulgated and came into effect and thus the establishment of the Commission on the Constitution was achieved.

LAW FOR THE COMMISSION ON THE CONSTITUTION

ARTICLE 1 (*Establishment*). The Commission on the Constitution is established in the cabinet.

ARTICLE 2 (*Assigned Affairs*). The commission shall study the Constitution of Japan, investigate and deliberate on related problems, and report the results to the cabinet and through the cabinet to the National Diet.

ARTICLE 3 (*Organization*). The commission shall be composed of not more than fifty members.

The members shall be appointed by the cabinet from among the groups listed below and within the limit of the numbers there set forth.

Diet members: 30

Persons of learning and experience: 20

The members shall be regarded as parttime appointees [to whom many government personnel regulations do not apply].

ARTICLE 4 (*Chairman and Vice Chairmen*). The commission shall have a chairman and two vice chairmen. They shall be determined by election from the members by the members.

The chairman shall preside over the affairs of the commission.

The vice chairmen shall assist the chairman in matters to be designated by the chairman. In the event of the chairman's incapacity, the vice chairmen shall carry out his duties in his behalf.

ARTICLE 5 (*Specialists*). In order to investigate technical matters specialists may be appointed to the commission.

Specialists shall be appointed by the prime minister from among men of learning and experience.

Specialists shall be discharged on the completion of the investigation of the matters falling within their specialties.

Specialists shall be regarded as parttime appointees.

ARTICLE 6 (*Secretary*). A secretary shall be appointed to the commission.

The secretary shall be appointed by the prime minister from among men of learning and experience or from among officials from related agencies.

The secretary shall aid the members in the matters for which the commission is responsible.

The secretary shall be regarded as a parttime appointee.

ARTICLE 7 (*Divisions*). As the necessity may arise, divisions may be created in the commission.

Assignment of members, specialists, and secretaries for the divisions shall be made by the commission chairman.

A chairmanship shall be established for a division, and the chairman will be elected by the division members from among themselves.

ARTICLE 8 (*Proceedings*). Necessary matters relating to the proceedings of the commission shall be determined by the chairman after consultation with the commission.

ARTICLE 9 (*General Affairs Office*). In order to handle commission business a general affairs office shall be established in the commission.

A director, other officials, and additional required personnel shall be appointed to the general affairs office.

The director, under orders from the chairman, shall be in charge of the business of the general affairs office, carry out the appointment, dismissal, promotion, and retirement of personnel and direct their activities.

The officials shall dispose of the business matters according to orders.

Exclusive of the director, the established number of employees in the general affairs office shall be nineteen regular employees, a number sufficient to discharge the responsibilities of the office, on permanent assignment to the general affairs office.

ARTICLE 10 (*Responsible Minister*). The responsible minister, as set forth in the Cabinet Law, for matters relating to the commission shall be the prime minister.

ARTICLE 11 (*Provisions relating to Charge*). Other than the matters stipulated by this law, necessary affairs relating to the commission shall be determined by cabinet ordinances.

BY-LAW. This law will be effective from the date of promulgation.

While the law was being passed, the Central Executive Committee of the Japan Socialist Party in January 1956 decided to expand greatly the national movement for the prevention of constitutional revision and to set up within the party a special committee for the protection of the Constitution.

On the other side, the Liberal Democratic Party Constitutional Investigation Committee released in April 1956 its "Problems of Constitutional Revision."

2. The Formation

THE COMMISSION WAS ESTABLISHED against the background described above, but the government strongly requested the participation of the Japan Socialist Party (JSP) because the composition of the commission had to be above party politics in view of its character and mission. However, the JSP did not change its previous attitude, and the commission set out without the JSP's participation.

In July 1956 the regular election for the House of Councilors was held and the Liberal Democratic Party emerged as the majority party. The JSP and the other progressive parties, however, won more than a third of the seats [enough to prevent revision]. The JSP secretariat then agreed informally that same month not to participate in the commission, which had already been established. The government held the view that in accordance with both the letter and the spirit of the law the commission should be organized and inaugurated with Diet members on a non-partisan basis and with men of learning and experience from various fields. Consequently, it was going to be forced to delay the start of the commission beyond the expected date of August if the participation of the JSP was to be obtained.

The JSP, however, at the August meeting of its Central Executive Committee decided the following: (1) that it would provide no members for the commission even if the government formally requested that it participate, (2) that scholars would be requested to fall into line with this policy, and (3) that the government be requested not to form the commission. Party Secretary Asanuma Inejirō reported this decision to the government. Thus, the start of the commission was delayed for some time.

Later, in December 1956, the Hatoyama cabinet resigned and the Ishibashi cabinet was formed. The latter also resigned in February 1957, after only nine weeks in office, and was succeeded by the Kishi cabinet.

In the same month Prime Minister Kishi Nobusuke before the Budget Committee of the House of Councilors in reply to a question from JSP Councilor Okada Shuji stated that he would like to have the commission get started at the earliest possible date.

Then in April, Kishi conferred with Suzuki Mōsaburō, the chairman of the JSP Central Executive Committee, and declared that he would like to have the JSP designate members for the commission so that it could speedily get started on a nonpartisan basis. After conferring with his committee, Chairman Suzuki replied formally to the prime minister that as a matter of policy it would be difficult for the JSP to comply. The committee met immediately thereafter and after discussion decided to refuse the prime minister's request. At the same time that the party told the government that it would not participate in the commission, JSP Representative Asanuma Inejirō and seven colleagues presented on the house floor a bill calling for the dissolution of the commission.

This bill was explained on the floor of the house on 16 May and two days later was carried over until the next session. In the following November at the twenty-seventh special session of the Diet it was referred without discussion to the twenty-eighth regular session in December. No action of any kind was taken during that session, before it ended in April 1958, and the bill died.

The government, after discussing the best means of handling the JSP's attitude, concluded that it had no recourse but to get the commission started while leaving vacant those seats allotted JSP Diet members, thus making possible future JSP participation in the commission. While proceeding with the selection of commission members from among men of learning and experience in July 1957, the cabinet requested the speakers of both houses of the Diet to nominate commission members.

In response, the House of Representatives in that same month decided that the allotted twenty members should be split between thirteen LDP and seven JSP nominees. However, the JSP reported to Speaker Masutani Hideji that it did not intend to fill any of its positions in view of the earlier party decision not to participate.

The House of Councilors at the same time decided to allot its ten seats as follows: LDP, five; JSP, three; Ryokufūkai [Green Breeze Society], two. Again, the JSP notified Speaker Matsuno Tsuruhei that it would not participate.

Both speakers then transmitted the lists of their nominees to the prime minister. On 30 July 1957 the government appointed thirty-nine commission members: eighteen Diet members from the LDP, two from the Ryokufūkai, and nineteen persons [including one woman, Sakanishi Shiho] of learning and experience. Thus, the commission began its existence without JSP participation.

Then on 31 July the People's Federation for the Protection of the Constitution issued a declaration and a protest criticizing the inauguration of the commission, stating that it was regrettable in the extreme that the government, which bears the responsibility for the defense of the Constitution, had established the commission in spite of the opposition of a majority of the people.

As described above, it was most regrettable that the commission was started without achieving a nonpartisan organization in view of its mission to examine constitutional problems from a national point of view. Thereafter the government and the commission appealed both to the JSP and to the Democratic Socialist Party (DSP) to participate in the commission. However, both parties continued their refusals.

The commission in its first plenary session, which was held on 13 and 14 August 1957 decided on its own to appeal to the JSP to participate. At its second plenary session on 19 September the commission set forth the principle that "when there is no unanimity of opinion even after serious deliberation the views of this commission will not be determined by a compulsory majority vote." It then adopted a resolution requesting the participation of the JSP. This resolution was delivered by Chairman Takayanagi Kenzō on that same day to Prime Minister Kishi and Chairman Suzuki of the JSP Central Executive Committee and on the twentieth to the speakers of the two houses of the Diet.

On 21 September the JSP replied that it could not participate on the grounds, among others, that the establishment of the commission within the cabinet was unconstitutional. The commission at its third plenary session on 2 October after deliberating on a reply to the JSP decided that it could not accept the JSP claim that the commission was unconstitutional and that the insufficiency of the argument should be pointed out in a statement from the chairman. The statement was issued on the same day.

On 26 June 1959 after the April general election that had followed dissolution of the House of Representatives, the government reappointed or appointed new commissioners from the lower house. The government again requested the JSP to participate; Mr. Akagi, the chief cabinet secretary, met with JSP Secretary Asanuma and transmitted the request to him. In addition, Chairman Takayanagi in his capacity as a private citizen met with Mr. Asanuma on 27 June and also requested JSP participation. But on 28 June the party again replied to the government and to Chairman Takayanagi that it refused to participate.

In view of the circumstances described above, the commission continued its investigations and deliberations without the JSP. In September 1961 the commission completed its general factual investigation of the circumstances of the enactment of the Constitution and of its actual operation and entered the new stage of deliberations on the problems related to the Constitution as revealed by the factual investigations.

Meanwhile in October 1959 the JSP split and the Democratic Socialist Party (DSP) was formed. In July 1960 the Ikeda cabinet succeeded the Kishi cabinet. Under these new circumstances and on the occasion of entering the new stage of deliberation in its operations the commission at its fifty-seventh plenary session on 20 September 1961 decided unanimously again to invite both the JSP and the DSP to participate.

On 22 September Chairman Takayanagi called on Prime Minister Ikeda Hayato and explained to him the commission's requests to the two socialist parties. During the same day he also called on Chairman Kawakami Jōtarō of the JSP's Central Executive Committee and handed over the request for JSP participation. The JSP again refused, however, and on the same day the Central Executive Committee released a document entitled "The Most Recent Developments in the Commission on the Constitution." On that same day the request was handed over to the DSP, and on 25 September Chairman Takayanagi called on Chairman Nishio of the DSP's Central Executive Committee and requested that the party participate in the commission. The party replied that it would be impossible to meet the request. Also after his interview with Chairman Takayanagi, Nishio released a document entitled "Comments on Non-participation in the Commission on the Constitution."

At the fifty-eighth plenary session on 27 September the commission received a report from its chairman on the details of the negotiations with the two socialist parties. Again, at the fifty-ninth plenary session on 4 October, the commission chairman announced, in reply to the JSP contention, that the commission was not unconstitutional.

3. External Developments
after the Commission's Inauguration

IN SPITE OF THE PROVISIONS of the law regarding the mission of the commission and the government statements to the effect that the commission was not designed to revise the Constitution, a segment of public opinion entertained the doubt that the commission did have the objective of revising the Constitution, as Prime Minister Hatoyama had stated on one occasion.

There was also the undeniable fact that the commission had begun its labors without the participation of the JSP. Public opinion held that this was regrettable for the commission and that its discussions would consequently be one-sided. Others believed there was little significance to be attached to the creation of the commission and that the above circumstances meant there were built-in limitations on both its significance and its role. But there were also those who believed that when the commission began its operations its first consideration would be to provide a basis for all the people to express candidly their will on constitutional problems, not to rush to a set of conclusions.

Thus, when the commission began its work, there was a generally critical attitude toward it, but, as reflected in newspaper comment, there was also a feeling that it was difficult to understand why the JSP refused to participate in the face of the government's generous invitation. Some not only felt that the JSP should reconsider and participate but also that the commission should demand its participation.

At the outset the commission adopted the following general principles of operation: (1) to call on expert witnesses in order to hear the views of scholars; (2) to have all meetings open to the public; (3) to hold public hearings in order to learn the views of the general public; and (4) not to resort to a majority decision in voting to decide commission views on the results of its investigations and deliberations. On this basis the commission again called on the JSP to participate.

In addition, as the basic policy for the pursuit of both investigation and deliberation, the commission decided that it would carry out factual investigations of both the process of the enactment of the Constitution and of its actual operation so that its deliberations would be based on the most objective factual basis possible.

With the above principles the commission carried out its judicious investigations and deliberations beginning in October 1957. Scholars who had been critical of the commission at the outset appeared as witnesses to express their opinions as the investigations and deliberations developed, and when the public hearings were held throughout the country after November 1958, representatives of labor unions gradually began to appear as witnesses.

In addition, the mass media gradually began to give full coverage to the commission's work and consequently aroused a great deal of public interest. As a result, it generally became accepted that the commission was not striving to revise the Constitution.

Meanwhile, in June 1958, the Committee for the Study of Constitutional Problems was established to provide the most accurate study of the basic principles and provisions of the Constitution, thus reflecting the critical attitude toward the commission. In October 1959, when the Democratic Socialist Party was formed as a result of the JSP split, Katayama Tetsu, the chairman of the National Federation for the Protection of the Constitution, withdrew from the federation and established the New National Council for the Protection of the Constitution on a broad popular basis with the aim of developing a genuine movement to protect the Constitution with a new scope and significance. This new council formally started on 3 May 1960.

In September 1961 the commission concluded its factual investigations and announced that it was about to begin drafting the various reports on the results. At that time, both in newspapers and in scholarly journals, there was favorable comment on the value of the material collected by the commission and numerous statements that it was an important contribution to the constitutional debate. Also there finally appeared in influential newspapers comment favorable toward the commission's approach to its deliberations, holding it to be both impartial and conscientious.

In that same September the commission entered the new stage of deliberation on constitutional problems. At that point it again asked both the JSP and the DSP to participate. Again, both parties refused. At the time there was a strong preponderance of critical editorial opinion against this attitude of the two parties.

In December, soon after beginning its deliberations on constitutional problems, the commission decided to invite representatives of the movement to protect the Constitution to attend a plenary session in order to discuss the controversy over protection.

At this same time the Federation for the Protection of the Constitution transmitted to the commission its desire to make a proposal. On 11 January 1962, Hara Hyō, a representative of the federation, presented a request to the commission that it forthwith suspend its current deliberations. Chairman Takayanagi replied from the chair as follows: "I would like to see the commission complete its discussions as rapidly as possible, and I believe also that I would like to carry out the mission entrusted to it by law. The JSP is not participating in the commission, but I am striving to do the best I can under the circumstances and to carry out careful and impartial investigations and discussions according to what the law calls for, requesting those who share the views of the JSP to appear as consultants or to testify as witnesses at the public hearings. In this spirit I would like to have consultants from the federation as well appear before the commission to explain their views on the protection of the Constitution."

In its reply to the commission on 23 January, the federation refused to send a representative as a consultant to a plenary session of the commission and also requested that the commission engage in a public debate on the issues. The commission responded by stating that it could not accept this request because for the commission to engage in debate with any organization that is engaging in political activities from a specific position would not be in accord with the commission's character.

In addition, the New National Council for the Protection of the Constitution similarly did not become directly involved in the activities of the commission. However, at this point in its deliberations, the commission, actively continuing its operations, decided on a positive educational campaign to be achieved by obtaining participation in the public hearings.

The commission, because it wished to hear the arguments for the protection of the Constitution, continued to request that both the federation and the council send consultants. On 24 January 1962 at the seventy-first plenary session, the council sent Katayama Tetsu, its chairman, and two other members to discuss their views.

On 22 February 1962, on the occasion of the first regional public hearing, that for the Kwantō region held in Tokyo, Advisor Nakamura Kōichi of the JSP called on the commission and presented a statement requesting it to suspend its activities and, in particular, to drop its plans for the regional public hearings. Both Chairman Takayanagi and Vice Chairman Yabe Teiji replied from the chair that the commission must complete the mission entrusted to it by law and that they had no intention of suspending the public hearings, which were a vital link in the investigations and deliberations then in progress.

The commission at its 113th plenary session in May 1963 set up its Drafting Committee and entered the stage of preparing the draft report for presentation to the cabinet and the Diet. It continued drafting the report and in January 1964 began to prepare the draft of Part Four, which would contain the results of the deliberations on constitutional problems. The federation at this point transmitted to the commission its intention of presenting another request to the commission. On 7 February, a representative of the federation, Secretary Narita Tomomi of the JSP, and the vice chairman of Sōhyō [Japan General Council of Labor Unions] and others called on the General Affairs Office of the commission and presented a demand that if the commission was to carry out a truly democratic and impartial examination of constitutional issues, it abandon the presentation of its report to the cabinet and the Diet and immediately dissolve itself. On 13 February the commission replied in writing that (1) it would continue to carry out the mission bestowed on it by law; (2) it would report impartially to the cabinet and the Diet, not deciding commission views by majority vote, on the opinions of individual commission members without regard to minority or majority views or to revisionist or antirevisionist sentiments; and (3) it could not accept the demand at this stage of the draft because it had to complete its mission on the basis of the policies outlined.

In addition, during the regional public hearings and the central public hearings in Tokyo between February and September 1962, some students engaged in activities designed to prevent the hearings by force. But the commission, while it continued its investigations and deliberations, was able to bring together the views of a number of organizations on constitutional problems and on the commission itself.

PART TWO

Duties, Organization, and Operation of the Commission

1. Duties

As THE LAW ESTABLISHING the commission provided, it was set up within the cabinet and had the duties of examining the constitution, investigating and deliberating on problems relating to it, and reporting the results to the cabinet and through it to the National Diet.

2. Organization

THE COMMISSION CONSISTED OF not more than fifty members of whom thirty were to be from the Diet and twenty were to be persons of learning and experience. They were to be appointed by the cabinet and considered as part-time appointees.

On 30 July 1957 eighteen Diet members associated with the Liberal Democratic Party, two members of the House of Councilors from the Ryokufūkai, and nineteen persons of learning and experience were appointed, leaving vacant the seats that were to have been filled by JSP Diet members. As has been pointed out, the JSP was invited to fill its seats several times, but refused. Consequently, the total number of members remained around forty. As a result of the July 1962 House of Councilors' election, the Kōmeikai [the political arm of the Sōka Gakkai, the militant Buddhist sect which became the professedly independent Kōmeitō (Clean Government Party) in November 1964] was assigned a single seat on the commission. However, it was never filled.

There were a number of changes in Diet membership of the commission because of dissolutions of the House of Representatives, the expiration of terms, appointments to cabinet ministerships or standing committee chairmanships, or death. However, there were few changes in membership among the persons of learning and experience.

At the first plenary session of 13 August 1957 Professor Takayanagi Kenzō was elected chairman, and Yamasaki Iwao and Yabe Teiji were elected vice chairmen, as provided for in the law. On several occasions Yamasaki left his positions as both member and vice chairman of the commission but was reelected as vice chairman each time he returned.

The commission also at its first plenary session adopted a set of standing rules and under their provisions set up a Steering Committee to deliberate on matters relating to the administration of commission affairs. The Steering Committee was composed of members appointed by the chairman, the vice chairmen, and the committee chairmen acting in conference. The chairman of the Steering Committee was the commission chairman.

The Steering Committee was appointed at the first plenary session. It consisted of thirteen members: the chairman, the two vice chairmen, and ten members appointed by the commission chairman. The number was later increased to fourteen when on 16 January 1958 the Subcommittee on the Process of the Enactment of the Constitution and on 17 September 1958 the First, Second, and Third committees were inaugurated, and one of the new committee chairmen, who was not already a member of the Steering Committee, was appointed. On 16 January 1964 another member was appointed, raising the total number to fifteen.

The commission carried out its investigations and deliberations primarily through its plenary sessions. For the effective prosecution of its investigations and deliberations, however, the commission was enabled by law to establish committees, subcommittees, and divisions as necessary. These and the plenary sessions carried out commission business. The principal committees and divisions were as follows: the Subcommittee on the Process of the Enactment of the Constitution, the First Committee, the Second Committee, the Third Committee, the First Division, the Second Division, the Third Division, the Special Division, the Arrangements Committee, the Committee on Draft Preparation, and the Drafting Committee. In the initial stages of its work the commission set up the subcommittee and the First, Second, and Third committees, but not the divisions, which were provided for in the law.

At the eighth plenary session the Subcommittee on the Process of the Enactment of the Constitution was established. It consisted of ten members appointed by the commission chairman. The subcommittee chairman was elected by the committee members. Hosokawa Ryūgen, a distinguished commentator, was named chairman.

At the fifteenth plenary session the three committees were established. With the exception of the chairman and the two vice chairmen, each member of the commission was to be a member of one of the three committees. The committee chairmen were to be elected by the committee members, and subcommittees could be set up in each committee. The commission members were given their committee assignments by the commission chairman at the sixteenth plenary session. The three committees then elected the following chairmen: First Committee, Mano Tsuyoshi; Second Committee, Saka Chiaki; and Third Committee, Takada Motosaburō. At the ninth meeting of the Second Committee, Ushioda Kōji was elected chairman to succeed Saka, who had died. In each of the three committees, subcommittees were created to act in the name of the committees until the new Diet members were appointed to the commission following the general election of October 1960.

The above subcommittees were appointed by the committee chairmen and each elected a chairman. The subcommittees were appointed from among the commissioners who were not members of the House of Representatives. The chairmen of the subcommittees were elected by the committee chairmen from among themselves.

The assignments of the three committees were as follows: the First Committee dealt with matters relating to the rights and duties of the people and the judiciary; the Second Committee covered matters relating to the National Diet, the cabinet, finances, and local selfgovernment; and the Third Committee studied matters relating to the preamble, the emperor, the renunciation of war, amendment, and the Constitution as the supreme law.

The subcommittee on the process of enactment and the three committees were abolished with the establishment of the three divisions in February 1961.

The commission established an Arrangements Committee at its fifty-fifth plenary session, when it entered the stage of deliberation on constitutional problems, in order to organize properly the problems that it was to discuss. This committee was composed of the chairman, the two vice chairmen, the chairmen of the subcommittee and the three committees, and either two or three members appointed by the commission chairman from each of the above committees. The commission chairman appointed the chairman of the Arrangements Committee from among its members.

At its eighty-fifth plenary session the commission concluded its deliberations on the general and basic questions which had been presented in the abstracts of the problems. It then decided to carry out by means of discussion its examination of basic constitutional issues and important matters which had been revealed in the investigations and deliberations up to that point. In order to frame the problems that were to be the object of these discussions, subcommittees of the Arrangements Committee were established. These subcommittees were composed of the two vice chairmen, the chairmen of the divisions [see below], and members of the Arrangements Committee appointed by the commission chairman. The subcommittee assignments of the committee members were made by the commission chairman at the eighty-sixth plenary session.

The Arrangements Committee and its subcommittees were abolished in June 1963 when the deliberations on basic constitutional issues and important related matters were concluded.

When the commission entered the stage of deliberations on constitutional problems it established the First, Second, Third, and Special divisions, the first three at the sixty-eighth plenary session, and the fourth at the sixty-ninth. These divisions were characterized as follows: (1) with the exception of the chairmen and the vice chairmen, all commissioners could be assigned to any or all of the divisions; (2) each division would have a chairman appointed from among the members, and an unspecified number of committee members would serve as permanent members and with the chairman would act as a group to confer on the management of division affairs; and (3) subcommittees could be set up in each division. Members were appointed by the commission chairman to the first three divisions at the sixty-ninth plenary session, and to the Special Division at the seventieth. At the first combined meeting of the divisions, the following division chairmen were elected: First Division, Takada Motosaburō; Second Division, Mano Tsuyoshi; Third Division, Ushioda Kōji; and Special Division, Hosokawa Ryūgen. These division chairmen then appointed permanent division members.

The responsibilities of the divisions were as follows: the First Division examined matters relating to the preamble, the emperor, the renunciation of war, amendment, and the Constitution as the supreme law; the Second Division dealt with matters relating to the rights and duties of the people and to the judiciary; the Third Division studied matters relating to the National Diet, the cabinet, finance, and local self-government; and the Special Division was responsible for all matters not properly to be discussed in the above three divisions or the combined divisions and assigned from a plenary session. (Matters assigned to the Special Division by a plenary session included the problems of the possible invalidity of the Constitution and of constitutional continuity.)

The above four divisions were abolished in July 1964 upon completion of the deliberations on the body of the final report to the cabinet and the Diet and of the supplementary documents.

At the ninety-second plenary session when the deliberations in the plenary session and the divisions on the basic and general constitutional issues were ended, and the deliberative discussions on the basic issues and important matters had been started, the commission established the Committee on Draft Preparation. This committee was responsible for making the necessary preparations for the preliminary draft of the report to the cabinet and Diet as decided at the eighty-fifth plenary session as set forth in the "Outline for the Organization of the Report to the Cabinet and the Diet" with respect to the sections dealing with the development of the investigations and deliberations. This committee was composed of the vice chairmen, the division chairmen, and commissioners designated by the commission chairman. He also appointed one of the vice chairmen to serve as chairman of this committee. These appointments were made at the ninety-third plenary session. In June 1963 this committee completed its mission by presenting to the Drafting Committee a partial draft of Parts One and Two and the first part of Part Three of the report. The committee was then dissolved.

The commission completed its deliberative discussions of basic constitutional issues and important related matters at its 112th plenary session. At the 113th plenary session it approved a paper entitled "The Development of Future Deliberations and Basic Organization of the Report to the Diet and the Cabinet." It then established a Drafting Committee, which had the assignment of preparing the final report. The Drafting Committee was composed of members of the Steering Committee (excepting the commission chairman) and the standing members of the various divisions. The chairman of the Drafting Committee was a vice chairman designated by the commission chairman. A subcommittee was established in the Drafting Committee to carry on its work until new committee members were appointed following the dissolution of the House of Representatives in October 1963. This subcommittee was made up of the members who were not from the House of Representatives, and the chairman of the Drafting Committee served as its chairman. The Drafting Committee was dissolved in July 1964 when the report was completed.

3. Operations

THE GENERAL MISSION of the commission as stated in law has already been set forth. It should be added, however, that the commission was completely independent in the execution of its mission, and although it was set up within the cabinet, it neither answered questions presented by the cabinet nor acted under its direction. Consequently the Steering Committee was set up within the commission to deliberate on matters relating to the operations of the commission, while the commission's plenary sessions deliberated on the plans and proposals generated by the committee. In addition, the commission as a whole decided on the general outlines of its proceedings, the establishment of its internal organization, policies relating to its investigations and deliberations, and other matters.

Because the Constitution sets forth both the organization and activities of the state and the basic norms for the life of the people, the commission, when it determined the basic policies relating to its own procedures, investigations, and deliberations, was careful to adopt a position common to that of the people in deliberating on constitutional issues and to make sure that its investigations and deliberations were both nonpartisan and impartial.

Consequently the basic approaches of the commission in the fulfillment of its responsibilities can be outlined as follows:

1. As has been pointed out already, in keeping with the aim of being nonpartisan, the commission repeatedly called on the JSP to participate in its work.

2. As a matter of principle, the meetings of the commission were open to the public so that its investigations and deliberations could be made widely available to the people and so that constitutional problems and opinions relating to them could be made understandable to the people. In this regard, minutes were kept of each meeting, were delivered to all

those involved in commission matters, and were broadly distributed in the same manner as the *Official Gazette* and other governmental publications. In a like manner a general outline of the commission's investigations and deliberations was assembled each year in the form of an annual report and was also broadly distributed.

3. Participation in the commission's investigations and deliberations was not limited to commissioners, specialists, and others within the commission. The commission's standing rules (Art. 6) provided that the chairman could ask for the appearance at commission meetings of appropriate persons and could request explanations or statements of their views. As will be pointed out later, the commission not only invited those involved in the actual operations of the Constitution and specialists in constitutional studies to appear and heard their discussions and opinions, without regard to their points of view, but also compiled for purposes of reference, with considerable dependence on those who appeared before it, different types of reference material relating to all aspects of the Constitution.

4. So that the voice of the people could be heard by the commission, the standing rules also provided that the chairman could invite any person who wished to testify to appear, provided that the request was regarded as being appropriate. In addition, also in accordance with the standing rules, the chairman could decide to carry out public hearings with a specified number of commissioners present and such public hearings were held throughout the country. In these public hearings particular care was taken to select witnesses in a fair and impartial manner, and they were nominated through the cooperation of a variety of organizations. These witnesses came from certain segments of the population and were selected without regard to their points of view.

5. In order that the investigations and deliberations be carried out on a broad basis involving constitutional conditions in other countries and constitutional trends in the contemporary world, the commission dispatched both commissioners and specialists to foreign countries where they investigated the actual operations of constitutions there and heard the opinions of scholars on various constitutional issues.

6. It has already been described how in the execution of its investigations and deliberations the commission established various committees and divisions, centering on the plenary sessions, which carried out in concert the effective execution of responsibilities. The plenary sessions also developed concrete plans for the public hearings.

7. Finally, in the preparation of its final report, the commission attempted to make the report as useful as possible for the understanding of the cabinet, the Diet, and the people. To that end it stated at one time or another that (a) it would at the end of its labors present a clear

statement of the views of each commissioner (standing rules); (b) in the event that any result of the investigation or deliberation or an opinion respecting them was to be voted on, it would be submitted to a plenary session after due consideration by the Steering Committee (standing rules); and (c) in the resolution (second plenary session) relating to the request to the JSP to participate it declared "in the event that there was no unanimous opinion after a serious consideration of the results of an investigative study, there would be no determination of a general commission opinion as in an ordinary plenary session but an impartial report of majority and minority opinions and of the reasons for and against revision in such a way that the results would be useful to the formation of a political judgment by both the Diet and the people." This, in essence, was reaffirmed at the fifty-fifth plenary session when the commission entered into its deliberations on the problems relating to the Constitution.

PART THREE

*The Investigations and Deliberations
of the Commission*

1. Basic Policy for the Investigations and Deliberations

IN ACCORDANCE WITH its legally established responsibilities, the commission's basic aim was to carry out serious and impartial investigations and deliberations. Because the commission was averse to making the constitutional issue into an instrument for partisan politics and to drifting into the controversy over constitutional issues, which tended to become emotional, it took particular care to base its work on facts, to carry out rational investigations and deliberations, and to contribute accurate information to the cabinet, the Diet, and the people useful for the attainment of political judgments on constitutional issues.

The commission in the pursuit of its investigations and deliberations began with objective factual investigations and followed three stages in its work. First, in view of the fact that the process of the enactment of the Constitution was unusual and had become one of the principal issues in the constitutional controversy, it carried out a strictly factual investigation of this problem. Second, because many wondered if the Constitution conformed to the conditions of the nation, and because this had also become a principal issue in the constitutional controversy, the commission spent four years in a wide and detailed factual investigation of the actual operation of the Constitution. Third, the commission spent about two-and-a-half years in painstaking deliberations on problems emerging from the previous investigations in order to determine whether the solutions to those problems required revision of the Constitution or improvements in its application. The results of those investigations and deliberations will be set forth here in abbreviated form.

2. The Progress of the
Investigations and Deliberations

THE COMMISSION, from its first plenary session in August 1957 to its third in October of the same year, deliberated on the basic principles for its procedures and on the basic aims for both investigation and deliberation. From that time forward until July 1964 for a period of about seven years it carried out its examination of the Constitution and of related problems.

The commission began its investigation of the circumstances of the enactment of the Constitution in October 1957 and of its actual operation in March 1958 and continued these two sets of investigations until September 1961. In that month it approved a paper entitled "Outline of Problems for Future Deliberations," which contained more than 120 problems for commission deliberation, drawn from a total of more than 200 which had been brought to light in the above investigations. Then until December 1962 the commission deliberated on those problems in order to determine whether they should be dealt with by constitutional revision or by an improvement in constitutional processes.

In January 1963 the commission, on the basis of the above investigations and deliberations, approved a paper entitled "Problems for Debate," which contained basic constitutional issues and ten important constitutional matters, and debated these issues and matters from then until May 1963. Following these debates deliberations began in June 1963 on the drafting of the final report. Finally, at the 131st plenary session in July 1964 the report was approved.

During its investigations and deliberations the commission invited 418 persons of learning and experience to appear as consultants to present their analyses and opinions, held 56 public hearings at which 487 witnesses appeared to present their views, and in addition made wide investigations abroad. In the process it met in 131 plenary sessions. Committees and divisions held some 319 meetings.

SECTION A.
INVESTIGATION OF THE PROCESS OF ENACTMENT OF THE CONSTITUTION

At the third plenary session in October 1957 the development of the investigations and deliberations was discussed and it was decided that the process of enactment of the Constitution would be investigated first. From the fourth plenary session in October 1957 through the tenth in February 1958 a general investigation was carried out which involved the calling of consultants and the hearing of their testimony. Deliberations were continued in the twenty-fourth plenary session in January 1959 and the twenty-fifth in February when the results of the overseas investigation of the problem of enactment were reported. Then in April 1960 at the forty-fifth plenary session the views of consultants were heard on the problem of the invalidity of the Constitution, an issue related to the process of enactment.

Meanwhile, at the eighth plenary session in December 1957, the Subcommittee on the Process of the Enactment of the Constitution was established. This subcommittee was entrusted with the tasks of putting into proper shape the materials and testimony presented at the plenary sessions, of carrying out thorough factual investigations, and of reporting the results to the plenary sessions. The subcommittee, between January 1958 and September 1961, held forty-nine meetings at which it heard and deliberated on the testimony of consultants. At ten of these meetings it dealt with the reports of the overseas investigation of the enactment of the Constitution. In addition, it compiled for research purposes various materials relating to the enactment which were given by Japanese and foreign scholars and men of affairs. The subcommittee completed its work when it presented to the fifty-sixth plenary session in September 1961 the results of its investigations in a report entitled "Report of the Subcommittee on the Process of Enactment of the Constitution."

SECTION B.
INVESTIGATION OF THE ACTUAL OPERATION OF THE CONSTITUTION

At the tenth plenary session in February 1958, it was decided that beginning with the next plenary session an investigation into the actual operation of the Constitution would be carried out. From the twelfth plenary session in March 1958 to the fifty-fourth plenary session in July 1961, a total of forty-two meetings, the commission carried out a general investigation of each chapter of the Constitution in order.

In July 1958 at the fifteenth plenary session the First, Second, and Third committees were created, and it was decided that these three committees would carry out additional detailed investigations of matters referred to them by the plenary sessions relating to the actual operation of the Constitution.

From the seventeenth plenary session in September 1958 to the forty-fourth in March 1960, the actual operation of the constitutional provisions, in the order given, relating to the judiciary, the Diet, the emperor, the renunciation of war, the Constitution as the supreme law, finance, basic human rights, the cabinet, and local self-government, was discussed. The testimony and materials presented at these hearings were put in order and referred to the committees having jurisdiction over these issues for the completion of the investigation and for reports to the plenary sessions.

Between September 1959 and July 1961 the total number of meetings of each committee (including subcommittee meetings) was as follows: First Committee, 54; Second Committee, 47; and Third Committee, 43.

In these committee investigations consultants were called in and heard, and Japanese and foreign scholars and men of affairs were called and research materials obtained from them.

These three committees completed their work by presenting between February and July 1961 the following list of reports to the plenary sessions:

"Report of the First Committee on the Actual Operation of the Constitution: (1) Rights and Duties of the People (Articles 10 to 30); (2) Rights and Duties of the People (Articles 31 to 40); (3) The Judiciary"

"Report of the Second Committee: (1) The National Diet; (2) The Cabinet; (3) Finance; (4) Local Self-Government"

"Report of the Third Committee: (1) The Emperor; (2) The Renunciation of War; (3) The Constitution as the Supreme Law"

SECTION C.
DELIBERATION ON PROBLEMS RELATING TO THE CONSTITUTION

At the fifty-fifth plenary session in July 1961 it was decided that the next step following the investigation of the enactment and operation of the Constitution would be the study of and deliberation on the necessity for constitutional revision as based on the investigations already completed. The same session also established the Arrangements Committee, which outlined the problems that should be studied and deliberated on by the commission.

The Arrangements Committee's approach can be described by the following three questions: For the future of Japan what kind of Constitution is most suitable? On the basis of experience with the actual operation of the Constitution, does it conform with national conditions? How should the process of the enactment of the Constitution be evaluated?

This committee also devoted additional study to the problems raised in the reports of the various committees dealing with the operation of the Constitution, broad, general questions relating to the Constitution (including the process of enactment), problems not yet studied (including the preamble and the amendment process), and the problem of whether new provisions should be added to the Constitution. The committee consolidated these problems, prepared a draft outline of them, and presented the outline to the fifty-seventh plenary session in the same month. It was immediately deliberated on, and the session approved the outline of the problems. [Omitted here is a long list of the problems. They are all repeated and considered in the following chapter.]

Between September 1961 and December 1962, both the plenary sessions and the commission divisions held deliberations on the problems described above. During that period at the eighty-fifth plenary session in September 1962 the commission approved a paper entitled "Outline for the Organization of the Report to the Cabinet and the Diet" and also determined the general outlines for the development of later deliberations. It was also decided that after January 1963 deliberations would be held on the basis of discussions of the basic constitutional and important related matters, using an interim report as the foundation. In order to examine the problems that should be discussed a subcommittee was set up inside the Arrangements Committee.

The subcommittee examined the problems between October and December 1962 and prepared a draft relating to problems for deliberation after January 1963 and presented it to its parent committee in December. The committee deliberated on that draft and after making a few revisions presented it to the ninety-first plenary session in the same month. In January 1963 at its ninety-second plenary session, the commission deliberated on the draft and approved it under the title "Problems to be Submitted for Discussion." [Omitted here is a long list of the problems. They are all repeated and discussed in the following chapter.]

At the fifty-eighth plenary session in September 1961 the method for developing discussion of the numerous questions was decided upon with the deliberations to be carried out in plenary sessions on both the general and the fundamental questions.

From the fifty-ninth plenary session in October 1961 through the sixty-seventh in November, the commission deliberated principally on the general constitutional questions. The deliberations on the general questions having been completed for the time being at the sixty-seventh plenary session, the commission entered deliberations on the basic questions at the sixty-eighth plenary session in December where it established the First, Second, and Third divisions for more effective deliberation on those problems. At the sixty-ninth session in the same month the commission set up the Special Division, and the deliberations on the basic problems were continued by the plenary sessions and the four divisions acting in concert.

The seventeen plenary sessions between the sixty-eighth and the eighty-fifth in September 1962 were devoted to deliberations on the basic problems. At the seventy-second plenary session in February, another basic question was added.

Between December 1961 and December 1962 the divisions held the following number of deliberative meetings: First Division, 21; Second Division, 18; Third Division, 24; and Special Division, 8.

The assignment from the plenary sessions to the Second Division was to study the question, Are there other matters that should be dealt with in the Constitution? For example, the basic principle of the rule of law, principles relating to the economic and social systems, a basic principle relating to education. In respect to the application and interpretation of the Constitution, should there be some kind of coordination or relationship among the cabinet, the Diet, and the courts?

The Third Division was also to examine the question, Are there other matters that should be dealt with in the Constitution? For example, a constitutional organ to guarantee fair elections (demarcation of election districts, supervision of elections), a constitutional organ to guarantee the status of public servants, political parties, and such systems relating to direct democracy as a popular referendum.

The Special Division was to review the question, How should we view the assertion that the Constitution is invalid because of the circumstances and procedures involved in its enactment and the dispute respecting its continuity with the old Constitution?

In addition to the above, seven plenary sessions (from the eighty-sixth in October 1962 through the ninety-third in January 1963) were devoted to deliberations on the general and basic questions in order to supplement those already held.

In the above sessions of the full commission and of the divisions the deliberations were carried out by expression of opinions by commissioners and by questions and debates centering on those opinions. Witnesses were also called to these meetings when doing so was regarded as necessary for the study of the issues, and materials for the deliberations were gathered both from foreign and from domestic scholars and men of affairs.

In addition to the deliberations on the general and basic problems the commission at its seventy-first plenary session in January 1962 heard witnesses on the controversy over the defense of the Constitution, and at its eightieth plenary session in July 1962 it also heard witnesses speaking on the Constitution of the Soviet Union.

Among the results of the deliberations both of the plenary sessions and of the divisions was an interim report on the deliberations on the general questions in the fifty-ninth through sixty-seventh plenary sessions. This was approved by the eighty-sixth plenary session in October 1962.

The results of the deliberations of the sixty-eighth through eighty-second plenary sessions and of the four divisions on the basic problems were prepared and presented in the form of interim reports to plenary sessions between July and December 1962 where they were accepted. The Interim Reports of the First Division included "Preamble," "Emperor," "Renunciation of War," "Amendment," and "Supreme Law." The Interim Reports of the Second Division included "Rights and Duties of the People: I (Articles 10 to 30)," "Rights and Duties of the People: II (Articles 31 to 40)," "The Judiciary," and "Basic Principles for Education and for the Social and Economic Systems." The Interim Reports of the Third Division included "The Diet," "The Cabinet," "The Cabinet: The Discussion of the Popular Election of the Prime Minister," "Finance," "Local Self-Government," "A Constitutional Organ to Guarantee Fair Elections (Demarcation of Election Districts and Supervision of Elections)," "A Constitutional Organ to Guarantee the Status of Public Servants," "Political Parties," and "Systems for Direct Democracy: National Referenda, etc." The Interim Report of the Special Division was entitled "The Controversy over the Invalidity of the Constitution."

The discussion of the basic principle of the rule of law, one of the matters assigned to the Second Division, was included in its interim report on the judiciary. Similarly its discussion of the problem of coordination among the cabinet, the Diet, and the courts by means of a constitutional provision was included in the First Division's interim report on the supreme law.

Also the four plenary sessions between October and December 1962 deliberated on the basic questions of the terseness, style, and organization of the Constitution, and the results were incorporated in an interim report, which was deliberated on and approved at the ninety-second plenary session in January 1963.

The deliberations on both the basic and general questions were largely completed by the end of December 1962, and in January 1963 at the ninety-second plenary session the general procedures for the future were agreed upon, particularly in respect to the problems that would be debated.

In the twenty plenary sessions from the 93rd to the 112th between

January and May 1963, the commission deliberated on the questions that were listed for debate. During this period there were no meetings of the four divisions. Then in the 114th and 115th plenary sessions in June summary discussions of the same problems were held in order to supplement the earlier deliberations. During this period the commissioners set forth their opinions and questions, and opposition views were presented. In addition, reference materials were also compiled where necessary.

Because there was some overlap between the discussions above and the earlier deliberations, the results of the discussions were gathered together at the 113th plenary session in May 1963; they were not issued, however, as separate reports but were incorporated into the divisional interim reports dealing with the general and basic questions. At that point the divisional interim reports were revised as necessary and coordinated in general.

The general coordination and supplementary corrections of the "Interim Report on General Questions" and of the divisional interim reports were carried out as outlined below.

The results of the ninety-third and later plenary session deliberations beginning in January 1963 on the questions of the kind of Constitution Japan should have and of the attitude toward revision and the results of the plenary session deliberations after the eighty-sixth session in October 1962 on the general questions were added to the "Interim Report on General Questions." This was then compiled as "The Report on Basic Problems in the Reexamination of the Constitution" which was deliberated on and approved at the 116th and 117th plenary sessions in July 1963. At that time materials relating to the organization, style, and terseness of the Constitution and to the application and interpretation of the Constitution and other matters were taken from other interim reports and added to this one.

Other problems submitted for discussion were deliberated on in plenary sessions following the ninety-eighth in February 1963, and certain basic problems were deliberated on in plenary sessions after the eighty-second in July 1962. The results of these deliberations were added to the divisional interim reports between May and September 1963 after due deliberation in the divisions regarding additions and revisions. This material was added to the appropriate divisional interim reports.

At this time the following changes were also made. The contents of the Second Division interim report, "Basic Principles for Education and for the Social and Economic Systems," were incorporated into that division's first report on the rights and duties of the people. Also the contents of the Third Division's interim reports on a constitutional organ to guarantee fair elections, political parties, and direct democracy were shifted to the same division's report on the Diet. Finally, the contents of the Third Division's interim reports on the election of the prime minister and on a constitutional organ for the guarantee of the status of public servants were shifted to that division's report on the cabinet.

SECTION D.
PUBLIC HEARINGS AND INVESTIGATIONS ABROAD

The commission at its eighteenth plenary session in October 1958 decided to hold public hearings in the major cities and all the prefectures and also decided on the basic policy to govern such hearings. When the commission entered the stage of investigating the process of the enactment of the Constitution and the actual circumstances of its operation, it held a series of meetings in the forty-six major administrative units of the country in order to hear the opinions of the public at large on important issues relating to the Constitution, especially as those opinions reflected their actual experiences with the operation of the Constitution. These meetings were held between November 1958 and March 1961. Then when the commission entered into the stage of deliberating on the constitutional problems that were revealed in the course of its investigations, it sponsored a series of nine regional public hearings in order to hear the opinions of the public at large on the issue of constitutional revision and on whether there should be improvements in the actual operation of the Constitution. These meetings continued from February to September 1962 in nine regions throughout the country; hence, they were termed the regional public hearings. Finally, a central public hearing designed to cover the nation was held in Tokyo.

The Holding of Public Hearings

The local public hearings were decided upon at the eighteenth plenary session (as indicated above), the thirty-second (July 1959), and the forty-first (February 1960). As a result, forty-six hearings were held throughout the country in locations decided by the unit of prefectural government involved in the period between November 1958 and March 1961.

The regional public hearings were decided upon at the seventy-first plenary session (January 1961) as indicated above. The nine regional hearings were held between February and August 1962 in the principal cities of the following regions: Kantō, Kinki, Kyūshū, Tōhoku, Shikoku, Chūgoku, Hokuriku-Shinetsu, Tōkai, and Hokkaidō.

The decision to hold the central public hearing was also made at the seventy-first plenary session and the eighty-fourth (September 1962) and was held for two days in the same month in Tokyo.

Circumstances of the Public Hearings

From the first through the ninth of the public hearings the witnesses represented labor, management, small- and medium-sized enterprises, agriculture, women, young people, the press, academic circles, and other groups and were simply selected on the basis of nominations by cooperating organizations representing the groups.

From the tenth hearing onward a representative was nominated from the legal field in addition to those above, and witnesses were also called from the public at large. At these hearings the witnesses were usually equally split between those nominated by the above organizations and those selected from the public by the commission itself. Usually there were four at-large witnesses selected from those who submitted written statements containing their age, occupation, and an outline of their testimony in response to public notices printed in the newspapers outlining the objectives of the hearings and indicating the items on which testimony was desired. The commission desired to have the witnesses split evenly between the two groups with as little overlap as possible in the fields they represented.

A total of 389 witnesses appeared at the local public hearings to make their views known, and of those 136 were from the public at large.

About ten commissioners attended each hearing, one of whom acted as chairman of the meeting. In addition, specialists and the director also participated. At the beginning of each hearing the chairman explained why the hearing was being held. Then witnesses would appear in order to state their views, following which there would be a question-and-answer period between the witnesses and the commissioners.

Witnesses were allowed about twenty minutes to state their views, centering on their experience with the operation of the Constitution. They could freely select the problems they wished to discuss under the general topic of "Important Problems relating to the Constitution" as heard by the commission; for example, the emperor, the renunciation of war, fundamental human rights, the House of Councilors, the Supreme Court, and local self-government. Attendance at the hearings was open to all, the only limitation being the size of the hearing room.

The regional public hearings differed from the local public hearings as indicated below. The witnesses were nominated by organizations representing the same fields as in the local public hearings, but with the addition of education. A total of eighty witnesses appeared at these hearings.

The regional hearing witnesses addressed the general issues of whether the present Constitution should be revised or whether there should be improvements in its application. They were free to select their topics from among those which had been discussed and deliberated on within the commission and which were listed as follows in the commission's "Topics for Statements in the Public Hearings":

1. The emperor: his position as a symbol; his functions

2. The renunciation of war: the right of self-defense and the Self-Defense Forces; the relationship between the renunciation of war and the system for international peace

3. The rights and duties of the people: the relationship between basic human rights (especially the freedoms of expression, assembly, and association; the rights of labor to organize, bargain, and act collectively; and the right of property) and the public welfare; the relationship between church and state; the family system; the inheritance of farm property; the guarantee of the right to a decent life; the guarantee of human rights in criminal procedure; and the duties of the people

4. The National Diet: the position of the Diet as "the highest organ of state power"; the bicameral system; the organization of the House of Councilors

5. The cabinet: the parliamentary cabinet system; the position and the method of selection of the prime minister; measures to be taken in a state of emergency

6. The judiciary: the judicial review of the constitutionality of legislation; popular review of Supreme Court justices

7. Finance: limitations on the utilization and expenditure of public property and funds

8. Local self-government: the coordination of local self-government and central government (the relationship between the state and local public entities; the organization of local public entities and the election of their heads); a system for wide-area administration

9. Miscellaneous: political parties and an organ to provide for fair elections

The central public hearing differed from the regional ones in the following respects. In addition to the fields represented in the regional hearings, religion and social welfare were added for the central hearing. Witnesses were selected from all fields in cooperation with the national organizations representing them. A total of eighteen witnesses appeared at the two-day central hearing.

Although all commissioners were to have attended the central public hearing, about twenty (including the member who served as hearing chairman) appeared during the two days. The specialists and the director also participated. In addition to the nine areas of general problems discussed at the regional hearings, a tenth was added for the central hearing: a general discussion of the Constitution and the problem of revision.

Following each public hearing an outline of what had happened was presented at a plenary session by the commissioner who had acted as chairman. In addition, minutes of each public hearing were compiled for purposes of commission investigation and deliberation. Finally, the "Report on the Public Hearings" was prepared, discussed, and approved at the 118th and 119th plenary sessions in September 1963.

Investigations Abroad

When the commission was in the stage of making its investigation into the process of enactment of the Constitution, it examined during November and December 1958 in the United States the circumstances as seen from the standpoint of the Allies. In the next stage when the commission was investigating the actual operation of the Constitution, it carried out research between September 1958 and March 1961 on the state of constitutional operations in Southeast Asia, Europe, the United States, and Latin America.

Later when the commission was in the stage of its deliberations on Japanese constitutional issues, it heard opinions from American, Canadian, and European scholars on Japanese constitutional problems. This took place between March and December 1962.

At the thirteenth plenary session in April 1958 at the time when it was investigating the circumstances of the enactment of the Constitution, the commission decided that it should study the circumstances from the side of the Allies and the United States. Then at the sixteenth plenary session in September 1959 it decided to send Commissioners Takayanagi, Inaba, and Takada and Secretary Ohtomo Ichirō to the United States.

As a part of this investigation Commissioners Takayanagi and Inaba and Secretary Ohtomo spent October and November 1958 in West Germany investigating that country's Basic Law. They were then joined by Commissioner Takada in the United States where they carried out their investigations in November and December.

Commissioner Takayanagi presented a comprehensive report on the investigations in the United States at the twenty-fourth plenary session in January 1959. Commissioner Takada then gave a detailed report on the same matter to the sixteenth through the eighteenth sessions (January and February 1959) of the subcommittee on the process of the enactment of the Constitution. At the twenty-ninth meeting of the same sub-committee in October 1959, Commissioner Inaba reported on the West German investigation.

At the same sixteenth plenary session when it was decided to send Commissioner Takayanagi and the others for investigation in the United States on the process of enactment of the Constitution, it was decided to carry out research on the current state of constitutionalism in the United States and other countries. Between September and December 1958 the same three commissioners conducted investigations in India, Italy, Yugoslavia, Switzerland, West Germany, France, England, and the United States on the current state of constitutionalism. Commissioner Takayanagi also reported on these investigations at the twenty-fourth plenary session in his report on their investigation in the United States on the process of enactment.

At the thirty-seventh plenary session in November 1959 it was decided to send Commissioner Nakamura Umekichi to various European countries; Commissioner Takayanagi to Southeast Asia; Commissioner Rōyama Masamichi to various countries in Asia, Europe, and America; and Specialist Satō Isao to the three countries of Northern Europe to study constitutional problems in those areas. Between January and March 1960 Commissioner Nakamura studied the relationship between the government and the parliament in Italy, Switzerland, West Germany, France, England, Holland, and Belgium; in January and February Commissioner Takayanagi studied democratic trends in the Federation of Malaysia, Indonesia, the Philippines, and Singapore; from March to July Commissioner Rōyama investigated constitutional trends in India, Pakistan, Italy, West Germany, France, Switzerland, and the United States; and from March to May Specialist Satō studied developments in monarchical systems in England, Norway, Sweden, Denmark, Holland, Belgium, Luxembourg, France, West Germany, Switzerland, Italy, Greece, and Egypt. Preceding the above investigations, Commissioner Tagami Jōji in March 1959 had studied monarchical systems in Sweden, Norway, Denmark, Holland, Belgium, and Luxembourg.

Reports on the development and results of the above investigations were delivered as follows: by Commissioner Tagami at the eighth meeting of the Third Committee in October 1959; by Commissioners Nakamura and Takayanagi at the forty-sixth plenary session in May 1960; by Commissioner Rōyama at the forty-seventh plenary session in August 1960; and by Specialist Satō at the twentieth meeting of the Third Committee in June 1960.

In addition, at the forty-eighth plenary session in January 1961 it was decided to send Commissioners Yabe Teiji, Nakasone Yasuhiro, Ushioda Kōji, and Ōnishi Kunitoshi to Central and South America for investigations into the actual operations of constitutions in countries of those areas. Between January and March 1961 the above commissioners carried out investigations in Mexico, Peru, Chile, Argentina, Uruguay, Brazil, and Venezuela in regard to provisions and the application thereof relating to the executive, legislative, and judicial branches and their actual operations and matters relating to the guarantee of and restrictions on fundamental human rights. Reports on the development and results of these investigations were given by Commissioners Yabe and Ōnishi at the fifty-first plenary session in May of the same year.

In addition to the above, scholars in several foreign countries were requested to submit opinions relating to the operation of the constitutions of their countries and this material was prepared for reference.

When the commission entered the final stage of deliberation on problems relating to Japan's Constitution, investigations were carried out abroad in order to ascertain the opinions of foreign scholars on those problems.

It was decided at the seventy-second plenary session in February 1962 to send Commissioners Takayanagi and Kojima Tetsuzō, Specialist Tanaka Kazuo, and Director Takeoka Kenichi to the United States and Canada. Between March and May 1962 the above individuals either interviewed or requested the written opinions of scholars in both countries. They circulated beforehand a long list of questions to those they expected to interview, together with a commentary in English on Japanese constitutional problems.

[Omitted here is the long list of questions. The questions and the English commentary may be found in *Comments and Observations by Foreign Scholars concerning the Constitution of Japan, 1946.*]

Commissioner Takayanagi reported on the development and results of this investigation at the eightieth and eighty-first plenary sessions in June 1962.

Then at the eighty-fifth plenary session in September 1962 and the eighty-sixth in October it was decided to send Commissioners Mano Tsuyoshi and Aichi Kiichi and Specialists Kuroda Satoru and Matsumoto Kaoru to Europe. Between October and December these four carried out investigations in Europe similar to the earlier one in the United States and Canada, using a slightly revised list of questions. They interviewed or obtained written opinions of scholars in England, France, Belgium, West Germany, Austria, Switzerland, and Italy. Commissioner Mano delivered a report on the European investigations at the 100th plenary session in March 1963.

The written opinions of the American and Canadian scholars, as well as the results of the investigations in those two countries, were compiled as materials to be used during the commission's deliberations. In addition, scholars from a few other foreign countries were asked to submit their criticisms of and opinions concerning Japan's Constitution, and these were also compiled for use during the deliberations.

The results of the above overseas investigations were compiled in "Report on Investigations Abroad," which was deliberated upon and approved at the 122nd plenary session in January 1964.

SECTION E.
THE DRAFTING OF THE REPORT TO THE CABINET AND THE DIET

[This section, pp. 81–95 in the original, is omitted here. It is an extremely detailed account of the drafting which adds nothing to an understanding of the nature of the work of the commission or the content of the report.]

3. The Investigations and Deliberations

The Investigations on the Process of Enactment
of the Constitution of Japan

The details of the investigation into the process of the enactment of the Constitution are supplied in the report of the subcommittee (Supplementary Document No. 2). However, a condensed outline of the principal matters covered in that investigation is presented below.

The investigations went back to the formation during the Second World War of Allied policy toward postwar Japan, as the source of the enactment of the Constitution, and dealt with the entire process including the completion and promulgation of the Constitution. Consequently, the report of the subcommittee on this problem is extremely detailed, and many sections in it contain thorough research and inquiry into special problems. Consequently, it is extremely difficult to present a condensed outline without deficiencies. Accordingly, for the details of the investigation reference to the appropriate sections of the subcommittee report is recommended.

[Omitted here is the table of contents of the subcommittee report which was included for the convenience of Japanese readers of the report.]

Below an extremely simplified and condensed outline of the principal problems is presented.

The Origin of the Problem of Constitutional Revision

Allied Postwar Policy during World War II. The direct origin and motive for the enactment of the Constitution of Japan lay in the acceptance of the Potsdam Declaration which was the result of military defeat. Because the declaration must be regarded as both the Allied

62

policy for the postwar handling of Japan and the achievement of the Allied war aims, its fundamental and special character as Allied postwar policy must be examined.

First of all, the fundamental characteristics of this policy will become clear when it is compared with the postwar policy of the victorious countries following World War I. Between the two there is a striking and fundamental difference. In contrast with the victors in World War I who did not raise directly either as a war aim or as postwar policy the reconstruction of the political systems of the defeated nations, the Allies in World War II not only set forth unconditional surrender as the war policy toward their enemies from the beginning of the war but also proclaimed that their principal aims were to destroy militarism, to reform the political systems supporting it and to reconstruct the nations involved. The basic principles were enunciated in such pronouncements as the Atlantic Charter and President Franklin D. Roosevelt's congressional message on the "Four Freedoms."

Thus, the policy of unconditional surrender was based on the premise of the broader principles outlined above. Accordingly, the unconditional surrender formula was connected to Allied occupation policy. Here we turn to the origins and significance of the unconditional surrender policy.

The origin of this policy flowed from President Roosevelt's statement at the Casablanca Conference, but in the process of the concrete realization of this concept in relation to Italy and other enemy countries, opposition developed even among the Allies on the grounds that its enforcement actually strengthened the enemy's will to war. However, Roosevelt adhered steadfastly to the policy. In regard to Japan, the policy was realized through the issuance and acceptance of the Potsdam Declaration. The investigation centered on these considerations.

The Potsdam Declaration was designed to present to Japan the conditions for unconditional surrender. At the same time it constituted the ultimate formulation of the basic objectives of postwar policy toward Japan. Under the circumstances of the time Secretary of War [Henry L.] Stimson's memorandum [of 2 July 1945 to President Harry S. Truman outlining a possible program for ending the war short of an invasion] has been described as the draft of the Potsdam Declaration. In essence, it is clear that Japan's surrender was unconditional, if "unconditional" means that Japan had no other choice than to accept the conditions of surrender presented unilaterally by the Allies. It is impossible to escape the fact that the policy of unconditional surrender, which had been firmly maintained by the Allies since the Roosevelt statement at Casablanca, was realized toward Japan.

In spite of the above circumstances, two opposing views emerged during the subcommittee's investigation into the characteristics and intrinsic nature of the Potsdam Declaration. The first view was this: unconditional surrender means "complete annexation by conquest" in disregard of all rules and usages of international law. It resembles the ancient Roman doctrine of *debellatio*, or the complete defeat and destruction of an enemy country. Thus, the authority of General Douglas MacArthur as commander of the occupation army was absolutely unlimited. Consequently, this view considered the Allied occupation of Japan as an absolute military dictatorship with the objective of complete control on the order of *debellatio*. This view was strongly advocated, particularly by Commissioner Kamikawa Hikomatsu.

In opposition, the second view held that *debellatio* refers to the complete military annihilation of the enemy nation and designates the situation where, in terms of international law, the enemy nation no longer retains its character as a nation. The second viewpoint maintained that this did not apply to Japan's situation. Moreover, the Potsdam Declaration was also binding on the Allies. This view was strongly held by Commissioner Takayanagi and Consultant Iriye Tetsushirō, professor at Seikei University.

In addition, according to the investigations of the group that went to America, an American official who participated in the drafting of the Potsdam Declaration made the following interpretation: "The provisions of the Potsdam Declaration had legal meaning; the Allies and Japan were bound together in a relationship of rights and obligations. Accordingly, in respect to the revision of Japan's Constitution during the occupation, the Allies had the right to demand it in accordance with the provisions of the Potsdam Declaration, and Japan had the obligation to carry it out in accordance with the same provisions."

Views were opposed, as indicated above, regarding the nature of the Potsdam Declaration. In respect to the connection between the declaration and the origin of the present Constitution, there were other views that raised questions such as the following: Was Japan's surrender unconditional? Is it worthwhile to decide whether the surrender was unconditional or not?

THE FORMATION OF BASIC POLICY TOWARD JAPAN IN THE UNITED STATES. It is necessary to consider developments from the formation of American policy toward Japan during the war down to the completion of the Potsdam Declaration. The drafting of policy respecting the postwar control of Japan had already begun by about November 1942, and various American government organizations developed draft plans for research by different groups. Ultimately, the so-called State, War, Navy Coordinating Committee [SWNCC] became the principal group and prepared a variety of basic documents. It also developed ideas relating to the methods and machinery for joint Allied control of post-surrender Japan.

In regard to the formative process, the circumstances surrounding the opposing views, both within the government and among the public, regarding the handling of the emperor system were investigated in a number of documents. In summary, it can be said that within the United States government the debate over what should be done about the emperor system remained unresolved even during the final stages of the war. The top levels of the State Department consistently maintained a policy of retaining the emperor system, but opposition to this policy was extremely strong. As the war entered its final stage the solution of this problem became a matter of urgency. At this point the preparation of the Potsdam Declaration through the [Joseph C.] Grew Draft (28 May 1944 [1945]) and the Stimson memorandum (2 July) came into the picture. In the process at this stage in the second part of paragraph 12 of the first draft of the declaration there was a provision to the effect that a "constitutional monarchy under present imperial rule" would be acceptable. But detailed inquiry revealed that this was eliminated in the final stage. It can be said that in the above process, however, Grew and Stimson played important roles in the retention of the emperor system, and the possibility remains that even though the last part of paragraph 12 of the declaration was eliminated, it permitted at the very least the later interpretation that the retention of the emperor should be left "to the freely expressed will of the Japanese people."

In relation to the investigation of the above matters the United States Department of State in June 1961 released the *Documents on United States Foreign Relations: The Potsdam Conference 1945.* One of these documents, entitled "A Comparative Examination of the Declaration of 26 July 1945 and the Policy of the Department of State," shows that there were several items of existing policy toward Japan, including the handling of the emperor system, to be included in the Potsdam Declaration that the State Department had to change. Clearly, the State Department arrived at the conclusion that existing policy as it related to the application and interpretation of unconditional surrender had to be changed. For example, the State Department had held that unconditional surrender was a unilateral act possessing no contractual elements of any kind, but the Potsdam Declaration did presuppose a surrender of a contractual nature.

JAPAN'S ACCEPTANCE OF THE POTSDAM DECLARATION. On the problem of Japan's acceptance of the Potsdam Declaration, two central questions were studied: How did Japan and the Allies treat the problem of the emperor system at the time of the acceptance of the declaration?, and How did Japan interpret "unconditional surrender"?

In respect to the role of the question of the emperor system in the acceptance of the Potsdam Declaration, three issues were dealt with: (1) the question of how to guarantee the "maintenance of the national polity [*kokutai*]," which was the matter of greatest concern to the inner circles [of Japan] at the time of the acceptance of the declaration; (2) the circumstances surrounding the request for an expression of Allied opinion regarding the emperor system at the time of the offer to the Allies to accept the declaration on 10 August 1945; and (3) the circumstances surrounding the issuing of the Allied reply on 11 August and the subsequent realization of the end of the war.

On the question of how the Japanese Foreign Ministry interpreted unconditional surrender at the time, Commissioner Matsumoto Shunichi, who was then vice minister of foreign affairs, declared that at the very least Foreign Ministry officials believed that regardless of what Roosevelt may have meant by the term when he originally used it, the idea of unconditional surrender came to an end with the Potsdam Declaration, which was nothing more than a presentation of concrete conditions for the surrender.

The Opening of the Question of Constitutional Revision

THE START OF OCCUPATION CONTROL. At the start of occupation control the question of constitutional revision still had not assumed a concrete form. As a matter of principle, the method of occupation control was indirect, but in exceptional cases direct control was also available. At the end of the war the machinery for policy-making for the control of Japan had not been organized. The Far Eastern Advisory Commission was only a temporary body that continued until the establishment of the Far Eastern Commission in December 1945.

In respect to the establishment of policy for the control of Japan, two documents must be examined: "United States Initial Postsurrender Policy for Japan" (22 September 1945) [formally approved by President Truman on 6 September 1945], and "Initial Basic Directive" [from the U.S. Joint Chiefs of Staff to General MacArthur] (1 November 1945). The question of constitutional revision was dealt with in this control policy in the following way: First, neither in the Potsdam Declaration nor in the above documents was there any provision that dealt clearly and specifically with constitutional revision. However, even though these documents are not interpreted as holding that the revision of the Meiji Constitution was unnecessary, the Allies, and especially the United States, must be regarded as having believed that the policy for the control of Japan naturally included the revision of the Meiji Constitution.

THE QUESTION OF CONSTITUTIONAL REVISION AT THE BEGINNING OF THE OCCUPATION. The Allied control of Japan began with the question of constitutional revision looming in the background, but in the closing days of the Higashikuni cabinet, concrete action was shown for the first time in a hint from General MacArthur to Prince Konoye Fumimaro. Under the circumstances neither the Higashikuni cabinet, which was responsible for handling the matter of the ending of the war, nor the press dealt with the issue of constitutional revision. In addition, the generally passive attitude of the time, particularly of the government, could not evaluate, accurately or adequately, the nature of occupation policy. There was no way of determining what the policy might be on constitutional revision.

Investigations were then made of SCAP's attitude at the time that it was necessary for the Constitution to be revised rapidly in order to achieve the objectives of the occupation and the corresponding necessity to awaken the attention of the Japanese government to the matter.

INVESTIGATION OF CONSTITUTIONAL REVISION IN THE OFFICE OF THE LORD KEEPER OF THE PRIVY SEAL. The commission examined the circumstances surrounding the inauguration of the investigation of constitutional revision in the Office of the Lord Keeper of the Privy Seal which was carried out by Prince Konoye, then a minister of state, in conjunction with Professor Emeritus Sasaki Sōichi. This followed a suggestion from General MacArthur on 4 October 1945 to Prince Konoye regarding the necessity for such revision and the presentation on 8 October by U.S. Ambassador George Atcheson, Jr., of twelve points relating to revision. [Atcheson had the title of ambassador, but was not accredited to the government of Japan.]

Then, in respect to the progress and conclusion of the above investigations of the Office of the Lord Keeper of the Privy Seal, the Konoye project and the foreign and domestic reactions to it were described. Also investigated were the circumstances surrounding the announcement on 1 [11] November from General Headquarters (GHQ), SCAP that the Allied authorities regarded as inappropriate the selection of Prince Konoye for the work of constitutional revision and the fact that a considerable amount of opposition to and criticism of Konoye's conduct had developed both at home and abroad. In the above investigation of the attitudes of both GHQ and the Shidehara cabinet toward Prince Konoye, the testimony of four associates of the prince at that time was obtained: Professor Emeritus Takagi Yasaku of Tokyo University; Professor Emeritus Sasaki Sōichi of Kyoto University; Ushiba Tomohiko, the prince's former secretary; and former Commissioner Tomita Kenji.

The principal points of the so-called Konoye and Sasaki drafts were produced, but during the investigation what is apparently the complete text of the Konoye draft was turned up. It can be considered to be the original text of the draft that Prince Konoye presented to the emperor.

THE PUBLICATION OF REVISED CONSTITUTIONS, AND TRENDS IN PUBLIC OPINION. The principal points of the drafts of revised constitutions released between October 1945 and March 1946 by the Liberal Party, the Progressive Party, the Socialist Party, the Communist Party, the Association for Constitutional Research, the Constitutional Discussion Group, and Dr. Takano Iwasaburō were presented to the commission, and the basic differences among them were outlined on such matters as the emperor system, the parliamentary system, the rights and duties of the people, and especially the social and economic provisions. Several items are worth noting. On both pacifism and demilitarization there is nothing in the above drafts that resembles what later became Article 9. Also only the draft of the Association for Constitutional Research, in its supplementary provisions, provided for what can be considered a provisional constitution by stipulating the following: "Within no more than ten years after the promulgation of this constitution a new constitution must be enacted by means of a national referendum."

On the problem of trends in public opinion, newspaper editorials dating from around the time of General MacArthur's statement regarding Prince Konoye and of the release of the news about the start of constitutional investigation in the Office of the Lord Keeper of the Privy Seal about 11 October 1945, editorials on the draft of the Liberal Party and the results of the public opinion poll of 3 February 1946 were presented to the commission. The results of the above public opinion poll showed the following: (1) on the method of constitutional revision an overwhelming majority demanded a constitutional revision committee to be selected by popular vote; and (2) on the emperor system, while support for it was definite, only an extremely small minority favored the placing of the emperor beyond government.

THE WORK OF THE SHIDEHARA CABINET IN CONSTITUTIONAL REVISION. The problem of constitutional revision was dealt with concretely for the first time under the Shidehara cabinet. The commission investigated the circumstances relating to such matters as the creation of the Committee for the Investigation of Constitutional Problems (the so-called Matsumoto committee) on the basis of MacArthur's suggestion to Prime Minister Shidehara Kijurō on 11 October 1945, the progress of the committee's investigations, and the process of the creation of the Matsumoto draft.

Among the above problems, especially on the progress of the work of the Matsumoto committee, the commission relied heavily on the testimony of Satō Tatsuo (former chief of the Bureau of Legislation), who was a member of the committee, relating to the discussions in the cabinet meetings under Prime Minister Shidehara. It also relied heavily on the records supplied by Mr. Iriye Toshirō (also a former chief of the Bureau of Legislation), who attended the cabinet meetings in his capacity as vice-chief of the Bureau of Legislation.

The Matsumoto committee, and especially Minister of State Matsumoto himself, unlike those around Prince Konoye, firmly maintained the position that it was not necessary to refer in any way to the views of GHQ. According to Professor Takagi, he advised Matsumoto to take into account the views of GHQ, but his opinion was disregarded. According to what Matsumoto said later, it was his recollection that he believed constitutional revision could be carried out completely independently by the Japanese, on the basis of such phrases as "the freely expressed will of the Japanese people" in the Potsdam Declaration and in the Allied reply to the Japanese query of 11 August 1945. However, from the vantage point of today it can be pointed out that Matsumoto's view was probably somewhat too legalistic.

The Preparation of the Draft Constitution in General Headquarters

THE PRESENTATION OF THE MATSUMOTO DRAFT TO GENERAL HEADQUARTERS. The problem of constitutional revision entered a critical stage and the situation underwent a complete change when "Gist of the Revision of the Constitution" (or the Matsumoto draft which had been drafted by him as a minister of state on the basis of the deliberations of his committee) was presented to GHQ. The commission went into the circumstances of the presentation of this "Gist of the Revision of the Constitution."

Its principal points can be ascertained through an examination of documents entitled "General Explanation of the Constitutional Revision" and "Proposed Revision of the Army and Navy Provisions in the Constitution." The contents of these were condensed and published by the commission.

GENERAL HEADQUARTERS' REJECTION OF THE MATSUMOTO DRAFT. The content of the Matsumoto draft had already been inferred by GHQ even before its formal submission on 8 February 1946. MacArthur had already decided on 1 February to reject it. In respect to what happened during that interval, the activities of GHQ at the time the Matsumoto draft was submitted are described in *Political Reorientation of Japan* which was compiled by GHQ's Government Section. The reasons for the rejection can be examined in that publication. Briefly, GHQ concluded that the Matsumoto draft was far more conservative than unofficial drafts prepared at the time and that consequently it was not representative of Japanese opinion.

THE POLICY OF THE AMERICAN GOVERNMENT TOWARD CONSTITUTION- AL REVISION. The reasons for GHQ's rejection of the Matsumoto draft were as described in *Political Reorientation of Japan*. However, SWNCC 228 [State, War, Navy Coordinating Committee, Document 228] which set forth the policy of the American government toward constitutional revision in Japan had already been delivered to GHQ. On the basis of SWNCC 228, GHQ believed that the Matsumoto draft was completely unacceptable and that this same document should be regarded as the most important guide when GHQ began its work on the so-called MacArthur draft. The commission first obtained the original text of SWNCC 228 when its research team went to the United States. It was the first to publish the complete text, especially the section entitled "Conclu- sions," and carried out a detailed study of its principal points.

The document dealt with the emperor system as the principal point. In "Conclusions" the fate of the emperor system was to be decided by the freely expressed will of the Japanese people. However, it was considered that the continuance of the emperor system as it was would be inconsist- ent with the general objectives set forth in the document. In addition, it stated that the Japanese people should be encouraged either "to abolish the Emperor Institution or to reform it along more democratic lines." Finally, if the people decided to retain the institution, then the necessary stipulations should be included to insure that it be democratic.

The document also made it clear that constitutional reforms were necessary and that the Supreme Commander should call on the Japanese government to make them; it also warned that there was the danger that such a request, if in the form of an order or coercion, would result in the ultimate failure of constitutional reform. Accordingly, methods should be used to facilitate the acceptance by the Japanese people of such constitutional changes, and the Supreme Commander should "order the Japanese government" to carry out the reforms "only as a last resort."

The commission also considered the problem of how, in this docu- ment, the American government dealt with the disarmament of Japan in relation to constitutional reform. SWNCC 228 had no provisions regard- ing Japanese disarmament which could be regarded as the sources of the later Article 9 of the Constitution. The following provisions appear in the document: ". . . formal action permanently subordinating the mili- tary services to the civil government by requiring that the ministers of state or the members of a cabinet must, in all cases, be civilians would be advisable"; and "the emperor shall be deprived of all military authority. . . ." These expressions can be interpreted as indicating that the existence of military forces was approved and that the necessary means for controlling them would have to be established. This is an extremely interesting point for debate: on the one hand, there are strong grounds for maintaining the opinion that SWNCC 228 did not anticipate the disarmament of Japan and that accordingly Article 9 was drafted on the basis of MacArthur's own policy; on the other hand, the opinion can also be put forth that since the same document included the policy of the permanent disarmament of Japan as a matter of course, the source of Article 9 was clearly in the unshakeable policy of the United States.

On this same question there is the problem of a possible connection between the "Draft Treaty for the Disarmament and Demilitarization of Japan," drafted at about the same time by the American government and delivered to Great Britain, the Soviet Union, and the Republic of China, and the constitutional provision for the renunciation of war. The research team that went to the United States concluded, however, that there was no ground for assuming that there might be such a connection.

THE RELATIONS BETWEEN THE FAR EASTERN COMMISSION AND GENERAL HEADQUARTERS ON CONSTITUTIONAL REVISION. In the investigation of the activities of GHQ, SCAP and MacArthur around the beginning of February 1946, the circumstances surrounding the establishment of the Far Eastern Commission at the Moscow Conference of late December 1945 were inescapable. After 1 February 1946, MacArthur took the following steps: (1) the decision to reject the Matsumoto draft; (2) the ordering of the speedy preparation of the so-called MacArthur draft; and (3) the delivery of that draft to the Japanese government. These steps can be interpreted as the result of his expectation that the FEC would impose certain limitations on his authority as Supreme Commander in regard to constitutional revision in Japan and his wish to make it into an accomplished fact before the commission held its first meeting on 26 February 1946. These measures by MacArthur were the source of the subsequent confrontation and friction between GHQ, SCAP and the American government on the one hand and the FEC on the other. In connection with the above circumstances, the commission investigated the course of the establishment of the FEC and the lines of authority between it on the one side and the Supreme Commander and the Allied Council for Japan on the other.

The commission first studied MacArthur's authority in the area of constitutional revision. On 30 January 1946, MacArthur had a private conversation with the members of the Far Eastern Advisory Commission who were then in Japan and indicated that the FEC had not yet assumed authority over constitutional revision, that the problem should be dealt with by the Japanese people themselves, and that GHQ, SCAP had not undertaken any work in this area. However, immediately after the advisory commission members had left Japan, MacArthur suddenly ordered his own draft. These developments constituted a dramatically sudden shift in circumstances.

In relation to MacArthur's steps as described above, the commission examined the 1 February memorandum to MacArthur by Brigadier General Courtney Whitney, chief of SCAP's Government Section. The essentials of that memorandum were: (1) that until the FEC made a policy decision on the matter, the Supreme Commander was under no limitations even in respect to constitutional revision; (2) that even if there were any restrictions, the Allied Council for Japan could impose restrictions only on the method by which the Supreme Commander's authority was exercised; and (3) that the FEC was empowered only to review the decisions of the Supreme Commander.

The circumstances under which the above memorandum was drafted are naturally not clear. However, the effect was that after 1 February MacArthur's actions can be recognized as having been based on the opinions set forth in this memorandum. Views conflict over the Whitney opinions. One holds that they were a distortion of the Moscow agreement and that MacArthur's actions were either *ultra vires* or an evasion of the law [agreement]. There is also the view that, leaving political and moral considerations aside, Whitney's interpretation was legally not in error. Another opinion is that MacArthur's presentation to the Japanese government of the draft revision of the Constitution in the form of a "suggestion" or "instruction" cannot be termed a violation of the Moscow agreement. However, in any case, it is an undeniable fact that these steps by MacArthur had to be accepted as a *fait accompli* at an important stage in the revision of the Constitution at the time when the FEC had not yet commenced its activities.

THE CREATION OF THE GENERAL HEADQUARTERS DRAFT. In relation to the process discussed above, the so-called three principles of MacArthur, the process of the drafting itself, and other noteworthy matters relating to the draft were considered. MacArthur's three principles were as follows [*Political Reorientation of Japan*, vol. 1, p. 102.]:

I.

The Emperor is at the head of the State.

His succession is dynastic.

His duties and powers will be exercised in accordance with the constitution and responsible to the basic will of the people as provided therein.

II.

War as a sovereign right of the nation is abolished. Japan renounces it as an instrumentality for settling disputes and even for preserving its own security. It relies upon the higher ideals which are now stirring in the world for its defense and its protection.

No Japanese Army, Navy or Air Force will ever be authorized and no rights of belligerency will ever be conferred upon any Japanese forces.

III.

The feudal system of Japan will cease.

No rights of peerage except those of the Imperial family will extend beyond the lives of those now existent.

No patent of nobility will from this time forth embody within itself any National or Civic power of government.

Pattern budget after British system.

In regard to the drafting process, especially in respect to the draft of the Committee on Constitutional Research, one of the unofficial Japanese proposals, investigations were made of the degree to which the composers of the MacArthur draft seriously considered and consulted them. Witness Suzuki Yasuzō (professor at Shizuoka University), who was at the time a member of the above research group, asserted that GHQ paid careful attention to the attitudes of the Japanese people on constitutional revision and that one manifestation of this was the GHQ draft itself. In opposition to this, however, Commissioner Kamikawa put forth the view that it was inappropriate to place excessive value on the above opinion, that the research group's draft should be regarded as nothing more than source material in the same sense that other source materials were used, and that it did not have a character that would permit its being regarded as having made a special contribution to the GHQ draft.

Next, the commission investigated the circumstances surrounding the determination of two of the outstandingly important points in the GHQ draft: the emperor system and the renunciation of war.

In regard to the emperor system, the policy of the American government had still not been decided in spite of SWNCC 228, and the approval of the continuation of the system in the MacArthur draft was based on the final decision of MacArthur himself. As a part of the background of that decision it can be said that there was also the attitude of the so-called pro-Japan group in the United States which consistently demanded the maintenance of the emperor system even during the war. In addition there was also the GHQ evaluation of the role played by the emperor in ending the war and during the initial stages of the occupation.

The following quotation from correspondence by General MacArthur to Chairman Takayanagi clearly reveals the strong stand he took in support of the emperor system: "The preservation of the Emperor system was my fixed purpose. It was inherent and integral to Japanese political and cultural survival. The vicious efforts to destroy the person of the Emperor and thereby abolish the system became one of the most dangerous menaces that threatened the successful rehabilitation of the nation." [As quoted in a speech by Professor Takayanagi, the text of which was published in the *Japan Times*, 16 March 1959, p. 8.]

The "vicious efforts to destroy" the emperor system mentioned above referred both to the domestic arguments for abolition put forth by the Japan Communist Party and others and to similar positions strongly voiced among the Allies in the Soviet Union, Australia, and elsewhere. These nations planned to demand in the FEC a republican system for Japan, but MacArthur's decision in this matter can be regarded as a successful effort to strike the first blow [in defense of the emperor system].

In respect to the reasons for including the renunciation of war clause, MacArthur's speech before the Allied Council for Japan on 5 April 1946, following the release of the government's draft of a revised constitution, can be offered. However, in the letter to Chairman Takayanagi referred to above, MacArthur also pointed out that the purpose for inserting Article 9 was to express the determination that Japan would not again engage in foreign aggression and that it would give spiritual leadership to the world. He also emphasized that from the beginning, Article 9 was considered as a prohibition on Japanese aggression and that it was never intended to deny Japan the military power necessary to counter a threat to its security.

Next the commission carried out detailed investigations, using oral statements of many witnesses and other materials, to determine whether MacArthur or Prime Minister Shidehara was the first to propose the renunciation of war provision.

On this point the testimony of a large number of witnesses falls into several categories. The following views are influential. Prime Minister Shidehara was the originator, but MacArthur was sympathetically impressed and probably wrote it into his three principles. Another view is that, at a minimum, there was a sympathetic meeting of minds between the two men. In opposition is the positive denial of the view that Prime Minister Shidehara was the originator. Both Minister of State Matsumoto and former Commissioner Ashida Hitoshi, who was a cabinet minister at the time, were of this school. Also, according to the hearings of the commission's investigative team that went to the United States, those attached to GHQ at the time were generally critical of the view of Shidehara as the source. However, Prime Minister Shidehara himself on many occasions and to many Japanese and foreigners stated that the renunciation of war provision was completely the product of his own initiative. In addition, Ōhira Kutsui, a close friend of the prime minister's and at the time an advisor to the Privy Council, supported the Shidehara argument, namely, that the prime minister was devoted to the preservation of the emperor system and believed that a Japanese declaration of the renunciation of war was the only means by which the wariness and the misgivings of foreign countries toward the system could be swept away. Mr. Ōhira pointed out that on this issue the views of the prime minister and the general came together. On this point the thinking that tied together Article 9 and the preservation of the emperor system was supported inside the commission by Chairman Takayanagi and former Commissioner Murakami Giichi, who had been a member of the Shidehara cabinet. In addition, MacArthur himself both in a speech before the Allied Council for Japan and on many other occasions repeatedly set forth the Shidehara thesis and described the same point in the letter to Chairman Takayanagi mentioned above.

To summarize, the considerable testimony and evidence are extremely tangled, and many interpretive and speculative opinions are not based on direct evidence. In addition, with Prime Minister Shidehara now dead, MacArthur's testimony alone comes from a direct participant in the events. There is also the opinion that the problem of who actually put forward Article 9 is not too important because the disarmament of Japan was the unshakeable policy of the Allies.

Finally, the commission considered three questions relating to the significance of the GHQ draft: (1) did the SCAP draft constitute an order to the Japanese government as "a last resort" as stated in SWNCC 228?; (2) did the draft deviate in content from SWNCC 228 or from past policy of the American government?; and (3) in actual fact to what extent did MacArthur exercise his individual discretion?

The Composition of the Japanese Draft and Its Presentation to the Diet

THE PRESENTATION OF THE SCAP DRAFT. The SCAP draft was presented to the Japanese government on 13 February 1946. On the basis of that draft a Japanese draft was prepared. The commission first carried out an investigation of the circumstances of the 13 February meeting based on materials from both the Japanese and the American sides.

The investigation centered on the important question of "the guarantee of the person of the Emperor"; that is, on the day of the meeting it is said that General Whitney told the Japanese side that if the SCAP draft was not accepted by the Japanese government, it would be impossible to guarantee the safety of the emperor.

The only Japanese record of what Whitney said is in the so-called Matsumoto notes, that is, the notes that Minister of State Matsumoto wrote after the interview. He also reported what was said at the cabinet meeting of 19 February and on the basis of his notes described the meeting at a session of the Liberal Party Constitutional Investigation Committee. Outside of what Minister Matsumoto said and wrote there is nothing which can be considered to be testimony on this point.

Among the American materials nothing that has been made public deals with the "emperor's person" issue. The research team that went to America inquired as follows of Whitney and other SCAP officials in regard to whether there had been such a statement or an occasion at which the matter might have been referred to: "Was it designed to put pressure on the Japanese? Or did it emphasize the tenseness of the international situation at the time? Or was it related to the possible summoning of the emperor to the Tokyo war crimes trial?" Whitney himself replied that what was reported as Dr. Matsumoto's interpretation was completely erroneous. He also replied to the effect that what he had said regarding the emperor on that occasion was designed to call attention to the critical state of affairs regarding the imperial institution at that time. Also others who were SCAP officials at the time answered that they had no recollection of the Matsumoto statement.

However, following the investigations of the research team in America, Mr. Milo Rowell, who had participated in the 13 February meeting, presented to Chairman Takayanagi the memorandum of the meeting which was drafted immediately afterward on the basis of the recollection of the American officials who were present. According to this memorandum, the phrases relating to the emperor's person were not included in what Whitney said.

On the basis of the above materials from both Japanese and American sources, Commissioner Takayanagi has expressed the following opinions: What Whitney said at the meeting might have been interpreted by Minister Matsumoto to be a threat. However, Whitney's real intention was to refer plainly and objectively to the grim international situation. Minister Matsumoto's view that Whitney's comment was a threat and the generally held opinion accepting that view must both be regarded as erroneous. Even though we have testimony from Minister Matsumoto as to how he felt at the time, we must also regard as important the testimony of the Americans regarding their thoughts at the time.

However, it was Commissioner Ōishi Yoshio's opinion that the question is not one of American intentions at the moment, but that under the objective situation of the time the fact was that Minister Matsumoto took Whitney's words to mean that if his side's proposal was not accepted then there was strong pressure to infer that the person of the emperor would be in danger. In addition, Commissioner Nakasone Yasuhiro was of the opinion that Minister Matsumoto's oral testimony and the American materials possessed equal value and that it would be regrettable to respect the American responses without qualification. These views were in opposition to Commissioner Takayanagi's. Also Commissioner Kamikawa Hikomatsu consistently put forth the view that the question as to whether there was coercion or pressure was not to be decided only in regard to the 13 February meeting, but that MacArthur's occupation policy itself had to be regarded as characteristic of an absolute military dictatorship.

Next the commission dealt with the Japanese government's reaction to the SCAP draft which had shocked it profoundly. On 18 February, Minister of State Matsumoto again explained the gist of his draft and presented a supplementary explanation to support a request for reexamination by SCAP. However, SCAP also rejected that. Whereupon on 19 February for the first time there was an explanation to the entire cabinet of the events until then. On 21 February a meeting between MacArthur and Shidehara took place, and on the following day Whitney and Matsumoto met. As a result, it was decided that a new Japanese draft would be prepared, paralleling the SCAP draft. The commission examined the details of the discussion that took place in a number of cabinet meetings during the above period, with particular reference to the records compiled by former Commissioner Ashida Hitoshi who was a cabinet minister at the time.

THE COMPOSITION OF THE JAPANESE DRAFT. The commission first looked into the Japanese attitudes at the time of the initiation of the drafting and then into the content of the draft. The fundamental attitude during the drafting was to follow the SCAP draft as closely as possible, to modify only the points that were completely unacceptable to the Japanese side, and to leave those points to future negotiation. A comparison of the SCAP draft with the principal points of the Japanese draft of 2 March was made on the basis of the testimony of Witness Satō Tatsuo who was involved in the drafting. Also set forth were the main points of the commentary on the SCAP draft which was submitted with the 2 March draft.

THE PRESENTATION OF THE 2 MARCH DRAFT TO SCAP. The circumstances surrounding the presentation to SCAP on 4 March of the so-called 2 March draft and whether or not it was tentative or provisional were next described to the commission. However, SCAP took the attitude that a final draft should be completed immediately and it was finished during 4–5 March, including an all-night session. Concerning the operations involved in the completion of this final draft, on the basis of the oral testimony of Witness Satō Tatsuo, who was primarily responsible on the Japanese side, the commission carried out a detailed examination of the process, which resulted in the approval of the draft. Satō stated that each chapter of the 2 March draft was revised on the basis of negotiations with SCAP.

THE RELEASE OF THE "OUTLINE DRAFT OF A REVISED CONSTITUTION." The Shidehara cabinet decided that there was no other course but to adopt the final draft that had been decided on as a result of the joint labors in SCAP on 4–5 March and to announce it in the form of a Japanese government draft; this is what was released as the "Outline Draft of a Revised Constitution." The process of the composition and release of this draft was examined with particular reference to the discussions in the cabinet meetings of 5 and 6 March on the basis of testimony by former Commissioner Ashida and the records presented by Witness Iriye Toshirō.

The committee next dealt with SCAP's reasons for the speedy release of the draft and the reasons why the Shidehara cabinet decided to release it. These sets of reasons were interrelated. In respect to SCAP's reasons for haste it was understood that it had been MacArthur's intention from the beginning to create a *fait accompli* in order to anticipate the involvement of the Far Eastern Commission (which had been inaugurated on 26 February) in the constitutional issue and consequently any delay beyond 4 March could not be allowed. Also it was revealed that Prime Minister Shidehara, in an off-the-record statement before a Privy Council meeting on 20 March, called special attention to the "international situation since about the end of February" and stated his beliefs that if the opportunity [for approving the draft] were lost there would be "great fear for the safety of our imperial house" and that "we are in a very critical situation."

In respect to the Japanese government's reasons for releasing the draft, a perusal of the testimony of the Japanese involved at the time will serve the purpose. On the issue of "the emperor's person" there is the testimony of Minister of State Matsumoto, mentioned earlier, and the statement by Prime Minister Shidehara, referred to just above. Shidehara also stated at a 25 March cabinet meeting that "events had speeded up unexpectedly" and that "since February 26 [when the Far Eastern Commission held its first meeting] we have stood on the perilous brink of losing the imperial house." Witness Narahashi Wataru, then chief secretary of the cabinet, also stated his thought that "if we rejected it [the draft], what could be done in the event that the Far Eastern Commission forced on us a constitution based on republican principles?" Also former Commissioner Murakami Giichi, who had been a minister of state at the time, testified to the effect that Prime Minister Shidehara was extremely committed to the preservation of the emperor system and believed that to preserve it the sacrifice of all else was justified, and that it was his own [Murakami's] interpretation that the emperor system and the renunciation of war were indivisibly related.

The commission then examined the domestic reaction to the cabinet draft. The true circumstances surrounding the composition and release of the draft were not made clear at the time. However, it was surmised that SCAP's powerful advice was behind the draft. In addition, in respect to the content of the draft all the political parties—including the Liberal and Progressive parties, but excluding a sector of radical individuals—and influential press comments generally either approved or went along with it. This was evidenced by a number of press comments, a Foreign Ministry survey of foreign and domestic comment, and public opinion surveys.

It must be remembered, however, that domestic public opinion at the time was under the control of the occupation authorities. It was a fact that prior censorship of newspapers was carried out by the occupation at that time. It can also be surmised that anyone expressing his views had to keep in mind more or less how they might relate to occupation policy. In reality, however, it is difficult to make a precise judgment on the extent to which the wishes of the occupation or a feeling of reserve in the face of them might actually have controlled views on the constitutional issue. Finally, the subcommittee also presented some materials relating to foreign reactions to the cabinet draft.

THE CODIFICATION OF THE CABINET DRAFT. In respect to the codification of the cabinet draft the subcommittee described the process in the following order: the negotiations with SCAP on the cabinet draft from the time it was released on 6 March to the completion of the draft of 17 April; the composition of the revised draft from the colloquial version; and the discussions relating to the time when the revised draft would be presented and to the procedure for bringing it before the Diet.

DELIBERATIONS OF THE PRIVY COUNCIL. The subcommittee described such matters relating to the Privy Council's deliberations as Prime Minister Shidehara's off-the-record explanation of 20 March, the work of the council's investigation committee, and developments in the full council, using principally the testimony of Witness Iriye Toshirō, then vice chief of the Bureau of Legislation, and Witness Morohashi Jō, then chief secretary of the Privy Council. Particular emphasis was placed on the questions and answers relating to the principal points of contention between the council members and the government authorities in the investigation committee sessions.

CONSTITUTIONAL REVISION AND THE GENERAL ELECTION. The general election for the House of Representatives held on 10 April 1946 possesses special significance for comprehending "the freely expressed will of the Japanese people" at the time. The subcommittee went into such problems as the circumstances surrounding the decision to hold the election on 10 April, the attitudes of the Far Eastern Commission toward it, and especially the extent to which constitutional revision was dealt with as an election issue.

The subcommittee took testimony from a number of individuals who were candidates in that election. However, the collective view seems to have been that constitutional revision was regarded as a secondary issue and that both candidates and voters were far more concerned with problems of food, clothing, and shelter.

The commission's secretariat carried out an investigation of the degree to which the candidates dealt with the constitutional issue based on a study of the official election bulletins, which contained the platforms of the candidates. The results were as follows: no more than 17.4 percent of the candidates mentioned the draft revision; only a very small number touched on constitutional revision itself; and on the other hand, 78.5 percent mentioned the emperor system, and 36.6 percent the renunciation of war.

RELATIONS WITH WASHINGTON AND THE FAR EASTERN COMMISSION. As the third section of the subcommittee's report shows, the relations between SCAP on the one hand and Washington and the Far Eastern Commission on the other were complex. After the release of the cabinet draft of 6 March, the relations between MacArthur and the FEC became far worse, and the American government found itself in an extremely uncomfortable position between the two. The subcommittee studied the shifts in this situation in some detail, principally on the basis of documents from Professors [Hugh] Borton, [George H.] Blakeslee, [Robert] Ward, [Theodore] McNelly, and others. [Note: These four American professors were involved in or have studied the issues here discussed.]

On this point documents such as the following were presented: the policy decision of the FEC on 20 March; General MacArthur's speech of 5 April to the Allied Council for Japan in response; the FEC's resolution of 10 March and its policy decision of 13 May; and MacArthur's response of 14 June to the latter. These exchanges reveal the profound depth of the opposition between the FEC and MacArthur. The sources of this friction are to be found ultimately in the opposing views of the two sides on such matters as the FEC's dissatisfaction with MacArthur's creation of a *fait accompli* [the draft constitution] without prior consultation with it, the related problem of the distribution of authority between the FEC and the Supreme Commander, and doubts as to whether the steps taken by MacArthur were in accord with the basic principle of "the freely expressed will of the Japanese people." Nevertheless, without a resolution of the above conflict, the schedule for the revision of the Constitution continued.

*Deliberations of the Constituent Assembly
and the Completion of Constitutional Revision*

GENERAL STATEMENT. The subcommittee reviewed the general outline of the course of the deliberations on the draft for the revision of the imperial Constitution in the so-called constituent assembly or the ninetieth session of the Imperial Diet.

On this matter Commissioner Takayanagi, who was then a member of the House of Peers, contributed points such as the following: that the draft revision was directly related to what had been written by American lawyers in SCAP was an open secret; that the Bureau of Legislation had to prepare a daily report in English of its proceedings and forward it to SCAP; that during the deliberations on the Constitution, for example, on the problem of popular sovereignty and on the requirement that cabinet ministers must be civilians, the motivating force for the government came in the form of positive proposals from SCAP; and that for all changes it was necessary to obtain the understanding of SCAP. Also, former Commissioner Ashida who served at that time as chairman of the Special House of Representatives Committee on the Revised Draft of the Constitution pointed out that in those cases where a demand from SCAP was involved, the point was not specifically made but the committee members surmised it by a sort of mental telepathy.

DELIBERATIONS IN THE HOUSE OF REPRESENTATIVES AND THE DECISION ON AMENDMENT. The subcommittee described in detail the process of the deliberations in the House of Representatives and the final decision in the following order: (1) the presentation of the draft of a revised constitution and the MacArthur statement relating to the deliberations on it; (2) the explanation of the reasons for and the deliberations on the draft in plenary sessions; (3) deliberations in the special house committee; (4) deliberations of the house subcommittee; (5) approval of the amendment by the special committee; and (6) approval of the amendment in plenary session.

Under those six items the subcommittee also presented the principal points of discussion that were dealt with as shown in the deliberations both of the plenary sessions and of the special committee. Also made clear were the questions raised by HR members and the answers provided by the government, particularly by Minister of State Kanamori Tokujirō. Among the principal points of discussion were the basis of the necessity for constitutional revision; the combined problems of the national polity [*kokutai*], the locus of sovereignty and the position of the emperor; the renunciation of war; and the basic rights of the people.

The revised draft was completed in the subcommittee, but the process was investigated in considerable detail, particularly in regard to the circumstances of the negotiations between SCAP officials and Minister of State Kanamori on the course of the revisions which resulted in a clear expression of popular sovereignty in Article 1 and the preamble of the Constitution; and the circumstances relating to the composition of the so-called Ashida revision of Article 9 [see p. 100].

DELIBERATIONS IN THE HOUSE OF PEERS AND THE DECISION ON AMENDMENT. There was no significant difference between the way in which the House of Peers dealt with the revised draft and the way in which the lower house had handled it. However, the House of Peers' deliberations involved the views of individual members to a greater extent than had the House of Representatives deliberations, where those who spoke represented, in general, the positions of their parties. In addition, there were a number of expressions of opinion from scholars who were members of the House of Peers. Also the latter on many occasions went fairly deeply into points that had already been covered in the House of Representatives deliberations.

The subcommittee also investigated the relations with SCAP in regard to the revisions recommended in the special committee in relation to the provisions on the guarantee of universal suffrage and on the limiting of cabinet offices to civilians and the circumstances surrounding the so-called Yamada–Takayanagi revision of Article 7 and the Tadokoro–Makino revision of Article 24, neither of which was adopted.

THE DELIBERATIONS IN THE IMPERIAL DIET. Here it is appropriate to point out what can be regarded as certain important characteristics of the whole process of the deliberations and the passage of the revision in the two houses as described above.

First, Witness Kanamori, who at the time was minister of state responsible for the constitutional problem, described the current attitude of the government toward the Diet. On that occasion, the witness pointed out, it was recognized that the Constitution had been written in large part by foreigners, but that he thought from the beginning, whoever wrote the Constitution did not have much bearing on the discussion of the rightness or wrongness of the results. Also he explained his attitude at the time in response to questions raised by Commissioners Nakasone and Kamikawa concerning the government's attitude toward the revision of Article 7 proposed in the House of Peers to which SCAP had no objection and which was expected to obtain approval but had failed because of strong opposition from the government. He stated that he had been unable, as a matter of principle, to support even a formal strengthening of the functions of the emperor, that he had taken into consideration the will of the House of Representatives, which had accepted the original version, and that there had been criticism of the proposed revision even inside the House of Peers.

In response to a statement from Commissioner Nakasone to the effect that the Liberal and Progressive parties had agreed to the Constitution with deep regret, former Commissioner Ashida declared that while it was difficult to provide a precise description of the atmosphere in the political parties at that time it was his impression that the Socialist Party supported the requirements of SCAP and that the farther one went to the right the stronger the feeling of passive resistance. Also Witness Morito Tatsuo, now president of Hiroshima University and then a socialist member of the House of Representatives, stated that he had a strong impression during the passage of the draft constitution that it had been bestowed on Japan, but that in terms of content it did not seem to have been forced on the country. However, since the draft contained few elements of a socialist constitution, as compared with the Socialist Party's draft, he had presented a draft of his own. He also said that his feelings were complicated because he could support the renunciation of war. He also favored a presentation of a revision that would set forth in a supplementary provision the requirement that the Constitution be reviewed after a stipulated period following its adoption, because it was difficult to believe that under the occupation the Constitution could be the result of the freely expressed will of the people. However, he finally dropped the idea because it was resisted on the grounds that SCAP would strongly oppose it, that the government party believed there were means of achieving [later] constitutional amendment even without a special stipulation along the lines he proposed, and that it was undesirable to convey the impression that the Constitution would be a provisional one.

As a general impression to be gained from the deliberations in both houses, Witness Kanamori thought that in the stage of deliberation (setting aside the issue of the origins of the draft) there was an adequate expression of popular feeling. However, this view was opposed.

In relation to the procedure in the constituent assembly, a debate was raised concerning the "Problems Relating to the Legal Continuity between the Old and New Constitutions and the Amendment Procedure according to Article 73 of the Old Constitution." What must be regarded as the SCAP view on this problem is to be found in a memorandum by Dr. Alfred Oppler of the Government Section [of GHQ, SCAP] addressed to the chief of the Government Section [General Whitney] under the date 25 August 1946 entitled "Authority of the Diet in relation to Constitutional Amendment under the Meiji Constitution."

THE COMPLETION AND PROMULGATION OF THE REVISED CONSTITUTION. The subcommittee report (pp. 574–78) describes the second referral to the Privy Council, the deliberations and approval, and the process of promulgation.

THE SITUATION IN THE FAR EASTERN COMMISSION. The commission investigated the difficult situation that existed between SCAP and the American representatives in the Far Eastern Commission when the constituent assembly was holding its deliberations and while the revised Constitution was being approved. For example, the FEC policy decision of 2 July on the basic principles of the new Japanese Constitution was based on SWNCC 228 and the content, in general, was identical. However, it was also based on the SCAP proposals to the Japanese government concerning an explicit statement of popular sovereignty and the provision that all cabinet ministers must be civilians. MacArthur in his 30 July response transmitted the view that the FEC's overly detailed directives might have an adverse effect on the achievement of Allied objectives.

In addition, the FEC's right of final review and approval of the draft Constitution became an issue. Here again the views came into conflict, the American government and SCAP holding that such approval was unnecessary, while the FEC held that approval by a formal vote was required. However, as the process of constitutional revision developed in Japan, the FEC discussions gradually gave tacit approval to the American position. Thus, while the revision of the Constitution was completed, it became necessary to salvage the situation and so the FEC achieved a compromise solution by means of a policy decision entitled "Provisions for the Review of a New Japanese Constitution," on 17 October 1946 which provided that the Japanese people should be afforded an opportunity in the future to review the Constitution. However, SCAP certainly did not greet this policy decision with any enthusiasm. Also, in actual fact, this "review" ended without either the Japanese government or the FEC making any positive effort toward realizing it.

General Considerations on the Process of Enactment

Finally, the subcommittee presented some general considerations relating to the process of enactment, offering the following comments regarding the importance of the investigation with reference both to its general and to its special features.

The process of the enactment of the Constitution of Japan is as has been described in the previous sections of this report. We are confident that we have made clear in respect to the enactment of the Constitution both its origins and the procedures by which it was realized under the domestic and international circumstances of the time.

In the investigations of this commission into the enactment process the opinions of all commissioners on the important points of the discussion were certainly not in complete agreement and there was a fair degree of conflict. On those points this [subcommittee] report simply presents the individual opinions and in respect to the historical facts out of which the opposing views originated it faithfully sets forth facts as facts. In general, it must be said that in the study of history some sections must be left to the judgment of historians of a later age. In this case also we were made to feel anew that it is not easy to clarify historical matters. In regard to the process of enactment of our Constitution this report attempts not only to deal with the results of previous investigative studies both at home and abroad, but also to acquire important new foreign and domestic materials, to study them, and to make clear the course of constitutional enactment in as accurate and as objective a manner as possible. By this means it has been possible in a number of cases to clarify circumstances that until now have not necessarily been clear. In this sense, it is our hope that this report will at least contribute to a correct understanding of the significance of the Constitution of Japan.

Below are set forth in abbreviated form the important topics of discussion relating to the investigation of the process of constitutional enactment:

1. How should we regard the significance of Japan's unconditional surrender to the Allies and, accordingly, the legal character of the Potsdam Declaration?

2. Should we regard the Potsdam Declaration as in itself requiring the revision of the Meiji Constitution?

3. In the preparation of the so-called MacArthur draft and its presentation to the Japanese government, did SCAP act in contravention to the freely expressed will of the Japanese people and did it thereby exercise compulsion against the Japanese government and people?

4. Should the measures relating to constitutional revision taken by SCAP, namely, General MacArthur, be regarded as infringing on the authority of the Allies, namely, the Far Eastern Commission?

5. Was the free will of the Japanese people properly reflected in the entire process of constitutional enactment, including the deliberations on constitutional revision carried out in the constituent assembly?

After having presented in summary form the opposing views revealed during the investigation of the above five points, the subcommittee report summarized the entire section in the form of a conclusion, which it introduced with the following statement:

> In essence, it is clear that the Constitution of Japan is the product of a lost war and that it was enacted under the very special circumstances of a military

occupation, as well as in the very center of the chaotic environment of the people's lives. In this sense, it is also clear that the enactment of this Constitution was carried out in an extremely unusual manner, if one considers what the form of enactment of a nation's constitution should actually be. That the basic source of the above situation lay in Japan's defeat is a fact, no matter how hard it may be to accept. It is not too much to say that Japan's fate was decided in reality by the acceptance of the Potsdam Declaration. In addition, the enactment of this Constitution took place in the midst of the delicate, even grim, international situation surrounding our country and as one of a series of confused events taking place in January and February 1946, the process of constitutional revision was extremely unusual. The circumstances under which the above procedure had to be adopted must be understood against the background of international politics at the time.

As described above, the process of the enactment of the Constitution was both extremely peculiar and abnormal and the facts were extremely complex. In respect to the problem of whether the process was either imposed or forced on Japan or, in other words, whether it was based on the freely expressed will of the Japanese people, the facts are by no means simple.

SECTION B.
THE INVESTIGATIONS OF THE ACTUAL OPERATION OF THE CONSTITUTION

The detailed content of the investigations of the actual operation of the Constitution is included in "Report on the Investigation of the Actual Operation of the Constitution: Rights and Duties of the People, and the Judiciary" (Appended Document No. 3); "Report on the Investigation of the Actual Operation of the Constitution: The National Diet, the Cabinet, Finances, and Local Autonomy" (Appended Document No. 4); and "Report on the Investigation of the Actual Operation of the Constitution: the Emperor, the Renunciation of War, and the Supreme Law" (Appended Document No. 5). Below, however, we describe the important items examined during the investigation, regarding the concrete operations and interpretation of the Constitution. We present those items in outline form, following the order of chapters in the Constitution.

The Emperor

In the investigation of the provisions relating to the emperor—for example, the origin of the term "symbol"—some matters were closely related to the investigation of the process of enactment of the Constitution. A number of investigations were carried out from both the historical and theoretical points of view of such matters as the history of the emperor system, the concept of *kokutai* [the national polity], the ideal nature of the emperor system as well as the concepts of the head of state and monarch, and the special character of contemporary European monarchies. The Report of the Third Committee is the best source of the results of the investigations of the points just listed. Here we shall describe in general outline the investigations of the problems produced in the actual working of the provisions relating to the emperor.

THE POSITION OF THE EMPEROR (ART. 1). The origin of the provision in Article 1 that the emperor is a "symbol" was investigated in the Subcommittee on the Process of Enactment of the Constitution. The Report of the Third Committee described the process, relying on the subcommittee report. Former Minister of State Kanamori Tokujirō recalled the debates in the constituent assembly on the position of the emperor, the question of *kokutai*, and other matters, and he set forth his own basic thoughts on those matters at the time.

Next, in regard to the actual position of the emperor, a member of the Imperial Household Agency (Vice Director Uriu Nobuyoshi) stated that at present the application of the provisions relating to the emperor follows the line set forth in the government's explanation in the constituent assembly, based on the principle that the position of the emperor is no longer that of the wielder of sovereign power. The witness declared that as the result of the above change the emperor's public activities, including the so-called private ceremonies, are fairly extensive and that some duties resemble those he had previously in relation to documents and other formalities. He stated, in addition, that the number of official reports to the throne, for example, had decreased markedly and that the emperor's involvement in state affairs had become extremely formalistic and mechanical. In addition, he said that the emperor has revealed in various activities his new significance as "symbol" and offered the conjecture that he was also actively performing a role in promoting the unity of the people while remaining above political confrontation.

On the sanctity of the symbol, Witnesses Satō Tōsuke (special adviser to the Ministry of Justice) and Satō Tatsuo, in discussing the manner in which the provision relating to the crime of *lèse majesty* was expunged by the revision (Law No. 124 of 1947) of the Criminal Code, stated that it was done at the extremely strong demand of GHQ, SCAP. On this same point, authorities of the Imperial Household Agency also stated that at the present time, as compared with the past, there have been a fair number of articles [possibly impairing the dignity of the emperor], and so forth, that have created problems but that they believed the good sense of the people and the press could be relied upon.

FUNCTIONS OF THE EMPEROR (ARTS. 3, 4, 6, AND 7).

The Scope of State Affairs Requiring the Advice and Approval of the Cabinet. There are no problems relating to the principle set forth in Article 3.

Certain technical questions, however, were examined: Does the appointment of the prime minister as stipulated in Article 6 require the advice and approval of the cabinet? Since the appointment and dismissal of ministers of state is the exclusive right of the prime minister, does their attestation likewise require the advice and approval of the cabinet?

On these questions Witnesses Satō Tatsuo and Suzuki Shunichi (vice chief of the Cabinet Secretariat) testified on the actual practice of the executive branch. On the first question, it was their interpretation that the advice and approval of the previous cabinet would be required. On the second question, they also held that on the basis of the provision of Article 7 the advice and approval of the cabinet are required, but particularly, in the case of the attestation of the dismissal of a cabinet minister in accordance with the principle of collegial action, an effective cabinet decision on attestation can be arrived at without the participation of the minister concerned, who would be directly affected.

Methods of Advice and Approval. Advice and approval are carried out by cabinet meetings. But since "advice" and "approval" are separate and distinct, does it necessarily follow that there must be two cabinet decisions: one on "advice" and another on "approval"? Or should they be treated as one and consequently require only a single cabinet decision? This point was in dispute in the Tomabechi appeal case. [In 1952 Prime Minister Yoshida dissolved the House of Representatives. Tomabechi Hidetoshi, a member of the opposition party, brought suit against him on the grounds that the action had been carried out in an unconstitutional fashion. The Supreme Court threw out the suit on the technicality that a decision would involve the Court's acting as if it were a constitutional court, which it is not. However, Justice Mano Tsuyoshi wrote a long concurring opinion which went into the advice and approval question in detail. See John M. Maki, *Court and Constitution in Japan*, pp. 366–83.]

According to Witness Suzuki Shunichi, in the actual operation of the executive branch on this matter, advice and approval are considered to be a single cabinet action. Consequently, it is not necessary to distinguish between the two and a single cabinet decision would achieve both.

Acts in Matters of State, and Public and Private Actions of the Emperor. In relation to Article 4, several commissioners set forth opinions on the interpretation of the difference between "acts in matters of state" and "powers related to government." A point that was emphasized was the scope of acts in matters of state, especially the relationship between state, public, and private acts.

First of all, in addition to the total of twelve acts in matters of state set forth in Articles 6 and 7, can the emperor perform other public acts? On this question Witnesses Satō Tatsuo and Takao Ryōichi (superintendent of the economy of the Imperial House) said that the usual practice of the executive branch was based on the interpretation that "acts in matters of state" are limited to the above twelve. The public acts of the emperor, however, fall outside the above acts of state. Such public acts can be performed as long as they are understood not to involve powers related to government or the responsibility of the cabinet. As examples, we can offer the emperor's appearance or statements at public functions such as the opening ceremony of the National Diet, domestic tours of inspection, and exchange of telegrams with foreign heads of state. Such acts are not properly private ones on the part of the emperor, but public national acts recognized as such on the basis of the emperor's symbolic position. The Constitution cannot be interpreted as forbidding them.

In regard to the above public acts the general interpretation is that the cabinet, through the Imperial Household Agency as an upper level administrative organ [The IHA is not a government ministry, but an executive agency attached to the Prime Minister's Office.], bears responsibility for them by making cabinet decisions which in a sense determine matters relating both to policy and to important matters.

This problem also involves the question of the difference between the public and private acts of the emperor, which relates to the allocation of duties among officials of the Imperial Household Agency who might either be civil servants or private employees of the emperor. In addition, there is the economic problem of the allocations between the Imperial Court budget (part of which involves administrative expenses) and the privy purse. In regard to these matters an administrative interpretation within the government was set forth in 1947. According to this, the imperial household possesses a private character in addition to the public one recognized by the Constitution. Private affairs arising from this private character are deeply influenced by the emperor's role as a symbol. For example, such matters as imperial visits, imperial audiences, and the education of the crown prince must be assisted by the state, through the Imperial Household Agency or the Imperial Court budget so that they may be properly carried out as private activities.

The purely private acts of the emperor lie outside the scope of Article 4, but even so a question remains as to whether the emperor and the imperial household are subject to restrictions different from those that apply to the general population. For example, the rights of suffrage and of election to office of the emperor and members of the imperial family are not at present clearly set forth in law but are dealt with somewhat irregularly by an interpretation of the supplementary rules contained in the Law for the Election of Public Officials. One opinion holds that, as a reflection of the basic principles of the Constitution, this problem should be decided by means of legislation.

Delegation of Acts in Matters of State. The law relating to the delegation of acts in matters of state as provided for in Article 4, paragraph 2 has not yet been enacted. Witness Uriu Nobuyoshi stated that the lack of such a law makes it impossible for the emperor to travel abroad even though doing so might be desirable as an act of international courtesy.

The Scope of Ceremony as an Act of State. In respect to matters of state as set forth in Article 7, the scope of ceremony has been regarded as a special question. Heretofore, four specific examples were stipulated by cabinet decision as matters that might be formally treated as "ceremony": the ceremonial institution of an imperial prince as heir to the throne; the coming of age ceremony of the crown prince; the celebration of the New Year; and the wedding ceremony of the crown prince. However, administrative officials raised the question of how such acts as imperial appointments to office, attestations, installations, and presentations should be treated.

A problem has also arisen as a result of the so-called separation of church and state and the abolition of state Shintō, namely, what action can be taken in regard to those ceremonies, as acts of state, which are inseparably related to former traditional religious rites. Officials of the Imperial Household Agency explained the circumstances relating to this matter.

The Functions and Position of the Emperor in Foreign Relations. The question of whether the emperor can, under the present Constitution, be regarded as occupying the position of head of state was dealt with on several occasions both theoretically and as a matter of comparative law. A debated question was whether or not the emperor possesses a certain function and position as head of state in foreign relations under international law in reference to such matters as the attestation of the credentials of ministers and ambassadors and of the ratification of treaties as set forth in Article 7 as acts in matters of state.

From the standpoint of the present constitutional functions of the emperor, it is doubtful whether he could be regarded as the head of state under international law. In addition, some commissioners set forth the opinion that since the situation is not in accord with international usage, it creates an obstacle in intercourse with other countries. An opposing view was set forth by Witness Iriye Keishirō, who stated that the emperor is far more limited than heads of state of other countries, but, in spite of being a special figure, he participates in certain diplomatic acts that are carried out by ordinary heads of state. Within these limits he must be considered as representing the nation, and under the present Constitution customary practice toward that end has been steadily accumulating. In addition, the same witness and Hagiwara Tōru, former chief of the

Treaty Bureau of the Foreign Ministry, stated their opinion that although there is no precedent for overseas travel by the emperor, there is no doubt that he would receive the courtesies extended to a head of state and would be accorded the usual privileges and exemptions. Also Witness Suyama Tatsuo, chief of protocol of the Foreign Ministry, and Witness Kokiso Motoo, head of the legal section of the Treaty Bureau of the Foreign Ministry, stated that in reality no foreign country has taken the attitude that the emperor is not the Japanese head of state and that they have taken special care to bring both the form and wording of such matters as ratifications of treaties and attestations of ambassadorial credentials into accord with documentary forms in international usage and to avoid departing from the language and forms under the old Constitution. Witness Hagiwara also expressed the opinion that since its enactment, the present Constitution has been interpreted as providing no real diplomatic obstacle even in attestation, and that even now there is no interference in the conduct of foreign affairs.

SUCCESSION TO THE THRONE (ART. 2). On the matter of succession the views of those involved in the drafting were described particularly in respect to the fact that neither female succession nor abdication is recognized in the Imperial House Law. A group of commissioners also expressed concern over the fact that at present only a few members of the imperial family are qualified to succeed to the throne and that it was widely accepted that members of the imperial family could remove themselves from the official family roster. Witness Takao Ryōichi of the Imperial Household Agency stated, however, that the problem of how the number of those qualified to succeed to the throne may be preserved is extremely difficult and that there is a question as to whether it can be solved by legislative means alone. He also expressed the view that a system under which one who had once left the roster of the imperial family could return to it and succeed to the throne is a dubious one and that in any event this problem is too difficult to be considered at the present time.

THE ECONOMY OF THE IMPERIAL HOUSEHOLD (ARTS. 8 AND 88). Concerning Articles 8 and 88, particularly their origins, Witnesses Satō Tatsuo and Takao Ryōichi, both involved in the matter at the time, testified that the occupation regarded the imperial family as one of the *zaibatsu* and that one of its important policies was the dispersal of its assets, as one aspect of the *zaibatsu* dissolution policy.

Also in respect to Article 8, Witness Takao described the current application of Article 2 of the Imperial Household Economy Law. Regarding the current status of the limitation on cash holdings, as stipulated in the law for the enforcement of the above law, he said that gifts were handled conservatively and that because contributions might easily give rise to such abuses as the traditional publicity-getting, they were dealt with very strictly. He added that he particularly felt there was no need to raise the limitation on contributions.

Concerning Article 8 Witnesses Takao, Uriu, and Satō made the following points:

1. It is not clear whether the first paragraph of this article is a transitional or permanent provision.

2. It is a difficult legal question to determine the extent to which the private assets of the emperor and the imperial family can be regarded as private holdings, even if they are treated as falling outside the application of this article.

3. The system has been set up under which former imperial property has become state property, some of which has been placed at the disposal of the imperial household. However, under Article 3 of the State Property Law, when property is acquired for the use of the imperial household, the approval of the National Diet is required. Consequently, in cases where the budget provides for new construction in the imperial palace this also becomes a case of acquisition of imperial household property, and the approval of the National Diet is required anew. In addition, the Diet becomes involved in extremely minute details because of votes taken under Article 8 and the votes on the budget of the imperial household.

4. It is difficult to determine by law the scope of what is referred to as "objects traditionally handed down with the imperial throne" and at the present time no attempt has been made to do so.

5. On the basis of the 1959 budget, the combined total of the imperial household and the Imperial Household Agency [budgets] was a little more than 20 percent of the prewar sum. Among the expenses of the imperial household those for the court are being handled economically, and unexpended surpluses are accumulated to meet unexpected expenses. In addition, the following matter is related to the principle of the separation of church and state. As a result of Article 89, the operating expenses of the Imperial Sanctuary, which is involved in the religious practices of the imperial family, are carried by the Imperial Court budget, not that for the Imperial Palace. In this respect there is the question of how the character of the Imperial Sanctuary should be regarded, a problem calling for study.

RESULTS OF THE INVESTIGATION. The content of the investigations on the actual operation of the provisions relating to the emperor has been summarized above. The most important points for later discussion and deliberation were as follows.

1. Should the word "symbol" in respect to the position of the emperor be retained unchanged?
2. In relation to the position of the emperor, is it necessary to rectify the provisions regarding acts in matters of state?
3. Should female succession to the throne and abdication be recognized?
4. What should be the limits of Diet control over the economic activities and expenditures of the imperial household?
5. How should property belonging to the imperial family be handled?

The Renunciation of War

Since only one article in the Constitution addresses the actual application of the provisions on the renunciation of war, the investigation differed from that for other provisions in that it could not be approached article-by-article. What was examined was the entire question of Japan's security, within which the question of the application and interpretation of Article 9 was set.

[Omitted here is a listing of the table of contents of the Report of the Third Committee on the renunciation of war which was included for the convenience of Japanese readers of the report.]

THE ORIGIN OF ARTICLE 9. For the general details of the origins of Article 9, we refer to the detailed discussions contained in the report of the Subcommittee on the Process of Enactment of the Constitution. In that report are set forth simply the changes in the wording of the provisions of that article between the issuing of the MacArthur draft and the final composition of Article 9. The various changes in the circumstances of the wording were also described, since they produced controversies in the later interpretation of the article.

POSTWAR CHANGES IN THE WORLD SECURITY PROBLEM. Witnesses Katō Yōzō (chief of the Defense Section of the Defense Agency) and Masuhara Keikichi (former vice chief of the Defense Agency) were the principal experts heard on changes in the defense situation with particular reference to the gradual increase in defense strength. They dealt with such problems as the circumstances surrounding the surrender and disarmament, the outbreak of the Korean conflict and the establishment of the National Police Reserve, the negotiation of the Japanese–American security treaty and the establishment of the National Safety Agency, the negotiation of the Japanese–American Mutual Defense Assistance Agreement and the Agreement on the Loan of Naval Vessels, the enactment of the Law for the Protection of Official Secrets, the establishment of the Defense Agency and the Self-Defense Forces,

American assistance to Japan and the outlook for defense expenditures, and the present state of the organization and equipment of the Self-Defense Forces.

Witness Masuhara, speaking on the circumstances at the time of the establishment of the National Police Reserve (NPR), pointed out the extreme urgency of the intentions of GHQ, SCAP and the rapidity of the Japanese action in the matter. He also stated that in this situation it could not be said there was an accommodation of views between the two sides even on such matters as the nature of the NPR.

In respect to "the outline of the present legal system relating to defense," Witness Katō presented explanations relating to such matters as the organization, activities, and authority of the Self-Defense Forces; measures relating to personnel and duties, preservation of secrets, obligations for defense, and states of emergency; and, in outline, the general body of current laws relating to defense.

THE CONCLUSION AND REVISION OF THE JAPANESE–AMERICAN SECURITY TREATY. Witnesses Okazaki Katsuo, former foreign minister, and Nishimura Kumao, former chief of the Treaty Bureau of the Foreign Ministry, as two principals on the Japanese side in regard to the security treaty, gave detailed explanations of the progress of the conclusion and revision of the treaty. They also touched on the problem of the attitudes of the Japanese authorities on the question of interpretation of Article 9. The following is the essence of their explanations:

1. Prime Minister Yoshida firmly held to the basic position that re-armament was impossible for both constitutional and policy reasons. They believed that his principal emphasis in this regard was on policy.

2. In the treaty negotiations the prime consideration was the desire to obtain a treaty of peace at the earliest possible moment with the resulting return of independence. The question of Article 9 was limited mainly to the point that the stationing of foreign troops in Japan did not constitute the maintenance of war potential. Hence, they thought that on the basis of the treaty any foreign troops retained in the country would obviously not be Japanese and that Article 9 would not prevent that.

3. The problem of the relation between Japan's right of self-defense and the right of collective self-defense set forth in the United Nations Charter became a matter of controversy after the conclusion of the treaty and only recently and so at the time was not gone into deeply.

4. The initial negotiations on the treaty came shortly after the enactment of the Constitution and the explanations of the government in the constituent assembly were considered. The domestic consideration of Article 9 was so careful that it went beyond even morbid sensitivity. However, by contrast, the government interpreted Article 9 very boldly indeed in respect to the United States, assuming the position that within

the limits of Article 9, paragraph 2, Japan could enter into a relationship of mutual assistance with the United States, namely, conclude a collective defense arrangement based on Article 51 of the United Nations Charter. However, this was denied by the United States because the Vandenburg Resolution took precedence and thus the original security treaty took the shape it did.

Witness Nishimura similarly explained the progress of revision and the constitutional points discussed in relation to the new security treaty.

THE SYSTEM OF SECURITY GUARANTEES. In the reexamination of Article 9 in respect to the system of security guarantees, it was necessary to take a point of view relating to the evaluation of Article 9 because of the trends in the system in contemporary international society. A historical study of the systems by which individual countries guaranteed their security was made on the basis of explanations of such witnesses in the field of international law as Yokota Kisaburō, professor emeritus at Tokyo University; Tamura Kōsaku, Chūō University professor; Tabata Shigejirō, Kyoto University professor; Takano Yūichi, Tokyo University professor; and Iriye Keishirō. In addition, the special character of the present Japanese–American security treaty was dealt with.

On "the prohibition of war and the development of a system of collective guarantee of security," such matters as the following were investigated: (1) before World War I the so-called individual approach under which each country would seek its own security through the exercise of individual national rights such as those of military preparedness, alliance, war, and neutrality; (2) as a result of the failure of the above approach, the realization of the League of Nations and the Anti-War Pact (the Pact of Paris) based on the concepts of the limitation of war and a system of the guarantee of collective security; (3) the special significance of the right of self-defense under the above; (4) as a result of the failure of the League and the Anti-War Pact, the creation after World War II of the United Nations and its own system of collective self-defense; and (5) the fact that there is still not an ideal system of collective self-defense because of the veto power in the hands of the five great powers.

Next, in respect to "the Charter of the United Nations and the right of collective self-defense" various academic theories relating to the formulation of Article 51 of the UN Charter, to the relationship between that article and "regional arrangements" [in Article 52] and to the "right of collective self-defense" were considered.

Finally, on the issue of "the special character of the Japanese–American security treaty" the following matters were examined: (1) the difference between this treaty before revision [in 1960] and similar treaties concluded by the United States with other free-world nations, even though it was also associated with Article 51 of the UN Charter; (2) the treaty as a special one which did not determine mutual defense responsibilities on a bilateral footing of equality between Japan and the United States; (3) the fact that the treaty, even after revision, is not completely identical with other treaties concluded by the United States with other countries even though it approaches them in form in that it sets forth the responsibility for mutual assistance between the two countries and for common defense activities and contains provisions relating to the UN Charter.

The above special characteristics of the treaty were revealed in the explanations of government officials relating to the right of self-defense as set forth in the treaty itself. Namely, the concept as in the treaty after revision was, they said, clearly adopted. Nevertheless, Witnesses Shimoda Takezō (former chief of the Treaty Bureau of the Foreign Ministry) and Hayashi Shūzō (chief of the Cabinet Bureau of Legislation) testified that the government thought it unnecessary to explain that Japan clearly possesses the right of collective self-defense. Their reasoning was as follows. The so-called treaty area in the new treaty is limited to "the territories under the administration of Japan." If an armed attack against Japan occurred, and if American armed forces in Japan had not yet come under attack, and if the United States took military action to deal with such an armed attack, then the United States would be exercising the right of collective self-defense. If, on the other hand, Japan initiated military action when American forces in Japan came under attack, then the circumstance would be that such an armed attack would also be one on Japanese territory, properly speaking. Thus, in this situation any armed action taken by Japan would be justified as an exercise of Japan's individual right of self-defense. Hence, at the time of the revision of the treaty it was the government's interpretation that there was no need to explain an invocation of the collective right of self-defense.

Witness Hayashi explained that even at the time of treaty revision no consideration was given the view that it would be impossible to explain the measures to be taken by the Japanese side without invoking the right of collective self-defense. Thus, on the basis of this interpretation, it came about that there was no fundamental difference between the right of collective self-defense as stated in the old, prerevision treaty and the new one. On the reason for this circumstance Witnesses Iriye and Takano explained that there were constitutional limitations in Article 9 on the Japanese exercise of the right of collective self-defense.

THE IDEAL FORM OF JAPAN'S SECURITY TODAY. The question of the need to guarantee Japan's security, from the standpoint of the character of contemporary war and defense against it, was investigated by hearing the opinions of specialists in military affairs and commentators on military matters. The principal witnesses were Saeki Kiichi, instructor and counselor of the Defense Agency; Tsuchiya Akio, director of the Institute for Research on Continental Problems; Ōi Atsushi, military commentator; and Tomioka Sadatoshi, director of the Institute of Historical Investigation. They explained the particular necessity for security in terms of the contemporary world. Witness Saeki also set forth the view that in this age of change in military technology, a policy of neutrality is practically impossible to maintain.

Next, on "the current stage of the disarmament problem," Witness Watanabe Seiki (editorial writer for *Asahi Shimbun*) explained such matters as the fact that under present conditions, where absolute weapons serve as a deterrent to war, disarmament has become necessary, and he explained also the reasons for the development of the disarmament program and the barriers to its achievement.

Finally, on "the necessities of Japan's security," Witness Saeki presented explanations of the drafting of the "Basic Policy on National Defense" (approved 20 May 1957) and of "Plan for the Perfection of Defensive Power" (approved 14 June 1957), and of the conclusion of the Japanese–American security treaty from the standpoint of the necessities of security today. However, on this issue Witness Hayashi Katsunari, military commentator, expressed opposing views, namely, that the security treaty does not serve the interests of Japan's defense and that under this treaty Japan does not enjoy true independence, a prerequisite for self-defense.

On the issue of whether Article 9 imposes any restrictions on cooperation with the United Nations, Witnesses Nishimura Kumao, Shimoda Takezō, Tabata Shigejirō, and others described their views on such matters as the House of Councilors' resolution (2 June 1954) relating to the sending of Self-Defense Force units overseas, the circumstances of Japan's entry into the United Nations, their regret that Japan did not participate in the international police force established by the UN at the time of the Congo rebellion (July 1960), and the problem of the so-called Matsudaira Declaration. On this general question Witness Ōhira Zengo, professor at Hitotsubashi University, expressed the view that because one of the cornerstones of Japanese foreign policy is participation in the UN, even in the interpretation of Article 9 it is not proper to argue that that article makes it impossible to cooperate with either the UN or its armed forces. In opposition, Witness Tabata pointed out that the UN armed forces, a UN police force, or an international police force can assume several different forms and that on the problem of cooperation with the UN or of placing central emphasis on the UN in foreign policy, it is necessary to consider them on the basis of the differences in the functions that the UN carries out.

THE IDEAL SECURITY SYSTEMS FOR THE PRESENT. The following points arose from the point of view that our country's system of Self-Defense Forces must also be examined in the light of the necessity for security systems at present.

First, in regard to "the primary basic conditions for defense organizations today" Witnesses Saeki and Fukushima Shingo, professor at Senshu University, set forth explanations relating to the security systems of the free nations, the communist nations, and the neutralist nations with reference to the possible systemization of two especially important principles relating to civilian control of the armed forces and their unification.

Next, "rearmament in West Germany and the revision of the Basic Law" was examined particularly from the angle of those matters that might be worth attention in Japan as well. The principal witness was Azabu Shigeru, legal researcher of the Defense Agency, who considered the following matters: (1) basic considerations relating to armed forces and military men; (2) limitations on the fundamental human rights of military men; (3) the right of supreme command of the armed forces; (4) control by the Federal Council; (5) relations between the military and the judiciary; (6) states of emergency; and (7) the National Defense Council.

Finally, on "the problems relating to the Self-Defense Forces" (SDF), the following topics were addressed: (1) civilian control; (2) the right of supreme command; (3) the unification of the armed forces; (4) the National Defense Council; (5) the morale and duties of the SDF; and (6) the activities of the SDF.

Among the points mentioned above, the right of supreme command of the SDF resides, under law, in the prime minister. Witness Yoshida Hidezō (former commander-in-chief of the Maritime Self-Defense Forces) expressed the opinion that on the basis of experience in order to make the SDF into well-disciplined units it would be best to make the emperor, who is the symbol of the nation, the supreme commander of the armed forces in name only. There were some commissioners who agreed with this idea, but a number of commissioners and witnesses opposed it.

Witness Masuhara also expressed the view, based on experience, that in order to raise SDF morale, it would be desirable to create a clear constitutional mission for the SDF, if there is occasion to revise the Constitution.

THE INTERPRETATION OF ARTICLE 9. The commission investigated both the process that produced disputes over the interpretation of Article 9 and the important points involved therein, particularly in respect to the manner in which the strength of Japan's defense structure increased both through the conclusion of the Japanese–American security arrangements internationally and through the SDF domestically.

First, on "the government's interpretation," Witnesses Hayashi Shūzō, an official of the Cabinet Bureau of Legislation, Takatsuji Masami, vice chief of the same bureau, and Satō Tatsuo explained the former interpretations of the following points:

1. Paragraph 1. Should the right of self-defense be renounced? If the right of self-defense is not renounced, within what limits should defense activities be recognized? Are the dispatch abroad of troops and participation in UN police units recognized? What is the relationship between paragraph 1 and the Japanese–American security treaty and the right of collective self-defense as set forth in the UN Charter?

2. Paragraph 2. What is war potential? Do the SDF constitute war potential? Is the possession of nuclear weapons recognized? What is the relationship between the nonrecognition of the right of belligerency and the right of self-defense?

Witness Hayashi delivered a full and detailed account of the government's interpretation of all issues, including the above points, and stated that the criticism that the government's interpretation is always changing or that it is far too broad misses the point.

The important points of the government's interpretation of the above matters can be summarized as follows:

1. Paragraph 1 of Article 9 does not deny the right of self-defense. Self-defense actions are not included in the phrase "means of settling international disputes." In sum, because of the right of self-defense, it is possible to take the measures involved in its exercise.

2. Constitutionally, the content of self-defense actions is recognized only within the narrow limits of the right of self-defense; consequently, it is impermissible to go beyond those limits by sending troops to foreign territory for a preventive attack. However, because the scope of self-defense action is not necessarily limited to a nation's territory or territorial waters, for example, when a missile attack has been launched from enemy territory and there is no other means to counter it, then there is no constitutional prohibition against attacking the launching sites within the necessary limits.

Mutual acts of assistance based on the right of collective self-defense set forth in Article 51 of the UN Charter are also included in the scope of the right of self-defense as properly recognized in the Constitution.

3. Force that does not reach the "capacity to wage contemporary war" or "the minimum force for self-defense" is not war potential as prohibited by the Constitution. In addition, the SDF today are not unconstitu-

tional to the extent that the term "war potential" cannot be applied to them in fact.

4. So-called latent war potential [e.g., industrial capacity that might be used to turn out war materiel] is not included in the term "war potential."

5. The phrase, "to accomplish the aim of the preceding paragraph," refers to the "aim" as set forth in paragraph 1 in its entirety. It is in error to interpret "the aim of the preceding paragraph" as was done in the so-called Ashida view [which held that the right of belligerency would not be recognized even in a defensive war].

6. The right of belligerency is a separate concept distinct from the right of self-defense. Self-defense actions based on the right of self-defense can be carried out even if the right of belligerency is not recognized.

7. Excluding the question of policy, in general, all nuclear weapons must be termed unconstitutional because of their nature.

8. As a matter of principle, participation in any collective security system, including the UN police forces, goes beyond the scope of the right of self-defense in the sense that it involves military assistance to another country. However, it does not follow that the dispatch of SDF units overseas in order to achieve a peaceful nonmilitary objective is necessarily and directly unconstitutional.

In regard to the government's interpretations as set forth above, differing opinions and doubts were expressed both by commissioners and by witnesses.

In its decision on the appeal of the lower court decision in the *Sunakawa* case handed down on 14 December 1959, the Supreme Court ruled that the stationing of American forces in Japan, on the basis of the Japanese–American security treaty (before revision) was not unconstitutional, thus quashing and returning the decision to the court of first instance (Tokyo District Court, 20 July 1959) which had held such stationing unconstitutional. The constitutional interpretations in both these decisions were compared and discussed. In the decision rendered after the return of the case (Tokyo District Court, 27 March 1961) there was no judgment rendered in respect to Article 9 because the district court was bound by Article 4 of the Court Organization Law ["A conclusion in a decision of a superior court shall bind courts below in respect of the case concerned"]. Also the Supreme Court decision did not touch on the problem of the maintenance by Japan of defensive military strength. However, this decision held that the legal meaning of Article 9, paragraph 2, did not provide for either nonresistance or defenselessness, and that it did prohibit the waging of offensive war by the military power of Japan itself.

RESULTS OF THE INVESTIGATION. The outline of the investigations on the actual application of the provisions relating to the renunciation of war is as summarized above. As a result of the investigation, several important points emerged for later discussion and deliberation.

A fundamental question was, What attitude should be taken toward Article 9 as it relates to the development of Japan's defense structure since the time of the establishment of Article 9 to the present? Attitudes on this seem to fall under two demands: that Article 9 should be revised to bring it into accord with the realities of the defense structure; and that the present defense structure should be harmonized to the greatest extent possible with Article 9.

These two demands were observable in the investigation. Also within these demands it is possible to perceive various nuances. It also appears as if it is possible to classify these two views—in favor and opposed to revision of Article 9.

Other principal questions were as follows: Should Article 9 be expunged, or should the existence and maintenance of the right of self-defense be made clear? Should a provision relating to international peace be enacted? How should the organization of a self-defense army be dealt with? Especially, to what extent should the authority of the National Diet in military matters be recognized? What provisions should be made regarding the people's responsibilities relating to national security and regarding limitations on the guarantee of fundamental human rights of military men?

Rights and Duties of the People: I (Arts. 10–30)

THE MEANING OF THE GUARANTEE OF HUMAN RIGHTS (ARTS. 11, 12, AND 13). On the issue of fundamental attitudes toward the guarantee of human rights, two opposing views can be observed: that which strongly proclaims the absolute value of human rights and that which stresses limitations on them by the [doctrine of] public welfare. Witness Kanamori asserted that the guarantee of human rights in the Constitution of Japan is not simply a dogmatic declaration of principle and that the decision regarding that fundamental policy was consistent with the development of the concept of the human rights of the people. There is the view that this basic policy, in addition to being a principle in nations under the rule of law which guarantees the rights and freedoms of the people against the negative exercise of state power, also requires that it be utilized together with the principle of the welfare state, which holds that the welfare of the people must be positively promoted [by the state] and also that because the excessive expansion of welfare administration carries with it the danger of an increase of executive power welfare can be sufficiently achieved under the present Constitution.

In respect to the inviolability of human rights, the current Constitution does not recognize human rights as being absolutely without limit, the explanation being that it also contains a guarantee of social benefit. Moreover, in respect to the guarantee of human rights, it was also pointed out that all human rights cannot be considered equal to each other and that there must be a recognition of differences among them according to their nature, as rights to a decent existence or as rights to spiritual freedom.

One problem that appeared was whether the provisions of the Constitution are weighted in favor of the guarantee of human rights and, consequently, whether it is necessary to enact other provisions on the duties and responsibilities of the people, thus providing a balance. On this point it was asserted that in addition to making even clearer the current constitutional responsibilities that accompany human rights, such as the duty to preserve them, the prohibition of the abuse of fundamental rights and the responsibility for their exercise, the following should also be clearly set forth: the duty to defend the country, the prescription of the responsibilities of honesty and loyalty in the execution of duty by public officials, the establishment of responsibility on the part of those who have been protected to support their guardians as a balance to the responsibility of the latter for the protection and education of women and children under their care, and the clarification of the duties and responsibilities relating to the freedom of expression.

The guarantee of human rights deals with the relationship between the state and the people; consequently, even though a problem may arise concerning the violation of human rights among private individuals, it does not directly involve unconstitutionality. However, it was explained that if a court approves such a violation, this action on the part of a state organ becomes unconstitutional. In the contemporary world where it is recognized that in a state under the rule of law it is a principle that there should be a positive intent to regulate the common good of society, it was explained, the requirement for the constitutional guarantee of human rights in the relations among individuals has also become a matter for serious consideration; but herein the constitutional requirement enters into the relations among private individuals through the mediation of law and the force of the Constitution does not directly extend into those relations.

The original concept of human rights recognized the right of resistance against oppression, but under the principle of popular sovereignty, resistance against the sovereign people is a contradiction in terms. Also, even though the right of resistance is a concept of natural law, to demand it subjectively is a denial of democracy, and there is the view that thoughtless recognition of the right is extremely dangerous. Thus, in order to prevent the exercise of such resistance it has been pointed out that there are such methods of protest as the referendum and recall, as means of direct democratic government, but since the principle of democratic government is representative democracy, it has been pointed out that direct democracy is strictly auxiliary.

LIMITATIONS FOR THE PUBLIC WELFARE (ARTS. 12, 13, 22, AND 29). Opinion was divided on the issue of whether human rights can be limited for the sake of the public welfare. The concept of the public welfare is vague and its meaning varies according to different points of view. First, there is the belief that under police states the public welfare has been used as an anti-human rights concept and that the guarantee of human rights thus negates it. From this standpoint, the requirement is for standards of regulation that are clearer, more reasonable, and more objective than the public welfare. For example, in respect to limitations on the freedom of expression, there must be a prohibition of prior restraint and the establishment of such standards as clear and present danger. Second, there is the view that the public welfare contains inherent limitations that must be recognized as arising from the very nature of human rights which reside in the common life of society itself. For example, even though the public welfare, as an abstraction, is not clear, its meaning can be clearly determined under concrete conditions. In addition, there is also the view that the public welfare through the historical development of the state under the rule of law has been endowed with a specific content and that broad discretionary power, either legislative or executive, is not recognized in respect to limitations on human rights.

In regard to the meaning of the public welfare under the broad provisions of Articles 12 and 13 and under the specific stipulations of Articles 22 and 29, there is an opinion that both have the same intent and another that sees the latter as having special meaning for the welfare state. In opposition to the first view which sees the public welfare as set forth in Articles 22 and 29 as a precautionary stipulation relating to the general provisions, the latter view recognizes the public welfare as based both on positive welfare policies of the nation and on a passive limitation on rights and freedoms.

In addition, there is the opinion that the general provisions are admonitory and that limitations by the public welfare doctrine can be recognized as applying to human rights only as determined in each individual case. This opposes the opinion that the general provisions can be applied to limit all human rights.

Accordingly, opinions were split on the issue of the establishment of provisions relating to limitations on human rights: Should they be in summary general articles, or is it necessary to set forth standards for limitation in specific provisions relating to human rights? From the point of view that there should be clear standards objectively determined it is desirable to determine standards of limitation on an individual basis; from the standpoint that such standards should not be fixed in the Constitution, it is preferable to clarify the standards through the accumulation of judicial decisions.

It is also believed that under a state of emergency it is possible to expand the concept of the public welfare and to impose strong restrictions on human rights. But there is also the view that if that idea is set forth in writing there would be even greater danger that an abuse of power would occur and that therefore it would be preferable to leave it unwritten. In addition, it was also stated that under a state of emergency it is possible to establish a constitutional basis for restrictions on human rights under the principle of necessity which is supreme even over law. Opposed to this is the opinion that because it is impossible to take measures to deal with an emergency in the absence of written provisions, the Constitution must be amended to remedy the deficiency.

EQUALITY UNDER THE LAW AND THE DIGNITY AND EQUALITY OF INDIVIDUALS IN FAMILY LIFE (ARTS. 14 AND 24). Equality under the law means equality in the application and in the making of the law. If law is interpreted to mean not simply general law, but also the Constitution and natural law, then the principle of equality is also binding on the legislative power, and laws containing unreasonable discriminations must not be enacted.

Concerning the dignity and equality of individuals in family life, the opinion was expressed that the relations between a married couple and their minor children are the basis of communal family life and that the significance of the Constitution lies in its maintenance of equality and respect for human rights within communal family life and in the objective guarantee through legislation of relations of equality within the family rather than in the relationship among individual rights in the family.

Changes in Communal Family Life and the Abolition of the Ie. Opinions were divided concerning whether constitutional provisions relating to the legal principles of communal family life within the household and the preservation of family life are necessary. Explanations were offered in respect to the following matters: (1) contemporary family life has changed to a limited household with the husband, wife and children as the core, and the old system of communal life of the *ie* [literally, "house" or "family," but the legal term for the extended, patriarchal family] has undergone a change; and (2) based on the results of a number of public opinion surveys, popular attitudes toward the former family system have also changed and there has been a real alteration in the communal life of the family. Thus, the view was expressed that the abolition of the system of the *ie* must be accepted, particularly in respect to the equality of the sexes and improved family conditions, and that the substance of the Constitution, relating to these matters, must be upheld.

Also asserted was the opposing opinion, which was critical of the present policy that centers on the individual in both the Constitution and the Civil Code and holds that there must be an improvement in morality and the spirit of mutual respect in communal family life and that family life itself must be preserved by the Constitution. In addition, it was also demanded that the communal nature of family life be recognized as it is, but without returning to the old authoritarian family system centered on the head of the household, and that such a family system as the *ie* be protected and respected through the Constitution. In regard to the preservation of family life, the view was also set forth that an economic guarantee to family life should be added, not stopping with the ethical and moral.

Responsibility for Support and Social Security. On the problem of the relationship between the private responsibility for support among relatives and public social security under the real condition of contemporary economic life, there is no way to avoid the expectation of a public system of social security. Consequently, it was said that it is necessary to reexamine the supplementation of the guarantee of livelihood under the present system. In addition, there were explanations of the actual situation relating to the provision of public assistance and the operation of the old-age pension system. On the relationship between these problems and communal family life, several views were set forth: Should not mutual support within the family be given first consideration? In addition to the protection of the livelihood of individuals, should not thought also be given to assistance for family life itself? Should not serious weight be given to the *ie*, which is a natural form of human communal life?

Inheritance. The system of inheritance, outlined in Article 24 of the Constitution, is based on commonality and equality. However, there were reports relating to such matters as the improvement of the positions of wives and mothers, the protection of children's rights of inheritance, and problems relating to wills and bequests. In respect to agricultural property, the right of equal inheritance is recognized. As a result, the atomization of farmland has occurred, and farm management has become difficult. Consequently, the view was expressed that special measures are necessary to deal with this problem. It was pointed out that even though for the sake of appearances the system of equal inheritance is followed, individual inheritance is what actually occurs in respect to both land ownership and cultivation and thus there has been a divergence between the actual relationship involved in rights and the legal relationships relating to property. Also pointed out was the necessity, in order to prevent the atomization of farmland, both to recognize exceptions relating to inheritance, and to provide some relief both financially and under the Tax Law.

INDIVIDUAL PROBLEMS.

Foreigners. There are no constitutional provisions respecting foreigners, such as their legal status and the effectiveness of their rights. Regarding those who possess rights and duties, the Constitution uses such expressions as "the people" and "every person." On this point the view was expressed that in the enjoyment of fundamental human rights, both the Japanese people and foreigners are jointly recognized. Foreigners must also be guaranteed the security of life, person, freedom, and property. It was also indicated that, unlike citizens who have a permanent tie to the nation, foreigners can claim only a relationship through residence and, consequently, there is no reason why they should necessarily be treated on the same footing with citizens. It was further explained that there are situations in which it is proper either to limit or to deny foreigners certain rights respecting immigration, emigration, conditions of residence, suffrage, and qualification for public office or to limit rights respecting occupation and property.

The Responsibilities of Public Officials (Art. 15). Articles 15 and 99 use the term, "public officials," while Articles 7 and 73 use simply "officials." Also, the Law on National Public Officials treats all those employed by or who receive compensation from the state as public officials, but its first article stipulates that it is a law which sets forth the standards to be applied to "officials." In addition, if the phrase "public officials are servants of the whole community" in Article 15, paragraph 2, is taken not to include Diet members, then it does not conform with the phrase in paragraph 3 of the same article, "election of public officials." The above indicates that it may be necessary to have a constitutional provision which clearly sets forth the scope of the phrase "public officials."

The stipulation relating to "servants of the whole community" can be interpreted to be even broader than a similar provision in the Weimar Constitution. It can be taken to mean not only a prohibition applying to those serving a specific political party, but also as providing a basis for limitations for the public welfare as in Article 13 and also for limiting the rights of public officials to bargain collectively and to strike. There is also the opinion that "workers" in Article 28 includes public officials and that the constitutional right to organize is also recognized in respect to the employees' unions referred to in the Public Officials Law. However, that concept of "public official" has been made unclear by the MacArthur letter [of July 1948] prohibiting labor unions for public officials, while under a revision of the Public Corporations and Governmental Enterprises Labor Relations Law, labor unions are recognized for ordinary workers in such enterprises as the national railways and telecommunications.

[There is no mention of Arts. 16 and 17 in the original.]

Freedom of Person (Art. 18). Because it is reasonable to assume that "punishment for crime" in Article 18 includes imprisonment with hard labor against one's will, the view was expressed that it is necessary to expunge the phrase "except as punishment for crime," in accordance with criminal law theory involving the principles of correction and reform.

[There is no mention of Art. 19 in the original.]

Freedom of Religion (Art. 20). The occupation directive relating to Shintō, of December 1945, separated Shintō as a religion from the state. That directive was based on the assumption of both freedom of religion and the separation of church and state, and it can be said that this was affirmed by Articles 20 and 89 of the Constitution. Some maintain that shrine Shintō is a religion of nature that has developed along with Japanese culture and that the Grand Shrine at Ise and Yasukuni Shrine in Tokyo, particularly, fall within the ambit of religious phenomena. There is also the view, however, that Shintō shrines should be regarded as nonreligious, state-related cults.

In respect to religious activities by the state or its organs, one view holds that education in public schools which favors any particular religious group or sect is unconstitutional, while religious education of a general nature designed to enhance religious cultivation is constitutional. In addition, there is the view that because religious freedom for the emperor is also recognized, any religious ceremony carried out in the Imperial Palace and worship at any of the Shintō shrines are simply individual worship on the part of the emperor and are private acts. There is the additional view that imperial proclamations calling for prayers for the peace of the nation are to be regarded as ceremonial acts of the emperor.

Freedoms of Assembly and Expression (Art. 21). The freedoms of expression and of political discussion must be guaranteed at a high level. In order for the state to adopt the best possible policy, every political opinion must be freely expressed. A free market for thought is a necessity. It is generally accepted that the foundation for majority decision lies in the opportunity to develop a majority opinion from among all shades of thought competing freely.

Meetings, parades, and mass demonstrations as defined in public safety ordinances include the expressions of thought and demands relating to politics, economic, labor, and world problems involving appeals to the general mass of the people. At the same time it is generally understood that such parades and demonstrations possess a special character in that they are supported by the power of a mass of people brought together as one, namely, a kind of latent physical power. In respect to limitation on such collective activities, there are the theories of prior restraint and precision [of terms of limitation] and, in cases where these cannot be agreed upon, the legal principle of "clear and present danger" can be invoked. In view of the provisions prohibiting censorship, the interpretation has been set forth that any prior restraint on freedom of speech or publication is unconstitutional. However, it is also believed, as can be seen in the case of the system of required prior reporting [of intention to engage in any of the above activities] in some public safety ordinances, that it cannot be said that prior restraints are all necessarily unconstitutional. The Supreme Court decision of 1954 in the *Niigata Ordinance* case held that to require the granting of prior permission was constitutional, even in respect to collective activities, provided it was done under clear and reasonable standards relating to specific places and methods. However, a similar decision in 1960 relating to the Tokyo public safety ordinances modified the Niigata decision. It held that if there was any need whatsoever to place legal restrictions on such collective activities, and excepting situations where it was clearly recognized that the carrying out of the activity would present a direct danger to the maintenance of public peace, then such provisions would be constitutional if they were regarded as unavoidable, regardless of whether the places where the activity was to be held were listed with some degree of generality or if they were to be held in any place whatsoever. [For the Niigata and Tokyo ordinance decisions *see* Maki, *Court and Constitution in Japan*, pp. 76–83 and 84–116.]

In respect to limitation on association, ordinances relating to the formation of organizations utilize the system of licensing. However, the Law for the Prevention of Subversive Activities recognizes prior restraints exercised by administrative committees and divides such committees into control and investigative organs. The said law widens the concept of criminal law as a condition for the control of organizations. The fact that it establishes instigation and incitement as separate crimes means control of speech and publication which might be against the public welfare. However, the explanation is that such control is constitutional because the conditions are clearly set forth.

Concerning freedoms of expression such as speech and publication, legal restrictions based on the public welfare can be imposed on expressions which violate public morals or instigate or incite violation of criminal or other statutes, are advertisements [of products] harmful to public hygiene, or constitute the infliction of injury on individual honor or feelings or privacy. In respect to the application of provisions of the Customs Rate Law to pictures or writings harmful to the public order or public morals, a problem arises relating to the examination and restriction of imported motion pictures by a customs office in consultation with a review committee. However, there is the opinion that because the prohibition of censorship is a guarantee of the freedom of expression, such examination and restriction can be declared to be not unconstitutional if an absolute minimum of exceptions on behalf of the public welfare is recognized. Concerning the secrecy of correspondence, there is an opinion that any report by the postal authorities relating to matters handled by postal stations, such as the name and address of the sender or the number of articles posted by him, is unconstitutional if done without the consent of the individual concerned.

The Freedoms of Occupation, of Residence, and of Citizenship (Art. 22). The freedom of trade, which includes the freedom to choose an occupation, is a fundamental principle of a free economy. Because this and the freedoms of residence and of change thereof are stipulated in the Constitution, there is the fear that limitations for the sake of the public welfare will be considered to center on the consumer, and that it is necessary to consider the well-being of the producer and the distributor. The Anti-Monopoly Law places restrictions on the freedom of trade and of property of a minority of monopolists for the sake of the public welfare. It is regarded as constitutional, however, because it protects the small and medium businessman, because it protects the interests of the consumer in the form of a supply of cheap and well-made goods, and indirectly, it also guarantees the well-being of labor through developing full employment. It is also believed, however, that when excessive competition results in harm to the public welfare, it may be necessary to modify the Anti-Monopoly Law in exceptional cases.

In the case of small and medium enterprises, forced association to prevent mutual failure is not a denial of fundamental free competition. It is also explained as being in accord with the public welfare through the elimination of public inconvenience arising from inefficient management and through modernization of labor-management relations. In essence, if legislation placing limitations on businesses leads to the most efficient operation of enterprises from the economic standpoint of the people, including producers, consumers, and distributors, then it must be considered as being in accord with the public welfare. However, there is the possibility, as in the case of the Public Bathhouse Law, of the development of a bias in favor of the protection of existing businesses. Also there is the opinion that, as in the case of the government's tobacco monopoly, to consider limitations on trade for financial reasons as being based on the public welfare as set forth in Article 22 is straining matters somewhat. [The argument here is apparently that to interpret government income from the tobacco monopoly as involving the public welfare is not really a justification for prohibiting private sales of tobacco which is clearly a violation of the right to choose an occupation.]

There is an interpretation that holds that a temporary trip abroad is included in the freedom to change one's residence, but this right is ordinarily taken to be a guarantee of something analogous to migration to a foreign country. There is no constitutional guarantee of the right to travel to countries not recognized by the government, as in the case of countries with which the United Nations has voted to break off economic relations. Consequently there is the view that it is possible to deny the issuance of a passport. The denial of a passport on the grounds that it may be injurious to the interests of Japan is a highly political question. A Supreme Court decision has held that this can be done in cases where such travel might be against the public welfare. [For this decision *see* Maki, *Court and Constitution in Japan*, pp. 117–22.]

Regarding the freedom to divest one's self of citizenship, unlike the English system where an Englishman is still treated as an English citizen even after becoming a naturalized American citizen, the United States, even though it strongly adheres to the right to divest one's self of one's citizenship, clearly does not include in this right situations in which a person becomes stateless [through renunciation of citizenship]. There is also the opinion that Article 10 of the Citizenship Law, which holds that the renunciation of citizenship is a condition for becoming a naturalized citizen of another country, is constitutional.

Academic Freedom (Art. 23). Such freedoms as those of research, of the publication of the results of research, and of teaching are included under the freedom of academic activity. The prescription of a specific academic theory by public authority is considered an invasion of the freedom of research. When a public announcement of research results is made, it is subject to limitation by the public welfare as in the case of the general freedom of expression. Unlike the freedom of education in the lower schools, the freedom of instruction in the universities is included in academic freedom. But this does not involve the teaching of a specific ideology; the opinion was expressed that it is limited to the purely academic sphere.

Academic freedom in the universities must be regarded as a freedom to be recognized by the state within the social system and to be based on the public nature of academic research rather than as a human right under natural law. The view was also expressed that university professors should be required to maintain political neutrality in both teaching and research on the basis of the spirit of both the Constitution and the Basic Education Law and of the objectivity of learning.

University self-government is based on respect for university autonomy in regard to such matters as teaching, research, personnel matters, and the management of student affairs and university facilities. Even though the government can provide general directions for the universities, the view is that it is impermissible for it to issue orders on minutely detailed concrete matters. On appointments of university faculty members, the minister of education does not possess the power of veto, but the responsibilities of the cabinet in this matter are unclear. However, it was explained that responsibility for appointment lies completely within the universities, which possess the right of selection. However, as the Supreme Court decision of 22 May 1963 in the *Popolo* case points out [For this decision *see* Hiroshi Itoh and Lawrence Ward Beer, *The Constitutional Case Law of Japan*, pp. 226–42.], student actions in resistance to the legal exercise of the police power on the grounds of university autonomy are not permissible and that the entry of police officers into universities in criminal cases is not an impairment of university autonomy. Also it was stated that an absolutist or totalitarian attitude on the part of academic researchers is in violation of democratic academic freedom, which is based on the relativity of the truth and the pluralism of academic research. It was likewise explained that it was necessary for universities to be circumspect about direct participation in politics in order to prevent political interference from the outside and to protect university autonomy. In this respect university autonomy resembles the independence of the judicial power. However, the view was also expressed that it could not be considered appropriate to recognize the independence of education as if it were a fourth power of government.

The Right to a Decent Existence and Social Security (Art. 25). Article 25 sets forth in writing what was formerly regarded as the moral right to a decent existence and is the most fundamental provision relating to social security. Other constitutional provisions concretely expressing this are Articles 27 and 28 relating to labor policy and Article 26 relating to cultural policy. Judicial precedent holds that Article 25 does not guarantee a direct and material day-to-day existence. However, it does recognize the right to a decent existence as a concrete right. There is the opinion that it is impossible to demand that right through resort to legal process. An additional opinion is that any government policy or act destructive of "the minimum standards of wholesome and cultured living" is illegal and invalid. Moreover, wholesome and cultured living should be judged to involve culture for low-income groups as well. The view is that by means of raising broadly the lives of all those who are currently the recipients of a guarantee of livelihood there should be no inequality between those of low income and others.

Social security is a concrete system for the protection of the right to a decent existence, at the center of which are public assistance and social insurance. Article 25 makes a distinction between social security, social welfare, and public health. In social security, in addition to the protection of livelihood as a form of public assistance, there are such guarantees of income as government pensions, welfare pensions, and pensions from public employees' cooperatives. It was also pointed out that there are medical guarantees such as health insurance and the national health plan. Welfare programs for children and mothers are included in social welfare and such laws as those relating to mental hygiene and tuberculosis prevention are central in public health. Legal assistance for the destitute also falls under social security in the form of expenses for lawsuits.

In our country where full employment and a minimum wage have not yet been completely achieved, a large part of the cost of social security has been allocated to the costs for the protection of daily livelihood. Under the Daily Livelihood Protection Law it is stipulated that support from private sources is given priority. However, since it can be considered that private support contradicts the concept of social security, there has been a tendency in practice to place major emphasis on public support as a matter of necessity. If Article 89 of the Constitution is regarded as having an inhibiting effect on the development of social security among the people, a problem results, since there is the opinion that local public entities carry out the actual execution of social security and that a problem is created by the strong assertion of the local position itself in opposition to that of the state.

The Right and Duty of Education (Art. 26). The guarantee of the right to receive an education is more than a guarantee of a simple individual right; it places the responsibility for education on the people and has been described as ultimately placing it on the state because education is something to be done by public bodies, not by individuals. In respect to the equality of educational opportunity, the outstanding results of the six-three system [six compulsory years of grade school, three of junior high] have been indicated, but there is still the necessity for opening as widely as possible the doors of the universities. Also in order to eliminate inequalities among schools, the opinion was expressed that it is the state's responsibility to establish definite standards for the school system by means of national planning and to increase supervision in order to contribute to their upkeep. The prohibition of discrimination on the basis of sex does not necessarily lead to coeducation, one explanation held, and such discrimination is permissible if educational necessity makes it not improper.

To clarify the basic policy for education it was thought more appropriate to set it forth in the form of law than in an imperial rescript and so the Basic Education Law was passed. However, the opinion was expressed that since the constitutional provisions relating to education are too brief, there is some ground for inserting the substance of the Basic Education Law into the Constitution. The prevention of educational bias and the guarantee of political neutrality in education are responsibilities of the state, but the opinion was also expressed that the Ministry of Education should go no further than the determination of general and basic policy and that current policy should hold that the concrete administration of education is the province of local education committees. However, the view was also expressed that the warning in Article 10 of the Basic Education Law, regarding the improper control of education, concerns the fact that the right of supervision in the administration of education possessed by the Ministry of Education, governors, and the mayors of cities, towns, and villages was not necessarily improper and that in general independent bodies for the administration of education should be established. Again, it was also explained that since under the same Article 10 education bears a direct responsibility to all the people and thus possesses a public character, those who are involved in education, including those in private schools, are servants of the whole community. Education committees have as their objectives the achievement of decentralization of authority over education in respect to interference and control from the central government, but they can be regarded as being directly related to Article 10 of the Basic Education Law because of their direct connection with the residents in each locality. The Basic Education Law holds that compulsory education is free and no tuition can be charged, but in reality parents must bear directly considerable expenses such as school facilities, teaching materials, school supplies, and parent-teacher-association costs. Even during the constituent debates the opinion was expressed that the government should assume the responsibility for expenses to the extent that national finances would permit.

The Right and Obligation to Work (Art. 27). The right to work has been called the guarantee of an offer of work to those who do not have the opportunity, even though ready and willing. To that end the Employment Security Law has been enforced, but recently there has been an insufficiency of skilled workers, and it has become necessary to perfect occupational training and to maintain the flow of the labor force. In addition, the Law for Special Provisions relating to Unemployed Miners and the Law for the Encouragement of the Employment of the Physically Handicapped provide for special treatment for unemployed miners and the physically handicapped and thus infringe on the freedom of administrative management possessed by employers and the freedom of the general population to choose its employment; but it is held that this special treatment is constitutional since it is a reasonable form of discrimination.

There is the problem of exactly how the obligation to work is related to Article 18 of the Constitution which forbids involuntary servitude, also prohibited by an International Labor Office (ILO) treaty. For example, there is a danger that this obligation might be used against strikes, and it is also argued that imprisonment is unconstitutional [because it negates the obligation to work]. As a result of such problems, the enforcement of the obligation to work is limited to such matters as, for example, the handling of those who refuse for no good reason to take employment by postponing job placement without paying unemployment insurance.

Such laws as the Minimum Wage Law and the Labor Standards Law address the conditions of labor, but there are many violations of the latter law in such matters as safety and hours of work. In regard to these matters it is said that leadership and education are more necessary than correction through penal provisions. The Constitution prohibits discrimination regarding human rights, but the Labor Standards Law prohibits discrimination on the basis of nationality, formerly a feature of labor relations, and also prohibits discriminatory treatment, particularly in salaries, on the basis of sex. Accordingly, there is the opinion that even though there may be discrimination in labor relations, it does not forthwith become unconstitutional. For example, there is an opinion that legislation permitting the discharge of a female employee for the reason of marriage is unconstitutional in the case of public employees, but another holding it to be constitutional in the case of private employees [under certain conditions].

Fundamental Rights of Labor (Art. 28). The fundamental rights of labor are differentiated from the constitutional right of association; they involve negotiations by workers on a footing of equality with employers for the maintenance and improvement of working conditions. Consequently, collective bargaining is regarded as being central. Thus, Article 87 of the ILO treaty provides for such matters, especially in regard to the right of organization, as the freedom to establish a union without official authorization, the freedom to join a union on the sole condition that it be in conformity with union rules, and the freedom to enact union rules and to elect representatives. In this sense, the view was set forth that the right of organization is paramount among the three rights of labor because it guarantees the right of association to workers, as possessors of the power of labor, against the employers as the bearers of the right of property.

Because organized workers control the labor market through their organizations, there is the opinion that it is necessary for those who belong to differing enterprises, the unemployed, and others to be able to organize broadly. Consequently the view is also asserted that even in respect to the provision of Article 4, paragraph 3, of the Labor Relations Law for Public Enterprises [that anyone who is not an employee of a public enterprise cannot be a member or an officer of a public enterprise union, a provision designed to protect a union official's position if he has lost his job through an illegal act, presumably by management, during a strike] the status of a union member should be given not only to officials within a union who have been dismissed, but to all union members who have left their jobs until such time that they are again employed and attached to another union. However, because enterprise unions were created in our country under the aegis of the occupation and because raises in nominal wages were easy due to extreme inflation, it was thought that the power of the unions became excessive. As a result, treatment according to one's status in a company was incorporated into the organization of the unions, and the unions shut off the employment of temporary workers; the view was expressed that therein lay the origin on the part of the company of such matters as the undesirability of persons other than employees becoming union officials and the tendency toward ideological contract struggles on the union shop and the raising of the wage base.

Both the Labor Union Law and the Labor Relations Adjustment Law predated the enactment of the Constitution and in 1949 were revised to make them consistent with it. However, because it was legislatively difficult to set proper limitations on strike activities, in addition to setting forth clearly the exclusion of violence from the immunity provisions of the penal law, these laws did not go beyond stipulating in the Labor Relations Adjustment Law such matters as emergency adjustment and the maintenance of safety installations generally relying on the judgment of prevailing social concepts. However, before the establishment of the rules for labor relations, as a result of three fairly advanced labor laws, it was said that there was a tendency to resort to the most extreme action permissible under law without retaining the previous orderly harmony under the civil law and with the misunderstanding that labor regulations did no more than set forth standards for hearings.

Regarding limitations on the right to organize, several points were made. First, there is the political activity of unions. The opinion was expressed that labor unions might possibly restrict the political freedom of some of their members by means of resolutions supporting political parties and that to expel members who acted contrary to such resolutions would be a violation of the guarantee of economic benefits to union members which is the principal concern of the right to organize. There is also a judicial opinion to the effect that to strike against the government to achieve a political objective and to suspend the operations of individual enterprises to that end are outside the scope of Article 28. The right to organize has as its objective the creation of organizations to control the labor market, and since strikes are a means for dealing with employers in order to determine collectively the conditions of work, they cannot be used as a means to achieve political objectives that do not contribute to work. Hence, there is also the view that employers can seek compensation for damages from unions in political strikes.

Second, the union shop system presents a problem. The opinion was expressed that ordinarily in our country even if a union is dissolved the employer should not dismiss the workers unless there is unavoidable necessity, and when a second union is set up by the company in the free exercise of the right to organize, notwithstanding the fact that there may be no union shop system, it is impermissible to resort to the strike [in protest against the new union]. It was also said that there is a question as to whether the union shop system infringes on the worker's freedom to choose an occupation in addition to his freedom to choose an organization or not to organize.

The third point concerns the public welfare. The courts have held that strikes are impermissible which obstruct by violence or threat any actions by an employer taken in pursuit of operations, which illegally restrain the employer's free will, and which obstruct the control of his property. In addition, there was also the opinion that in order to prohibit such abuses of labor's basic rights, there should be a constitutional provision specifically limiting these rights in the name of the public welfare. An opposing view held that a law limiting strikes would be going too far and that there is no necessity for a prohibition of strikes by law, if there is no fear, even if guards are withdrawn, of destruction of the place of work which must be restored to the owner at the conclusion of the strike.

On the fourth point, the problem of the harmony between these rights and other fundamental rights, the following opinions were expressed: infringement through strikes on the right of the employer to manage his facilities and property is an infringement of the right of property; the prevention of the movement of products by those other than union members is an infringement of the right of operation; picket lines are limited to peaceful persuasion and cannot impede by force the freedom to work of nonunion members.

The Right of Property (Art. 29). The right of property in Article 29 was interpreted to include all rights of property under both private and public law, freedom in the utilization and disposal of both consumers' and producers' goods, the freedom of contract and the right of private ownership. In addition, the opinion was expressed that a guarantee of the rights of management and of enterprises themselves should be added to the Constitution. However, a counterview held that there was no need to add the right of management because it is related both to the right to work and the right of property.

The opinion was also put forward that in view of the history of the development of the system of private property, the first paragraph of Article 29 [the inviolability of the right to own and hold property] might be too strong and that there might be doubts about it from the standpoint of human rights. But since the phrase "the public welfare," appears in the second paragraph, there was the opinion that this constitutes a recognition of a principle of socialism. There was also the view that in order to make clear the social character and public nature of the right of property, a provision to the effect that the right of property is accompanied with responsibilities might be inserted and such a provision might be substituted for the present first and second paragraphs. But there was also the view that nothing was particularly inappropriate about this article, regarded as a whole, in respect to the gradual realization of the welfare state.

Another view is that the use of paragraph 3 of this article on behalf of the public welfare is limited to situations in which there is acquisition of parcels of land on a purely local basis and does not include the acquisition of farmland as applied broadly to the landlords of all the nation [as under the land reform program]. However, there is the additional view that even when, as a result of expropriation, specific individuals in concrete situations do become the beneficiaries, if the comprehensive objective of the expropriation is the public benefit, then it is constitutional. Also there is the opinion that expropriation carried out by the state, a local public entity, or a public housing corporation for a housing project comes under the provision for public use in this paragraph because it is publicly authorized by the national housing policy, even though the actual beneficiaries are the individuals who obtain housing, and that expropriation for the acquisition of industrial sites is also constitutional if it is necessary from the standpoint of immediate national industrial policy.

As for just compensation, the courts have held that an appropriate sum calculated reasonably based on a price arrived at under the economic conditions existing at the time of surrender for public use is acceptable and that it need not necessarily conform completely to normal pricing standards. But there is also the opinion that the compensation should correspond to an objective value possessed by the property in question on a concrete, individual basis. In respect to assets held abroad, the explanation has been made that since the government went no further than to refrain from exercising the right to protect [the interests of] Japanese nationals abroad as a result of the application of Article 14 of the Treaty of Peace [involving the Allied seizure of Japanese assets abroad] and did not act directly to take away the right of ownership, no problem arises with respect to paragraph 3 of Article 29 [regarding just compensation for private property taken for public use]. In respect to the methods of compensation, it was held that in addition to making the standards of compensation clear and explicit, it is necessary to develop the ideas of both fungible compensation and payment in kind as against cash compensation; and, in addition, it was declared that ex post facto payment is not unconstitutional.

If the interpretation is made that to limit corporate earnings or to keep them at a low level is not unconstitutional, even if compensation is made on the basis of those levels, the socialization or nationalization of heavy industry may be easy. There is the opinion that the control of earnings produces no harmful effects, if it is subjected to limitations for the public welfare according to the second paragraph of Article 29 or if it is subjected to the additional limitation for the public welfare under the third paragraph.

[There is no discussion of Art. 30 in the original.]

RESULTS OF THE INVESTIGATION. The essential points of the investigations regarding the actual application of the provisions relating to the rights and duties of the people in Articles 10 to 30 are as outlined above. The following questions were raised as the most important for future consideration:

1. Is it necessary in regard to the provisions relating to the rights and duties of the people to reexamine them with reference to the Universal Declaration of Human Rights? In addition to those now listed, should any rights and duties be added or expanded? Are there any constitutional provisions that should be eliminated?

2. Is it acceptable to indicate general limitations on fundamental human rights by a concept such as the public welfare, or should there be individual limitations on each human right?

3. Is it necessary to provide stipulations relating to the principles of common life within the family or to guarantee family life?

Rights and Duties of the People: II (Arts. 31–40)

In the investigation of the application of the provisions relating to the rights and duties of the people, as set forth in Articles 31–40, opinions were expressed initially on the problem of whether these provisions might be too detailed, and then investigations of each provision were carried out, particularly by means of statements from consultants.

THE NEED FOR SIMPLIFICATION OF THE PROVISIONS. Provisions in the Constitution relating to the judicial guarantee of human rights are fairly detailed in comparison both with foreign constitutions and with the degree of detail of others of its own provisions. Consequently, the argument, both for and against, has been made that the provisions relating to human rights before the courts are too detailed and should therefore be expunged from the Constitution in large part and transferred to the Code of Criminal Procedure. On the one hand, a special adviser to the Ministry of Justice argued that because they guarantee the freedoms of the people, it is of significance that these detailed guarantees are set forth in the Constitution. In contrast, two other consultants expressed the opinion that revising the provisions of both the Constitution and the Code of Criminal Procedure is an urgent matter because of the fear that true criminals might go free due to the over-emphasis on the guarantee of the rights of suspects and the accused and because due consideration is not given to the protection of victims and to the maintenance of the public welfare. It is worth particular attention that even among lawyers who were witnesses at the public hearings, there was more than one who expressed the view that it was unnecessary for such detailed provisions to appear in the Constitution.

However, those holding this opinion did not believe that if the provisions relating to the right of silence were removed from the Constitution, their intent should be not retained, but only argued that it was not necessary to go as far as a constitutional guarantee. Those with the opposing view declared that without a constitutional provision the guarantee would be weakened and that would be undesirable.

THE GUARANTEE OF LEGAL PROCEDURE (ART. 31). Is the guarantee of legal procedure limited only to cases involving criminal punishment? Or does it extend also to cases involving the deprivation of liberty by methods other than criminal punishment? The legal wording is by no means clear on these questions. A system of protective custody which involves restraint of freedom without resort to criminal punishment is under consideration for possible inclusion at some future date in the Criminal Code. If and when it is adopted, failure to extend the guarantee of legal procedure into this area would fall short of the guarantee of human rights. Consultant Hirano Ryūichi, professor at Tokyo University, was of the opinion that a provision containing such a guarantee should be clearly stipulated in the Constitution.

In Article 31 only the phrase "life or liberty" appears, with no reference to property. Consultant Hirano was doubtful that there is a guarantee of legal procedure in respect to property. It is likely, however, that to interpret the intent of the article to include property may be understood in the actual application of the Constitution.

This problem was dealt with after the commission had largely completed its investigations into the actual operation of the Constitution. In regard to the penalty of confiscation of property, for example, for a violation of the Customs Law, the law had held that goods belonging to a third party ignorant of the circumstances would be subject to confiscation once the sentence of the offender was handed down (the so-called third-party or indiscriminate confiscation). However, there was a question as to whether confiscation without the opportunity of such a third party to offer opinions or to make a plea or to attack the prosecution or defend himself in court proceedings, especially in regard to his own rights, involved unconstitutional deprivation of the guarantee of legal procedure. In the first case before it, the Supreme Court did not pay particular heed to this issue (decision of 19 October 1960: appeal denied on the grounds that it would not result in benefit to the appellant). However, on 28 November 1962, the Supreme Court held that such confiscation was unconstitutional. This was the first time that the Supreme Court had declared a law to be unconstitutional. [For this decision *see* Itoh and Beer, *Constitutional Case Law of Japan*, pp. 58–73.]

THE RIGHT OF ACCESS TO THE COURTS (ART. 32). Naturally, the right of access to the courts includes the right to bring actions in the courts in civil and administrative cases. But the discussion of this guarantee concentrated on criminal cases in general. The system of legal assistance which has been in the process of gradual development since 1952 involves civil, administrative, and criminal cases. This system makes real the constitutional guarantee by assisting those who cannot obtain judicial protection for their just rights because of poverty, thus making it possible for them to obtain their rights.

The Constitution simply guarantees access to the courts and does not touch on the problem of their composition. Hence, there has been some question as to how their composition should be understood. Does "courts" here mean only those composed of professional judges who possess qualifications set forth in law, or are courts permissible which include laymen such as jurors and *sanshin* [under the German system, *Schöffen*, laymen elected or chosen by lot to sit on the bench with judges]?

As a problem of constitutional interpretation, there are two views: the affirmative one holds that since the Constitution stipulates simply "courts," the introduction of the jury or *sanshin* system would not be unconstitutional; the negative one holds that since there is no stipulation regarding these systems, they would be impermissible. Among those who favor the adoption of a new system, many set forth the special condition that a jury, for example, should be composed of those of high intelligence. In addition, there was the view, related to the criticism of the current trial system, that even though justice is handed down by professional judges alone, popular confidence in the courts is still not strong. Consequently, any new system must be accompanied by a deepening of the popular understanding of the judiciary. This view was held both by lawyers and officials of the Justice Ministry.

Opponents criticized support of the new system as evasion of responsibility of the authorities under the present one. A lawyer who appeared as a consultant presented the following arguments against a jury system: juries would be limited to the preliminary determination of the facts; as amateurs, jurors would be easily swayed by public opinion; the system is not suitable for dealing with complicated matters; and it does not conform with the Japanese national character.

Another problem discussed in respect to Article 32 was the guardianship of juveniles. Under the current system, such guardianship is the responsibility of the courts, but the question was raised as to whether it should remain under the sole authority of the courts. In defense of the system it was argued that guardianship should remain a court responsibility because it has a great bearing on the human rights of juveniles. Those opposed to the current system pointed out that actions involving the restraint of persons are entrusted to administrative organs by such laws as the Mental Hygiene Law and the Law for the Administration of Emigration and Immigration, and thus there is probably no good reason why guardianship must be entrusted to judicial organs alone. It was also argued that the old system, in which guardianship was entrusted to administrative organs such as the former juvenile courts, was superior both in terms of efficiency and of the intrinsic nature of guardianship itself and that it was changed under the compulsion of the occupation.

It was also argued that matters of guardianship should be entrusted to administrative organs because the word *trial* as applied to guardianship proceedings not only has a bad connotation for the young, but also tends to impair the dignity of the courts as judicial offices. It was also pointed out that in the case of an adult who might be involved in a juvenile case, there would be a loss of equal treatment for the juvenile under current practice because guardianship can be carried out in secret without the involvement of a prosecutor and because there is no way to place a complaint with a prosecutor.

In respect to the investigation which must be the basis for a guardianship and which is carried out at present by a family-court investigator, it was argued on the one hand that from the standpoint of the judicial function reasonable competence cannot be expected from the investigator and, on the other hand, that if juvenile cases are the responsibility of the judicial and prosecutorial systems, then the absence of trained investigators will be a serious defect.

THE REQUIREMENTS FOR ARREST (ART. 33). Is arrest possible without a warrant when a crime is not actually being committed? Under the Code of Criminal Procedure, arrest on the spot (Article 210) and arrest for offenses just committed (Article 212, paragraph 2) can be made without a warrant, but this fosters doubt as to whether such arrests fall under "arrest with warrant" as one would expect under the Constitution. However, a judicial precedent (Supreme Court decision, 14 December 1955) holds as follows: "The recognition of arrest . . . under strict limitations, only in respect to serious, specific crimes and under urgent and un-avoidable circumstances, is not contrary to the intent of the stipulations of Article 33 of the Constitution." This, in effect, means that such arrests are not unconstitutional because the common sense of society would recognize them as being undeniably necessary.

Ultimately, however, a question would arise as to whether they would remain constitutional when, after the fact, warrants still were not obtained, thus resulting in the absence of an important requirement. The opinion was expressed that the Constitution should be amended in order to exclude the possibility of such a violation. However, even among those who did not advocate a need for a constitutional revision, there were two opposing views of approval of arrest on the spot without a warrant: that it is a necessity in actual fact, and that it involves the possibility of the abuse of the power of arrest.

In regard to the actual facts regarding the utilization of the power of arrest, a national police official explained that, according to national police statistics up to 1958, there was a tendency toward a decline in unnecessary detention, and that in 1958 some 58 percent of criminal violations were handled by investigations without arrests. A prosecutor offered the criticism that there are many instances in which judges wrongfully refused prosecutors' requests for warrants. However, judicial officials pointed out the problem of deficiencies in the cases of the investigative authorities. There was no resolution of this confrontation.

Government authorities offered the interpretation that warrants are not necessary in administrative procedures. However, there is a lower court decision to the effect that to punish a failure to respond to an order to appear before an administrative body responsible for regulating organizations is in violation of the constitutional requirement of a warrant, for the reason that such an appearance has the character of a true criminal investigation (decision of the Tokyo High Court, 16 July 1956). The case went to the Supreme Court where it was dismissed, however, without a ruling.

GUARANTEE AGAINST ARREST AND DETENTION (ART. 34). Article 34 guarantees the right to counsel, and on that basis Article 39 of the Code of Criminal Procedure was enacted. However, in actual practice the investigative authorities have limited interviews between suspects and their lawyers without observers present, for the reason that observers impede investigations. One lawyer also complained that interviews are not easily arranged and that they have been unreasonably short.

As a legislative device to realize constitutional guarantees, the system of required bail was instituted for the first time following the promulgation of the Constitution. However, because of apparent shortcomings in the system, many dangerous criminals were set free and so legislation was passed which increased the number of exceptions. The criticism was also offered that many suspects jumped bail because it was set too low. Nevertheless, it was also argued that the principle of required bail must be followed.

After the Habeas Corpus Law was enacted in accordance with constitutional provisions, procedures for showing the cause for detention and imprisonment were provided for in the Code of Criminal Procedure. However, this seemed to provide a propaganda tool which some defendants used for a struggle in open court. Consequently, one consultant expressed the opinion that the system of showing cause for detention or imprisonment should be either abolished or revised. Others urged a fundamental reexamination of the system from the standpoint both of prosecutors and of judges. One consultant declared that the present procedure has the effect of putting judges in the position of having to defend themselves. However, a legal scholar argued that in view of the fact that under the old system there were many wrongful imprisonments, the retention of the procedure for the showing of reasons for detention and imprisonment is necessary.

THE INVIOLABILITY OF THE HOME AND SEARCH AND SEIZURE (ART. 35). It has been the consistent view of the government that there is no constitutional requirement for a warrant for administrative inspection and search, but as an element of proper procedure under law the official involved is required to carry on his person proof of his identity. But, in fact, legislation has established that, as in Article 2 of the Law for Handling Evaders of Indirect National Taxes, even though a criminal procedure is not involved, it is necessary to obtain a writ of authorization from a judge. The Supreme Court has ruled (decision of 11 July 1952) that such a writ of authorization falls within the meaning of a warrant as provided for in the Constitution.

In the matter of search and seizure, the Constitution stipulates that the place and the objects must be specified; but in practice it is difficult to specify individual objects, and so the method has been devised under which the specification of the place and the case has the effect of specifying the objects. In addition, "separate warrant" is taken not to mean a so-called general warrant, which is lacking in the specification of an objective, and it is understood that the intent of the law is to prohibit such general warrants. A decision of the Supreme Court (19 March 1952) placed no hindrance to the inclusion in a single warrant of provisions for both search and seizure.

THE PROHIBITION OF TORTURE AND CRUEL PUNISHMENT (ART. 36). A key problem discussed here was whether capital punishment falls under what is termed in Article 36 "cruel punishment." The Supreme Court has held (decision of 12 March 1948) that capital punishment in itself cannot be said to fall directly under "cruel punishment." [For this decision see Maki, *op. cit.*, pp. 156–164.] It has also held that hanging, which is currently in use in our country, cannot be regarded as an especially cruel form of punishment when compared with methods used in various foreign countries (decision of 6 April 1955). A criminal law scholar stated that capital punishment must be retained in order to maintain the moral and legal order as it is today.

Twelve different forms of disciplinary punishment are provided for in the regulations relating to the deprivation of freedom in our country. Major solitary confinement is no longer used because it was regarded as excessively harsh, but reduced rations and minor solitary confinement continue in use. In regard to whether or not such forms of punishment as reduced rations for those who break prison rules are cruel, a professor of comparative law stated that the West German constitutional court has held that such punishment cannot be regarded as the impairment of the dignity of man and that it can be approved within the necessary limits for the maintenance of public welfare and of special discipline within certain relationships.

The United States Constitution prohibits excessive bail. One consultant set forth the view that in Japan, too, fines and bail bonds, excessive in terms of the financial resources of the accused, could be considered cruel punishment.

THE RIGHTS OF THE ACCUSED IN CRIMINAL CASES (ART. 37). The Supreme Court has pointed out (decision of 5 May 1948) that "impartial tribunal" in Article 38 means "a court without possible bias in composition or otherwise." Consultant Ono Seiichiro explained that this provision denies arbitrariness in trial or punishment by the authorities and requires a lawsuit for the person involved. Consultant Kishi Seiichi added that in the concrete operation of criminal procedure, both the voluntary nature and the reliability of the documentary evidence must be thoroughly investigated and that the prosecution's method of utilization in court of the documents so compiled must also be considered for anything that might be improper. Consultant Takahashi Ichirō presented for consideration such other matters regarding the right of prosecution as the utility of the system of the stay of prosecution, the necessity for the revision of the system of investigation boards for the prosecution, and the discrepancy of views between the family courts and prosecutors in the disposition of juvenile cases.

Efforts to insure speedy trials have been made through the enactment of provisions in the Code of Criminal Procedure and other laws, but the ever-present striking delays in justice have not been eliminated. One result has been an excessive lengthening of the period of detention. The following causes for delay were listed: (1) an insufficient number of judges, prosecutors, and courts; (2) a concentration of cases in the hands of prominent lawyers; (3) the complex legal process, particularly the excessive exclusion of hearsay evidence and the lack of a system of arraignment; (4) the weakness of the hearing system; and (5) unreasonable appeals. Naturally, attempts have been made to speed up trials. Consultant Kishi suggested the following remedies: (1) concentrated trials based on sound preliminary preparation; (2) the decisive resolution of disputes by procuring sufficient evidence beforehand; (3) the broadening of simple trial procedures; (4) the adoption of a system under which delayed prosecution would be dismissed without permitting a retrial; (5) a system for disciplining judges guilty of delay; and (6) the use of the system of court-appointed counsel for the accused in order to speed up trials.

The Supreme Court has recognized (decision of 6 March 1950) that guarantees in criminal procedure do not extend to the system of cross examination, and the Code of Criminal Procedure (Article 304) provides that cross examination is an exceptional method of interrogation. In actual practice, however, cross examination is used. According to Consultant Kishi, the technique of interrogation is still considerably underdeveloped.

In the interpretation of the constitutional right to interrogate witnesses, the Supreme Court has held that the right does not mean that each and every witness requested by the litigants must be summoned, but that it is sufficient if all witnesses appropriate and necessary to the trial appear (decision of 23 July 1948 and others). The legal provisions regarding the exclusion of hearsay evidence which originated in this provision have been set forth in the Code of Criminal Procedure, but because these provisions have gone too far and been abused, two views have been expressed: that they must be revised along the lines set forth in the Law relating to Emergency Measures in the Code of Criminal Procedure accompanying the Coming into Effect of the Constitution; and that they must be revised in accordance with the principle that the accused through his attorney can question any witnesses. On the other hand, it has been charged (Consultant Kishi) that the provisions relating to the exceptional approval of hearsay statements (Code of Criminal Procedure, Articles 226 and 227) have been abused and this abuse has become virtually established as a principle.

Because for some years it had been clear in actual practice that some witnesses found it difficult to testify in front of the accused, the Diet in 1958 enacted a new provision to the effect that "during the testimony of a witness the accused may be taken from the court" (Code of Criminal Procedure, Article 281 (2)). At the time it was concluded that this provision was not unconstitutional because at the conclusion of the testimony the gist of the statement would be reported to the accused and he would be given the opportunity to question the witness. But there were both support and opposition regarding this device.

One consultant declared that "competent counsel" is usually taken to mean simply a person who has the qualifications of a lawyer, but if it is not interpreted to mean a lawyer skilled in criminal defense, then the human rights of the accused will not be safeguarded. Another consultant said that the system of legal advocacy is being violated because a large proportion of criminal cases involve summary justice and snap judgments with some 30 percent of public trials involving no defense attorney. This results from the absence of the jury system and from the fact that the courts have not lived up to their intention of adopting generally the system of investigation by a court officer prior to the handing down of a decision. Also in regard to actual practice relating to court-appointed counsel, the following difficulties were pointed out: the assignment of such counsel to defendants of sufficient means, the general and lamentably low level of such counsel, and the insufficiency of compensation.

THE PROHIBITION OF FORCED TESTIMONY AND THE ADMISSIBILITY OF CONFESSION (ART. 38). Some suspects and defendants will not give their names and addresses in the exercise of their right of silence. Not surprisingly, one view recognizes this practice as a proper right and another calls for its control as an abuse. One consultant pointed out that the right of silence is not too often utilized in open court and also turns out to be useless because the probative value of the prosecution's documentary evidence is recognized and proof can be established without the testimony of those who remain silent.

In regard to the right of silence, investigative officers are desirous of a revision of both the Constitution and the relevant laws on this point. The reasons offered were that criminals have become more skillful and less material evidence is left behind and, in addition, proof of intent is difficult in the face of silence.

Another problem is whether the practice of informing a suspect of his right to remain silent goes too far. Consultant Dandō Shigemitsu strongly defended the practice because in its absence it is difficult to exercise the right of silence. On the other hand, investigative authorities were strong in their criticism of the duty to notify a suspect of his right to be silent. They maintained that because the existence of the right of silence is widely known today, and because the point has been reached where the right is abused even by members of terrorist groups, notification is no longer necessary. They argued that to burden investigative officers with the duty of notification through provisions in the Code of Criminal Procedure would be going even beyond constitutional requirements.

Doubts have been expressed as to whether under the current system of notification it is possible to obtain confessions. However, one consultant pointed out that the difficulty has been solved through the exercise of material or immaterial force such as arrest, detention, the presentation of conclusive evidence, and interrogations extending over a considerable period of time.

The question was also raised as to whether testimony is currently being obtained by force. It was claimed that testimony is given involuntarily during the investigative phase either through harsh examination or the promise of release if confession is made. Although force and torture in the obtaining of evidence have been strikingly reduced as compared with the old system, they have not been completely eliminated, according to one witness. One reason, he said, is that some investigators fail to consider that testimony which is contrary to their expectations might be only one small part of the case presented.

One school of thought has maintained that reliance on scientific investigation to produce physical evidence is a means of correcting the abuse of overemphasis on confessions. One consultant pointed out that scientific investigation is not the answer because many crimes, such as bribery, do not produce physical evidence. He argued that it is impossible to expect unsolicited confessions on a completely voluntary basis and therefore it is necessary to give some consideration to the limitations of relying on voluntary confession. He concluded that the attitude of the courts which willfully relies on the unrealistic defense of human rights is improper.

The Supreme Court has held (decision of 20 April 1949) that, as a matter of constitutional interpretation, there is no requirement of corroboration for confession made in open court. Subsequently legislation was passed concerning the Code of Criminal Procedure which provides (Article 329, paragraph 2) for corroborative evidence "regardless of whether there has been confession in open court" and this provision has been applied.

Because under the Anglo–American system of arraignment evidence is presented before the case itself is tried, there is the opinion that no question of unconstitutionality is produced even though the evidence is actually accepted. There are those who maintain that because the arraignment system can be interpreted to be unconstitutional, since in many cases a verdict of guilty may be handed down only on the basis of confession, some revision is desirable so that the system can be utilized without raising this difficult point. Consultant Dandō opposed the system on the grounds that it violates the essence of criminal justice because it is based only on the idea of the disposal of the cases themselves.

The phrase in Article 38 that no person "shall be convicted or punished" has been criticized as being redundant and clumsy. But according to Consultant Ono in recent criminal procedure, the determination of guilt and the passing of sentence have been separated, and the thinking has developed that in regard to the former strict proof is required, but that for the latter there is no reason for not basing it on a prejudgment investigation. Thus, from this point of view the above expression is entirely fitting.

In view of the adoption of a system that does not attach considerable importance to confession as a matter of procedural law, the problem arises as to whether it is necessary to have a different attitude toward the establishment of facts. It is possible to establish facts by circumstantial evidence without reliance on confession. But it cannot be denied that great limitations exist on the establishment of facts through reliance on circumstances in the absence of testimony from the person involved in cases where the facts of the case include such matters as the motive for the crime, intent, or negligence, which involve subjective, psychological factors. If it is necessary to establish minute points, proof can be exceedingly difficult in the absence of testimony by the person involved. Consequently, voices have been raised, particularly by criminal investigators, pointing out the contradiction in this matter arising from the fact that our procedural law has become Anglo–American, while our substantive law has remained continental.

Because Anglo–American substantive law is satisfied by the establishment of the externals of an act, there is a tendency to regard proof of objective facts as sufficient in litigation. Because under our substantive law there are many cases where it is necessary to press for proof of subjective internal facts of the offender, such as one involved in willful negligence, proof is difficult under Anglo–American-style procedural law, which recognizes the right to challenge testimony. Under these circumstances it is easy to resort to forced confession. Some consultants emphasized the need to reconcile our and the Anglo–American approaches.

In addition to the above, other problems relating to Article 38 were pointed out. Consultant Hirano asserted that our current judicial practices recognize that proof based on evidence arising from forced confession has probative value. Consultant Honda Masayoshi expressed the view that because judges have a tendency to feel relaxed about the establishment of facts in the absence of a confession and because both they and prosecutors must avoid overemphasis on confession, it is necessary to school judges in the fact that they can hand down judgments based on circumstantial evidence alone. The same consultant pointed out that, although lawyers have a strong claim to the examination and copying of documents produced in an investigation, prosecutors are not inclined to comply. The reason for such a lack of response is that if the documents must be presented as testimony in court as proof, then because confidence in their content will be even greater than that in oral testimony, the objective of the trial will not be realized, from the prosecutor's viewpoint, because premature permission to examine and copy such material would provide too much advance warning for the accused.

[No reference to Art. 39 appears in the original.]

COMPENSATION FOR CRIMINAL ACTION (ART. 40). According to judicial statistics published in 1961, claims for compensation following criminal actions numbered more than 300 for the entire country. Most of the cases involved those found not guilty, of whom some 30 percent were found to be completely innocent. In comparison with some 95 percent of those who placed claims for reasons of innocence and who received compensation, the percentage of those obtaining compensation who had put in claims because they had been acquitted or because the prosecution had been dismissed was far smaller. As for the amount of compensation, those receiving the legal minimum of 200 yen were numerous, comprising 35 percent of the whole. Consultant Satō Tōsuke expressed the opinion that the present maximum of 500,000 yen, set as the compensation to the survivors of a person who may have erroneously suffered capital punishment, is too low and should be reconsidered legislatively at a proper time.

RESULTS OF THE INVESTIGATION. The substance of the investigations relating to the actual operation of the constitutional provisions relating to human rights in the administration of justice are as summarized above. The principal points raised as problems for future discussion are given below.

The fundamental issue was whether certain provisions should be eliminated because they are too detailed as compared with similar provisions in constitutions of other countries. On the one hand was the view that in the basic law of the nation it is not appropriate to have such detailed points and therefore these provisions should for the most part be eliminated from the Constitution and transferred to such laws as the Code of Criminal Procedure. On the other hand, it was asserted that, considering our country's past history, it is necessary to have provisions guaranteeing human rights as detailed as those now appearing.

The principal individual problems were the following:

In regard to "procedure established by law," should Article 31 be revised to cover other than criminal actions?

Because many voices have been raised concerning the possibility of the unconstitutionality of arrest on the spot, should it be clearly sanctioned in Article 33?

Should the abolition or the limitation of capital punishment be clearly provided for in the Constitution?

Because doubts have been raised as to whether the provisions of Article 38, paragraph 3, recognize the competence of confessions made in open court, should this point be made clear?

Because the provisions of Article 38, paragraph 1, relating to the right of silence have tended to be abused by tricky criminals, should they be modified or stricken?

In order to correct the activities of investigative agencies, should there be restrictions on the competence of evidence collected illegally?

The National Diet

The operation of the constitutional provisions relating to the National Diet includes matters such as the great influence of the circumstances at the time of the enactment of the Constitution on the House of Councilors system, for example, and also the considerable number of issues relating to the indivisible relationship between laws and constitutional provisions such as in the election system. In addition, there are other matters of considerable import for the Diet system, including problems of legislation (e.g., the National Diet Law), such as the central position of committees in Diet operations. The ideal form of political parties has an important connection with the operation of both the Diet system and the cabinet system. The investigation of the actual operation of the constitutional provisions relating to the Diet was carried out in a number of areas but what is dealt with below is limited to those matters which were recognized as being especially important.

THE POSITION OF THE DIET (ART. 41). Article 41 reads as follows: "The Diet shall be the highest organ of state power, and shall be the sole law-making organ of the State." Because problems revolving around the phrases "highest organ of state power" and "sole law-making organ" were discussed in relation to other provisions concerning the actual operations of the Diet and the cabinet, the discussion is described in the sections relating to those provisions. [See Index.]

THE BICAMERAL SYSTEM (ARTS. 42 AND 43). Problems relating to the bicameral system were taken up with particular emphasis on the issue of the House of Councilors.

From a Unicameral to a Bicameral System. Consultant Satō Tatsuo testified as follows on the process of change from the unicameral system, as in the MacArthur draft, to the bicameral system and on the deliberations on the House of Councilors held in the constituent assembly.

The MacArthur draft provided that the Diet be unicameral, but upon the request of the Japanese it was changed to the bicameral system, with the House of Representatives and the House of Councilors. However, on the point of the membership of the House of Councilors, the Japanese request was not honored. In the 2 March draft prepared by Minister of State Matsumoto, it was proposed that the House of Councilors be composed of two groups of members: those elected according to locality and profession, and appointed members (appointment to be made by a vote of a joint committee from both houses); but this proposal was not accepted by GHQ. From the time of the outline of the revised draft, it was provided that both houses be composed of members elected to represent the people in general. Dissatisfaction with this was expressed during the discussion of the draft revision in the constituent assembly, but under the objective conditions of the time there was no movement to return to the line set forth in the Matsumoto draft. The Special Committee for Constitutional Revision in the House of Representatives, in a supplementary resolution, recognized the principle that the House of Councilors also should be composed of members elected as representatives of all the people; but on its composition the view was expressed that serious consideration should be given to facilitating the election of men of knowledge and experience from various social groups and professions. Chairman Abe of the Special Committee for Constitutional Revision of the House of Peers in his report strongly set forth the view that the two houses should be as different as possible in their composition in view of the import of the bicameral system.

The Electoral System for the House of Councilors. According to the testimony of Consultants Satō Tatsuo and Kōri Yūichi, who at that time was head of the Regional Office of the Home Ministry, deliberations on the revised draft of the Constitution and examination of the system of election for the House of Councilors were carried out during the constituent assembly, and three different drafts were prepared by the Home Ministry, the Bureau of Legislation, and the Emergency Committee on Legislation. All three drafts concentrated on how the House of Councilors could be given its own special character distinct from the House of Representatives by means of the electoral system. At an early stage the concept of the double system of national and local constituencies came into being, and the central problem was the nature of the national constituency. Ultimately, the problem narrowed down to a system of recommendation of candidates with an element of functional representation, but this failed to obtain GHQ approval, and a system of direct popular elections from local and national constituencies had to be adopted. However, there was some expectation that in the operation of the national constituency system there would be a flavoring of functional representation. There was a general tendency to favor a minimum age of forty for candidates, but this was reduced to thirty. Generally, in both the government and the Diet there were uneasiness and apprehension as to whether such an electoral system could actually produce a difference in the character of the House of Councilors.

At the time the House of Peers, particularly its secretariat, produced several drafts regarding an electoral system for the House of Councilors, as explained by Consultants Kobayashi Jirō, former secretary-general of the House of Councilors, and Teramitsu Tadashi, former chief of the Proceedings Division of the House of Councilors.

Operation of the Electoral System of the House of Councilors. According to Consultants Fujii Sadao, chief of the Local Administration Bureau of the Local Autonomy Agency and former chief of the Election Section of the Home Ministry, and Matsumura Kiyoyuki, chief of the Election Bureau of the Local Autonomy Agency, during the earliest period the national constituency did not meet the expectation that persons with national reputations for outstanding learning and experience and persons with professional and intellectual achievements would be elected. In addition, there was no particularly strong partisan political flavor to the elections. They added that as elections continued the following tendencies appeared: (1) a decrease in the election of persons who were simply well-known but without organizational backing; (2) an increase in the election of those with special organizational backing, such as from labor unions or government offices; (3) increasing involvement of political parties; (4) the maintenance to a certain degree of the expectation of functional representation, but with a particular emphasis on representation of interest groups; and finally, (5) the failure to eliminate confusion among electors in choosing candidates, a weak point that has existed from the beginning.

ELECTIONS (ARTS. 44 AND 47).

Qualifications of Members and Electors. The interpretation of the phrase "social status" in the proviso that there shall be no discrimination "because of race, creed, sex, social status, family origin, education, property, or income" in Article 44, which deals with the qualifications of members and their electors, has been a problem in actual operations.

In regard to the problem of whether the adoption of functional representation would result in discrimination on the basis of social status, Consultant Matsumura declared that the system of functional representation involved the phrase "members, representative of all the people" [Article 43] rather than social status. Consultant Satō Tatsuo said also that, although the various drafts which included functional representation in the electoral system for the House of Councilors failed to gain acceptance by GHQ, its view was that a method involving recommendation by occupational organizations would probably be acceptable if such candidates were recognized along with independent candidates.

On a number of occasions, legislative devices to limit the candidacy of high-ranking public officials have been discussed, but none has been adopted. On this point Consultant Matsumura pointed out that because such a limitation might involve the constitutional problem of "social status" there might also be constitutional doubt about the right of equality under Article 14 and the freedom to choose one's occupation under Article 22. Moreover, the same consultant expressed the view that a question of unconstitutionality might arise in respect to limitations on the candidacy of high-ranking public officials if they were limited to specific positions, such as the chiefs of certain bureaus of the Construction or Agriculture and Forestry Ministries or persons in certain positions relating to subsidies and authorizations and not stipulated by such general abstract terms as bureau chiefs and vice ministers in each ministry and agency.

A Political Parties Law. The question of the need for a political parties law was also dealt with because of its relation to elections. On this issue Consultants Minakawa Michio, chief of the Election Section of the Local Autonomy Agency, and Matsumura testified as follows.

In the first general election in 1946, political parties entering candidates numbered about 260, and because there seemed to be a need for the limitation of qualifications for political parties, the Home Ministry prepared a draft law to that effect. However, opposition developed in the cabinet conference on the draft and no government bill was presented. About November 1947 in the Special Committee on the Election Law and the Political Parties Law, a political parties bill cooperatively drafted by members of the Liberal, Democratic, Socialist, and National Cooperative parties was agreed upon. This draft also imposed certain limitations on candidates, but was not finally enacted into law. The draft then appeared in a different form in the 1948 Law for the Control of Political Funds. This law was reexamined in 1954 by the Diet, and at the same time a Progressive Party bill on political parties was also drafted. Each of these proposals for a political parties law was criticized as being either unconstitutional or an abuse for unnecessarily imposing restrictions on the freedom of both elections and party activity.

In the Second Committee, Consultant Tsuchiya Shōzō, former special researcher of the National Diet Library, was heard on the 1956 Argentine Political Parties Law and the 1959 West German Political Parties Bill which has not yet been enacted into law.

PRIVILEGES OF DIET MEMBERS (ARTS. 50 AND 51).

Right of Exemption from Apprehension (Art. 50). Article 50 provides as follows: "Except in cases provided by law, members of both Houses shall be exempt from apprehension while the Diet is in session, and any members apprehended before the opening of the session shall be freed during the term of the session upon demand of the House." Exceptions set forth in law (Article 33, National Diet Law) approve the apprehension of Diet members caught while committing crimes and in certain other criminal situations.

In actual practice there have been two instances in which a house has not approved an apprehension when a request has been made. But there were other cases in which approval was granted. An example of a withdrawal of a request for approval of apprehension came when the member involved resigned during deliberations thus rendering further action unnecessary.

Two special cases involving requests for approval of apprehension have occurred: one concerning the exercise of the right of command of the justice minister; and the other, approval with a time limit. Consultant Takahashi Ichirō discussed these cases as follows. The case involving the right of command developed during the nineteenth ordinary session of the Diet in 1954. The chief prosecutor of Tokyo requested through the attorney general that the justice minister issue an instruction on whether or not it would be acceptable to request a warrant for the arrest of a certain member of the Diet. In response it was pointed out that the justice minister, exercising his right of command, could postpone the matter. This case did not involve a request for approval of an arrest directed to a house of the Diet, but it did involve several elements related to that issue.

The other case concerned approval with a time limit and also arose during the nineteenth Diet session. This case involved the approval by the House of Representatives of a request for the arrest of a certain Diet member, but with a time limit attached. Several questions arose concerning the validity of the time limit on such an approval. There was also a conflict of academic opinion on this. A decision of the Seventh Criminal Section of the Tokyo District Court on 6 March 1954 held that the right of the house to approve arrest involved the authority to reject a wrongful and unnecessary arrest after weighing the legality and necessity of an arrest of a Diet member and recognized that "a higher necessity" was required in the case of a Diet member than in the case of ordinary suspects because of the importance of deliberations on national policy. But it held that "while approving apprehension itself, measures such as placing a time limit on the approval are illegal because they disregard the essential nature of the approval of apprehension."

Consultant Takahashi described two views on approval of arrest: that because the right not to be apprehended is naturally designed to prevent the abuse of the power of arrest, apprehension must be approved only if there is no abuse of the right involved; and, that comparing the legal benefits from the standpoint of deliberations on national policy, not granting approval is acceptable.

Immunity of Diet Members for Speeches and Votes (Art. 51). There is no instance in which a Diet member has been held liable outside the Diet for "speeches, debates, or votes cast inside the Diet." However, there is the question of whether or not the immunity provided for in Article 51 is applicable to violence, the infliction of bodily harm, or interference in the discharge of duties of public officials which might be incidental to actions involved in the execution of the duties of a Diet member. This issue was dealt with in criminal court actions arising out of two cases of violence in the House of Councilors in 1955 and 1956, in relation to whether or not charges lodged by the Speaker of the House or by a member could be regarded as legal actions. In the 1956 case, the chief judge of the Second Criminal Section of the Tokyo District Court expressed an opinion (25 April 1961) on a hearing in such a case in which he held that it was not illegal for a prosecutor to bring charges without waiting for a complaint by either the speaker of a house or a house itself. Also in relation to the 1955 case, a similar decision was rendered on 22 January 1962, by the Third Criminal Section of the Tokyo District Court.

DIET SESSIONS (ARTS. 52, 53, AND 54). A number of opinions were expressed by consultants on various problems relating to Diet sessions.

Continuous Sessions. Consultants Yamasaki Takashi, vice secretary of the House of Representatives, and Kondō Hideaki, former secretary-general of the House of Councilors, described a number of problems arising from the principle of continuous sessions in both houses. One problem relates to bills and other matters subjected to intermittent investigation while the Diet is not in session, but currently this has been solved entirely by legislation.

The Principle of One-Time Deliberation. Article 39 of the Meiji Constitution stated: "A Bill which has been rejected by either the one or the other of the two Houses shall not be again brought in during the same session." In neither the current Constitution nor the National Diet Law is there such a provision. According to the testimony of Nishizawa Tetsushirō, head of the Legislative Bureau of the House of Representatives, the draft of the National Diet Law prepared by the secretariat of the House of Representatives contained such a provision, but it was stricken at the direction of GHQ. The reason given was that there might be situations in which such action would have to be taken in accordance with changes of circumstances during long sessions of the Diet. However, the same consultant stated that fundamentally this principle had to be followed and that there were demands that it be set forth explicitly in law, but that there are technical difficulties involved in trying to determine the extent of its application.

Calling an Extraordinary Session. Former Commissioner Ozawa Saeki described a number of cases involving the difficult problem of attempting to place a limit on how soon an extraordinary session could be assembled when the Diet members themselves convoke one. Consultant Nishizawa Tetsushirō stated that on a number of occasions when the National Diet Law had been revised, the question of inserting a provision relating to the time within which an extraordinary session had to be convened came up, but that although opinion in general was agreed, a conclusion had not been reached.

The Length and Extension of Sessions. Consultant Yamasaki testified on cases involving the application of Articles 11 and 12 of the National Diet Law bearing on the length and extension of sessions. [Those articles provide that the length and extension of extraordinary and special sessions shall be determined by resolutions passed by both houses.] There were questions relating to the interpretation of provisions, but they were dealt with as political issues, and were finally resolved by legislation through a revision of the National Diet Law in 1955.

VARIOUS PRINCIPLES RELATING TO SESSIONS (ART. 56).

Quorums. Paragraph 1 of Article 56 provides that in neither house can business be transacted or votes be taken "unless one-third or more of the total membership is present." Foreign constitutions require that a quorum for voting be a majority of those present, but Article 56 does not.

According to the testimony of Consultant Nishizawa, under Diet practice the basis for determining quorums is the legally specified number of Diet members, not the actual number. Also the determination of a quorum in the House of Representatives is within the authority of the speaker of the house, and in the House of Councilors it can be obtained through a demand for a count of those present.

Determination of a Majority. When a vote is to be taken by written ballot, the question arises of what constitutes the basis for a majority. The

Constitution says that it should be "a majority of those present," but that is not the actual practice. Consultant Nishizawa testified as follows. The written ballot vote is calculated by taking the total count of ballots and then determining the ayes (or white ballots) and nays (or blue ballots). But in the actual vote count there are situations in which it cannot be said that the total number of votes is that of "those present" because of invalid ballots or abstentions. There are a number of examples of how invalid votes are dealt with, but members who cast invalid votes are generally excluded from the number of those present. The same consultant stated that in reality notwithstanding the constitutional provision that Diet business be determined by a majority of those present, the current practice is close to the West German method where decisions are made by a simple majority of valid votes cast.

INTERNAL ORGANIZATION AND PROCEEDINGS OF THE DIET (ART. 58).

National Diet Law and House Rules. Details regarding the internal organization and proceedings of the Diet are set forth in the National Diet Law and the House Rules.

During the enactment of the National Diet Law, the directions of SCAP had a great influence. Consultant Nishizawa, who was in charge of the drafting of the National Diet bill by the secretariat of the House of Representatives, received detailed instructions from SCAP on numerous occasions during the drafting of the bill. For that reason alone there was a decisive influence from the American congressional system, as shown particularly in the committee system.

Consultant Teramitsu Tadahiko made a similar point regarding SCAP influence on the House Rules. He stated that the rules of both the House of Representatives and the House of Councilors were enacted by house members, but the close resemblance of most of the details in each arose from the fact that SCAP instructions were relayed to each house.

The Committee System. Consultant Nishizawa testified as follows on the committee system. Diet proceedings underwent a great change when the shift was made from an emphasis on the plenary session to one on committees, particularly the standing committees. During the enactment of the National Diet Law, there were a number of changes in the instructions from SCAP on the committee system, but the final fixed sections included the establishment of standing committees, the stipulation by law of specific committee titles, the abolition of the system of three readings of a bill, and the immediate assignment of a bill by the speaker of the house to the appropriate committee. In addition, only in committee can bills be given treatment resembling rejection. Namely, paragraph 3 of Article 56 of the current National Diet Law provides: "A bill which a committee decides not to submit to a plenary session of the house shall not be submitted. However, when demanded by twenty or more members within seven days . . . from the date of the committee decision, it must be submitted to a plenary session." This was based partly on a misunderstanding of a SCAP instruction. The said instruction was as follows: "A committed bill can be directly considered in a plenary session when the committee concerned has accepted it and when twenty or more members of the committee support it." In other words, the misunderstanding lay in believing that consideration in a plenary session was allowed without awaiting the completion of committee discussion. The error was remedied by a revision of paragraph 3 of Article 56 of the National Diet Law in 1948 when a provision was added providing for interim committee reports, a limit was placed on committee consideration, and direct consideration on the house floor was made possible. Consultant Kinoshita Kōkyo, chief of the Research Section of the Legislative Bureau of the House of Councilors, compared the system above with the British Parliamentary committee system, which utilizes the three-reading system and emphasizes the importance of consideration in full session.

THE PASSAGE OF BILLS: THE SUPREMACY OF THE HOUSE OF REPRESENTATIVES (ART. 59).

Supremacy in the Passage of a Bill. Consultant Yamasaki provided a detailed explanation of the actual operation of this article in relation to the passage of bills.

Members' Bills. Consultant Nishizawa testified as follows regarding the unified system of research experts in the standing committees, as provided for in the National Diet Law, the Legislative Research Bureau of the National Diet Library, and the Legislative Bureaus of the two houses stressing members' bills. This system was provided for in the SCAP instructions on the first draft of the National Diet Law prepared by the secretariat of the House of Representatives. Also in those instructions was the requirement that there be Rules committees in both houses. These were to be composed of Diet members and were "to advise the Cabinet and both Houses on legislative problems and needs." They were also to lay stress on members' bills. However, the same consultant declared that it could not be concluded that SCAP intended that only members' bills could be recognized and that the right of the cabinet to present bills would be denied. He also stated that the fact that the Rules committees in both houses could also advise the cabinet could not be understood without the premise that the cabinet possessed the right to introduce its own bills.

Until the tenth ordinary session of the Diet, there were not many members' bills, but these steadily increased thereafter reaching the highest point in the sixteenth extraordinary session. Consultant Kondō Hideaki stated that this was because, following the return to Japan of a group of Diet members who investigated the American congressional system in 1950, there was a demand made to the speakers of both houses for the principle of members' bills in respect to general legislation.

Consultants Kondō and Ōike Makoto, former secretary-general of the House of Representatives, pointed out that the consent of a specific number of members was required for motions relating to bills in the 1955 revision of the National Diet Law; that there was a particularly large increase in the number of members consenting to the introduction of bills accompanying the budget; that the two preceding points were regarded as placing a limitation on members' bills; and that there had been in the past various criticisms of members' bills accompanying the budget.

THE SUPREMACY OF THE HOUSE OF REPRESENTATIVES AND BUDGET APPROVAL AND TREATY CONCLUSION (ARTS. 60 AND 61). Consultant Yamasaki gave a detailed explanation of instances relating to the supremacy of the House of Representatives and budget approval and treaty conclusion. In regard to the budget there are a fair number of cases in which there was automatic approval. In respect to treaties, cases in which they were first presented in the House of Representatives were in the majority and in only a few instances was there prior consideration by the House of Councilors. However, in all cases Diet approval was obtained. There were three cases of automatic approval [in which approval by the lower house becomes Diet approval if the upper house fails to act in thirty days] of treaties in the thirtieth extraordinary session of the Diet. Also in this category was the renewal of the Japanese–American security treaty of 1960.

THE RIGHT OF INVESTIGATION IN RELATION TO GOVERNMENT (ART. 62). The two houses have differed in the scope of the investigations in relation to government they have carried out. Consultant Ibaraki Junichi, head of the Records Division of the House of Representatives and former head of the Committee Division, testified as follows on cases in the House of Representatives.

In that house the exercise of the right of investigation in matters of government produced no problems in respect to preparation for legislation or the supervision of administration. Investigations concerning the latter have the character of inquiry. Naturally, investigation of matters relating to government extends to administration of criminal affairs. Special limitations are placed on the right of investigation in government in respect to the exercise of the right of prosecution which possesses a quasi-judicial character. In relation to the Audit Committee's investigations, continued after 1953, into the Japan Development Bank's investments in shipbuilding, there was a request from the justice minister in February 1954 that the committee temporarily suspend its investigations because of the necessity arising from the investigations being carried out by the prosecutor-general's office. Subsequently, in April 1954 the justice minister's right of command was invoked. In this case the Audit Committee limited its investigation to that part which related to the exercise of the right of prosecution. There is no case in which investigation of actual trials has been carried out.

Consultant Watanabe Takeshi, head of the Committee Affairs Division of the House of Councilors, testified as follows on cases of investigation into governmental affairs in that house.

There was one case in which the House of Councilors in 1948 conducted an investigation of a trial. The Judicial Affairs Committee investigated the so-called Urawa Mitsuko affair. This committee carried out its investigation of this case of infanticide by Urawa Mitsuko and prepared a report containing conclusions expressing dissatisfaction with the finding of facts by both the prosecutor and the judge in the case and stating that the punishment inflicted was improperly light. The Supreme Court took exception to the committee's report, holding that it was an infringement on the independence of the judiciary and that it went beyond the scope of the right of investigation. The committee countered by saying that the Diet is the highest organ of state power and the sole law-making organ of the state, that the right of investigation of governmental affairs was not limited to preparation for legislation but extended to all matters of government, and that it made possible both investigation and criticism of matters involved in the administration of justice which is an aspect of governmental affairs. However, subsequently, the Judicial Affairs Committee took the position that the right of investigation extended neither to matters in litigation nor to decisions already handed down.

Consultants Higuchi Katsu and Mano Tsuyoshi, justice of the Supreme Court, represented the opinion of the Supreme Court in the matter of the right of investigation. This right possessed by both houses is a supplementary power involving necessary materials relating to the exercise of authority in matters of legislation and the consideration of the budget, and any announcement of an opinion resulting from reexamination of the propriety of a finding of fact or the imposition of punishment or any action that might lead to a reprimand of a judge who has made a decision would be an infringement of the independence of the judiciary. Moreover, the Supreme Court seems to have taken the view that because the House of Councilors has not again undertaken an investigation similar to that in the *Urawa* case, a custom in actual fact has been established.

Consultant Tsuda Minoru stated an opinion on the right of prosecution as it is related to the right of investigation of governmental affairs.

His view was that the exercise of the right of prosecution has a quasi-judicial element resembling the independence of the judicial power and that perhaps those investigations which either by method or scope might directly influence the independent execution of duties in accordance with the conscience of a prosecutor might be inadmissable.

IMPEACHMENT COURTS (ART. 64). In regard to organs for the "public impeachment" of judges the Law for the Impeachment of Judges provides for two: an impeachment court, and a Committee for the Prosecution of Judges. Both are composed of members of the two houses. Explanations concerning problems were heard from Consultant Kobayashi Kenji, secretary of the Committee for the Prosecution of Judges, on matters relating to that committee and from Consultant Sumai Akira, secretary of the Impeachment Court, on matters relating to that court.

A major question in the Prosecution Committee which did not come to prosecution was the *Suita* case of 1953. This case was also related to the issue of judicial independence. There were a number of cases in which impeachment resulted from prosecution by the Impeachment Committee.

RESULTS OF THE INVESTIGATION. The results of the investigations into the actual operation of the constitutional provisions relating to the National Diet were as summarized above. The following were the principal points raised for future discussion and deliberation: (1) Should the expression to the effect that the National Diet is "the highest organ of state power" be retained just as it is?; (2) Is the bicameral system acceptable as it is? Especially, how should the House of Councilors be organized?; (3) Should the basic principles for the internal management of the Diet be set forth in the Constitution? Especially, is there any necessity for a revision of the committee system as the core of Diet administration?; (4) Should the current system of sessions be retained as it is?; and (5) Should there be some constitutional provision relating to political parties?

The Cabinet

The investigation of the provisions relating to the cabinet in many cases was carried out from a theoretical point of view involving such matters as various types of parliamentary cabinet systems, the link between the parliamentary cabinet system and political parties in their ideal form, and the relationship between party politics and the electoral system. The content of the investigations relating to the above points is left to the Second Committee Report. Set forth below is an outline of the investigations of the problems produced by the actual operation of the constitutional provisions relating to the cabinet. In addition, the opinions cited here of the commission members and of the specialists attached to the commission are limited to what they have stated in their capacities as consulting witnesses.

POSITION OF THE CABINET (ART. 65). The executive power is vested in the cabinet. The principal problems in the operation of the Constitution relating to the exercise of the executive power by the cabinet are as follows.

The Cabinet Law. The organization and functions of the cabinet are set forth in the Cabinet Law as well as in the Constitution. Specialist Satō Isao testified that at the time of the enactment of the Cabinet Law, strong doubt was expressed as to its necessity. The reasons for this doubt were that the content of the Cabinet Law in many places simply repeated the Constitution and the belief that executive power could be provided for simply by the internal rules of the cabinet itself. Consultant Ide Seizō, former vice chief of the Bureau of Legislation, who at the time was head of the First Section of the bureau and as such was responsible both for the drafting of the Cabinet Law and for negotiations with SCAP concerning it, testified as follows. The content of the Cabinet Law was strongly influenced by SCAP instructions. In those instructions, the following beliefs appeared: that the Diet was supreme over the cabinet and other administrative organs; that executive power was inferior; and that its authority should be limited. SCAP produced a draft of its own in opposition to that presented by the Japanese side, and to a certain extent the SCAP draft had to be accepted. Articles 1, 6, and 11 of the current Cabinet Law were inserted in accordance with the SCAP draft.

Cabinet Meetings. Consultant Suzuki Shunichi testified as follows regarding the form of cabinet meetings, the time period for cabinet decisions, and the method by which cabinet decisions are made.

There are regular and extraordinary cabinet meetings. In addition, there are *mochimawari* sessions [literally, "carrying around" sessions, where instead of full formal sessions the opinions of individual cabinet members are sought out privately]. Decisions, understandings, and reports may be arrived at or approved at cabinet meetings, and in all cases the necessary documents must be prepared.

Documents relating to cabinet decisions are signed and sealed by cabinet ministers and finally by the prime minister. The seal attests that the opinions of the ministers of state are in accord on the matter before the cabinet meeting. The date on which the ministers of state agree and the date of the signature of the prime minister may differ, but in such a case the date of the prime minister's signature is the date of the cabinet decision.

Because matters before a cabinet meeting can be coordinated with the ministers up to the day before a decision, a minister who is absent from a meeting because of illness, official travel, or such can express his opinion in the event that he is opposed to the matter. Also, when there is no expression of opposition, and when the prime minister who chairs the cabinet meeting recognizes that cabinet ministers, both present and absent, agree on a matter, he may affix his signature to the document without the signature of an absent minister, and the decision is made.

Cabinet agreement is based on the principle of unanimity. When there is disagreement, cabinet meetings are repeated, deliberation is carried out fully, and ultimately an opinion is arrived at through an accommodation of views. When accommodation is difficult and there is no time to spare, the prime minister hands down a decision. Ordinarily, a dissenting cabinet minister is also bound by this decision, but if not, either there is no cabinet decision or the prime minister has no recourse but to exercise his power of removal [of the dissenting minister] under Article 68.

The same consultant also expressed the opinion that although there has been criticism of the principle of unanimity in cabinet decisions, it may be possible under legislative theory to establish a quorum for cabinet meetings and to adopt the system of the majority decision. Administrative practice on methods of cabinet decisions has become set, and to create overly formal stipulations [respecting decisions] might not be appropriate from the standpoint of unified group action by the cabinet.

Administrative Committees. There may be some constitutional doubt concerning the role and the competence of administrative committees because of their somewhat independent position vis-à-vis the cabinet, which enjoys executive power under Article 65, and because of the cabinet's position of collective responsibility to the Diet under paragraph 3 of Article 66. On this point consultants expressed the following views.

Consultant Takatsuji Masami stated the view that it might be possible to grant such committees a certain degree of independence from the cabinet in regard to matters where it is recognized that there is a social requirement for impartial, nonpartisan, and fair neutrality in the disposition of a problem in the absence of controlling policy or other measures. Consultant Tanaka Jirō, professor at Tokyo University, also expressed the view that it is not necessarily contrary to the spirit of the Constitution to recognize the independent nature of administrative committees under conditions where the government reserves its rights in personnel and budgetary matters. In opposition to this, Consultants Aichi Kiichi, former cabinet chief secretary, and Tanaka Eiichi, former cabinet vice chief secretary, expressed the view that in all frankness administrative committees have no proper reason for being, even though such questions as their possible efficiency in government operations or the locus of executive responsibility in respect to them should be examined.

Also Consultant Ide Seizō stated the view that it might be desirable to add to the Constitution some basic provision that would enable administrative committees to be established by some such method as a Diet resolution passed by a special majority when the creation of such a committee might be necessary. He based his view on the fact that even though administrative committees might operate effectively, there is some doubt about their position because of Article 65 and because Article 72 provides that the prime minister exercises control and supervision over all executive organs.

ORGANIZATION OF THE CABINET (ARTS. 66, 67, AND 68). The cabinet consists of the prime minister, who is its head, and the ministers of state. The following points were indicated as operational problems related to the organization of the cabinet.

Designation of the Prime Minister (Art. 67). The prime minister shall be designated from among the members of the Diet by a vote of the Diet. In actuality such designated members, until now, have come from the House of Representatives, not from the House of Councilors. Commissioner Rōyama Masamichi said that there is no problem regarding the method of designation itself, but that there may be one in the Japanese practice of designating as prime minister the person who is president of a political party. He declared he sympathizes with the criticism he had heard in the United States that the election of a party president as prime minister is not simply a question for party members to decide but should involve the people themselves.

Appointment and Dismissal of Cabinet Ministers (Art. 68). Cabinet ministers are appointed by the prime minister and may be dismissed at his discretion. To date there have been two cases involving the dismissal of cabinet ministers. There is no question involving dismissal in itself, but Commissioner Noda Uichi has pointed out that the prime minister's possession of the right of dismissal has made cabinet reorganization simple, and that the majority of cabinet reorganizations have originated from considerations of faction [that is, the appointment of cabinet ministers from factions favored by the prime minister]. Commissioner Yoshimura Tadashi remarked on the ease of cabinet reorganization, and pointed out two examples of cabinet reorganization which had been carried out immediately after the dissolution of the House of Representatives and before the required general election, stating that the problem was a theoretical one contrary to the principles of the parliamentary cabinet system.

The Number of Cabinet Ministers (Art. 66, 1). There is no provision in the Constitution for a fixed number of ministers making up the cabinet, the matter being left to law. Specialist Satō Isao and Consultant Okabe Shirō, vice chief of the National Diet Library and former head of the Administrative Management Office of the Administrative Management Agency, both stated that Article 2 [of the Cabinet Law] provides for a fixed number of cabinet ministers, sixteen including the prime minister, the same as that under the Meiji Constitution. In regard to the appropriateness of this number, Consultant Tanaka expressed the opinion that it should be increased, and Consultant Aichi the opinion that it should remain as it is.

The Provision regarding Civilians (Art. 66, 2). The provision that the prime minister and the other ministers of state must be civilians was added as a revision by the House of Peers during the constituent assembly on the demand of the Far Eastern Commission. The Japanese term *bunmin* is a translation of "civilian." Consultant Kobayashi Jirō, who was at the time chief secretary of the House of Peers, explained the process of the selection of the term *bunmin* in the House of Peers.

There have been conflicting interpretations of the meaning of "civilian" since the constituent assembly. In 1954, when the first Hatoyama cabinet was being formed, consideration was given to the appointment of former Admiral Nomura Kichisaburō. Consideration was dropped because of doubt over the interpretation of the term "civilian." Consultant Hayashi Shūzō, explaining the government's interpretation, stated that it was the government's understanding that this provision did not exclude all former professional military men, but that the intent of the peace Constitution is that only those professional military men whose thinking was militaristic should be excluded.

THE COLLECTIVE RESPONSIBILITY OF THE CABINET (ART. 66, 3). The following matters were pointed out as operational problems relating to the cabinet's collective responsibility to the Diet.

The Prime Minister's Position and Collective Responsibility. The prime minister occupies a powerful position within the cabinet, as is shown by his right to appoint the other ministers and especially by the right of dismissal at his discretion, but Commissioner Yoshimura described the contradiction between this position and the cabinet's collective responsibility to the Diet.

The Cabinet's Collective Responsibility and the Individual Responsibility of the Ministers. Commissioner Rōyama testified as follows on the actual operation of the Constitution in cases during the past ten years in which there was an indistinct separation between the cabinet's collective responsibility and that of individual ministers and cases in which it was difficult to draw a distinction. Under Article 3 of the Cabinet Law, each cabinet minister is in charge of his respective administrative affairs and consequently he can be held responsible within the scope of those assigned administrative matters. However, it is extremely unclear as to whether that responsibility is to the cabinet and how it is related to the cabinet's collective responsibility to the Diet as constitutionally stipulated. This has frequently been shown in cases of resignations or shakeups in cabinet organization. In situations in which the Diet may produce resolutions of nonconfidence in individual cabinet ministers, it is also extremely unclear whether such responsibility is limited only to the affairs for which the minister is responsible.

Problems appear in this area and difficulties arise in operations. The lack of collective responsibility in the cabinet is no reason for individual cabinet members to evade responsibility for matters under their jurisdiction, but situations occur in which it is unclear whether the responsibility lies in an individual minister or in the cabinet as a whole. Herein lie problems arising from the exercise of the right of command over prosecution by the justice minister. In a situation where a specific minister has erred in his responsibility for affairs for which he is clearly responsible, it seems to be extremely unclear whether he should resign under responsibility to either the cabinet or the prime minister even before his conduct becomes an issue in the Diet.

DISSOLUTION OF THE HOUSE OF REPRESENTATIVES AND THE RESIGNATION OF THE CABINET (ART. 69). Article 69 reads: "If the House of Representatives passes a non–confidence resolution or rejects a confidence resolution, the cabinet shall resign en masse, unless the House of Representatives is dissolved within ten (10) days." The problem that arises under the application of this provision is this: Is dissolution of the House of Representatives limited to Article 69, or is dissolution possible without reference to it?

Consultant Satō Tatsuo said he understood that when Minister of State Matsumoto and the Japanese side were preparing their draft on the basis of the MacArthur draft, the English system was being followed, and that the exercise of the power of dissolution could be carried out in any situation, not simply under a nonconfidence resolution. Consultant Kanamori Tokujirō also stated that at the time of the constituent assembly, he was completely confident that dissolution could be carried out on the basis of a direct interpretation of Article 7 [which provides that the emperor can carry out, as an act in matters of state, the dissolution of the House of Representatives with the advice and consent of the cabinet] without direct reference to Article 69.

On looking at the actual operation of this article we see that the first dissolution (23 December 1948, fourth ordinary session of the Diet) was the result of a nonconfidence motion. This was based on SCAP's constitutional interpretation at the time, and with SCAP's approval the nonconfidence motion was passed. The second dissolution (28 August 1952, fourteenth ordinary session of the Diet), the so-called surprise dissolution was carried out without reference to Article 69. The third dissolution

(14 March 1953, fifteenth extraordinary session of the Diet) was based on a nonconfidence resolution. However, from that time on a number of dissolutions were carried out without nonconfidence resolutions.

Consultant Hayashi Shūzō explained the government's interpretation of dissolution, namely, that it is not limited to situations under Article 69. In the *Tomabechi* case regarding the "surprise dissolution" [Tomabechi Gizō, a Socialist member of the House of Representatives, brought suit against the government charging that Prime Minister Yoshida's 1952 dissolution of the House of Representatives was unconstitutional.], the court of first instance (decision of 19 October 1953, Third Civil Section, Tokyo District Court) held that the dissolution was invalid, but the court of second instance (decision of 22 September 1954, Second Civil Section, Tokyo High Court) upheld it. The decision of the court of first instance was that the cabinet's advice to the emperor was defective and there was no basis for holding that the exercise of the right of dissolution was limited to situations under Article 69. The Supreme Court decision in this case (Grand Bench decision, 8 June 1960) applied the theory of the act of state and rejected the appeal [of the Tokyo High Court decision].

THE PRIME MINISTER'S FUNCTIONS (ART. 72). A point involved in the application of Article 72 was whether "bills" submitted by the prime minister, representing the cabinet, include the drafts of laws. This was dealt with in the form of the question as to whether the cabinet has the power to submit drafts of laws.

This point has been at issue since both the constituent assembly and the first extraordinary session of the Diet. The government has consistently taken the stand that the cabinet enjoys the right to submit draft laws. Consultant Hayashi explained the government's position, the interpretation being a legislative one based on the Cabinet Law, but the ultimate reasons are that it is a part of the parliamentary cabinet system and that the "bills" of Article 72 should be considered as not being doubtful because the term is related to the provision that the National Diet is the sole law-making organ.

THE CABINET'S FUNCTIONS (ART. 73). The principal matters dealt with in the actual operation of Article 73 related to the conclusion of treaties and their subsequent approval by the Diet (item 3), to the administration of the civil service (item 4), and to the enactment of cabinet orders (item 6).

The Conclusion and Diet Approval of Treaties. Two problems were pointed out in relation to the actual operation of this provision: the scope of treaties for which diet approval is regarded as required, and approval by the Diet.

Consultants Hayashi, Takatsuji Masami, and Nishimura Kumao made it clear that the approval of the Diet is not required in all cases involving agreements with other countries. For example, there are matters which are dealt with under the management of foreign affairs as stated in item 2 of Article 73 in which there is agreement with another country which does not require the approval of the Diet. Included here are trade agreements and agreements relating to payments which do not bear on the Diet's legislative power or its power to approve the budget. There are also administrative agreements. In regard to the administrative agreement under the former [1951] security treaty with the United States, procedures requiring approval, which was a problem in the Diet, were not adopted. The new security treaty [1960] refers to a "separate agreement, replacing the Administrative Agreement [under the old treaty] . . . and . . . such other arrangements as may be agreed upon." These were measures that required Diet approval at the same time as the new security treaty itself.

Consultant Nishimura stated that a desirable system would be to stipulate clearly in the Constitution, speaking from the standpoint of the realities of diplomacy, those treaties in which the intervention of the legislative branch was regarded as necessary, such as those having a direct bearing on the rights and duties of the people or those involving changes in the national boundaries or other treaties having an extremely important political significance, and to leave all others to the executive branch to conclude.

An important question relating to approval of treaties by the Diet is the issue of whether revision as a part of the approval process is possible. The new security treaty of 1960 with the United States involved this problem. Consultant Hayashi set forth the government's reply to this point as follows: The power to conclude treaties is constitutionally the cabinet's; the cabinet requests the approval of the Diet for treaties; the Diet must answer yes or no to them; it cannot revise them in the course of granting approval.

Administration of the Civil Service. The problem relating to the actual operation of the provision on civil service administration is ultimately a problem of the National Public Servants Law. Paragraph 2 of Article 1 of that law sets forth "standards for the administration of the civil service" as referred to in Article 73 of the Constitution. In this law a National Personnel Authority (NPA) is established under the "jurisdiction" of the cabinet.

A number of constitutional issues arise from the strongly independent position of the NPA. According to Consultant Okabe Shirō, the NPA enjoys its position because of (1) a strong guarantee of status for personnel administrators; (2) the double budget system; (3) the right of advice to both the Diet and the cabinet; and (4) the right to determine its own rules. Although it is under the jurisdiction of the cabinet, the latter possesses the rights of direction and supervision over it only in respect to the appointment of its members.

On the other hand, on the basis of item 4, Article 73 of the Constitution and paragraph 4, Article 12 of the Cabinet Law, the right of personnel administration is reserved to the cabinet, and the NPA appears as no more than an advisory organ to the cabinet. It is also said that in this contradiction between the strong independence of the NPA and its character as an advisory organ, constitutional problems emerge in respect to the cabinet's collective responsibility toward the Diet and other matters.

Cabinet Orders: The Problem of Delegated Legislation. Item 6, Article 73, has produced a number of problems in actual operations. One point is whether or not cabinet orders directly enforcing the Constitution are possible without legislation. This is an academic question. The revision of the Awards Order is the only case. Consultant Takatsuji described the view that the government's position in this matter is not unconstitutional.

Another problem is delegated legislation. That the provision of item 6 of this article does not deny the delegation of legislation to cabinet order is believed by some, but Consultant Satō Tatsuo stated that the Bureau of Legislation realizes the situation is different from that under the Meiji Constitution and that in the drafting of bills such delegation must be limited to very specific circumstances indeed and referred to some examples of this.

Consultant Tanaka Jirō said that administrative legislation in the form of delegated legislation plays an important role in all countries and that the existing system under which important matters are determined entirely by national law, which is a tendency in all postwar countries, has been criticized and that this cannot be overlooked from the standpoint of the actual situation in Japan as well. He observed that from the constitutional standpoint administrative legislation is subject to fairly strict restrictions but in terms of foreign examples even where there is no constitutional basis which broadly recognizes administrative legislation, in actuality, in accordance with the demands of necessity, problems are solved as the occasion may require. In the case of Japan this point must also be given serious consideration.

Consultant Satō Tatsuo testified on the issue of what measures might be taken under the present Constitution in respect to emergencies and disasters. He stated that under the Meiji Constitution, there were emergency imperial ordinances and a system of emergency financial measures, but nothing similar exists under the present Constitution. There are emergency sessions of the House of Councilors, but if, for example, it is impossible because of a great disaster for either the Diet to meet or for the House of Councilors to gather in an emergency session, what can be done? This point has caused anxiety among government leaders from the time of the promulgation of the Constitution. In order to prepare emergency measures to meet such situations, is it not necessary to consider a system in which delegation of legislation might be handled beforehand? Consultant Tanaka has set forth the view that in such situations, on the basis of common sense, there is no reason to say it is impossible to interpret the Constitution as not permitting true emergency measures. He could not agree that prior provision should be made in law for executive measures in such situations.

RESULTS OF THE INVESTIGATION. The outline of the investigations relating to the actual operation of the provisions on the cabinet is as summarized above. The following were the principal points raised for future discussion and deliberation: (1) Should the parliamentary cabinet system be continued or should it be abolished and a system of direct public election of a prime minister be adopted?; (2) Should the position and the powers of the prime minister be continued as they are under the present parliamentary cabinet system?; (3) Is it necessary to stipulate in the Constitution special measures to deal with emergencies or disasters?; and (4) Is it necessary to have constitutional stipulations relating to the scope of delegated legislation or to ex post facto Diet review of such legislation?

The Judiciary

The provisions of the new Constitution relating to the judiciary differ from those of the old in many respects. For example: (1) the establishment of administrative or other special courts is prohibited (paragraph 2, Article 76), accordingly, administrative disputes are also dealt with in ordinary courts; (2) the Supreme Court is given the authority (Article 77) to establish rules of procedure; (3) the system of popular review of Supreme Court justices is established (paragraph 2, Article 79); (4) the Supreme Court is given the power to nominate judges of the inferior courts (paragraph 1, Article 80); and (5) the courts are given the power to review the constitutionality of laws (Article 81). Consequently, the investigation of the provisions relating to the judiciary naturally centered on the operation of these innovations. Below is a summary of the important points of the investigation on the actual operation of the provisions relating to the judiciary.

JUDICIAL POWER (ART. 76).

Scope of the Judicial Power: Litigation in Administrative Cases. Under the old Constitution litigation could be assigned to administrative courts set up separately under law and was accepted not only by judicial courts. In the new Constitution there are no provisions to that effect, but it is provided that no extraordinary courts can be established (paragraph 2,

Article 76). Consequently, under the new Constitution litigation in administrative matters is handled in the ordinary courts. As a result, administrative litigation is extremely delayed in comparison with other litigation.

Consultant Sawada Takejirō, formerly a councilor of the old administrative court and later a Supreme Court justice, compared the handling of administrative litigation under the old system of administrative courts and under the new Constitution and found the procedure under the former to be much superior (especially in terms of the benefit to the plaintiff). He set forth a policy for the improvement of administrative litigation under the new Constitution. One measure would be to continue the Supreme Court as the court of final appeal in administrative litigation as well, but to establish a special court (an administrative court) as a court of first instance, composed of expert judges similar to the councilors of the old administrative courts and enable them to dispose of cases in accordance with the official powers vested in them. Other consultants described the following opinions: (1) judgments in administrative litigation on the level of a court of first instance could be entrusted to administrative organs; (2) even if the Constitution were revised, administrative litigation should be removed from the responsibility of judges; and (3) there are no constitutional barriers to the establishment of administrative courts as lower courts under the jurisdiction of the Supreme Court. The opinion was also expressed that there is no barrier to appointing individuals with specialized experience to positions as judges in lower courts and creating special sections of those courts in large cities to handle administrative litigation.

Judicial actions by executive organs (paragraph 2, Article 76), namely, the so-called quasi-judicial function of executive organs were also investigated.

The Power of Judicial Administration. The new Constitution has no specific stipulation on the locus of the power of judicial administration, but if, as under the old one, the supreme power of judicial administration is exercised by the government, it would be impossible to guarantee complete autonomy and independence to the judicial power; consequently, the power of judicial administration reverts in the broad sense to the courts. That this is in accord with the spirit of the new Constitution was the consensus held by consultants (Iwamatsu Saburō, former Supreme Court justice and special adviser to the Justice Ministry; Kobayashi Shūzō, former Supreme Court justice; and Kaneko Hajime, former Tokyo University professor, former chief of the Judicial Research and Opinions Section of the Attorney General's office). The provisions of the Court Law were also created with that as a premise. However, concerning the extent to which the power of judicial administration should lie in the courts, there were some problems. For example, at present, administration relating to the Prosecutors' Deliberative Council and to judicial training is carried out by the courts, but there is a question as to whether in theory it must be so. This view was described by Consultant Aichi Kiichi, former justice minister.

The power of judicial administration is exercised, in the broad sense, by the courts, but the power to prepare the budget of the courts resides in the government (Finance Ministry), and the power to draft laws relating to the courts and to present them to the Diet resides in the government (Justice Ministry). Consequently, the courts are particularly sensitive to the inconvenience involved in this situation. Especially, the question of the power to present drafts of bills was discussed at the time of the revision of the Law relating to the Compensation of Judges in 1959 during the thirty-first ordinary session of the Diet. Some judges were of the opinion that the courts also should be given the power to present bills. In opposition to that view another consultant stated that because under the provisions of the National Diet Law it is stipulated that "the Chief Justice of the Supreme Court or his designated representative can on his request appear and offer explanations to a Diet committee, approval of the committee having been obtained" (item 2, paragraph 2, Article 72 of the National Diet Law), this would suffice in case of necessity.

The power of judicial administration according to the Court Law is exercised by the courts, through a judicial assembly, except in the case of the summary courts, but consultants described a number of opinions relating to the appropriateness of a collegial exercise of the right of judicial administration, on such problems as efficiency and the preservation of secrecy, a possible increase in the already heavy responsibilities of judges in general, and, even more, the delay of justice as a consequence.

RULE-MAKING POWER (ART. 77).

The Relationship between the Rule-Making Power of the Courts and the Legislative Power of the National Diet. Concerning the rule-making power of the Supreme Court, especially in its relationship to the legislative power of the National Diet, there are a number of debatable points. While Article 77 bestows the rule-making power on the Supreme Court in relation to specific matters, Article 41 stipulates that the "Diet shall be . . . the sole law-making organ of the State" and places no limitation on its legislative power. Also, in relation to the power of local public entities to enact regulations, Article 94 stipulates that such local public entities "have the right . . . to enact their own regulations within law," but in Article 77 there is no such condition. Consultant Tanaka Kōtarō, who was then chief justice of the Supreme Court, described how the Court, in the exercise of its rule-making power established rules within the limits of the law while paying due caution not to infringe upon the Diet's legislative power.

In examining procedures in litigation, the current situation is that laws (the Codes of Civil and of Criminal Procedure) cover matters in comparatively detailed fashion, and the rules of the Supreme Court (Rules of Criminal Procedure, Rules of Civil Procedure) determine what might be called by-laws within the limits of the above laws. Opinions were split on whether that was either acceptable or necessary.

Paragraph 1, Article 77, stipulates: "The Supreme Court is vested with the rule-making power under which it determines the rules of procedure and of practice, and of matters relating to attorneys, the internal discipline of the courts, and the administration of judicial affairs." Regarding the matters listed, a question arises as to whether this legislative power is vested exclusively in the Supreme Court to the exclusion of the Diet. On this matter there is a Supreme Court minority opinion (Grand Bench decision of 24 June 1950, minority opinion of Justice Mano Tsuyoshi). Justice Mano held in relation to the Law on the Status of Judges that because the reprimanding of judges falls under "the internal discipline of the courts" as stated in Article 77, it must therefore be determined by the rules of the Supreme Court and that consequently the law involved is unconstitutional and void because it provides for reprimands. Also among the consultants the view was expressed that because both the machinery and the powers of the Supreme Court are matters touching upon its peculiar functions, except for those matters which the Constitution has determined must be provided for by law, all else must be entrusted to the rules of the Supreme Court. Opposed to this is the decision of the Supreme Court's Second Petty Bench of 22 April 1955 to the effect that "the determination by law of the procedures in criminal matters is not in contravention of Article 77 of the Constitution." This is based on the opinion that the enactment, as legislation under the new Constitution, of the new Code of Criminal Procedure and the new Law relating to Lawyers, even on matters listed in Article 77 as quoted above—at least in the overall sense—was not excluded from the Diet's law-making power.

Also, even among the enumerated matters, there is the view that some items must be determined by law. What is particularly in question here is the relationship to the provision in Article 31: "No person shall be deprived of life or liberty, nor shall any other criminal penalty be imposed, except according to procedure established by law." Even among the consultants there was the view that if it is held regarding the relationship with Article 31 that at least criminal penalties must be in accordance with the law, then the phrase "procedure established by law" has the meaning of the American "due process of law"; that it is also to be interpreted to include the rules of the courts and is not limited to law in the formal sense; and that the procedure of the imposition of punishment is acceptable even without a basis in Diet–enacted law.

In Article 77 there is the broad phrase "matters relating to attorneys." Because the stipulation of matters relating to the duties, qualifications, and status of attorneys is related to the freedom of choice of occupation set forth in Article 22, there is the opinion that these should be dealt with exclusively by law. In regard to "rules of procedure and of practice" there is also the opinion that such matters, whether what is involved is the fundamental structure of those procedures or matters relating to the important interests of the accused, or whether they are related to the rights and duties under substantive law, must be left to law.

Moreover, in respect to the enumerated matters, even if the law-making power of the Diet is not excluded, the stipulation of every detail, as for example in the Codes of Criminal and of Civil Procedure, and the minimization of the area for the operation of rules do not conform with the spirit of the Constitution.

Supremacy of Validity between Court Rules and Law. In situations where conflict is recognized between the Supreme Court rule-making power and the legislative power of the Diet regarding provisions of law and provisions of rule, the problem of supremacy of validity between the two appears. On this issue there are three views: the supremacy of law, the supremacy of rule, and equality between the two. According to the equality view, the later law always supersedes the earlier one, regardless of whether the legal form is that of law or of rule.

The majority of the consultants held the view of the supremacy of laws enacted by the Diet, which is the highest organ of state power and the sole law-making organ of the state, as being proper. However, Consultants Kaneko and Tsuda Minoru and Commissioner Mano pointed out that there was abundant evidence for the feeling that the Supreme Court may believe that the efficacy of rules is not necessarily as weak as indicated above. As one example, the following was set forth. The original form of item 1, Article 10, of the Court Law provided that one situation in which a petty bench of the Supreme Court could not hand down a decision was "when it had to be judged on the plea of the concerned party whether a law, order, rule, or action is or is not constitutional." Article 9 of the Supreme Court Rules for the Handling of Judicial Affairs established a rule in accordance with the above. However, on 1 April 1948 the Supreme Court revised the rule as follows: "In applying item 1 of Article 10 of the Court Law, a petty bench can render a judgment . . . when the opinion is that the said judgment is in accord with a Grand Bench judgment which previously held that a law, order, rule, or action is constitutional." Thus, when a Supreme Court rule is made which differs from the provisions of a law it must be considered to have been based on either the doctrine of the supremacy of rule or the equality view. However, on this point item 1 of Article 10 of the Court Law was revised later in December 1948, thus eliminating the conflict between law and rule.

THE STATUS OF JUDGES AND THE ORGANIZATION OF THE COURTS (ARTS. 78–80). The status of judges, particularly in relation to disciplinary action and the guarantee of change of station, was investigated. Here, the principal results of the investigation of the organization of the courts will be described.

Organization of the Supreme Court. Paragraph 1, Article 79, states that the number of judges on the Supreme Court will be determined by law, but consultants expressed the opinion that this should be determined by the Constitution itself.

In respect to the Supreme Court the delay of cases was frequently mentioned as a problem. Appeals to the Supreme Court are under some limitations as compared with the old Court of Cassation. While the responsibilities of the Supreme Court, as compared with the Court of Cassation, have been broadened in respect to such matters as constitutional review, rule-making, the appointment of judges of inferior courts, judicial administration, and the handling of administrative suits, the number of judges is only one-third that of the Court of Cassation. Consequently, the number of unsettled cases has increased; at the end of 1951 the number of such cases had exceeded seven thousand. The Japan Bar Association strongly demanded that the structure of the Supreme Court be improved, that the disposition of cases be speeded up, and that the door for appeals be widened. On the basis of a report by the Committee for the Investigation of the Legal System, the government in 1957 at the twenty-sixth ordinary session of the Diet introduced a bill for the structural reform of the Supreme Court, but it did not become a law. The essence of that bill was to create new inferior courts that would be called petty benches of the Supreme Court (but would differ in character from the present petty benches which are made up of Supreme Court justices), and would have a number of sections to review and pass judgment on ordinary civil and criminal appeal cases. Consultant Tanaka Kōtarō, former chief justice of the Supreme Court, expressed the opinions that any structural reforms of the Supreme Court should be consistent with the mission and character assigned to it by the Constitution and that the Court should not be simply converted to the old Court of Cassation by increasing the number of justices.

Appointment of Supreme Court Justices. The chief justice of the Supreme Court is appointed by the emperor as designated by the cabinet (Article 6, paragraph 2), and the other justices are appointed by the cabinet

(Article 79, paragraph 1). The first appointments were made in August 1947, and, in accordance with paragraphs 4 and 5 of Article 39 of the Court Law, in consultation with the Advisory Committee on the Appointment of Judges. Later in 1948 the above paragraphs were eliminated because the necessity for consultation with an advisory committee might possibly cloud the authority of the cabinet as determined by the Constitution. Since the second round of appointments, the selection has been made exclusively by the cabinet. Recently the suggestion that an advisory committee on appointments be set up has again been made and the bill mentioned above as having been introduced at the twenty-sixth Diet session has been revived.

Of the first Supreme Court justices, five were appointed from among judges and prosecutors, five from among lawyers, and five from among men of learning and experience; this proportion has generally been maintained. Some consultants held that selection from the three groups is a strong point, but others felt that it might possibly be contrary to the spirit of the Constitution, particularly in cases where a vacancy is filled by a person coming from the same group as the previous occupant [presumably because such appointments would involve discrimination against those from other groups].

Popular Review of Supreme Court Justices. The appointments of Supreme Court justices shall be reviewed by the people at the first general election for the House of Representatives following their appointment (or after a lapse of ten years following the first review), and when a majority of the voters favors the dismissal of a justice he shall be dismissed (paragraphs 2 and 3, Article 79). This is a type of recall. The provisions for carrying out this review are contained in the Law for the Popular Review of Supreme Court Justices. If a voter favors the dismissal of a justice, he places an X after his name on the ballot. If he does not favor dismissal, he makes no mark after the justice's name. If he is undecided as to whether a justice should be dismissed and simply leaves his ballot unmarked, that becomes a vote against dismissal. On this matter a Grand Bench decision of the Supreme Court on 27 February 1952 held that the above provision is in accord with the intent of the Constitution "because the system involves dismissal from office, the votes are divided into two groups: those positively favoring dismissal and those not favoring it." [The case referred to involved a complaint that to attribute approval to a voter who was undecided involved a violation of his freedom of thought. In effect, the court ruled that dismissal should be based only on votes clearly favoring it.] In respect to this system of popular review, both commissioners and consultants split on the issue of its desirability.

Appointment of Judges of Inferior Courts. Judges of inferior courts shall be appointed by the cabinet from a list of nominees presented by the Supreme Court (paragraph 1, Article 80). One problem related to this system is whether the cabinet has the rights of rejection and choice. The MacArthur draft called for cabinet appointment from among a list of two or more nominees [for each position], and the 2 March draft called for appointment from a list of nominees numbering twice the positions to be filled, but at the time of the revised draft and later, the phrase "numbering twice the positions" disappeared. According to Consultant Suzuki Chūichi, former chief of the Personnel Office of the Supreme Court, the actual practice is to compile a list containing a number of names equal to the number of appointments to be made plus one, even when a number of appointments are to be made (in case of judges for summary courts, the additional name is not added) with a seal imprinted above the names of the persons desired by the Supreme Court, and with the cabinet making the appointments accordingly.

Consultant Aichi expressed the opinion that the exercise of the cabinet power of appointment in this purely formal manner might undermine the intent of the Constitution.

Concerning the appointment of judges, there was, even under the old Constitution, a demand for the unification of bench and bar, that is to say, judges should have the qualifications of lawyers and judges should be appointed also from among lawyers and others with professional experience other than that of judges; under the new Constitution the demand has become even stronger. Commissioners Masaki Akira and Mano and Consultants Tsukamoto Shigenori, a lawyer, and Suzuki Chūichi described the following as the principal reasons preventing the unification of bench and bar: the extremely low compensation of judges as compared with the income of outstanding lawyers; no special consideration for judges after retirement; and the great difficulty for anyone without many years of experience in preparing judicial opinions in the commonly accepted form.

According to the testimony of Consultant Kaneko Hajime, who was the chief of the Legal Research and Opinions Section of the Attorney General's Office when the Court Law was being drafted under the new Constitution, the thought was that lawyers, prosecutors, and those with ten years of experience in legal matters without having been judges would be appointed to judgeships, but midway in the discussion it was felt that there would not be sufficient manpower, and so the system of assistant judges was adopted on the grounds that there seemed to be no reason why younger persons should not become members of collegial courts. It was felt that there was no reason why these assistant judges, with the passage of years, should not all be promoted to judgeships.

Among consultants there was also the opinion that the unification of bench and bar would still be premature without a dissenting voice being raised, even if it were achieved in accordance with the original concept and the system of assistant judgeships were abolished, and even if as a result judges were given especially good treatment, different from that accorded administrators.

Recently the number of those wishing to become judges has shown a tendency to decline and it appears difficult to guarantee the necessary minimum number of judges. In order to consider a policy for the solution of this situation, an Emergency Committee for the Investigation of the Judicial System was set up within the cabinet in September 1962. The committee's objective is to investigate and deliberate on matters relating to the unification of bench and bar and other items such as the appointment of judges and prosecutors and the system of compensation.

THE POWER OF CONSTITUTIONAL REVIEW (ART. 81).

General Theory of Constitutional Review. Article 81 of the new Constitution provides that the Supreme Court is the court of last resort with the power of constitutional review, even of [Diet-enacted] laws. This provision is particularly significant because the new Constitution strengthened the guarantee of fundamental human rights and, in contrast to the old Constitution where the guarantee of rights was mainly within the limits of the law, it is related to the principle that restrictions cannot be imposed even by law. This principle has made this constitutional guarantee truly effective.

The creation of Article 81 was somewhat complicated. In particular the MacArthur draft provided that the Supreme Court decisions would be final on questions involving the constitutionality of laws and official acts relating to fundamental human rights, but in regard to the constitutionality of other laws and acts the Diet was given the power to review Supreme Court decisions and could reverse them by a vote of two-thirds of the members. But this system of Diet review was eliminated in the revised draft of the Constitution.

In reviewing actual experience with the power of constitutional review, assertions of unconstitutionality in legal actions have been carried out in a number of ways. Supreme Court judgments holding unconstitutionality have been extremely few. It has held only one law to be unconstitutional. In a Grand Bench decision of 28 November 1962, the Supreme Court held that provisions of paragraph 1, Article 118, of the Customs Law relating to the seizure of the property of third parties were in violation of Articles 29 and 31 of the Constitution. [For this decision *see* Itoh and Beer, *op. cit.*, pp. 58–73.]

Is Abstract Constitutional Review Permissible? Two questions arose in respect to Article 81: does Article 81 recognize the review of constitutionality of laws and acts only within the limits necessary to resolve concrete suits?; and, does this article provide authority for the review in the abstract of the constitutionality of laws and acts without relation to a concrete suit? The Supreme Court has adopted the former view and has said (Grand Bench decision, 8 October 1952): "If, as the plaintiff argues, the Supreme Court has the power to issue abstract declarations nullifying laws, orders, and the like, then, since anyone could bring before the Court suits claiming unconstitutionality, the validity of laws, orders, and the like, would be frequently assailed and there would be the danger of the Court's assuming the appearance of an organ superior to all other powers in the land, thereby running counter to the basic principle of democratic government: that the three powers are independent, equal, and immune from each other's interference." [For this decision *see* Maki, *op. cit.*, pp. 362–65.]

There is also the view that even under the present Constitution there is the possibility of abstract constitutional review. In particular, the former Right-wing and Left-wing Socialist parties and the Farmer-Labor Party jointly presented a bill in 1955 at the twenty-second extraordinary session of the Diet under the title "A Bill for the Revision of a Section of the Court Law," which would have provided the Supreme Court with the power to review constitutionality in abstract cases. In addition, in 1956 the Socialist Party at the twenty-fourth ordinary session of the Diet presented a bill entitled "A Bill on Procedures for Constitutional Review," which incorporated the earlier bill and also would have determined the procedure for constitutional review in abstract cases.

Among the consultants the majority view was that the present Constitution does not provide the power of constitutional review in abstract cases, but there was also the opinion that what Article 81 particularly establishes is the power of constitutional review in matters other than concrete cases. Also there is the interpretation which holds that although the Constitution does not provide for constitutional review in the abstract, such review must be recognized as a matter of legislative theory. In order to bring about that recognition, thought should be given to the following methods: the establishment of constitutional courts, and the furnishing in some supplementary fashion of the Supreme Court with the character of a constitutional court. In addition, there is also the view that the second method is preferable because constitutional revision would not be needed since it could be done by law. There is the opposing view that even though from the standpoint of legislative theory the power of abstract constitutional review should be recognized under the present Constitution, the Supreme Court cannot be provided with the character of a constitutional court through the enactment of a law.

In connection with abstract constitutional review, the problem of the system of the advisory opinion as carried out in the Commonwealth of Massachusetts in the United States was dealt with. Only the view that such a system should not be adopted was set forth; but opinions were split on the issue of whether such a system, if it were to be adopted, would be possible under our present Constitution.

Do Lower Courts Also Have the Right of Constitutional Review? On the question of whether the lower courts possess the power of constitutional review, the Supreme Court has held affirmatively (Grand Bench decision, 1 February 1950) as follows: "When a judge decides whether a law or ordinance is in accord with the Constitution when making a judgment applying a law or ordinance in a concrete legal dispute, the function and the authority to do so are bestowed on the judge by the Constitution; this applies equally whether to a Supreme Court justice or a judge of a lower court."

In respect to the utilization by the lower courts of the power of constitutional review, Consultants Iriye Toshirō, justice of the Supreme Court, and Honda Masayoshi stated that if a lower court were to hold the opinion that a certain law is unconstitutional, the case should be transferred to the Supreme Court for a judgment. The reasons would be the difficulties created if the lower court were split on the unconstitutionality of the same law or if an unstable situation were created between an inferior court and the Supreme Court if a court of first instance rendered a judgment of unconstitutionality while the Supreme Court upheld constitutionality. Consultant Kaneko Hajime expressed the view that the present arrangement should be continued, that is, that even in constitutional questions, after the trial in the lower court had been conducted and the examinations and the pleas of both sides had been completed the Supreme Court would then render the final judgment on the solution within the necessary limits.

Objects of Constitutional Review. Article 81 lists "any law, order, regulation, or official act" as objects of constitutional review. The question as to whether treaties can become the object of review will be left to the explanation of Article 98 relating to the Constitution as the supreme law. However, one consultant regarded the regulations of local public entities as being included in the above "regulations," and one judicial decision (Grand Bench decision, 8 July 1948) held that judicial acts, namely, judgments, were included in "official acts."

The Supreme Court in respect to cases "having a highly political nature" has held that even in situations where legally a judgment of validity is possible, the power of constitutional review of the courts extends only to cases where there is "clearly obvious unconstitutionality or invalidity." This is shown in the Grand Bench decision of 16 December 1959 relating to the Japanese–American security treaty [the so-called *Sunakawa* decision; *see* Maki, *op. cit.*, pp. 298 ff., especially pp. 305–6] and the Grand Bench decision of 8 June 1960 relating to the dissolution of the

Diet. In the former decision it was stated: "It is proper to interpret this primarily as a matter that must be entrusted to the decision of the cabinet, which possesses the power to conclude treaties, and of the National Diet, which has the power to approve them; and it ultimately must be left to the political review of the sovereign people."

In the latter decision it was stated: "Under the system of the separation of powers in our Constitution the exercise of the judicial power cannot escape certain limitations and what are known as acts in matters of state cannot forthwith be judged to be the objects of an unlimited judicial review. . . . Restrictions on this judicial power arise from the principle of the separation of powers in view of the highly political nature of the competent acts of state, the character of the courts as judicial organs and the procedural restraints that necessarily accompany trials. There are no special provisions set forth in writing, but it must be understood that the restrictions are inherent in the nature of the judicial power as set forth in the Constitution." However, an opposing view is to be found in the dissenting opinions set forth in the above decisions themselves.

PUBLIC TRIALS (ART. 82). The proviso of paragraph 2, Article 82, reads: ". . . trials of political offenses, offenses involving the press, or cases wherein the rights of the people as guaranteed in Chapter 3 of this Constitution are in question shall always be conducted publicly." This is because in regard to the guarantee of human rights it is considered that the possibility of public surveillance is always necessary. However, there was also the opinion that it would be well to have public trials not only in the situations enumerated, but in others as well.

RESULTS OF THE INVESTIGATION. The basic points raised for future discussion and deliberation as the result of the investigations described above are as follows: (1) the prohibition of administrative and other special courts; (2) the system of review of unconstitutional legislation; (3) the rule-making power; (4) the power of appointment of judges of the lower courts; and (5) the locus of authority for judicial administration. These all related to the broadening and strengthening of the judicial power as adopted in the Constitution and to whether they should be maintained as they are. The principal individual issues were as follows: (1) Should the provisions of paragraph 2, Article 76 relating to the prohibition of extraordinary tribunals be retained as they are?; (2) Is it necessary to add provisions making clear the relationship between the rule-making power of the Supreme Court and the law-making power of the Diet?; (3) Is it or is it not necessary to provide in the Constitution for the organization of the Supreme Court?; (4) Should the method for the appointment of Supreme Court justices be retained as it is? For example, is it necessary to establish an advisory committee?; (5) Should the popular review of Supreme Court justices be retained as is?; and (6) Should

the system of judicial review of unconstitutional legislation be retained as
it presently exists? Should the establishment of a constitutional court be
considered? Or is it necessary to establish a system of advisory opinions
on constitutional issues?

Finance

GENERAL PROBLEMS. In regard to Article 83, which deals with the
power to administer national finances, two positions were advocated:
that the National Diet possesses the power to decide matters relating to
the national finances; and that finances are handled by the government
and the decisions of the Diet do nothing more than to create the conditions for the government's management of finances. The concrete
efficacy of this article is to be found in such matters as: the nonrecognition in the new Constitution of the system set up under the old Constitution in Articles 66, 70, and 71 [all of which had the effect of placing the
power of finance in the cabinet]; the nonrecognition of the responsibility
for the disbursement of a surplus as carried out under the old Constitution; and the necessity for either a law or a Diet resolution in respect to
such items in Article 3 of the Finance Law as the compulsory collection
of surcharges and the prices set for the products of the national
monopoly enterprises [such as salt and tobacco]. While the former position holds that the present article is a strong point of the present Constitution, the latter criticizes it because emphasis on the powers of the
Diet harms unification of financial affairs and invites laxity.

Concerning taxes as set forth in Article 84, there is a question as to
whether the requirement of "law or under such conditions as law may
prescribe" does not completely recognize the authority of the National
Diet as compared with a situation in which only the requirement of law is
set forth. There is the view that "such conditions as law may prescribe" is
to be interpreted to mean that delegation is possible to the extent set by
law. But there is also the view that existing tax law leaves far too much to
[cabinet] orders, that extremely broad delegation of authority is set forth
in law especially in regard to local taxes where there are independent
taxes not determined by law, and that the phrase "conditions as established by law" is adopted in such cases only to relax the principle of
taxation by law.

Related to this matter are two other opinions: (1) also in respect to
local taxes, that the power to levy taxes is bestowed on local public entities by law; and (2) that the power to levy taxes is inherent in the right
of local autonomy possessed by local public entities, entirely apart from
Article 84, and that laws which establish conditions, as set forth in Article
84, are nothing more than a limitation on the exercise of the right of

local autonomy. Consequently, there was also the suggestion that a constitutional provision should be established, separate from Article 84, as the basis for the levy of local taxes. Moreover, there was much criticism of the current system of tax administration under which much is done only on the basis of official notices. It was also stated that to the extent that administration can be made elastic through the use of such notices, the provisions of law become abstract and general.

PROBLEMS RELATING TO THE BUDGET.

The Form of the Budget and Its Legal Character (Arts. 83–86). According to Article 86 and item 5 of Article 73, the document at the point where the cabinet prepares and presents it to the Diet is not the "budget bill" but "the budget." On the nature of this term there were three opposing views. The first holds that this document is no more than reference material prepared for the exercise of the Diet's power of decision and that it must become law (the budget law) at the stage where the Diet makes its decision. The second position views the interpretation that the Constitution directly requires the budget to be regarded as law as questionable and holds that there must be a resolution of the contradiction between the principle of Diet power to decide as set forth in Article 83 and the expression in Article 86 of the principle of the centrality of the cabinet in the budget process. The third view treats the budget as a matter which belongs inherently to the executive branch. In actual practice the budget is passed as something different from a law and is not regarded as the object of promulgation and of signature and countersignature as set forth in Article 74. It was also stated that during the drafting of the Finance Law, absolutely no consideration was given to the question of whether the system involved a budget law. Moreover, there are two more conflicting opinions: one that, though not holding to the theory that the budget is a law, regards the budget as having the form of law and therefore requiring promulgation; and the other that regards the budget as a type of official instruction not requiring promulgation.

According to the theory that the budget is a law, the principle in Article 84 that taxes are levied by law means necessarily that there cannot be permanent taxes because the approval of a yearly budget law makes possible the determination of the conditions for the collection of taxes, but government officials have adopted the principle of permanent taxation.

Concerning what is called expenditure of state funds in Article 85, there is the opinion that under past practice the decision of the Diet was obtained in the form of a yearly budget, but that the British–American system of the permanent appropriation must be adopted. There was also the proposal, concerning obligatory expenditures relating to the national debt or other expenditures required by law, that these can be made without annual Diet approval, as a kind of permanent budget. Also in relation to the state obligating itself as mentioned in the same article, the old Constitution recognized a special form, but the current Finance Law holds that such obligations must be incurred in the form of law or the budget and that the government requires the prior approval of the Diet for everything. This has been explained thus because it was believed that to handle the matter by a special procedure relating to budget approval as set forth in the present Constitution is proper. It was also thought that decisions on acts by the national treasury relating to financial responsibilities in the form of a budget would be simpler than the procedures involved in approving a law, and the Finance Law limits to five years expenditures in accord with decisions of this type.

Consideration of the Budget. The present budget adopts the principle of accounting based on expenditures, and the opinion is that, in contrast with the method under which the required funds are collected and then completely spent, the procedure of capital management, assets, and liabilities is followed and this must be stipulated by the Constitution. Under the old Constitution, the prevailing thought was that, rather than the Diet's deciding the budget, only the acceptance by the Diet of the budget drafted by the government was required; it was pointed out that this position continues in actual practice today. Also in this connection the opinion was expressed that, in accord with the principles of the Constitution, the government party should stop its involvement in each detail at the stage of the compilation of the budget and revision should be carried out during Diet deliberation. Moreover, because Article 60 limits the House of Councilors' deliberation on the budget to thirty days, the opinion was expressed that during the deliberations of the House of Representatives preliminary investigations in the Budget Committee of the House of Councilors would be necessary, but it was also explained that such action would be difficult because of the appearance in the lower house of ministers and government committee members.

In Article 19 of the Finance Law and Article 13 of the National Public Officials Law there are provisions relating to the so-called double budget system. [Under this system both houses of the National Diet, the Supreme Court (acting for the court system), the Board of Audit, and the National Personnel Authority, as so-called independént agencies, must submit reports on their estimated expenditures to the cabinet for use in the compilation of the national budget. In the event that the cabinet recommends a reduction in the estimated budgets of the independent agencies it must submit with its budget the estimates of the affected agencies.] Concerning expenses for the courts in the 1952 budget a request from the courts was withdrawn and a duplicate budget was submitted. The opinion was expressed that only the budget of the courts was treated as a stepchild. Also there was the opinion that although the double budget existed only as a system, it possessed a real significance.

Whether the Diet can increase the total amount of the budget, or whether it can revise by adding new sections and items has become a real problem. The double budget system recognizes within its own limits the rights of the Diet to increase and to revise. In 1948 the Legal Committees of both houses issued reports to the effect that, from the standpoint of the principle of the central role of the Diet, it could not only simply increase the budget but also had the right to revise by adding sections and items. Today there is still that opinion in the Diet, but there is also the opinion that in its relations with the cabinet it is impermissible to infringe upon the cabinet's right to present the budget by adding items and sections or changing by revision the nature of the budget. There is a similar clash of opinion in the academic world as well. In contrast to the fact that there is no precedent for the addition of sections and items, there are precedents for revision involving an increase in the total amount of the budget. Some of the bad effects of accompanying members' bills involving increases in expenditures were criticized following the coming into effect of the peace treaty, and through the 1955 revision of the National Diet Law it was determined that majority approval and the government's opinion were required for revisions involving increases and members' legislation accompanying the budget.

On this matter the opinions of consultants were split into three groups. The first held that the revision was necessary for the harmonious operation of the parliamentary cabinet system between the government party and the cabinet. The second was that the introduction of bills revising the budget upward should be prohibited. The third was that restrictions should be placed on the right to introduce such changes. Among the suggestions of consultants which called for restrictions on the right of introduction were the following: a requirement for an indication of the source of the funds for any increases; a requirement that in all cases of increase the consent of the House of Concilors be obtained; the government's recognition of the necessity for such increase; and the carrying out of concrete revisions as a responsibility of the government and only with the approval of both houses of a resolution calling for the revisions. In regard to the latter there was an opinion holding that it should be stipulated either in the Constitution or in the Finance Law, and also an opinion which went no further than setting forth a desire for the establishment of customary usage in that regard. It was also pointed out that in certain foreign countries in the late 1950s, as compared with thirty years earlier, there was a growing tendency toward the prohibition of the power to introduce increases in the budget. On a number of occasions it was also pointed out that in regard to the abuse of the increase in expenditures the role of the Diet lies in reducing the burden of the taxpayer. The opinion was also expressed that restrictions should be placed on Diet legislation involving the reduction of taxes in order to maintain the balance between income and outgo and also a just sharing of the national expenses.

Continuing Expenditures. The pros and cons of establishing a system of continuing expenditures were debated in the constituent assembly, and such a system appeared in an early draft of the Finance Law, but SCAP approval was not granted. In 1952 at the end of the occupation, both continuing and carry-over expenditures were added in the revision of the Finance Law, but the limit on the payment of continuing expenditures was set at five years, and it was also stipulated that in the budget consideration in the fiscal year following the establishment of the continuing expenditure the Diet could review it. The statements of the consultants all recognized the necessity for the system of continuing expenditures, but there were opinions that it could be left to the Finance Law without revising the Constitution and that even though constitutional stipulations relating to continuing expenditures should be set up, there should be limitations relating to such matters as the amount of money and purposes.

Reserve Funds, Emergency Financial Action, and Nonapproval of the Budget (Art. 87). In the constituent assembly Minister of State Kanamori Toku-jirō stated that the reserve fund of Article 87 could be used as a source of emergency expenditures at such times as when the budget was not approved, but for that purpose a reserve fund independent of the yearly budget was necessary. The Finance Law stipulates that the reserve fund must be appropriated in the budget covering income and expenditures and, as a measure to be used when the budget is not approved, a provisional budget must be put into effect with the approval of the Diet. In respect to the utilization of the reserve funds, the Finance Law stipulates that Diet approval must be requested at the next regular session. But because such utilization may become the reason for the compilation of a supplementary budget, the opinion was expressed that it was desirable to develop the custom that any such utilization during a Diet session be reported to the Budget Committee.

Even though it is recognized that there might be a revival of the system of emergency financial action, the opinion was that there should be extremely narrow restrictions on it. Also, even if the system of responsibility for disbursements is established, because it is related to the operation of the reserve fund and financial acts for which there is an obligation on the state treasury, the government should not act alone. If advisory procedures are required, there is also the opinion that they would have no real meaning as compared with the present system of expenditures with the convocation of the Diet.

There have been two occasions where a vacuum has been produced at the beginning of a fiscal year without the establishment of even a temporary budget. Opinions as to what should be done on such occasions are divided into four categories. First, there is the opinion that the principle of Diet approval should be respected and that prior to deliberations on the budget, there should be, customarily, an agreement on a provisional budget. The second opinion is that there should be a revival of the system of the continuation of the budget of the previous year as under the old Constitution, but many also recognized that such a system must be fitted into some kind of a framework. The third view is that for a certain period the budget be continued as a temporary one at the monthly rate of expenditure of the previous year's budget, and the said rate should be regarded as not requiring a vote of the Diet. The fourth view is that the problem be solved by a system of accountable expenditure such as payments from an emergency reserve fund or from a permanent liquid reserve. In addition, it was also thought that the establishment of a permanent appropriation would be a solution in such situations.

INDIVIDUAL PROBLEMS.

Regarding Article 88. Because Article 8 recognizes that the imperial house may possess purely private property, the property of the imperial household referred to in Article 88 means only property of a public character as under the old Constitution. However, because the property of the former princely families is regarded as private property, the "imperial household" of Article 88 is different from that of Article 8 and is interpreted as not including royalty outside the imperial family. Also there is the opinion that in accord with the general view of this article as a transitional stipulation, it means a prohibition of a revival of imperial household property as under the old Constitution and that constitutionally in the future a similar provision must be maintained. There is the view that if, on the contrary, this article is regarded as permanent, then one cannot anticipate future large property holdings because there will be no way for an increase of the assets of the imperial household; the only means of increase will be the accumulation of the surplus over expenses and contributions approved by the Diet.

Expenditure of Public Property and Limitations on Its Use (Art. 89). The government's view that because Yasukuni Shrine [where the spirits of those who fell in battle in modern wars are believed to be enshrined] has a religious character, its management by the government is impermissible, and the fact that the expenses for the management of the ancestral shrine in the Imperial Palace are paid from the privy purse (imperial household expenses) can be said to be in accord with the intent of the separation of church and state in this article. However, the view was also expressed that this stipulation has no real parallel in foreign countries. Moreover, the interpretation has been made that it is possible to approve expenditures for subsidies for national treasures and for buildings which are important cultural assets because their religious character is separate.

The prohibition on expenditure or use granted to any "charitable, educational, or benevolent enterprises not under the control of public authority" is a provision that presents great problems in both interpretation and operation. The government's public interpretation is that the "public control" of this article does not include control not based on public authority, and also renders it insufficient for a public organ to possess only an abstract authority and that it is necessary that law specify concrete authority for the actual control of such enterprises. After the passage of the Law on Private Schools, other laws on the same pattern were enacted, such as the Law relating to Social Welfare Enterprises and the Law for Child Welfare, but there is the opinion that control to this degree does not fall under the "public control" of this article.

Auditing Review and the Board of Audit (Art. 90). Final accounts and the report of the Board of Audit are submitted to the Diet. Matters such as whether these are submitted to each house individually and whether they should be resubmitted when consideration of them is not completed in both houses during a Diet session are treated as so-called information items. Opinions differ on these matters. First, some feel that because the final accounts are only an indication of actual past income and outgo, to treat them simply as information items is appropriate and even though the Diet votes acceptance of the final accounts no legal effect is thereby produced. Another view is that because the Constitution stipulates that the final accounts must be submitted to the Diet, then the Diet must accept them by means of a joint resolution of the two houses. A third opinion is that while the Constitution does not specify methods by which this matter should be handled, from the standpoint of parliamentary government it is desirable that it be handled by a Diet resolution. In respect to the second and third opinions above, in those cases where the resolutions of the two houses are in disagreement then it is possible to apply by a law the procedures set forth in Article 60 of the Constitution [providing for the supremacy of the lower house decision on budgetary matters].

In regard to Diet bills for the approval of the audit one opinion is that they provide force to the review of the audit and have great political effectiveness, but another view is that on the contrary they weaken political criticism.

The current Law on the Board of Audit, in addition to guaranteeing an independent position for the auditors, provides for autonomous authority in personnel matters and for the rule-making power and recognizes the board's independence from the cabinet. In this regard one opinion holds that placing the Board of Audit in a position very close to that of the Diet is natural, but there is also a strong demand that the above independence be clearly spelled out in the Constitution.

Regarding Article 91. In regard to the system of reports on the national finances in this article, two opinions were expressed: that it is sufficient to depend on the provisions of the Finance Law, and that it should be set forth in the Constitution because of the importance of informing the people and the Diet of matters relating to economic planning.

RESULTS OF THE INVESTIGATION. An outline of the content of the investigation into the actual operation of the provisions relating to finances is as summarized above. The principal points which, as a result, were raised for future discussion are as follows:

1. Should the provision that authority for the management of the national finances must be based on Diet resolution be retained as it is?

2. Should the provisions concerning the functions of the Diet in respect to such financial matters as the budget and the audit also be retained unchanged?

3. Is it necessary to establish provisions which would make clear the relationship (form, procedures for passage, validity, etc.) between the budget and law?

4. Should Article 89 remain unchanged?

Local Autonomy

WHAT LOCAL AUTONOMY SHOULD BE. On the question of what is included in the "local public entities" of Chapter 8 opinions were divided. First, on the premise of the double structure of the major administrative units (Tokyo Metropolis, Hokkaido, Osaka and Kyoto cities, and the prefectures) and of the minor ones of cities, towns and villages, the view is that local autonomy is broadly guaranteed to all units as complete and comprehensive local public entities; the second and opposed opinion is that basic local public entities are indispensable, but that such questions as to whether the above double structure is to be maintained or how such local public entities are established are, under the Constitution, left to the law.

["Local public entities" through conventional usage has become the rather awkward translation for the Japanese original. The word *dantai*, translated as "entities," could equally well have been translated "organizations" or "bodies." Perhaps the preferable translation, at least from the American point of view, might have been "units of local government." What is involved in these local public entities is aptly rendered by the Japanese phrases, *todōfuken* and *shichōson*. The former can be broken down as follows: *to*, Tokyo Metropolis; *dō*, the island of Hokkaido; *fu*, the cities of Osaka and Kyoto; and *ken*, the prefectures. The latter phrase consists of the following: *shi*, cities; *chō*, towns; and *son*, villages. Here the Japanese terms, *todōfuken* and *shichōson*, will be used instead of the English equivalents.]

Even in the first opinion, it is held that whatever the *todōfuken* and the *shichōson* may have been at the time of the enactment of the Constitution, there is no requirement that they must be maintained as they are and that it is not unconstitutional to consolidate them gradually in order to achieve their better functioning as "wide area units."

The establishment in the present Constitution of the provisions relating to local autonomy constituted a criticism of the development of the former local government system, recognized the significance of local autonomy as an underlying theme of democratic government, and provided a constitutional guarantee for true local autonomy for both residents and their organizations. Following the end of the occupation a number of tendencies developed such as the emphasis on the national character of administration and efficiency and the strengthening of direction and supervision by the state. For example, these tendencies were manifested in the reform of the police system, the changes in the system of school committees, the abolition of elections for the heads of special wards in the cities, the drastic amendments of the Local Autonomy Law in 1952 and 1956, and the draft report on the local system issued in 1957 by the Fourth Investigative Committee on the Local System.

At the time of the enactment of the Local Autonomy Law, the government authorities considered special wards as well as special municipalities to be local public entities under the Constitution, but at the time of the revision of the law they regarded them as subentities under the basic entity which is Tokyo Metropolis and not as local public entities as set forth in the Constitution. Under the present system relating to Tokyo Metropolis, the bad effects involved in the double administration in the relations between cities and *fu* and *ken* were dealt with by the tie between Tokyo and its special wards. It was said that no consideration was paid to Tokyo as the capital and to its relationship with the government and no differentiation was made between its functions and its governor and those of other *fu* and *ken*. In regard to this issue opinions were that the capital should not be regarded as an autonomous unit, that its chief official have the status of a cabinet minister and that wards be established as autonomous units in place of *shichōson*, but there was also the opinion that constitutionally the capital is also a local public entity. Moreover, in respect to the abolition of special municipalities, there is the opinion that a sufficiently efficient management of the large cities is impossible under the present distribution of business matters and that it is necessary to establish a special system that will recognize the idiosyncratic nature of large cities.

In addition, the opinion was also expressed that to consider local autonomy to be independent of the national executive power and to seek after cabinet responsibility in matters that the Diet has entrusted to local autonomy by law are not in accord with the spirit of the Constitution.

INDIVIDUAL PROBLEMS.

The Principle of Local Autonomy (Art. 92). The principle of local autonomy as set forth in Article 92 is explained as having arisen from the two principles of the local autonomy of residents and of organizations. It was also said that the three principles at the time of the revision of the local government system, which was first carried out after the war, were the expansion of the rights of local residents, the independence of local public entities, and the strengthening of local self-rule and that the impartial guarantee of administration of local public entities means the objectification of the principle of local autonomy.

However, laws that determine matters relating to the organization and operation of local public entities are unconstitutional where they are in opposition to the principle of local autonomy, but it is by no means clear that simply to state that it is unconstitutional for the central government to handle matters involving only the area in question and that have no direct relation to the nation as a whole and to direct and supervise such a local area can be used as a standard to be applied to concrete questions. On this issue there is the opinion that the concept of the principle of local autonomy is not to be interpreted rigidly, but politically and developmentally and with a certain elasticity. There is the additional view that limitations on the principle of local autonomy must be recognized from the standpoint of the good of all and the development of and benefits to the nation. There is a court decision on the problem of legislative policy involved in whether provisions should be enacted in respect to so-called taxpayers' suits to the effect that they would not be in violation of the principle of local autonomy even if such provisions are not enacted.

Also in the Diet and elsewhere questions have been raised as to whether such matters as the new Police Law, which abolished the autonomous police of the *shichōson* and unified the police of the *todōfuken*, and the Special Law for Provisions relating to the Reconstruction and

Promotion of Local Finances, which provided for the power of direction in the head of the Local Autonomy Agency in respect to reconstructed public organizations, were not in violation of the principle of local autonomy. The government's reply was that they were not unconstitutional.

The Regional System. In the 1957 report of the Fourth Investigative Committee on the Local System, there were opposing views in respect to the reform of the *fuken* system. The so-called regional system proposal involved the abolition of the present system of the *fu* and *ken*, the establishment of intermediate entities to be called "regions" between the nation and the *shichōson*, the provision to them of the character of coordinated branch offices of the central government in addition to their character as local public entities, and the strengthening of government direction over them. In opposition to this was the proposal for the so-called consolidation of a number of *fu* and *ken*. This would have grouped together a number of them in accordance with social and economic circumstances without touching their present character as *fu* and *ken* or the basis of their organization and would have provided these larger *fu* and *ken* with appropriate administrative, financial, and political powers.

In this commission as well there was opinion supporting the regional system. Among the reasons given were: it is inappropriate to give *fu* and *ken*, as local public entities, broad powers in a country as small as Japan; it is desirable to make the *fu* and *ken* links of a national administrative structure in order to coordinate administration; the present *fu* and *ken* are not suitable for the maintenance of a uniform level of administration throughout the entire country; the regional system is appropriate for the administration of social security; and the regional system is necessary because the *fu* and *ken* no longer coincide with the spheres of life and economics of the residents. Also an opinion based on the proposal for the consolidation of the *fu* and *ken* held that it is necessary to reconstruct the present *fu* and *ken* so that they may become appropriate bodies for region-wide administration. The reasons are that it is necessary that regional administration in such situations be carried out as a reflection of the desires of the residents and that under such a system also the people must enjoy the greatest opportunity possible to participate in local government. Very recently discussions have developed concerning the consolidation of Aichi, Gifu, and Mie prefectures, of Shiga prefecture and Kyoto *fu*, and of Wakayama prefecture and Osaka *fu*.

Direct Public Election of Executive Officers (Art. 93). The system of executive officers and assemblies as stipulated in Article 93 has as its special characteristics a division of function and authority between the assemblies and the executive organs and their autonomous operation from mutually independent positions. However, in reality the method of operation under the form of the prewar parliamentary cabinet system has not been eliminated and during sessions of the assembly, the hands of the executive branch are generally tied by the assembly and there are many obstructions to the proper execution of duties. For that reason there is the opinion in the executive branch that there must be some limitation on the set number of assembly meetings. In addition, it is said that in Japan's local assemblies there is a difference from the true system of executive officer and assembly and that the standing committees are not provided with a sufficient number of functions.

In regard to the direct election of governors of *todōfuken*, both scholars and those involved in local public entities believe that democracy is more important than either rationality or efficiency and most of them support the view that because, if a system of appointment of governors is adopted, then the *fu* and *ken* would be converted into branches of the central government and even the autonomy of *shichōson* would be endangered, it is necessary to respect the direct connection between the residents and local autonomy by means of public elections. In opposition to that opinion there are not a few who hold that the election system should be abolished because the *fu* and *ken* must play a strong liaison and coordinating role of an essentially national character, because the administration of elected governors is carried out for the sake of election promises, because politics would become linked to local bosses and pressure groups, and because personnel administration would be lacking in stability because of the awarding of jobs to the party faithful. Thus, there are supporters of a system of appointment by the cabinet on the recommendation of impartially organized selection committees and of a system of [indirect] election by the local assemblies. In regard to the problem of whether the abolition of the public election system would require the amendment of the Constitution, government authorities hold that if the character of the *fu* and *ken* as organs of local government under the Constitution were changed, then it would not be unconstitutional to abolish the public election of governors of the *todōfuken*.

Concerning the direct public election of the heads of *shichōson*, in general the heads themselves find it desirable while the assemblies favor indirect election. As for the consultants, the majority supported the continuation of the present system, but there were also those who thought that the assemblies should select the heads because the implementation of policy by directly elected heads would follow election platforms and because of the fear that unnecessary friction would develop when the political positions of the head and the assembly would differ. In addition, because to determine a uniform organizational structure for all local public entities might be unrealistic, there is the view that the provisions of the Constitution should be given some elasticity so that it would be possible to adopt some appropriately simple organization in towns and villages such as a committee system or a town manager system. In addition, the view was also set forth that the public election of heads might develop too close a relationship between local politics and the political parties, and yet even if the elections were so politicized it would still be necessary to protect the independence involved in local government.

Article 93 recognizes the election of "other local officials as may be determined by law" in addition to the heads, but since the abolition of the public election of school board members there has been no case of an application of this provision. It was said that at the beginning GHQ suggested the election of vice governors and other assistant officials, but it was also said that this came from a confusion between a vice governor and a [American] vice president. The public election of other officials gives them an independent position and individual responsibility to the residents, but the supposition was voiced that because in the local public entities elective offices other than those of the heads and assembly members were not considered, this provision of the Constitution would not operate in the future.

Direct Petition by Residents. The system of direct petition set forth in the Local Autonomy Law, unlike the election of heads, was adopted by the Japanese side relatively independently. This system in the beginning was somewhat abused because of its novelty and because of the extreme feeling of liberation in the immediate postwar period. In the 1948 amendment of the law, matters relating to the imposition and collection of local taxes and charges were excluded from the objects of petition for the enactment and change of regulations. Also in the 1950 revision provisions were added relating to such matters as the examination of the petition rolls, the invalidity of signatures, and penalties for the illegal collection of signatures.

Also because residents have become accustomed to the operation of this system, it is said that the abuses are gradually disappearing. The number of petitions is steadily decreasing each year, and the number on the *todōfuken* level is much less than it is on the *shichōson* level. The system of direct petition should be highly praised as a guarantee of the rationalization of both representative democracy based on the system of elected headship and the operation of various types of administrative committees. An overwhelming majority of opinion held that even though it might not be necessary to promote the system directly in the Constitution, to abolish it would be inappropriate.

The Functions of Local Public Entities (Art. 94). Except in those cases where law reserves matters for the state or for other local public entities, there is no stipulation to the effect that all local public affairs are to be managed under the responsibility of local public entities; but taken together with Article 92 which guarantees the principle of local autonomy, Article 94 can be regarded as guaranteeing systematically all their functions. The Local Autonomy Law at the beginning generally followed the same thinking in regard to the distribution of business affairs as in the prewar system. However, the later revisions of the law set forth concrete examples of affairs for the local public entities and provided that they must manage them except for matters particularly provided for by law. But in reality the matters particularly provided for by law are many, and even in cases where affairs are administered locally many are carried out without control by the local assembly but under the direction and control of the state as matters entrusted to the responsibility of the office of the head of the local public entity.

Affairs based on the responsibility of the state, including the responsibilities of both the government office and the entity, total about 70 percent of those actually carried out by local public entities with the percentage rising to 90 in many cases. The reason for this tendency is that the central government offices have no confidence in local autonomy and believe that the management of affairs with central responsibility is both more rational and more efficient. There is also the opinion that there are examples of elected governors carrying out administration on their own even though the areas of the present *fu* and *ken* are not suitable for regional administration and that local public entities are lacking the organization for receiving the transfer of affairs as shown in their lack of joy in receiving such transfers for which there is no financial guarantee. Accordingly, for the solution of this problem it is said that in addition to a change of thought in government authorities in regard to local autonomy, it is necessary for local public entities to prepare an organization to receive affairs by means of the consolidation of the *fu* and *ken*.

National Direction of Local Public Entities. Because among the matters that might be transferred to local public entities there are many that possess the character of national matters, a certain degree of national direction flows naturally from the constitutional responsibilities of the cabinet. There is the opinion that it is not contrary to the principle of local autonomy to add national direction to the minimum degree necessary to the affairs of local public entities in order to insure that the state guarantees the unification of administration and maintains a specified level in it. But there is also the opposing view that to demand that the government positively direct and control the affairs of local public entities, due to the recent general tendency for administration to take on a considerable national character, is against the principle of local autonomy. In respect to future state direction of and participation in local affairs, one opinion holds that it is desirable to avoid as much as possible influential participation which would take a broad view of affairs as the responsibility of government agencies, to emphasize noninfluential participation such as advice and recommendation, and to specify in individual laws those matters which are to come under direction and supervision.

It is also said that the division of affairs into three types—public, delegated, and administrative—would become meaningless if there is the speedy abolition of affairs delegated to agencies which would lead to the supervision of the *fu* and *ken* agencies by the state and of the *shichōson* agencies by the *fu* and *ken* and if there is concrete stipulation of the necessary supervisory measures by individual laws.

Authority to Enact Regulations. The fact that Article 14 of the Local Autonomy Law comprehensively authorizes penal provisions in regulations creates a problem when compared with the proviso of item 6, Article 73 [Constitution], which prohibits general authority for penal provisions in cabinet orders. Both current theory and judicial decisions have held it to be constitutional, because regulations established by local assemblies are democratically enacted legislation and because the regulations differ in character from penal provisions applied from the unique position of the executive branch. Consequently, it is also held that penal provisions based on such regulations are not in contravention to Article 31 of the Constitution [guaranteeing procedures established by law in criminal cases]. But there is the additional opinion that there should be a clear provision in the Constitution permitting penal provisions in [local] regulations.

We have left to the section on finances the question of whether regulations relating to local taxes are in violation of the principle of taxation under law as set forth in Article 84 of the Constitution. In regard to whether it is possible to impose restrictions on the people's fundamental rights by means of so-called administrative regulations has been disputed in regard to public order ordinances, but court decisions have held them to be constitutional. In regard to affairs where constitutionality has been disputed, the opinion, however, is that it is more desirable to determine the matter by [national] law than by [local] regulation. In addition, as policy questions, the following issues were raised: the inadequacy of the legislative competence of local public entities; the acceptability of the approval in regulations of severe penal provisions; and the lack of unification among the various localities in such matters as the objectives of and the forms of control by regulations.

Local Taxes and Finances. The questions of whether financial authority centering around the power of taxation in local public entities has a direct basis in Article 92 or of whether it is bestowed by law as based on Article 84 are left to the section on finances. Also there is the opinion that in order to strengthen the independence of local public entities in addition to making specific financial grants it is necessary to adopt strong measures to redress the imbalances in financial resources. It is also necessary to adjust and consolidate the financial assistance tied to government agencies and to change the forms of financial grants based on objective standards.

Special Laws on Local Public Entities (Art. 95). It was declared that laws based on general standards, even if the organizations to which they are applied are extremely small in number or if they can ultimately be regarded as being exceptional, do not fall under [the prohibition of] Article 95 of the Constitution. Also, as in the case of the Hokkaido Development Law, the same thing holds true in cases where, even if the name of a local public entity is used in a law, the situation is one in which there is nothing more than the simple indication of a geographical name. Also the controlling opinion is that a law, which at the least in respect to basic conditions of organization and operation of a local public entity provides for a treatment different from that of local public entities, in general can be regarded as a special local autonomy law; but one which is beneficial to a local public entity or to the residents under it does not come under this provision.

However, there is the opinion, regarding precedents for this kind of special law, that they do not come under Article 95 if the principal content is that the state will provide some kind of financial assistance to a specified local public entity, and if it does not set up a special stipulation relating to the organization or the authority of the local public entity. If a name is to be given to a specific public entity by law, it is necessary to follow the formalities of Article 95, but there is also the opinion that it is a shortcoming of this article that there is no necessity to go through the formalities, if the law is simply to make general and abstract stipulations, and if the designation of individual local public entities is to be left to government order.

RESULTS OF THE INVESTIGATION. The outline of the content of the investigations into the actual operations of the provisions relating to local autonomy is as summarized above. The principal points which were raised as problems for later discussion and deliberation are the following:

1. Should the scope of "local public entity" be stipulated?

2. Is it necessary to express clearly the meaning of the phrase, "the principle of local autonomy"?

3. In respect to all local public entities is it desirable to determine a standard of organizational structure? In conformity with the different types of local public entities, should some room be left for the selection of different types of organizational structure or different methods of selection of heads (direct election, indirect election, or appointment)?

4. Should some concrete stipulations be set up in relation to the scope of affairs falling under the authority of local public entities?

[The report contains no discussion of Article 96, which deals with amendment.]

The Supreme Law

The investigations of the provisions relating to the Constitution as the supreme law were for the most part carried out on an article-by-article basis, but because there were few problems relating to Articles 97 and 99, particularly involving their operation, interpretation, or actual state, the investigation did not go beyond the expression of opinion by a few members of this commission. What was regarded as important was Article 98, particularly the relationship between treaties and the Constitution in its second paragraph. All opinions and explanations of the consultants generally related to this problem. Consequently, what appears below is principally related to this question.

THE SIGNIFICANCE OF ARTICLE 97. In regard to Article 97, a few commissioners expressed the following view: this article is not only unnecessary because it duplicates Article 11, but it makes it absolutely impossible to restrict fundamental human rights for reasons of "the public welfare" and hence it results in the interpretation that constitutional revision to make clear the basis for restriction of fundamental human rights is impermissible; as a result of the foregoing interpretation the evil of the abuse of fundamental human rights is produced and this article must be eliminated.

On the other hand, a few commissioners said that the above interpretation of this article was in error. They also expressed the view that this article is significant in that it emphasizes the rationale for the respect of fundamental human rights.

THE RELATIONSHIP BETWEEN TREATIES AND THE CONSTITUTION IN ARTICLE 98. The investigation centered principally on Article 98, and the relationship between treaties and the Constitution was dealt with in particular. Because there were comparatively few problems either in fact or in court decisions relating to the actual operation of this article, the investigation principally concerned points of debate in academic theory and comparative law in the fields of constitutional study and international law. The important points are set forth below.

The Formation of Article 98. Consultants Hagiwara Tōru and Nishimura Kumao offered explanations on the details of the insertion of the second paragraph dealing with the faithful observation of "treaties and established laws of nations" by means of revision in the House of Representatives in the constituent assembly. Consultant Nishimura particularly explained that the above revision was designed to clarify Japan's intention to adhere firmly in the future to respect for international law and that consequently it could not be denied that this paragraph should be interpreted to be a provision which recognizes that treaties and the laws of nations possess validity in domestic law. Authorities of the Foreign Ministry at the time also expressed the opinion that the intent of the above paragraph should be interpreted as emphasizing the political aim of making clear the objective of respect for international law.

The Validity of Laws and Ordinances under the Old Constitution. In regard to the operation of paragraph 1, Article 98, Consultant Takatsuji described how the executive branch and the courts interpreted this paragraph as possessing a transitional significance regarding the validity of laws and ordinances existing previous to the enforcement of this Constitution. ["Existing legal enactments, such as laws, regulations, ordinances, or by whatever name they may be called, shall, so far as they do not conflict with the present Constitution, continue in force."] Thus, under this paragraph, the interpretation at the time was that when the new Constitution became effective existing laws and ordinances under the old Constitution continued to be valid as a matter of principle, except for those contrary to the principles of this Constitution. On this point a particular problem was the validity of the so-called Potsdam Emergency Imperial Ordinance (Ordinance 542 of 1945), but this was a special problem relating to the occupation.

The Relationship between the Constitution and Treaties. In regard to the operation of paragraph 2, Article 98, the problems dealt with included the validity of treaties in domestic law; validity in the relationship among treaties, laws, and the Constitution; and the right of constitutional review of treaties. There were a number of theoretical, academic, and comparative law problems in these matters, but below is first set forth what Consultants Takatsuji and Nishimura said concerning the interpretation and actual operation by the courts and the executive branch (the Bureau of Legislation and the Foreign Ministry authorities).

First, in respect to the validity of treaties in domestic law and the relationship between the validity of treaties and domestic law the executive branch holds that, just as under the old Constitution, treaties as a matter of course are valid in domestic law from the time of their proclamation and their validity is treated as superior to that of law.

Next, in relation to the validity of treaties and domestic law, the executive branch emphasized the point that treaties could not possibly be interpreted to have a force above that of the Constitution because the procedure for the conclusion of treaties is simple as compared with that for the revision of the Constitution and that the so-called theory of the supremacy of the Constitution was treated as consistent. On this same point, in academic theory, the view of the supremacy of treaties was influential, but in the investigations of the Third Committee, in addition to Consultants Takatsuji and Nishimura, Consultants Kuriyama Shigeru (former justice of the Supreme Court), Tabata Shigejirō, Takano Yuichi, and Ukai Nobushige (Tokyo University professor) all supported the theory of constitutional supremacy.

Because under the premise that our country is in a position where it must obey the principles of international society and because the phrase means that as a matter of course the said basic principle must be protected, there is no ground for conflict between the "established laws of nations" and the Constitution, and this arises essentially from our acceptance of the Constitution.

Finally, in respect to the constitutional review of treaties, the executive branch holds that even though the word "treaties" does not appear in Article 81, treaties also become the objects of the power of judicial review.

The above is the past practice of the executive branch, and the attitude of the Supreme Court can be ascertained through the appeal decision in the so-called *Sunakawa* case (Grand Bench decision, 16 December 1959). That decision did not touch directly on the problem of the relationship between the validity of treaties and the Constitution, but in opposition to the argument of the appeal by the government that generally speaking the power of review does not extend to treaties, the decision held that in respect to treaties possessing a highly political character, the legal judgment as to whether or not their content might be unconstitutional lies outside the power of review except where it is recognized that it is "clearly unconstitutional and invalid." This view can be interpreted to mean, regarding it from the other side, that as a matter of principle treaties are the objects of the power of review.

Points in Dispute in Theory and in Comparative Law. In regard to the relationship between treaties and constitutions, a number of disputed points were dealt with in the fields of theory, academic opinion, and comparative law. The principal ones are as follows: (1) the problem of whether treaties concluded in contravention of constitutional proce dures possess validity in international law; (2) the problem of whether the content of a treaty which is in violation of a constitution possesses validity in international law; (3) academic theory regarding the relationship between international law and domestic law; (4) the dispute over the conclusion of the EDC treaty under the Constitution of the French Fourth Republic and the provisions of the Constitution of the French Fifth Republic; (5) the attitude which the courts should take in cases of the constitutional review of treaties; and (6) the relationship between the Constitution and acts of state possessing a highly political character.

THE SIGNIFICANCE OF ARTICLE 99. Among the commissioners the opinion was expressed on Article 99 that it was improper for this article, without mentioning the people's responsibility to uphold and respect the Constitution, to place that responsibility on the government and all organs of the state and that this article has also resulted in the interpretation that a request for constitutional amendment from government officials or from members of the Diet is unconstitutional. Many commissioners pointed out that this article originally established the system of oaths of allegiance by the emperor and all other public officials and would have had some meaning if this had been a Christian country. As a result of the fact that it was revised and enacted as it now appears in the Constitution, however, so that it simply determines a responsibility to uphold and respect the Constitution, it has become both meaningless and unclear.

RESULTS OF THE INVESTIGATION. The summary of the content of the investigation of the actual operation of the constitutional provisions relating to the supreme law is as outlined above. The principal points raised for future discussion and deliberation are outlined below.

1. Should Article 97 be eliminated as unnecessary and harmful? Or should it remain, with some positive significance attached to it?

2. Should all of Chapter 9 be eliminated, with Articles 97 and 99 and Article 98, especially its first paragraph, being regarded as unnecessary? Or should it remain and its value be highly acclaimed?

3. Is it necessary to reexamine paragraph 2, Article 98, particularly as it relates to Article 81, especially in order to clarify the relationship between the validity of treaties and the Constitution? Or is it necessary to reexamine that paragraph with the aim of linking it to the problem of Article 9 and to stipulations on participation in international organizations for peace and with some limitation on sovereignty also for the sake of peace?

4. Should Article 99 be eliminated? Or should it remain, with some positive significance attached to it?

[There is no mention of Chapter 10: "Supplementary Provisions," containing Articles 100–103. This chapter deals only with certain ephemeral measures relating to the coming into effect of the Constitution.]

SECTION C.
THE CONTENT OF THE DELIBERATIONS ON CONSTITUTIONAL PROBLEMS

The content of the deliberations concerning problems of the Constitution of Japan is omitted at this point because it is contained in Part Four of this report: "The Opinions of the Commissioners," and in "Opinions of Individual Members of the Commission on the Constitution" (Appended Document No. 1). In regard to the details, see Appended Documents Nos. 6–10.

SECTION D.
THE PUBLIC HEARINGS

Opinions Revealed in the Public Hearings

The opinions set forth, as well as the circumstances and the execution of the *todōfuken*, regional, and central public hearings are as described in the "Report on the Public Hearings" (Appended Document No. 11). Below we summarize in outline form the opinions of various sectors of the people as revealed in those public hearings.

SUMMARY OF OPINIONS.

The Operation of the Public Hearings. While the commission was investigating the enactment of the Constitution and its actual operation, the *todōfuken* public hearings were held between November 1958 and March 1961. These concentrated on public opinion regarding actual experience with the Constitution. Consequently, the witnesses were not requested to express their opinions on constitutional revision. The witnesses freely expressed their opinions on problems that they had freely selected from among those already considered by the commission on matters connected with "Important Questions relating to the Constitution," such as the emperor, the renunciation of war, basic human rights, the House of Councilors, the Supreme Court, and local autonomy.

When the commission was deliberating questions which had been revealed as a result of its investigations, the regional and central public hearings were carried out between February and September 1962. These hearings concentrated on the opinions of the public on whether they considered constitutional revision to be necessary or whether they believed constitutional operations should be improved in relation to the above important points. Consequently, witnesses were presented beforehand with appropriate items from among those which the commission had to deliberate on so that the opinions of the people at large could be heard. The principle followed was to request the freely expressed opinions of the witnesses on matters which they themselves had selected.

Problems Considered in the Todōfuken *Public Hearings.* In the *todōfuken* public hearings, as described above, the witnesses expressed their opinions and experiences with the operation of the Constitution on problems they had freely selected. Consequently, the problems dealt with by the witnesses and the content of their testimony covered a great deal of ground. They did not stop with the matters set forth in each article and chapter of the Constitution, but offered a rich variety of comments on problems relating to laws based on constitutional provisions and on daily experiences, impressions, and simple doubts, far removed from legal debates.

However, the problems dealt with by the witnesses can, in general, be classified according to topic, and the number of witnesses who testified on each topic and the percentages of the total number (389) that they represent can be presented. According to classification by topics, the points dealt with by a particularly large number of witnesses are as follows:

Topic	Total	Percentage
Renunciation of war	250	64.3
Process of enactment of the Constitution and general content	149	38.0
Constitutional revision	123	32.0
Family life	95	24.0
House of Councilors	87	22.4
Position of the emperor	79	20.3
Supreme Court justices	75	19.3
Fundamental rights of labor	71	18.3

These figures do permit, to a certain extent, a reading of the degree of interest among the witnesses on certain constitutional issues.

Problems Considered in the Regional and Central Public Hearings. In the regional public hearings the witnesses freely selected certain problems from among those which had previously been presented as "Topics for the Hearing of Testimony in the Public Hearings" (see p. 70 in the "Report on the Public Hearings") as being appropriate for the expression of general opinions and described their opinions particularly on the issue of constitutional revision. In the central public hearings "Topics relating to the Question of Constitutional Revision and to the Constitution in General" was added to the above "Topics for the Hearing of Testimony in the Public Hearings."

In both the regional and the central public hearings, as indicated above, the topics on which the witnesses were to testify were determined beforehand, but the opinions of witnesses were many and varied, and many witnesses expressed opinions on other topics.

The problems, by topic, dealt with by the witnesses in the regional and central public hearings, the number of witnesses heard on each topic, and the percentage of the total (98) are given below:

Topic	(Regional)	(Central)	Total	Percentage
Right of self-defense and the Self-Defense Forces	73	11	84	85.7
Constitutional revision and the Constitution in general	56	10	66	67.3
Position of the emperor	47	10	57	58.2
Relation between fundamental human rights and the public welfare	42	8	50	51.0
Relation between the renunciation of war and the structure of international peace	32	6	38	38.8
Functions of the emperor	25	6	31	31.6
Family life	20	6	26	26.5
House of Councilors	16	6	22	22.4

These figures, at least to a certain extent, permit a reading of the degree of interest among the witnesses on certain constitutional problems.

Classification of the Opinions of Witnesses. In respect to the categorization of the opinions described by the witnesses, the "Report on the Public Hearings" followed the policy set forth below.

1. The arrangement was according to the following divisions: *todōfuken* public hearings, and the regional and central public hearings.

2. Particular emphasis was placed on the content of the testimony on each problem, which could be regarded as representative, rather than on statistical analysis or description as might be done with public opinion surveys. The reasons for this procedure are that in the first place the public hearings were not carried out primarily with the intention of making them into opinion surveys and, in the second place, the *todōfuken* public hearings took place over a period of almost two and one-half years and thus it would have been inappropriate to handle them in the same manner as public opinion surveys, which are carried out at a

specific point in time. Next, although the witnesses were selected from all the *todōfuken*, and the selection was not based on a scientific sample, it would be difficult to say that the testimony of the witnesses was representative of the opinions of all communities and levels of the people. Accordingly, to interpret the opinions which might be revealed as in themselves being the attitudes and the opinions of the people might be incorrect.

3. [Here is omitted more than a page of description of the purely mechanical details relating to the presentation of testimony.]

Opinions Revealed in the Todōfuken *Public Hearings*

An outline of the opinions on the principal problems dealt with by the witnesses in the *todōfuken* public hearings is given below.

CONCERNING THE PREAMBLE. Among the opinions favoring the preamble, one offered blanket support because it sets forth the principles for the interpretation of the Constitution, thus focusing on the content of the preamble. Most of the views which did not support the preamble concentrated on its style and expressions. Such phrases were used as "sounds like a translation," "wordy, bad writing," "foreign-sounding," "apologetic writing," and "imploring." Other opinions used phrases such as "humiliating content," "declaration of penitence toward the war," "lacking in independence," and "Completely outside the current of our history, this Constitution will mark the end of Japanese history."

CONCERNING THE EMPEROR.

The Position of the Emperor as "Symbol." Among the opinions which supported the emperor's position as a "symbol," there were many that held it to be in accord with Japanese history and the feelings of the people, and also that to lay hands on his symbolic position would mean a return to the old times. There was also the view that the word "symbol" at first had a strange sound to it, but that today the meaning can be sensed directly without an explanation. Another opinion was that there is a feeling of joy in the full recognition of the significance and the value of the symbol and in the support of the emperor system.

Those who did not support the emperor as a symbol set forth as their reasons such things as the absolute destruction of the traditional emperor system by the occupation, the difficulty and obscurity of the word, and its lack of accord with the feelings of the people.

The Position and the Functions of the Emperor. Even from the standpoint of those who supported the position of the emperor as a symbol there was the view that it is necessary to treat more thoroughly his acts in matters of state. From those who did not support the symbolic position of the emperor, there were opinions that the term should be changed to "head of state" and that functions should be added which are appropriate to a head of state. In addition, there were the following views: that the emperor should be granted minimal political functions; that in times of emergency it would be desirable to return to the emperor temporary rights of sovereignty; and that there should be a return to the system of imperial sovereignty.

CONCERNING THE RENUNCIATION OF WAR. On the renunciation of war varied opinions were expressed: those arguing about the significance of the origins of Article 9; those interpreting Article 9 by centering on the right of self-defense and the Self-Defense Forces; and those debating Japan's defense policy from the standpoint of the current world situation and the present state of the structure of international peace. But on these points views were in direct opposition to each other, and consequently there was a split between those who favored and those who opposed revision of this article.

Among the above views were some which expressed naive feelings or frank impressions based on individual experience from which the following can be listed:

1. Regardless of the fact that during the term of a non-aggression pact there was an attack on a defenseless rear and the people suffered considerable casualties [a reference to the Soviet declaration of war in August 1945], to renounce war immediately thereafter and rely on international justice was simply unavoidable under the occupation. Subsequently, there were such developments as the problems of East and West Germany, North and South Korea, and the Hungarian incident. The firm establishment of the right of self-defense must at this time be clearly expressed in the Constitution.

2. To denounce the members of the Self-Defense Forces who are diligently drilling and seriously defending our soil as being unconstitutional or outside the law and to force humiliation on them is wrong. I, who observed with my own eyes with deep feeling the activities of the Self-Defense Forces when Typhoons Number 7 and 15 hit our prefecture last year, believe that the Self-Defense Forces can be active in many areas, not only externally but internally as well, in such matters as the opening up of land and industrial development. I would like to see these matters clearly set forth in Article 9.

3. Self-defense is a responsibility of all the people; it is not only a question of conscription. While we are neighbors with a country in which we cannot have confidence and a country which seizes our innocent fishing boats, frankly, there are people who selfishly say that in a time of emergency we can be defended by an international police force or with the assistance of a friendly country, but we should not now be involved in such deception. I would like to have a constitutional provision appropriate to an independent country.

4. The Ministry of Education provides direction in constitutional education

for all the teachers in primary and secondary schools, pointing out the road toward education for peace by saying, "From now on we possess nothing that can be used to wage war." On this basis postwar compulsory education has been comprehensively developed. Now, twelve years later the Ministry of Education has altered its policy of leadership to one of support for war and this tendency has been revealed in all educational materials. As teachers who are devoting themselves to education firmly committed to the road toward peace and who believe that it is preferable for the country not to possess the right of self-defense and that children should not again be sent to the battlefield, we must oppose such things as the Self-Defense Forces and any interpretation opposed to the spirit of peace in the Constitution.

5. I believe that without war potential there is no easy way to maintain Japan's independence and to protect our honor and the improvement of the people's livelihood, but we must possess full determination to do so. However, during the past fifteen years what efforts have been made through the operation of the Constitution to seek the cooperation and the understanding of the people in this regard? Has there been only the beginning of the discussion of revision and simple broad interpretation without any real effort? Have we not been involved only in the empty pursuit of fancies about the former military industry and the politics of the old military clique?

6. As a resident of Nagasaki on which an atomic bomb was dropped, I wonder if this our Constitution which arose from a sea of blood should be changed in accordance with the feelings of our leaders and suggestions from many countries? It is stupid to cut back unreasonably on the poor economy of our defeated country at the behest of the United States and demand more military potential than what is necessary for self-defense. I want to scream out that I do not want to be reminded of my fellow Japanese who sacrificed their lives in defense of the country by being told that the present camouflaged and limited Self-Defense Forces are working legitimately and splendidly for the sake of another country. I think that I would like to see the billions of yen spent every year on defense applied to social security so that Japan could become a welfare state on the level of the Scandinavian countries.

CONCERNING THE RIGHTS AND DUTIES OF THE PEOPLE. Opinions concerning Chapter 3 in general ranged from those that pointed out such evils as the excesses of individualism and the dilution of the concept of social order to those that pointed out there are still insufficiencies in the positive assertion of rights.

Many views were expressed on the relation between basic human rights and the public welfare. On the concept of the public welfare there were many self-serving interpretations on both sides: those who supported rights and those who would restrict them. Many opinions expressed the intent that it was necessary to set forth clear and concrete limits on both the concept itself and on fundamental human rights.

In respect to specific issues relating to Chapter 3, there were a number of opinions on the freedoms of assembly and expression, family life, the right to a decent life, education, and the basic rights of labor.

On the above problems were many opinions relating to the freedoms of assembly and expression, and among them a number emphasized such things as the many evils involving their abuse, the necessity for a strengthening of restrictions on them, and the need for a new system of censorship in the name of the people.

In regard to family life, particularly among the women, there were many opinions supporting Article 24. Also there were opinions to the effect that the source of the tragedy of discord between young wives and their mothers-in-law and between parents and children under the same article lay ultimately in family poverty and that the number one priority should be the raising of the level of the people's livelihood. In opposition there were views which did not support Article 24. Among these was the strong opinion that Article 24 through its philosophy of European/ American individualism was undermining the ideal of Japanese family life which is based on the harmony between husband and wife and parents and children. Also there were many opinions which pointed out that the system of equal inheritance was producing a number of unhappy results such as the atomization of farm land, part-time farming and the decline of agriculture. In addition, there was the view that measures are necessary which recognize that the inheritance of farm land should be a special exception to the principle of equal inheritance.

In regard to the right to a decent life in Article 25 there was the view that because the article is in fact nothing more than an empty phrase it should be regarded as providing a concrete right of claim and there were a number of opinions which called for its complete realization through the offering of various concrete realities of a system of social security.

In the field of education also the right to receive an education as in the above case of the right to a decent life was regarded by many as not being adequately guaranteed in reality and many also asserted the necessity for providing completely free compulsory education. In addition, there were many who described the necessity for the firm establishment of political neutrality in education.

A great many opinions were also expressed about the basic rights of labor. Among those who supported Article 28 were many who asserted, among other things, that the government infringed on the rights of workers by such things as the Government Officials Act, antistrike laws, public order ordinances, and the sabotage of the ratification of Article 87 of the International Labor Organization Treaty. They also claimed that there is abuse of the concept of the public welfare in order to limit the basic rights of labor.

On the other hand, those who did not support Article 28 expressed the following opinions: that it is necessary to enact clear provisions involving the reconciliation between the three rights of labor [to organize and to bargain and act collectively] and the public welfare; that it is necessary to establish provisions which limit collective bargaining and strike actions involving organized violence and which would protect injured parties; and that it should be clearly set forth that Article 28 does not recognize political strikes. Additionally, there was the view that the benefits of Article 28 flow only to that sector of workers who are in large enterprises and another that public officials should be excluded from workers properly speaking and be set apart from the application of Article 28.

CONCERNING THE NATIONAL DIET. In regard to the position of the National Diet there was the opinion that in view of the disorders and irregularities that characterize its activities it is not worthy of its position as "the highest organ of state power" and that this is one of the tragedies of our political scene. Most of the views, however, concerned the House of Councilors.

Among those who supported the present system of the House of Councilors were those who placed a high value on its role and said that serious consideration should be given to positive and constructive proposals for enhancing its role. In opposition, among those who do not support the present system were the following positions: because the bicameral system has been adopted, both houses should be on a footing of equality in matters other than the right to consider the budget; there should be a differentiation of function between the two houses; the six-year term should be made four years as in the case of the House of Representatives in order to eliminate idleness; the House of Councilors should be made nonpartisan; the system of direct election of members should be dropped; and the national constituency should be abolished. In addition, the opinions were expressed that in the interests of the simplification of operation of national affairs and of limiting the expense of government, the unicameral system should be adopted and that many petty disputes occur only in the House of Representatives.

CONCERNING THE CABINET. Compared with the opinions expressed on the National Diet and the courts there was only a very small number regarding the cabinet. Opinions regarding the election of the prime minister were both pro and con.

CONCERNING THE JUDICIARY. Opinions regarding the judiciary were many, particularly in regard to the popular review of Supreme Court justices. There was a conflict between two views regarding this system: one strongly asserting its connection with the idea of popular sovereignty and holding that it must be continued by all means as a precious heritage; the other holding that the present system is meaningless and must be replaced. Opinions typical of the latter view are as follows:

1. No one among my friends or colleagues is satisfied with it. They are simply left with the bad feeling that they have been forced to cast a ballot. Moreover, each time this review is carried out it costs more than a hundred million yen in national funds. Also because it is mixed in with a general election it does nothing more than confuse the electorate at the polling places. It sullies the dignity of the Supreme Court justices and is a harmful and worthless system.

2. The actual situation in which the fate of judges is determined by a haphazard "yea" or "nay" vote by all the electorate must be regarded as truly regrettable. Consequently, I have never voted on this. It is a completely impossible matter with no meaning for the people.

There were numerous opinions related to the power of constitutional review. The standard of the present system under which the power is exercised on the premise that the decision must involve a concrete case was held by some to be appropriate, but a number of opinions also held that an abstract review of constitutionality might be preferable. There was also the opinion that treaties should clearly be made the objects of review since they might in practice result in revision of the Constitution through the recognition of the doctrine of acts in matters of state, as in the Supreme Court decision in the *Sunakawa* case. Another opinion was that treaties should be reviewed by the Supreme Court prior to their conclusion.

CONCERNING FINANCES. On finances, opinions dealt mostly with the advisability of the limitation on the expenditures of public funds as in Article 89 and the opinion was strong that it should be abolished or revised on the ground that it does not conform with reality.

CONCERNING LOCAL AUTONOMY. In regard to the chapter on local autonomy, in general the views expressed involved the relationship between local autonomy and the centralization of government power. However, a number of witnesses related actual facts concerning the finances and administration of local public entities with which they were connected and averred that local autonomy had in fact been emasculated. For example, in local affairs, delegated matters, especially those delegated to organs of the central government, were in the overwhelming majority; in budgetary matters disbursements from the national treasury and tax grants to local governments comprise the overwhelmingly larger part; accordingly, the evil of dependence on central authority is strikingly evident. There was also the view that in order to deal with these phenomena it is necessary to set up much clearer provisions in place of the "principle of local autonomy" in Article 92. Another opinion held that constitutional revision would not be necessary if operational improvements were achieved through such devices as a distribution of administrative affairs and the adoption of the broad-area system of administration.

In regard to Article 93 pro and con opinions were expressed centering especially on the problem of the election of governors.

CONCERNING AMENDMENT. On the amendment procedure set forth in Article 96, there were such opinions as the following: a change should not be made because of the principle of popular sovereignty; consideration should be given to a loosening of the procedure; and there should be a provision which would prohibit revision during occupation by a foreign army. There was the additional opinion that it would be unreasonable to deal with the revision of all the provisions of Article 96 in an identical and uniform manner and that revision should be carried out to make the difficulty of amendment vary with the significance of the constitutional provisions involved.

CONCERNING THE CONSTITUTION AS THE SUPREME LAW. Concerning the chapter on the Constitution as the supreme law, there was the opinion, especially, that the unequal relationship between the Constitution and treaties should be clearly set forth. In regard to the fact that the phrase *the people* does not appear in Article 99 there were two opinions: one that it is preferable to keep it as it is, and the other that *the people* should be added.

OTHER PROBLEMS. In addition to the above opinions concerning the preamble and the chapters of the Constitution, there were others suggesting additions and improvements, pointing out deficiencies, and calling for the insertion of new provisions. Examples of such provisions or matters are as follows: a provision clearly setting forth the principle of popular sovereignty; a provision regarding the central importance of the United Nations; an organization for the development of the nation's territory; the protection of agriculture, medium and small enterprises and the middle class; the establishment of the right of management; the creation of a House of Women in the National Diet; a prohibition against political party membership by Diet members; the creation of an independent constitutional organ for the supervision of elections for Diet members; a system of recall of Diet members; the independence of the Prosecutors' Office; the right to education as a fourth constitutional right; and the establishment of a Committee on the Constitution.

CONCERNING GENERAL PROBLEMS RELATING TO THE CONSTITUTION. A number of witnesses described their opinions on general or broad constitutional questions, but it is possible to divide their opinions into two categories, those relating to the process of enactment of the Constitution and those relating to the content and the fruits of the Constitution.

The Process of Enactment. The views of the witnesses on the process of the enactment of the Constitution all centered on whether the Constitution was enacted on the basis of the freely expressed will of the Japanese people. The views were split between those which affirmed that it was and those which denied it.

As an example of an affirmative opinion, the following can be offered: "The occupation policy for Japan at the time did not call for the complete smashing of the country and found impermissible the order under the Meiji Constitution which, needless to say, ignored human rights and pursued imperialistic aggression, but was carried out in accordance with the Potsdam Declaration which called for the liberation of the people into a life of peace. Moreover, the Japanese people were already conscious of the contradictions of the order under the Meiji Constitution and could not overcome them on their own. They did, however, possess an adequate but latent consciousness of human rights, peace, and democracy. What brought this to light was the draft of the Constitution under foreign leadership; it cannot be said that it was imposed on Japan."

In contrast, the following negative opinion can be offered: "The Japanese people at the time this Constitution was manufactured were in a state of profound prostration. Consequently, they were under the illusion that the [outcome of the] Pacific War had served Japan well and had fallen into a regrettably servile attitude toward the victorious nations. Both legislation and administration were without autonomy, and disturbances such as disorder in the National Diet and mass violence have been transmitted down to the present day. Acts taken under conditions of fraud, threat, or mental derangement are invalid in either private or public law, and it is similarly necessary to undertake a reexamination of the Constitution of Japan which was enacted under conditions of collapse."

The Content and Results of the Constitution. The general opinion of the content of the Constitution for the most part was related to the actual results of its operation. Opinions were both positive and negative.

Among the affirmative views the following can be listed: those that regard the ideals of the present Constitution as something to be admired by the world; those that discovered a life worth living due to this Constitution which sets out the course for the Japanese people to follow; those that regard today's prosperity as having come from the Constitution; and those that regard it as a bible for women.

Typical of the dissenting views was the following: "The vagueness of the language of the text, the unintelligibility of the preamble, and the quality of expression are all half-baked. Not only is the Constitution hard to stomach, but it strikingly reveals an insufficient recognition of the

national character and illusions about the international situation. It is a
major cause of social disorder."

There were these additional opinions: that the present Constitution
has produced the extreme egotism of the people, and that there is a
tendency for politicians to look down on the Constitution. In addition
there was the view, based on the results of investigations attempted by
one witness himself, that there was an extreme lack of awareness of the
Constitution among the people.

DEBATE CONCERNING CONSTITUTIONAL REVISION. Opinions were divided equally over whether the Constitution ought to be revised. The
following are typical antirevisionist opinions:

1. The threat and uneasiness which are felt in respect to the recent discussion of constitutional revision lie in the fact that it has been produced by
external demands. For example, the National Police Reserve was created
under a directive from MacArthur, and Japanese military tendencies since the
revival of munitions production did not come about from the requirements of
domestic politics. Moreover, the results are incompatible with democracy and
respect for fundamental human rights, and we have moved away from the
world opinion which pleads for international peace. The present Constitution
cannot be regarded as perfect, but the movement for constitutional revision
must be opposed.

2. At present we are at the stage where we should not be thinking about
revision, but should be seriously considering how to deal with the points where
the Constitution is not working properly. Statesmen must act faithfully and
protect the Constitution. Moreover, we have reached the inescapable point in
time where for the first time the movement for constitutional revision has
arisen among the people.

3. Because the question of constitutional revision has already become en-
gulfed in political struggle and has become the seed of political warfare, the
situation is such that constitutional revision cannot be regarded as an impartial, proper issue involving all the people. The present senseless situation is
one in which the pro–American Liberal Democratic Party says that because the
Constitution was forced on us it should be revised, while the anti–American
progressive parties say that the Constitution must be protected. Consequently,
the time is extremely bad for constitutional revision.

As examples of revisionist opinion the following are offered:

1. The thinking that holds that the present Constitution, called the "MacArthur Constitution," should be revised in accordance with the spirit of popular
sovereignty and the freely expressed will of the people in order to reflect our
country's history and tradition is nothing more than proper and commonsensical.

2. In this Constitution there are empty, abstract phrases which emphasize
idealism, and in short passages there are points that must be called peculiar in

expression, no matter what one's point of view might be. I think that revision is necessary in order to correct these matters in substance.

3. No matter what one might think of the process of the enactment of the Constitution, those passages which should be changed will naturally be changed, leaving the good points unchanged. I think that it is preferable to stop with that.

In regard to when revision ought to occur, the following opinions were expressed: that the time has already arrived; that a conclusion should be arrived at only when public opinion has of itself matured along one line; and that revision should wait until the National Diet has been normalized and the people have developed confidence in it.

Also in regard to the manner of revision, the following opinions were expressed: that the Liberal Democratic Party and the Socialist Party should each prepare a draft revised constitution and the people should be asked to vote on them; and that after an outline of a draft constitution is published a general election should be held and the proposed constitution be submitted to the National Diet created as a result of the election.

In addition, many described their impressions and wishes about what both the Commission on the Constitution and the public hearings should be like.

Opinions Revealed in the Regional Public Hearings and the Central Public Hearing

Because in the regional and central public hearings the witnesses described their opinions on the pros and cons of revision in relation to "Matters for Statements in the Public Hearings," which had already been determined by the commission, below are recorded the views of anti-revisionist and revisionist groups.

CONCERNING THE PREAMBLE. Concerning the preamble, there were no particular opinions holding that revision is unnecessary. Among the revisionist opinions were those which held that articles centering on patriotism, beautiful traditional customs, and respect for Japanese culture should be added, while support should be continued for the three principles of democracy, pacifism, and liberalism proclaimed in the preamble. There were also opinions that the style of the preamble is not appropriate.

CONCERNING THE EMPEROR.

The Position of the Emperor as Symbol. Among the antirevisionist opinions on the position of the emperor as symbol were the following: the word *symbol* is meaningful and in accord with the historical sentiments of the people; to change it to *head of state* might result in political misuse; and "as a person born in the Meiji period, I understand the feeling for the change to *head of state*, however, that might be too much of a good thing and so by far the best procedure is to continue as is."

Opinions favoring revision on this issue include the following: because even under the present Constitution the emperor plays the role of the head of state he must be treated as such and it is nonsense to think that the world will come to an end if he is made the head of state; in view of the fact that the emperor's position as a symbol improperly holds him in contempt there should be established a provision expressing his dignity as a person; and because the authority which would strengthen the unity of the people in a time of emergency cannot be expected anywhere outside the emperor, in order to increase his authority it is clearly necessary to set forth his position as *head of state*.

The Functions of the Emperor. Among the opinions against revision on the functions of the emperor are the following: since the emperor should be placed in a position independent of governmental affairs, his functions should be kept as they are at present; because the emperor is recognized as a symbol, his functions as they are serve as a limitation; and if the emperor is given more functions than at present, this might become a means by which persons in certain positions would evade their responsibilities and there might be the danger that advisory organs close to the emperor and outside the cabinet might be revived.

Among the opinions favoring revision were many which held that there must be an ordering of the emperor's functions in foreign relations and that it is necessary to make clear his position as head of state.

THE RENUNCIATION OF WAR. Opinions concerning Article 9 on the renunciation of war in general fell into two categories: those centering on problems relating to the right of self-defense and to the Self-Defense Forces, and those centering on problems of the machinery for international peace. These of course are split between revisionist and antirevisionist opinions.

The Right of Self-Defense and the Self-Defense Forces. Among the antirevisionist opinions on the right of self-defense and the Self-Defense Forces were a number such as the following: it is improper to think of the right of self-defense and [possession of] war potential as being equivalent; and it is possible to interpret such things as the existence of the right of self-defense, the maintenance of the Self-Defense Forces, and the participation of the latter in the international police actions of the United Nations as being permissible under Article 9 as it stands and since revision of the article might result in friction and confusion at home and abroad, revision is accordingly unnecessary.

Another opinion held: "It would be better for Japan not to have an army and that would better serve the country's self-defense. Various international problems today cannot be solved by armies. Japan has the mission of serving the role of mediator in the confrontation between the United States and the Soviet Union. This is a difficult matter, but Japan must have the right to protest against the war preparations of the rest of the world."

There was also another opinion: "At this point in time before there has begun a marked increase in the capacity for self-defense the question of whether or not to revise Article 9 means a determination of whether or not to possess arms. However, today when the Self-Defense Forces are firmly established, I believe the question of the revision of Article 9 is not a question of the complete abolition of the Self-Defense Forces, but whether we should assume the position of achieving peace or stand on the premise that war is unavoidable. Thinking along these lines, obviously Article 9 should not be revised in order that we can achieve the principle of peace. Also from the international point of view revision is not a desirable policy."

In the latter opinion there is the feeling that the right of self-defense is firmly established. Notwithstanding that fact, it was pointed out that there has never been a general election in which the existence or abolition of the Self-Defense Forces was directly at issue and consequently the following proposal was made: "To find a practical solution to these questions, could a general election be held, with the Self-Defense Forces Law as the direct point of dispute? Or could continuance of the Self-Defense Forces Law be determined by a national referendum? Could the national will be determined in either of these fashions and could this question be settled finally?"

Among the opinions in favor of revision a number held that as an independent country Japan possesses the right of self-defense, that under this right it is proper to possess the minimum amount of arms necessary for self-defense, and that as a result it is necessary to make this point clear in the Constitution. In addition, there was the following opinion: "At a time when we are being threatened by an external force which would deny us the rights and freedoms recognized in the Constitution of Japan, enjoyed equally by all the people, and which aims to establish a despotism, we certainly possess the right to exercise the right of self-defense and to defend with all determination this Constitution which guarantees the rights and freedoms of the people. To renounce the means of self-defense while proclaiming the defense of the Constitution is a most striking example of self-contradiction."

Another opinion held: "To assert that rearmament will call forth a revival of militarism is to downgrade the significance of popular sovereignty." Also there was the opinion that it is necessary to set up an organ by which the nation itself will be able to carry out administration of the army as in the case of the National Public Safety Commission [which is in charge of the administration of the police system].

The Renunciation of War and the Structure of International Peace. Among the antirevisionists were many who held that while the necessity for self-defense is natural, one method of achieving it is to appeal positively to the whole world through the principles of Article 9. Several opinions were as follows:

"In today's age of nuclear war there is only one capability for the defense of one's country: to establish firmly the ideal of peace and to defend steadfastly the freedom of spirit."

"The ideal of peace set forth in the Constitution is too precious to be tampered with. I believe that to realize such an ideal may be the position that Japan is in today or, rather, that is its realistic situation."

"The renunciation of war in this Constitution will never be firmly established without assuming the existence of a world federation. . . . If we are ever to avoid war, it is necessary to devote just one ten-thousandth of the passion we have for war for the achievement of world federation. That will bring us closer to a solution of the problem."

Many revisionists argued that because Japan, which has cooperation with the United Nations as a central element of its foreign policy, is caught in the contradictory situation in which it cannot participate in or cooperate with United Nations armed forces, it is necessary to resolve this problem constitutionally.

On this point the following opinion was offered:

> I am opposed to the belief that the de facto existence of the Self-Defense Forces must be made constitutional, but it is necessary to add a provision to recognize them since we are moving toward a level where nations will transfer their right of self-defense to an international organization above the nation itself. Accordingly, it is necessary to set forth clearly the following matters: (1) the limitation of the mission of the SDF to the defense of our territory, the maintenance of internal order, and disaster relief; (2) preparation for cooperation in the establishment of international peace machinery and the transfer of the right of self-defense to such machinery when it is set up; (3) no adoption of the conscription system; and (4) the location of the right of supreme command in the prime minister.
>
> As a condition for obtaining the consent of both our own people and foreign countries to the possession of the Self-Defense Forces, it is necessary for them to be completely independent and to limit their war potential strictly to a level that will not arouse suspicions among Asian nations, in particular.
>
> In essence, at the present time when complete disarmament is the ideal in all countries, the SDF must be in a transitional state until that ideal is achieved. In this sense it is not simply a question of changing constitutional provisions regarding the SDF; they themselves must be gotten off to a fresh start.

CONCERNING THE RIGHTS AND DUTIES OF THE PEOPLE. Opinions expressed in regard to Chapter 3 on the rights and duties of the people were extremely complicated but they can be classified under a few problems and can be presented as follows as revisionist and antirevisionist opinions.

The Relationship between Fundamental Human Rights and the Public Welfare. Among the antirevisionist opinions concerning the relationship between fundamental human rights and the public welfare were the following: that the problem of that relationship can be solved by legislation and in actual operations; that revision of Chapter 3 is unnecessary, while a curbing of the tendency for many laws to go against the spirit of Chapter 3 is necessary; and that prevention of the abuse of rights requires consideration of the limitations inherent in such rights and of the self-restraint of the people, thus avoiding the possibility of limiting fundamental human rights by the public welfare.

In opposition, there were a number of revisionist opinions which held that the present Constitution does recognize the public welfare but gives the rights of the individual supremacy over it. Consequently, the demand for individual rights has taken priority and the intent of the Constitution is not being realized; therefore it is necessary to provide clear constitutional stipulations regarding limitations on rights and freedoms. There was also the opinion that there should be a provision honoring the rights of management as a balance to the rights of labor. Another opinion held that in addition to a provision placing a specific responsibility on enterprises for the maintenance, improvement, and advancement of the economic welfare of all the people there should also be a clear stipulation placing restrictions on the three rights of labor for the sake of the public welfare.

The Relationship between Church and State. Among the antirevisionists there were a number of opinions concerning the relationship between church and state that held that to provide Shintō shrines with a national character might lead to another deification of the emperor and would also infringe on the freedom of religion. In addition, there was the following opinion: "Too much emphasis on the separation between church and state may lead national organs, particularly the schools, to resist encouragement of the religious spirit; this point and going beyond Article 9 of the Basic Education Law [which provides that no national or local school shall carry out religious education or activity] can be corrected. Shintō shrines have a religious character, but it is necessary to recognize their extremely special characteristics and if this point is given sufficient consideration, I believe it will be possible to treat them within the framework of the present Constitution."

On the revisionist side were a number of opinions which held that because the Yasukuni Shrine holds a position in the folk tradition and that the Ise Grand Shrine [the most important of the Shintō shrines] is a spiritual heritage related to the existence and the culture of the Japanese race, the principle which holds that these should be treated in the same manner as ordinary religions should be changed.

The Family System (Family Life). Among the antirevisionist opinions concerning the family system was one which held that Article 24 is the holy writ of the women of Japan, and another which held that such issues as the lack of harmony between parents and children, the increase of divorce, and the unhappiness of old people are not to be attributed to the Constitution, but are really problems of education and social security. Another opinion was as follows: "The misapprehension that it is all right to destroy the family through the abolition of the [old] family system is fairly widespread. Consequently, it might be well to establish an ethical provision expressing the importance of family life; however, this is essentially not a constitutional issue, but a problem of both politics and education."

In opposition there were many who supported revision, holding that because as a result of Article 24 the friendly sentiments of the traditional Japanese family relationships have been lost, the ethics of immediate relatives have declined, and the integrity of family life is lacking, it is necessary to establish provisions concerning the relationships among direct blood relatives, the principle of cooperative family life, the maintenance of tranquility in the family, and the preservation of family life.

The Succession to Agricultural Property. Among those against revision on the issue of succession to agricultural property there was the opinion that in order to prevent the evil of the atomization of farmland, it should be possible to take measures, such as a system of special loans without special [constitutional] provisions, without resorting to means in the form of limitations on fundamental human rights but giving prior consideration to providing adequate conditions for farm management. An additional opinion was that because this same problem arose in respect to medium and small enterprises and small-scale merchants, the constitutional principle of equality should not be demolished only for the protection of agriculture.

In opposition a revisionist view pointed out the evil of the atomization of farmland and held that it is necessary to recognize exceptions to equal succession in respect to the inheritance of agricultural property, and if that involves the possibility of unconstitutionality, then revision is necessary.

The Guarantee of the Right to a Decent Life. Among those against revision concerning the guarantee of the right to a decent life there was the opinion that it is necessary to strengthen that guarantee, that anything that might weaken it is unnecessary, and that it would be preferable for the government to endeavor to give life to Article 25. However, it is not a problem calling for the revision of the Constitution.

Among those who favored revision were the following opinions: because Article 25 sets forth a responsibility of the state and has been regarded as the basis of the arguments of labor unions in the struggle for wage increases, it should be clarified; and there should be a clarification of the responsibility of the state in regard to social security and an even stronger move toward the welfare state.

The Guarantee of Human Rights in Criminal Procedure. Among the opinions holding that revision concerning the guarantee of human rights in criminal procedure is unnecessary is the following: "Because excesses in and the improper exercise of state power are the greatest threat to fundamental human rights, detailed provisions must be set forth in the Constitution; they cannot be left to law passed by a simple majority of one. Only provisions which can be considered to be impediments to the practices of police and prosecutors are necessary for the people."

Opposing views favoring revision included many which held that the provisions from Articles 31 to 40 should all be put in order so that they would be more in accord with a constitutional style and some which held that the right of silence has been carried too far.

The Duties of the People. Among antirevisionist views concerning the duties of the people was one which held that rights and duties should go hand in hand, but that the problem is simply to await the development of the people's awareness, not to add binding provisions relating to duties.

Among the opposition favoring revision were views which held that in order to correct the evil of overemphasis on human rights, provisions relating to such duties as loyalty to the nation, respect for law, the defense of the country, and respect for the fundamental human rights of others should be included.

In addition to the above opinions relating to existing rights, there were others involving education, the people's right of resistance, the guarantee of human rights in private relationships, the phenomenon of discrimination, the granting of honors, and the protection of agriculture and small and medium-sized businesses.

CONCERNING THE NATIONAL DIET.

The Diet's Position as "the Highest Organ of State Power." Among those feeling that revision concerning the position of the National Diet is unnecessary was the view that the appellation "highest organ of state power" is a desirable one showing a good sense of legal wording and should be maintained as is, but in the mutual relationship between the Diet and the cabinet it must be applied so as not to produce a one-sided concentration of power. In opposition there was the revisionist opinion that held that since "highest organ" is an ambiguous phrase, it should either be expunged or changed.

The Bicameral System and the House of Councilors. Among the views against revision concerning the bicameral system and the House of Councilors was one which held that there are doubts about the ideal form of the present House of Councilors, but it is sufficient under the present Constitution to consider such matters as a change to the system of vocational representation carried out by indirect elections.

In opposition there were a number of revisionists who held that the bicameral system should be maintained, but in order to assure the differences between the House of Representatives and the House of Councilors members should be added to the latter by recommendation and that provisions should be added concerning the method of election of such members.

CONCERNING THE CABINET.

The Parliamentary Cabinet System and the Position and Method of Selection of the Prime Minister. Among the opinions holding that revision is unnecessary were a number which were critical of the proposed system for the election of the prime minister. There were also a number of opinions to the effect that while the election of the prime minister is worth a careful hearing, in view of the fact that the political awareness of the people today is still low and that there are weaknesses and corruption in elections, one would feel uneasy if it were put into effect but there is room for working toward the smooth operation of the parliamentary cabinet system. In addition, there was the opinion that if an elected prime minister became the center of an upsurge of national consciousness and of the unity of the people there would be opposition.

Among the revisionist views were the following: that because the current parliamentary cabinet system gives the impression that the cabinet is subordinated to the Diet, it is necessary to consider a change to a form in which the legislative branch does not dominate the executive and judicial branches; that there is a certain fascination in the system of electing a prime minister; and that there is approval for the election of the prime minister, but the problem is one of timing.

Measures for States of Emergency. Among the antirevisionist opinions concerning measures for states of emergency was the following: "In regard to situations producing a state of emergency, there is an opinion that even under the present Constitution it is possible to limit fundamental human rights and another opinion that since that is impossible a provision permitting it must be inserted into the Constitution. I cannot agree with either view. This Constitution in itself is to bring into being a Japan in which there will be no occurrence of a state of emergency such as a revolution or a coup d'état. Because the realization of such a nation is the responsibility of the people, there should not be established any provision on the supposition that such emergencies will develop."

The opposing view supporting revision holds that to guard against a ten-thousand-to-one chance, the cabinet should be granted the power to deal with states of emergency but under strict limitations and conditions.

CONCERNING THE JUDICIARY.

The System of Constitutional Review. Among antirevisionists were some who supported the present system of constitutional review because, where the sense of law is not firmly established there is no true democracy, and there can be no danger from the intrinsically passive nature of the judicial power even if it is recognized as possessing a certain degree of supremacy. An additional opinion held that various evils would result if the present Supreme Court is given the character of a constitutional court or if a separate constitutional court is established.

An opposing revisionist view held that in addition to the courts of justice a constitutional court should be established with an organization similar to that of the constitutional council of France; and another view asserted that because a constitutional court is unnecessary and because Article 81 gives the impression that only the Supreme Court carries out constitutional review, there should be a revision to indicate that this is not the case.

Popular Review of Supreme Court Justices. Opinion against revision held that the popular review of Supreme Court justices should be supported because of the principle of popular sovereignty and that it should be maintained because of its significance in raising popular consciousness of both the law and justice.

Among the revisionists was the view that since this system is idealistic, formalistic, and unrealistic and can be subjected to political abuse, it should be abolished. As counterproposals the following were offered: the establishment of an independent nominating body for appointments, a system of review by the National Diet, and a system for the election of a supreme judicial official from among judges and prosecutors.

CONCERNING FINANCES. There were no opinions holding that revision of Article 89 concerning finances is unnecessary. Among those supporting revision was the view that since the article does not conform with social realities it should be either expunged or modified.

CONCERNING LOCAL AUTONOMY. Among those antirevisionist opinions concerning problems of coordination between local autonomy and the centralization of power and of broad-area administration were a number which held that today's problems of local autonomy, such as the evils of centralized authority, the reliance of local finances on the central treasury, the complexities of local administration, and the cramped size of *todōfuken* boundaries are all not problems of the Constitution itself and should be resolved by legislation.

Among the views supporting revision was the opinion that broad-area administration is a worldwide trend but the boundaries of the *fu* and *ken* do not conform to current requirements and the Constitution should clearly set forth some provision relating to administrative units organized on a wide-area basis. Concerning the organization of local public entities, there was the view that determination of whether local deliberative organs should be assemblies or committees should be by a vote of the local residents.

CONCERNING AMENDMENT. Concerning amendment procedures, there was only disagreement with the argument for relaxation.

CONCERNING THE CONSTITUTION AS THE SUPREME LAW. Concerning the Constitution as the supreme law, there were the opinions that the present three articles should be woven into either the preamble or Chapter 3, as appropriate, and another that since Article 97 has been used as a basis for the abuse of fundamental human rights it should be expunged.

OTHER PROBLEMS. In addition to the views expressed above concerning the preamble and the various chapters of the Constitution, the following opinions were offered on other problems: that there should be provisions relating to a national flag and a national anthem; that an independent Inspectorate of National Administration should be established; that there should be a provision relating to political parties; and that measures should be adopted to insure the fairness of elections.

THE CONSTITUTION IN GENERAL, THE PROCESS OF ITS ENACTMENT, AND THE DEBATE OVER CONSTITUTIONAL REVISION. Among the antirevisionist views on the Constitution in general were the following: that some matters arising from the actual operation of the Constitution might appropriately be amended, but these are trifling and do not require urgent attention, while other matters relating to the fundamental principles of the Constitution must not be returned to the old system; and that while the present Constitution has its shortcomings, observing the problem of timing, the question of revision should be dealt with at the earliest only after treaties of peace have been concluded with all the nations of the world [an indirect reference to the absence of such treaties with the Soviet Union and the People's Republic of China], after security treaties and foreign bases have disappeared, and after Japan has become completely independent.

Another opinion was as follows: "Present-day Japan is confronted with the question of whether the Constitution should be revised, but it cannot completely escape the dangers that are concealed in revision. The problem is deeper than that. It lies in whether or not the Japanese people will in a positive way either nurture or kill the extremely precious content possessed only by the Constitution. We must not waste precious time on whether there should or should not be revision, rather, I believe we should pour our entire effort into policies that arise necessarily from the core of the Constitution, especially the pursuit of a positive policy of peace and another emphasizing world federation."

Among the revisionist views were many especially favoring revision because of the process of enactment of the present Constitution. There was also the opinion that revision is necessary but that it must be limited to the most important points, that serious consideration should be given to both timing and method, and that it is necessary to divide the points into three kinds according to the degree of importance: (1) the amendment of Article 9; (2) the adoption of the system of election for the prime minister, the elimination of the provision making the National Diet the highest organ of state power, the creation of a provision relating to powers under a state of emergency, and the clarification of the relationship between the three rights of labor and the duties of teachers and public officials; and (3), for example, the ideal organization and structure of the House of Councilors. Measures for dealing with the above might include clarification by constitutional interpretation, the strengthening of its operation, or the improvement of law.

There were also opinions relating to the debate over the validity of the Constitution, its style, and the Commission on the Constitution itself.

[The section in the original (pp. 304–66) containing the opinions of foreign scholars on the Constitution is here omitted. These opinions have been published by the commission under the title *Comments and Observations by Foreign Scholars on Problems concerning the Constitution of Japan, 1946.* Most of this report is in English, but the opinions of the European scholars appear in the original languages.]

PART FOUR

The Opinions of the Commissioners

1. Introduction

AFTER HAVING COMPLETED its investigations and deliberations as described in Part Three, the commission began deliberations on such questions as whether the Constitution required amendment or whether it was necessary to improve its operation in relation to the large number of problems uncovered as a result of the above investigations. This fourth part is devoted to a description of the various opinions revealed in the deliberations relating to problems involving the Constitution of Japan.

First, the following three basic problems for a reexamination of the Constitution of Japan, as set forth in Chapter 2 of this Part, were addressed:

What kind of constitution should Japan's be?

How should the process of the enactment of the Constitution be evaluated?

How should the interpretation and application of Japan's Constitution be viewed?

Next, concrete constitutional issues, as described in Chapter 3 of this Part, were confronted, such as the preamble, the emperor, the renunciation of war, and the rights and duties of the people. There is a description of the various opinions revealed in the deliberations on the problems which emerged from the detailed examination of the preamble and each chapter in addition to questions such as states of emergency, political parties, elections, and national referenda.

Moreover, the opinions relating to the above basic questions as well as the important issues covered in the preamble and the chapters are, of course, related to the question of constitutional revision. Usually, the opinions of each commissioner were set forth as inseparable from the problem of revision. The general drift of opinions concerning revision makes up Chapter 4. The various opinions relating to the necessity for and the methods of the revision of the Constitution of Japan are also described in a general sense in that chapter.

In the deliberations on the above problems each commissioner expressed a large number of opinions. The individual opinions of each commissioner are set forth in outline form in "Opinions of Individual Members of the Commission on the Constitution" (Appended Document No. 1). In Part Four the various views as revealed in the above are described, and are arranged according to groups on the basis of content.

There were considerable differences among the opinions of the commissioners. Among them were opinions held by all, nearly unanimous opinions, and joint opinions held by a specific number of commissioners.

In the deliberations of the commission all members did, of course, express their opinions freely as individuals and, moreover, the deliberations themselves were carried out in accordance with a policy of debate. Accordingly, some issues were dealt with by all of the commissioners or by a majority, while others were mentioned only by specific commissioners. In addition, the opinions were in endless variety and on detailed points they can be separated only in terms of the number of commissioners who held them. However, on fundamental or general issues as distinct from detailed matters there was an unexpectedly large number of opinions which were unanimous or near-unanimous or held by a fairly large number of commissioners. Also at the conclusion of the stage during which the individual commissioners expressed or debated their individual opinions, Commissioner Yagi Hidetsugu and sixteen others presented a joint declaration entitled "Toward Constitutional Revision" which was to be consulted during the drafting of this report. In this joint declaration are differences of individual opinion on various points relating to revision but in general it can be regarded as their collective thinking; that is, these seventeen commissioners, leaving aside minor differences, here presented their joint, unanimously held opinions. Moreover, a fair number of commissioners in addition to those seventeen expressed concurrence with both the content and the main outline of that joint declaration.

The seventeen commissioners were as follows: Yagi Hidetsugu, Takada Motosaburō, Kojima Tetsuzō, Ōnishi Kunitoshi, Yoshimura Tadashi, Ushioda Kōji, Kōri Yuichi, Aichi Kiichi, Kimura Tokutarō, Sasamori Junzō, Ota Masataka, Kogure Bidayu, Yamasaki Iwao, Uetake Haruhiko, Aoki Masashi, Tanaka Isaji, and Chiba Saburō. Among those commissioners the following eight were responsible for drafting the declaration: Yagi, Takada, Kojima, Ōnishi, Yoshimura, Ushioda, Kōri, and Aichi.

In addition, Commissioner Nakasone Yasuhiro and twenty-eight others later presented a paper, entitled "Joint Opinion relating to the

Conclusions in the Report of the Subcommittee on the Process of the Enactment of the Constitution," to be similarly consulted during the drafting of this report. Moreover, former Commissioner Araki Masuo and seventeen others added their agreement with this joint declaration. This declaration revealed the joint opinion of these forty-seven commissioners on the evaluation of the process of the enactment of the Constitution of Japan.

The twenty-nine signatories of the declaration were: Nakasone Yasuhiro, Aichi Kiichi, Aoki Masashi, Ide Ichitarō, Inaba Osamu, Kojima Tetsuzō, Shiikuma Saburō, Sudō Hideo, Chiba Saburō, Nakagaki Kunio, Noda Uichi, Furui Yoshimi, Yamasaki Iwao, Uetake Haruhiko, Kimura Tokutarō, Kōri Yuichi, Kogure Bidayu, Sakomizu Hisatsune, Sasamori Junzō, Uemura Kogorō, Ushioda Kōji, Ōishi Yoshio, Ōnishi Kunitoshi, Kamikawa Hikomatsu, Tagami Jōji, Takada Motosaburō, Hirose Hisatada, Yagi Hidetsugu, and Yoshimura Tadashi. The eighteen who added their agreement were: Araki Masuo, Ueki Koshirō, Ozawa Saeki, Kiyose Ichirō, Kosaka Zentarō, Tanaka Isaji, Takahashi Teiichi, Nakamura Umekichi, Nishimura Naomi, Fujieda Sensuke, Aoyanagi Hideo, Ota Masataka, Kajiwara Shigeyoshi, Sugiwara Arata, Tachi Tetsuji, Tenbo Hirohiko, Murakami Giichi, and Tomita Kenji.

The fact that there were opposition and differences among the various interpretations concerning the basic issues of the Constitution and the important problems relating to the preamble and chapters is a result of the differences in the arguments, the attitudes, and the fundamental positions of the commissioners. Accordingly, in the description of their interpretations it is not enough simply to present their conclusions; emphasis must be placed on the basis of their differences in respect to their positions, attitudes, and arguments.

In relation to the question of revision, a broad division of opinion between those for and those against can be made, but among these opinions there is certainly no identity of position, attitude, or argument. Also, among those favoring revision were differences in respect to scope, timing, and manner of revision; similarly among those against revision were differences regarding the steps that should be taken in case there was no revision.

For example, among those favoring revision there were such differences on the problem of scope as a proposal for a systematic draft for revision, which would involve a broad revision of each chapter, and a partial revision limited only to some provisions. Also in respect to the timing and manner of revision there were the following differences: that even though it is natural to be prudent it is already time to set out on revision; that revision should be carried out by lumping together all the points for revision; that it is necessary to prepare public opinion for revision; and that it is necessary to consider carefully special methods for carrying out revision, such as establishing stages according to a certain order [of importance]. Also among those against revision were differences such as between those who held that special proposals should be made regarding political and legislative measures that should be taken if there is no revision, and those who felt that no such special proposals would be needed.

2. Basic Problems of the Constitution

THE FOLLOWING ARE the three fundamental problems relating to the Constitution of Japan: What kind of constitution should Japan's be?; How should the process of the enactment of the Constitution be evaluated?; and How should the operation and the interpretation of the Constitution be regarded?

These general problems take precedence over those relating to the individual chapters of the Constitution. That is to say, in examining whether revision of concrete provisions in the preamble and the various chapters is necessary, the foundation must be the manner in which these basic problems are regarded.

These three problems must be regarded as general, fundamental, and antecedent to the various concrete problems in the preamble and the body of the Constitution, but the two groups are, of course, inseparable. When the commissioners expressed their opinions on these three problems usually they simultaneously described their opinions relating to the revision of the preamble and the various chapters.

SECTION A.
WHAT KIND OF CONSTITUTION SHOULD JAPAN'S BE?

The opinions of the commissioners on the question of what kind of constitution should Japan's be were generally cast in an abstract form, but they did touch on various points of contention, and differing points of view were expressed in accordance with differences in standpoint and points of emphasis. Consequently, it is possible to offer the following three viewpoints as sharing for the most part in interpretations of the majority: (1) the constitution of Japan must be one freely enacted by the Japanese people themselves; (2) the constitution must conform both to the universal principles of mankind and to the history, tradition, individuality, and national character of Japan; and (3) it must be a realistic, practical constitution in conformity with world trends.

The three viewpoints above are interrelated and the opinions set forth by a majority of the commissioners, even though differing in points of emphasis, touch to varying degrees on them. These three viewpoints can be said to be the opinion of the majority of the commissioners who voiced opinions. However, some gave particular emphasis to only one or two of the three. Moreover, the above viewpoints were advocated particularly by those commissioners who demanded revision. For example, some expressed the view that the constitution which Japan should have should be an ideal one and, judged by that standard, the current one has defects and shortcomings, making revision necessary.

On the other hand, some antirevisionist commissioners expressed no particular positive view on the question of what kind of constitution Japan should have. For example, they completely affirmed the present Constitution and therefore felt that there was no need to discuss the ideal constitution for Japan; they saw the problem as a question of how the ideals of the present Constitution can be made into a living reality. In addition, there was also the position which held that the question of the ideal constitution should be argued concretely in terms of the preamble and the body of the constitution and that it is necessarily inappropriate to discuss it as an abstract issue.

The general trend of the opinions on this question is as shown above. Below are presented the various views on this problem centering on the three specific points that were set forth above.

The opinion that the Constitution of Japan must be one freely enacted by the Japanese people themselves.

This opinion was expressed by a majority of those commissioners who supported revision. Others did not touch directly on this problem. They did not deny it, but rather recognized it as a natural premise. Consequently, it can be said that this view was unanimously held by the revisionist commissioners.

An excellent example of this opinion is found in the joint opinion of Commissioner Yagi Hidetsugu and sixteen others, "Toward Constitutional Revision" (hereafter termed the "Joint Declaration"), which sets forth the argument as follows:

First of all, as is appropriate from the fact that the Constitution of Japan is to be the constitution of an independent nation, it must be enacted completely freely after having, of course, come from the free initiative of the people and having gone through a free study leading to approval concurred in by the convictions of the people. This is also a requirement arising from the principles of democracy; it is also a necessary condition for an independent and sovereign nation; and it is also the highest principle based on the importance of a constitution, which is the fundamental law of a nation. In order for it to be a constitution in which all the people can take pride as something of their very own and which they can look up to as the symbol of brilliant development toward the future, not simply with a passive attitude of loyal protection, it is necessary that it be gladly enacted by the general will of a free people, acting with undeniable independence.

Two additional opinions were that generally a nation's constitution must flow naturally from its people and it becomes something belonging to that people if it is regarded as having come from their blood (Commissioner Kamikawa); and that generally a nation's constitution must be written in the best vocabulary of that nation and in the best style. That is the first requirement for a constitution made by the people themselves. From that a constitution which is appropriate to a nation can come (Commissioner Ushioda).

Revisionist commissioners of this opinion stood on the judgment that the present Constitution was not enacted independently on the basis of the freely expressed will of the Japanese people and consequently they demanded that it is necessary to revise the Constitution independently. This opinion, in general, dealt with revision abstractly and usually did not touch on the particulars of an ideal constitution. However, most felt that the present Constitution has many points that do not conform with Japanese history, tradition, and individuality because it was not enacted by the freely expressed will of the people, thus leading to their view that independent revision is necessary. As a result this view is related to the question, "How should the process of the enactment of the Constitution of Japan be evaluated?" (see Section B of this chapter) and the opinion to be dealt with next.

The opinion that the constitution must conform both to the universal principles of mankind and to the history, tradition, individuality, and national character of Japan.

This opinion can also be regarded as held unanimously by those favoring revision. Also among the antirevisionist commissioners, it was impossible to discover anyone who was particularly opposed to this opinion in itself. The division of views concerned the concrete content of the "universal principles of mankind" and the concrete manner in which these and the national peculiarities of Japan could be reconciled.

In this opinion "the universal principles of mankind" designate, in short, democracy and pacifism which are the fundamental spirits of the present Constitution. Of course, the revisionist commissioners were unanimous in their respect and support of these principles as well as to how they could be broadened and developed. In this they were joined by the antirevisionist commissioners. Accordingly, this opinion as a general matter was unanimously held by all the commissioners.

Notwithstanding the above, what actually constituted the division of opinion between those for and those against revision related in the cases of pacifism and democracy to their concrete content. In addition, the difference also related to what kind of a concrete system should be realized to bring together these universal principles of mankind and Japan's history and tradition. Accordingly, it is necessary to treat this view in parallel with the concrete opinions on the wide variety of questions relating to the preamble and the chapters of the Constitution.

As representative of this view, for example, the Joint Declaration held that the principles of pacifism and democracy must be highly valued, but at the same time it declared that the constitution "must be simultaneously the instrument for transmitting the heritage of Japan's long tradition and for making the principles fit in with the individuality of Japan," and "by taking root in the patriotism, the independence, and the tradition of the Japanese people it can be treated as a 'constitution of the Japanese, for the Japanese and by the Japanese.'" From this standpoint the declaration is for revision covering all aspects of the preamble and the body of the present Constitution.

Also, as another example, Commissioner Hirose agreed in general but also stated that the entire body of the constitution must be based on the fundamental character of the Japanese nation and must contribute to its complete development. Therefore, he asserted that both democracy and pacifism in addition to the emperor system and the structure of sovereignty must be studied on the basis of the standard of whether they will in some way contribute to the full development of the nation.

The following view among those on this topic, that of Commissioner Ōishi, is one which emphasized the special character of the emperor system in the history and tradition of the Japanese race:

> No matter what the constitution, the most fundamental issue is where the spiritual foundation of the nation is to be found. In that spiritual foundation is the core for the unification of the communal society of the nation. Thus, in Japan, the historical emperor system which has been firmly established within the history of the Japanese race exercises the authority which is central to the unification of the people. Therein lies the special character of Japan's historical and traditional emperor system. Nevertheless, the policy of the occupation destroyed this spiritual foundation of Japan. The primary reason for a reexamination of the Constitution of Japan is the reestablishment once again of the spiritual foundation.

However, this view (that the restoration of the emperor system is of prime necessity) was not the majority view of those favoring revision, but was held by only a very small minority.

The following is a special view of the nature of the universal principles of mankind:

> In the contemporary world where the great problem is the establishment of world peace and world order every individual is required to be faithful to "the highest conscience of mankind" as well as loyal to his nation and his people. It is natural that the Constitution of Japan be based on "universal principles," but in reality it is extremely difficult to seek out principles in which all peoples without exception can believe. Also the classical Anglo–American liberalism and democracy and the Soviet-type socialism as they are cannot become "universal principles" either now or in the future. True universal principles must be those which transcend even those which might be built on a synthesis of those mentioned above. (Commissioner Kamikawa)

Others argued that the universal principles of mankind are, in general, those of pacifism, democracy, and others which have been adopted by the Japanese Constitution.

Another opinion, which follows, raises the issue of what has been termed the "living constitution" as compared with the usual emphasis on constitutional provisions.

> No matter how logically perfect a constitution may be, it can be no more than a blueprint. The fundamental principles of the Constitution of Japan, as a blueprint, are held in common with other free, democratic nations, and they are proper for setting the direction that Japan's government must follow. In addition, the emperor system which is the most characteristic feature of the Japanese nation is already preserved in a form appropriate to the present age and by this means the historical continuity of the Japanese nation is firmly established. The other fundamental principles of the Japanese nation are held in common with free, democratic countries and there is no need to add a special Japanese character to them. Into a "living constitution" of the Japanese nation which develops on the basis of the blueprint contained therein, the character of our people will be automatically woven. A Japanese democracy which has been developed in this way will have its own special color different from that of English, French, American, German, or any other democracy. In respect to the relationship between national character and a constitution, it is important to regard a "living constitution" as the core, not a constitutional blueprint. (Commissioner Takayanagi)

This opinion is based on the view that the Constitution need not be amended, but among the opinions of others against revision there was agreement on the point that in the present Constitution provision has already been made for the reconciliation of the fundamental principles of mankind and Japanese history and tradition and that there is no need for revision which would add a special Japanese character.

In addition, the following opinion particularly emphasized the point that Japanese history and tradition must not be stressed to the point where the universal principles of mankind are downgraded: "Because every nation has its individuality, it is natural that such individuality and special character must appear in its constitution. However, by overemphasizing this point and playing down the universal principles of mankind we must not end up by following a retrogressive course. We must adopt the thinking that we can add Japanese individuality and special characteristics to the foundation of universal principles." (Commissioner Furui)

The view that the constitution must be realistic and practical and in conformity with world trends.

The revisionists agreed on this view. Also among the antirevisionists no opinion appeared which opposed this view in itself. Divisions among those who held this view appeared over concrete issues.

What is referred to in this view as "a constitution in conformity with world trends" for most meant, in concrete terms, a constitution which would reveal the following two tendencies: toward a constructive, positive contribution to world peace, and toward the realization of the contemporary welfare state. The following view is representative.

> The so-called "protect the Constitution" position which asserts that the present Constitution must be protected through all time as a uniquely superior one is negative and retrogressive. Because the living today bear a responsibility toward future generations it is necessary to adopt a forward-looking attitude, namely, that an independent constitution aimed at the new age must be written out. Thus, a newly written constitution must be one which will retain the strong points of the present one, establish a welfare state, and express a strong ideal and desire for the realization of international peace, thus dealing with world conditions both now and in the future. (Commissioner Aichi)

Similarly, even among those who took the position that there should be a contribution toward world trends and toward the development of mankind, there were some, such as the following, that placed particular emphasis on special points.

> In the fifteen years following the promulgation of the present Constitution three changes have come about in world affairs. The first is the amazingly rapid development of science and technology; there must be a speeding up of governmental processes to match this rapid rate. The second is the unusual advance of the Communist bloc; in view of this advance we must devise greater governmental efficiency in Japan, which is a member of the free nations. The third is the strengthening of the authority of the United Nations; in accordance with this, Japan must firmly establish a cooperative attitude toward the United Nations. In essence, in order to make possible the development, stabili-

zation, and efficiency of national affairs in response to the above three great changes, constitutional modernization is a necessity. (Commissioner Chiba)

In the post–World War II world new conditions have been produced such as atomic energy, nuclear weapons, and space development and, moreover, these are advancing daily. What the attitude of the nation and its people should be toward these new situations must be clearly set forth in the constitution. Also it is necessary to adopt new principles which are in accord with new domestic political conditions. For example, today is the age of mass democracy and the power of the highest political leaders has become so great that it controls the fate of all mankind. Reflecting this change, the importance of the fundamental rights of the people does not lie in freedom from authority as in the past, but must be shifted to the freedom to create directly the power of the government. Namely, it is necessary to adopt a system under which the people possess the right to select directly the highest political leaders. (Commissioner Nakasone)

However, the view just presented, even though it is prorevisionist, was held only by a minority.

What is referred to as "a realistic, practical constitution" means one which does not simply set forth ideals but a realistic, concrete one which establishes systems and methods which make possible the realization of ideals. Opinions along this line set forth the requirement that it is necessary to express clearly a realistic, practical attitude toward the realization of world peace. For example, the principle of the renunciation of war in Article 9 is too idealistic and conceptualistic and thus it is necessary to adopt an attitude of cooperation for international peace and a practical, realistic defense which will make possible the realization of the ideal. This point was unanimously held by the revisionists.

The view which favored a "realistic, practical constitution" included similar demands respecting fundamental human rights and the structure of government, not simply Article 9.

The following view is typical of those which demanded that the constitution be realistic and practical and that it must provide effective systems and measures which would serve both as a check on the shortcomings of democratic government and as a guard against its destruction.

The majority of the democratic constitutions enacted after World War I were destroyed before World War II. One of the reasons is that they were not provided with effective means for limiting the shortcomings of democratic government; even though it is the highest form of governmental organization, it is not completely faultless. Its shortcomings include the difficulty of achieving a compatibility between liberty and equality, the reduction of government [to rule] by numbers alone, the lowering of efficiency in governmental affairs, the creation of waste in government spending, and tyrannical rule by demagogues and agitators. If constitutions are not provided with effective safe-guards against such defects, democratic government will become nothing more than a democratic concept and in the end will fail. In view of the above history, the present Japanese Constitution is really strikingly deficient in its consideration of matters such as those mentioned above. Also a similar situation exists in regard to pacifism. Consequently, the Constitution of Japan must adopt measures to prevent a rush toward mere conceptual democracy. (Commissioner Ōnishi)

The view presented above was revealed in revisionist opinions, but on the same issue the following antirevisionist view was expressed:

Using as a base the ideal constitution for Japan in the future, the problem is how to provide a demociatic constitutional order with the equilibrium, the elasticity, and the efficiency necessary for both its stability and development so that it will not end in failure in the face of anticipated political, social, and economic crises. Thus, in coming to grips with this problem, the following three points must be given special consideration:

1. Is the constitution appropriate to foreign and domestic realities in the face of contemporary upheavals?

2. If a deadlock is created in the relations among the organs of government, is the constitution provided with means by which a solution in accord with the will of the people is possible without falling into dictatorial government?

3. Are the processes of constitutional amendment appropriate as may be required by political, economic and social changes? (Commissioner Rōyama)

This view on the ideal constitution also held that the provisions and ideology are not the only considerations, but that laws and social conditions are also important if the constitutional order is to endure. Consequently, it was also asserted that excessive reliance should not be placed on ideology and value judgments.

World affairs are complex and strange, to say nothing of agitated. At this stage to consider what kind of constitution would be suitable for the Japan of the future is an extremely difficult task. However, it is clear that it is the wish of the great majority of the people that Japan should be associated with the camp of liberalism and capitalism. Consequently, there can be no disagreement with the fact that we should be tied to the group of modern countries which recognize the universal principles of mankind under the form of a democratic nation which centers on freedom and equality in accordance with respect for fundamental human rights. Considered in this way, I am confident that the Constitution of Japan is a good one for the future of our country. (Commissioner Mizuno)

In summary, the ideal constitution for Japan, according to the commonly held view among the commissioners, should be one that is: freely enacted by the Japanese people; in accord with Japanese history, tradition, individuality, and national character as well as the universal principles of mankind; and realistic and practical in conformity with world trends.

The view that Japan's Constitution should be of the above nature was positively set forth as a reason for revision by revisionist commissioners. On the other hand, even though there were cases among the anti-revisionists where this view was not particularly set forth, such commissioners were not necessarily opposed to it in itself. In this sense, it would be regarded as being unanimously held by the commissioners.

Within this apparently unanimous view there were the following principal differences:

Since Japan's Constitution has defects and shortcomings that cause it to fall short of the ideal, should it be revised? The differences on this question produced a confrontation between those favoring and those opposing revision.

What is the concrete meaning of such words and phrases used in the above discussion as "independent," "universal principles of mankind," "the history and tradition of Japan," "world trends," and "realistic and practical"? On this question the commissioners differed as to what the meaning should be.

The differences among these opinions were brought out particularly on the following points: (1) Should the present Constitution be regarded as one enacted freely by the Japanese people?; (2) Should it be regarded as placing too much emphasis on the principles of pacifism and democracy and other universal principles of mankind and thereby as lacking in respect for the history and tradition of Japan, particularly in regard to such matters as the emperor system?; and (3) Should the present Constitution especially in its principles relating to such matters as pacifism, democracy, and fundamental human rights be regarded as not being in accord with the present trends toward international peace and the contemporary welfare state and thus as leaning too far toward conceptualistic ideals? From the differences of opinion on these points arose the confrontation on the issue of revision. Consequently, these points were related to the views on the problem of the evaluation of the process of enactment of the Constitution and on the important issues relating to the preamble, the emperor, the renunciation of war, and the rights and duties of the people.

To what extent is it necessary to provide for constitutional ideals within the Constitution itself? On this question the following differences of opinion were observable: (1) all constitutions should be provided with sufficient provisions which will clearly set forth their ideals; and (2) this question should not be overemphasized, rather it is necessary to focus on the issue of the so-called "living constitution" and make the ideals live through legislation and social conditions. Here again confrontation developed on the issue of revision.

SECTION B.
EVALUATION OF THE PROCESS OF ENACTMENT

The evaluation of the process of enactment is indivisibly linked to the investigation of the process itself. The results of the investigation carried out by the commission in order to clarify the process of enactment are set forth in detail in "The Report of the Subcommittee on the Process of the Enactment of the Constitution" (Appended Document No. 2). In addition, a summary of that report is given in Part Three of this report (Chapter 3, Section A).

The commissioners' evaluation of the enactment process was linked closely to the discussion of revision itself, and the commissioners who expressed their opinions on enactment did so in relation to the question of revision. The views revealed in these opinions can be divided into the following three broad categories which show the clear conflict among them: the opinion that since the present Constitution was not enacted on the basis of the free will of the Japanese people, it should be independently reviewed and revised; the opinion that the present Constitution was not enacted on the basis of the free will of the Japanese people, but revision should be decided on the basis of its actual operation and content; and the opinion that while it cannot be said that the present Constitution was not enacted on the basis of the free will of the Japanese people, revision should be decided on the basis of its actual operation and content.

The first opinion was, of course, that of the commissioners who favored revision. Almost all who held the second opinion favored revision. However, among the latter, two (Commissioners Mizuno Totarō and Nakagawa Zennosuke) did not favor revision. Also the third opinion was expressed by all those who were against revision except for the two just mentioned. These commissioners believed that revision was unnecessary even from the standpoint of the content and actual operation of the Constitution. Among them, however, there was one dissenter, Commissioner Hosokawa Ryūgen, who thought revision necessary on the basis of both content and operation.

In relation to the evaluation of the process of enactment the problem of the so-called invalidity of the Constitution was also dealt with. This question, in view of the process and the formalities involved in the enactment, was a double one: whether the present Constitution is essentially invalid in law or whether, at least, it lost its validity with the end of the occupation.

The invalidity argument was, in essence, based on the following three reasons: as a general rule a constitution cannot be enacted during an occupation; the measures that General MacArthur took in regard to the enactment of the Constitution were in violation of international law; the Constitution is invalid because it was enacted merely as a revision of the Meiji Constitution notwithstanding the fact that it went beyond the limits of revision as set forth therein.

Only Commissioners Kamikawa and Ōishi and ex-Commissioner To-mita argued the invalidity of the Constitution, but even they did not support the argument as being correct in itself. Ōishi and Tomita simply stated that the possibility of invalidity should be examined because it contained matters that demanded attention. Kamikawa stated that the Constitution possesses certain legal characteristics flowing from occupation control, and that it consequently became invalid under international law with the end of the occupation, but that it did not, as a matter of course, become invalid under domestic law. He added that the discussion of the legal validity of the Constitution possessed no more than a secondary significance and that the real issue was whether the enactment was possessed of political and historical legitimacy. Except for these three, all other commissioners were against the invalidity argument. Thus, it can be said that no commissioner wholeheartedly supported the issue of invalidity. Accordingly, we shall stop with the above brief discussion and not return to the problem.

Was the Constitution Enacted on the Basis
of the Freely Expressed Will of the Japanese People?

The opinion that the Constitution was not enacted on the basis of the free will of the Japanese people.

This opinion, in essence, was that the present Constitution was enacted under the occupation and under duress from GHQ, SCAP, not on the basis of the free will of the Japanese people. It was held by a majority of the commissioners.

The basis of their argument is already clear from the results of the investigation of the enactment process. For example, the Joint Declaration offers the following three points:

1. General MacArthur not only transmitted to the Japanese government his desire for constitutional revision, but prepared his own so-called MacArthur draft and presented it to the Japanese government by fiat and compulsion.

2. General MacArthur avoided the appearance of forcing constitutional revision on the Japanese government and wanted it on the surface to take the form of an independent revision according to the free will of the Japanese people. It was also the policy of the American government that to issue orders to the Japanese government was limited to the last resort. Moreover, following the establishment of the Far Eastern Commission, constitutional revision fell under its authority. Thus, General MacArthur relied on direct orders and compulsion under the necessity for creating the fait accompli of hasty constitutional revision before the start of the FEC.

3. The Japanese government on the basis of the above MacArthur draft prepared its own draft, but even this process was carried out under the strict direction of SCAP and there was neither freedom nor autonomy on the Japanese side. The same was true of the process of deliberation and revision in the constituent assembly.

In close agreement the common opinion of Commissioner Nakasone and twenty-eight other commissioners plus eighteen former commissioners, totaling forty-seven, set forth the following view:

> In our consideration of the process of enactment of the Constitution we cannot agree that it was enacted by the free will of the Japanese people. It cannot be said that proper procedures were followed in the enactment because of the objective situation at the time that the draft was handed over by GHQ, SCAP, particularly because of such matters as the psychological state of the Japanese side, the purge of public officials, the considerable number of Japanese who had not yet been returned to Japan, and the necessity for obtaining the approval of GHQ, SCAP for the preparation of the government draft and all changes therein made by the assembly. It must be stated that the above made the expression of free will extremely difficult.
>
> Among constitutions which have appeared since World War II are some which have provisions prohibiting constitutional enactment or amendment under a foreign military occupation. However, in the Japanese situation it must be recognized that constitutional enactment took place under a military occupation by a foreign country to which such provisions would be truly applicable and under conditions where there was no guarantee of the free will of the people.

Commissioner Sakomizu Hisatsune provided additional arguments for this view as follows:

> The action followed by General MacArthur at the time of the enactment of the present Constitution involved the presentation from SCAP of a draft in the form of a recommendation and the request for an opinion from the Japanese side, but only those matters which accorded with his views were adopted. . . . It is clear that SCAP's fundamental position was that it would not recognize a

Japanese opinion which was not in accord with its own and for that reason this method, in its results, did not differ in actual fact from one in which unilateral orders were issued.

In essence, the process of enactment included the following elements: (1) both the times and the circumstances were such that everything was under the supervision and direction of the army of occupation with no independent Japanese action allowed; (2) the main element in constitutional revision was completely American; (3) the Japanese side was in a position because of both direct and indirect pressure where it could do nothing but resign itself to the situation; (4) as a result of the above there are sections in the Constitution which in reality were forced on Japan. Expressing these matters frankly, it must be said that this Constitution was forced or imposed on Japan. Considering the problem from the standpoint of SCAP or the United States for the moment, it can be said that it was their intent to cooperate in the creation of a constitution through the joint effort of both sides. Even so, from the Japanese point of view there was not on their side at the time a positive feeling that an independent constitution was being created through cooperative effort with the United States. Therefore, taking only the Japanese position, it is impossible to call this Constitution the result of Japanese–American collaboration.

As an argument against the views described above, it has been set forth that it is necessary to place considerable importance on the fact that preparations for the MacArthur draft took into account and drew on various unofficial Japanese drafts, public opinion, and items in the press at the time. But in opposition it was argued that at the time the press was under the strict supervision and control of the occupation, that there is no conclusive proof that public opinion was drawn on, and that even if any Japanese drafts were consulted, it amounted to no more than mere reference. It was asserted that to regard the above matters as an expression of the free will of the Japanese people simply does not accord with the facts.

The view that it cannot necessarily be said that the present Constitution was not enacted on the basis of the free will of the people.

The supporters of this view argue neither that the Constitution is based on the completely free will of the Japanese people nor that the power of the occupation or of a foreign nation was completely ignored. Rather, it was held that the Constitution was supported by the people at the time and in this sense their free will was reflected in it, that it should not be rejected because it was enacted under an occupation, and that the lost war and the occupation are facts that are hard to bear.

This opinion was well expressed by Commissioner Mano as follows:

> The assertion which emphasizes that the present Constitution was forced on Japan is ultimately only a face-saving or formalistic argument. For example,

rather than thoughtlessly to reject the enactment of the Constitution because it was based on the hard facts of defeat and occupation it is necessary to reflect on the experience of those facts.

Thus, if we regard the issue from the point of view of the content of the present Constitution, it is a fact of history that this Constitution was both approved and welcomed by the people at the time. In addition, it may be said that because its content is also in accord with the feelings of the people, their free will is well reflected in this Constitution. This kind of a constitution would probably not have been possible if it had been freely enacted. Namely, it can be said that a constitution with such a content was possible only because it was enacted under the circumstances of an occupation.

Commissioner Takayanagi spoke strongly both against the "imposed constitution" opinion and for his own concept of collaboration.

If we make a generalized judgment on the basis of the circumstances which have become clear as a result of the investigation of the facts carried out by this commission, then it is unfair to characterize the present Constitution as having been imposed by an army of occupation.

The question of whether or not the Constitution was "imposed" must be discussed from a number of different aspects. The first is that of the acceptance of the Potsdam Declaration. Because there can be no doubt that it can be regarded as the fountainhead of the present Constitution and that it was accepted by the government of Japan as a result of a lost war, it can be said that the declaration was forced on Japan by the Allies. Also it was enforced by the Japanese government under the supervision and direction of SCAP. Accordingly, because the power to decide whether the draft constitution prepared by the Japanese government was in accord with the provisions of the Potsdam Declaration resided in SCAP and ultimately in the Far Eastern Commission, the fact that the Japanese government was not completely free will be contested by no one. Regarded from this aspect, it can be said that the enactment of the present Constitution was forced on Japan.

The second aspect is that of the so-called transmission of the MacArthur draft. The emphasis of the "imposed constitution" argument is on whether that draft was imposed, ordered, or recommended. But it is impossible to conclude directly that there was force in this second aspect from a recognition that there were elements of force in the first aspect above.

Thus, the problem here concerns the powers of General MacArthur but in this case also a distinction must be made between the legal dimensions of his authority and its actual exercise. Thus, it is a fact that General MacArthur possessed the legal authority to impose orders and force on the Japanese government. But this is a problem of two different dimensions, namely, the fact of legal authority itself and his actual exercise of it.

If we look at the aspect of the actual utilization referred to above, General MacArthur's actions at the time of the enactment of the Constitution assumed the following form: the presentation to the Japanese government of the MacArthur draft as the first draft, the request for the opinions of the Japanese side in respect to it, and the acceptance and inclusion of the items in those opinions which could be endorsed. This differs from a one-sided imposition of orders; moreover, the fact that GHQ acted in accordance with this strict differentiation between these two forms can be recognized because at the time of the transmission of the MacArthur draft it was very definitely stated that it was not an "order," but "advice." Considering the matter thus, it is erroneous to view the MacArthur draft as having been forced on the Japanese side by SCAP. The present Constitution must be termed a result of the collaborative efforts of Japan and America.

Even when we turn our attention to the content of the Constitution, it must be considered a Japanese–American collaborative Constitution. For example, at the same time that, politically, a considerable effort on General MacArthur's part went into the maintenance of the emperor system and on the technical legal side the efforts of the GHQ legal experts were worked into the present Constitution, also on the Japanese side the efforts of Prime Minister Shidehara must be highly valued both in regard to his expounding to General MacArthur of the principle of the renunciation of war, but also in regard to his decision to follow the line of the MacArthur draft in order to defend the emperor system. Also on the technical legal side the wishes of the Japanese side were realized. As a reflection of facts like these, the Constitution was not something forced on us by an army of occupation. It was also not something created by the Japanese alone. In this sense, it must be considered as a constitution resulting from Japanese–American collaboration.

On the Basis of the Process of Enactment, Is Revision of the Constitution Required?

The three points of view on revision on the basis of the process of enactment are discussed below.

The view that the present Constitution, not having been enacted on the basis of the free will of the people of Japan, should be independently reexamined and revised.

This view holds it is only natural that today after the restoration of independence the people of Japan should freely reexamine the Constitution and revise it. Thus this opinion asserts that the Constitution was imposed by the occupation and places primary importance not on its content but on the method of its enactment.

Therefore, the common demand which can be observed in this view is that there should be a distinction between the method of enactment and the content and that the way of thinking which holds that "if the content is good, then the method is immaterial" is in contradiction to the true nature of a Constitution and, moreover, is opposed to democracy. This assertion was clearly expressed by all commissioners who held the view here being discussed and they also treated it as a natural premise.

The Joint Declaration stated the position well:

> Among those arguing for the protection of the Constitution there are not a few who, as might be expected, do not recognize the facts of the process of enactment; the view that "if the content is good, the method is immaterial" is still fairly strong. Even though the facts of the Constitution's having been imposed must be recognized because there is no help for it, there is a tendency either to disregard them or to play them down. However, this is clearly in error. The reason is that what is called democracy emphasizes not only content and results, but also method and procedure. Some argue that content and procedure are separate, but neither the argument that it is acceptable if the content is good even though the procedure was bad nor the reverse argument that it is acceptable if the procedure was good even though the content is bad should be accepted as being democratic. It does not follow that if the content is good then the procedure also becomes good. Moreover, as far as the present Constitution is concerned, it cannot even be said that the content itself is good.

From the standpoint of those who, as above, attach primary importance to the procedure of constitutional enactment and therein seek a reason for the necessity for a reexamination of the present Constitution, another opinion can be observed which recognizes significance in the reexamination in itself and, accordingly, believes that the significance is not lost even if as a result of such reexamination one reaches the conclusion that there is no necessity for revision of the present Constitution.

Those of this opinion also pointed out a variety of shortcomings in the content of the Constitution. Thus, all commissioners holding this view favored revision on the grounds of both procedure and content. Accordingly, this opinion, in theory, recognizes the significance of reexamination based on free will in order to correct the shortcoming that the procedure of enactment was not so based and does not place particular store on the results of such reexamination. In actual fact, this same opinion holds that at the same time there is an inseparable relationship with a regular evaluation of the content of the Constitution. Accordingly, this view, in substance, stands as a second one in which the Constitution is regarded as an imposed one regarding which the question of revision can be solved by resort to the real state of its content and operation. Thus, it does not differ from the opinion that revision will be necessary as a result of reexamination, and the two views are compatible.

This opinion also holds that in theory there is a distinction between content and the procedure of enactment, but that as a result of the fact that enactment was carried out under the occupation and was not based on the freely expressed will of the Japanese people, the content is opposed to Japanese history, tradition, individuality, and national character and disregards the state of affairs in the country. In addition, the content also was nothing more than an expression of the surrender

policy of GHQ, SCAP and of General MacArthur. A frequently mentioned example of the disregard for nation and people was the emperor
system. In addition, another frequently mentioned example of the expression of surrender policy was Article 9, providing for the renunciation of war.

Also on this point there were a number who said that the fact that the
composition of the GHQ draft was completed by a small number of
military men who possessed no specialized knowledge either of constitutions or of Japan in a very short period of time accounts for both the
shortcomings and deficiencies of the present Constitution.

Commissioner Hirose presented the following view, which combines
approaches to both the process of enactment and the content of the
Constitution:

> I believe that in looking at the enactment of the present Constitution and the
> Constitution itself, there are both pluses and minuses in the enactment and
> good and bad in the content.
>
> For example, in regard to enactment what must be regarded as by far the
> greatest plus is the maintenance of the emperor system. Also the greatest
> minus in respect to the Constitution, which is the basis of our government, is
> that constitutional revision, which was not clearly dealt with either theoretically
> or formally in the Potsdam Declaration, was carried out contrary to the princi-
> ple of self-determination that was clearly set forth in the Declaration.
>
> Next, what must be regarded as a plus in the Constitution is the pointing out
> of the past errors of militarism and the excesses of the police state. Again, what
> must be regarded as minuses are the unnecessary distortions of the emperor
> system, the fact that the road to the realization of pacifism is a complete
> daydream, and that the achievement of democracy is to be by means of a
> mischievous bias toward rights, freedoms, and equality.
>
> A minus in respect to enactment is the continued adherence to the Consti-
> tution as it is, simply unchanged. This fact means its continuation in its
> unstable state; no misfortune of our country is greater than this. The minuses
> in the content of our Constitution will create difficulties in our domestic and
> foreign policies, as far as it is continued unchanged, and this will be regrettable
> for both national independence and the unity of the people.
>
> Accordingly, a constitution revised so that it will be a praiseworthy one
> which will play a role in the development and realization of the ideal of the
> best Japan as an independent country must be given the highest value, rising
> above the present Constitution and its process of enactment. Thus, I believe
> we must recognize the facts concerning the enactment of the present Constitu-
> tion and the Constitution itself as historical and deal with them as the objects of
> high reflection based on the national formation of an independent Japan.
>
> The above political reflection can be added as one basis for the revision of
> the Constitution, but I am confident that starting with a general revision we
> must advance toward the firm establishment of a constitution which will serve
> an independent Japan.

The view that although the present Constitution was not enacted on the basis of the free will of the Japanese people, nevertheless the necessity for revision should be decided on the basis of the content and actual operation of the present Constitution.

Commissioners holding this view recognized that in essence the enactment of the present Constitution was not based on the free will of the people, and while defects in the method of enactment do require a reexamination of the Constitution, nevertheless, the necessity for revision must be initially determined on the basis of that reexamination in contrast with the first view which held that the process of enactment alone justifies revision.

The following opinion of Commissioner Yagi clearly sets forth the above point:

> The fact that the Constitution is said to be "imposed" and the question of revision are separate. For example, even granting for the moment that the Constitution was imposed, if the content is good, then there is no necessity for revision. To put it another way, even though a constitution may have been freely enacted, if in the light of its operations there are imperfections and inadequacies, then the people should consider revision on their own initiative. The circumstances of enactment are important to an understanding of the content, but they are not the best standard. Generally speaking, constitutions can best be evaluated not in terms of their origins, but of the actual situation relating to the value of their content and their application.

Adopting this view, it is possible to arrive at one of two conclusions— one holding revision necessary, and the other holding it unnecessary. Almost all the commissioners holding this view favored revision, while only two commissioners concluded that revision is unnecessary (Commissioners Mizuno and Nakagawa). The following opinion of Commissioner Nakagawa exemplifies the latter conclusion:

> There is the argument for an independent constitution which holds that revision is necessary because the present one was imposed. But whether there should be revision must be considered on the standard of the content of the Constitution; the problem of the process of enactment is secondary. Also in a certain sense it can be considered that this Constitution was created precisely because there was foreign pressure and I think that even though it was imposed, it is a good Constitution if its content is good.

The view that because it cannot be said for certain that the present Constitution was not enacted on the basis of the free will of the people, the question of revision must be settled on the basis of the content and actual operation of the Constitution.

This view, it goes without saying, is completely opposed to the first view. In addition, virtually all of the commissioners who held this view concluded that revision is unnecessary. Only Commissioner Hosokawa, while adhering to this opinion, was in favor of revision. As pointed out above, there were some who, while holding the second view, believed that revision is unnecessary, but almost all of those opposed to revision stood by this third view.

Commissioner Sakanishi Shiho expressed an opinion illustrative of this view:

> The argument that says the present Constitution was born under the occupation and criticizes its "birth" and "lineage" corresponds to that way of thinking that judges the value of a man on the basis of "birth." The value of a constitution as well should not be decided in terms of heredity on the basis of "birth"; it must be decided in terms of its content.
>
> In addition, in an age like the present where ideas are complexly interwoven, even in regard to a country's constitution, the value resides not in such things as whose independent or original ideas went into it, but in the variety of ideas and the degree to which they were gathered together and synthesized. I think that arguments about the "birth" of the Constitution and its originality are not worth very much.

General Summary

The evaluation of the process of the enactment and revision were viewed as related problems and, in general, the discussion revolved around whether the Constitution was enacted on the basis of the free will of the Japanese people. The various opinions therein revealed can be summarized as follows:

As shown in the Joint Declaration, the majority opinion was that the present Constitution was not enacted on the basis of the free will of the people.

Commissioner Takayanagi opposed the majority opinion and held that the Constitution was the result of Japanese–American collaboration. However, most of the other commissioners who held the view that it could not be said that the present Constitution was not enacted on the basis of the freely expressed will of the people held that for the most part the people's will was reflected in the Constitution and asserted as proof the fact that it has since been supported by a majority of the people, but did not use the phrase "Japanese–American collaboration" to characterize the enactment process.

As the principal basis for the view that the Constitution was not enacted on the basis of the freely expressed will of the people, the following points were offered: (1) the fact that the enactment was the materialization of Allied occupation policy for Japan and that GHQ or General MacArthur possessed absolute authority over the Japanese government in the implementation of occupation policy; (2) the fact that the inspiration for the enactment was in GHQ, that it presented a draft, and that the preparation of the Japanese government's draft which was based on the GHQ draft and the revisions in the Diet were all under the direction and guidance of GHQ; (3) the fact that even though there were occasions when Japanese views were taken into account, that happened only to the extent that they were in agreement with occupation policy, namely, the basic policy of GHQ, and that from the standpoint of the entire process of enactment they cannot be valued very highly; (4) the fact that even granting for the moment that the GHQ draft was presented as "advice," in reality it was an order, and the fact that, viewing the general environment at the time of the presentation and the position of the Japanese government in which it was subject to the orders of GHQ, the Japanese government had to accept that draft under duress or orders; and (5) the fact that even granting for the moment that the intentions of GHQ arose out of goodwill, this is an issue differing from the fact of compulsion.

Most of the opinions which held, in opposition to the above view, that it cannot be said that the Constitution was not enacted on the basis of the free will of the people were as follows:

1. Concerning (1) and (2) above, as a result of the fact that the enactment of the Constitution was based on the surrender document which accompanied the acceptance of the Potsdam Declaration and was carried out as an obligation of our country, it is recognized that it was done under the authority of GHQ or General MacArthur but within the scope of the Potsdam Declaration.

2. Concerning (3) above, this opinion recognizes the fact that the Japanese views were accepted within the limits of the basic policy of GHQ. While this point should not be slighted, that the will of both the Japanese government and its people was reflected to a considerable degree in those matters must be fully appreciated.

3. Among the above five points, (4) is accepted. However, in addition to the preceding point it must be emphasized that even though the Japanese government accepted the GHQ draft as indicated, the representatives in the constituent assembly, political parties, other private organizations, and the people certainly did not accept the draft just as it was; not only did they freely discuss it but there were many who not only welcomed but supported it. In addition, it is impossible to discuss the question of whether the present Constitution was forced on Japan without taking this into account.

4. Concerning (5) among the above five points, it must be appreciated that the will of GHQ was not imposed on Japan backed by its power, but arose out of good intentions for Japan's sake.

Commissioner Takayanagi accepted (1) and (2) among the points offered by those who held that the will of the Japanese people had not been consulted. His opinion concentrated on point (4), which centered on whether the MacArthur draft was "advice" or an "order." He argued that it was advice, not an order, and, as such, it fell within the ambit of basic occupation policy and, therefore, the Constitution was not imposed on Japan. Also, since Japanese views were accepted, the draft was the result of "Japanese–American collaboration."

Those who opposed his view argued that in accepting points (1) and (2) he accepted the view that the Constitution was imposed; that to argue the distinction between "advice" and "order" was formalistic and dealt only with a technical legal point; and that his narrow approach did not evaluate the historical facts that run through the entire process of enactment.

The evaluation of the process of enactment was treated entirely as a problem of whether or not the Constitution was enacted on the basis of the free will of the people and the central point at issue was the relationship between the Japanese side, especially the government, and GHQ. Arising from the view that the Constitution was not based on the free will of the people were two views concerning revision: one, that that fact alone was sufficient to make revision necessary; the other, that it was simply one important reason for revision. The opposing view frequently argued that revision should not be decided simply on the process of enactment but on the standard of its content and that it could not be said that the Constitution was not necessarily based on the will of the people.

It can be asserted that at the bottom of the confrontation between these two views are two approaches to the value of all constitutions: one that places primary importance on the origin and process of their enactment, the other on the nature of their content.

Section C.
The Interpretation and Application of Japan's Constitution

The treatment of the question of the interpretation and application of Japan's Constitution was related to the issue of revision and was dealt with in the form of two other questions: Should various problems currently arising in respect to the Constitution be disposed of by interpretation and application without necessarily resorting to revision? Or should they be dealt with by revision without resorting to interpretation and application?

There were two different approaches to these questions. A few commissioners set forth their opinions on the basis of the ideal interpretation and application of constitutions in general. Some views were based on assumptions regarding the case of the Japanese Constitution. Among the latter were some which were accompanied by an evaluation of the actual state of the interpretation and application of the Constitution since its enforcement. Accordingly, in relation to the problem of revision we describe below the various opinions which were set forth on how the interpretation and application of the Constitution should be regarded.

In general, the opinions on this question can be divided into the following conflicting groups: (1) the view that there are limits to the interpretation and application of a constitution and therefore the present Constitution should be revised; and (2) the view that constitutional interpretation and application should be elastic and therefore it is not necessary that the present Constitution be revised.

Those holding the first view did not fail to recognize that there are certain areas for interpretation and application and, likewise, those of the second view recognized certain limitations on interpretation and application. What set them apart was that the first group viewed interpretation and application very narrowly and the second viewed them very broadly. In this opposition of views it can be said that there was also an opposition of thought on the principle of a written constitution. But there was also opposition based on each individual's concept of a constitution and his attitude toward constitutional interpretation. However, this confrontation also revealed a confrontation on the evaluation of the actual facts of the interpretation and application of the Constitution. For example, those of the first view held that it is impossible to resolve the shortcomings of the Constitution by interpretation and application and that revision is necessary because their utilization has already gone beyond their limits. Those of the second view held that the various problems arising from the Constitution can be dealt with through interpretation and application and since this method must be followed, revision is absolutely unnecessary.

Article 9 was frequently mentioned as an example of the problems involved in interpretation and application, but the position of the emperor and the relationship between fundamental human rights and the public welfare were also raised in this connection. Another problem was the style of the Constitution, namely, the form and wording of some of its provisions. There were numerous demands for revision because the illogicalness and the obscurity of some provisions create disputes over interpretation. In opposition to this view it was argued that the special style of the Constitution lies in the fact that it does not conform to strict, classical legislative technique and that interpretation should be flexible, taking into account that special style. But this argument was countered by the view that the special style came from the occupation and should be changed to be appropriate for a Japanese constitution.

The opinion that constitutional revision is necessary because of limitations on both interpretation and application.

What can be perceived in common in the opinions of the commissioners who set forth the view that constitutional revision is necessary because of limitations on both interpretation and application is that in the interpretation and application of all constitutions there are natural limits set by their very natures and that interpretation and application which go beyond those limits lead to the destruction of a constitution. Consequently, because when there are intrinsic shortcomings in a constitution they cannot be corrected by interpretation and application, and beyond that, if the attempt is made to dispose of them in that manner, the constitution will be destroyed; therefore, in such cases the constitution must be revised. According to this view, the present Constitution has truly reached this stage.

The opinion that there are limits on interpretation and application was frequently put forward, especially as an assertion that such limits flow naturally from the principle of a written constitution. Representative of this view are the following two opinions.

"All written constitutions must not be broadly extended by interpretation and application; if there is a constitution which must be so extended, then it is not worth the name of a written constitution." (Commissioner Ōnishi)

"There is the claim that, while recognizing the possible existence of points in the content of a constitution that should be revised, revision is still unnecessary because they can be handled by interpretation and application. However, even though there are countries which have adopted unwritten constitutions or the common law or the law of precedent, it should not be forgotten that in our country, which has adopted the principle of the written constitution, there are natural limitations on interpretation." (Commissioner Kamikawa)

This general view also points out that to rely on interpretation and application while leaving unchanged any inherent shortcomings in the Constitution will lead to many undesirable results. Among these were offered the following: the development among the people of irresponsible constitutional disputes; the use of the Constitution as a tool of political controversy; the use of constitutional problems as obstructions to the unification of national policy; the assumption of judicial supremacy through the power of judicial review; and the people's loss of a sense of respect and confidence in the Constitution. In addition there was the strongly held opinion that to rely on the application of the Constitution was dangerous in that it forced reliance on the politicians of the moment and another that to continue the shortcomings of the present Constitution by application and interpretation amounts ultimately to nothing more than continuing the "imposed constitution."

This view holds that the above evils are already strikingly revealed in the present Constitution and offers Article 9 as a concrete example. Commissioner Kimura pointed out that although it is possible to interpret the Self-Defense Forces as being constitutional, the opposing view is strongly held, resulting in the disruption of defense policy and the destruction of SDF morale. Commissioner Kamikawa argued that the enactment of the Self-Defense Forces Law both trampled on the original interpretation of Article 9 and completely denied the principle of a written constitution. He then added that if the Constitution were a completely independent one, it might be correct to develop it through interpretation, but this should not be done with the present one.

This view does not place a very high value on the system of official constitutional interpretation by means of court decisions, particularly by the Supreme Court. For example, in the situation where there is a serious confrontation of views as in respect to Article 9, the following two views were offered: "It is doubtful that the people can be truly persuaded by a decision that is not comprehensive." (Commissioner Kimura) "The efficacy of a judicial decision extends only to individual cases and is ex post facto. The efficacy of a law is general and preventive. The two should not be compared. The foundation of national policy must be in law. It is impossible to leave problems of the interpretation and application of the Constitution solely to judicial decisions." (Commissioner Hirose)

Those holding this view often set forth the arguments that in general the form of the provisions of the present Constitution and its modes of expression are lacking in conciseness, are not logically precise and are unclear; that the meaning of some provisions is unclear because they are unnecessarily complicated; and that such shortcomings in legislative technique have produced a variety of disputes over interpretation. Frequently mentioned examples were the following: the misuse of the terms "every person" and "all the people" in Chapter 3; the misuse of the terms, "use of these rights," "guarantee of these rights," and "refrain from abuse of these rights" in the same place; and numerous repetitions in the text in Articles 11, 12, 13, 97, and others. In addition, there are imprecisions in respect to the position of the emperor in national affairs, particularly as to whether he is head of state, and in respect to Article 9, whether the utilization of the right of self-defense and the maintenance of war potential for self-defense are recognized.

Thus, because the present Constitution possesses a number of defects in legislative drafting technique as indicated above it is difficult to judge matters relating to the application of the Constitution, and the people may become confused as to what they should follow, and it may become impossible to achieve any unity in constitutional interpretation. Accordingly, if we should rely on the interpretation and application of the Constitution, then there can only be a multiplication of confusion in national affairs.

The opinion that constitutional revision is not necessarily required because both interpretation and application must be flexible.

The common thread in the opinions of those commissioners who supported this opinion that constitutional revision is not necessarily required is the view that it is theoretically acceptable to say that there are limits on constitutional interpretation but there must be appropriate flexibility in such interpretation so that by this means a harmony in application can be achieved. Thus, if it is possible to make the Constitution operable by these means in responding to the demands of the actual situation today, there is all the more reason not to revise it. This view also holds that the constitutional system is already operating in this way, thus eliminating the necessity for revision.

This view also holds that the attitude of adhering too closely to the text of the Constitution itself is inappropriate and attaches importance to the roles of the courts and the legislative and executive branches which must deal with the interpretation and application of the Constitution. Illustrative of this position is the joint opinion of Commissioners Yabe and Takayanagi which follows:

> The attitude taken on constitutional revision is closely related to the constitutional view of each person, but one should not regard only the text of the Constitution as the Constitution itself. If one observes only the provisions of the Constitution, even though there may be contradictions, repetitions, deficiencies, unclarities and such, it is possible to a considerable extent to compensate and adjust for the errors by such means as interpretation, application, and legislation, and if disputes arise over these matters, the Supreme Court hands down a decision. Of course, the text of the Constitution is the foundation, and makes it possible to structure a living, concrete constitutional order.
>
> If there are no special obstacles to its actual applicability to such a living constitutional order, then there is no particular necessity to adhere [exactly] to the wording of the Constitution. Also as far as the many strains observable in Japan's society today are concerned, rather than to attribute them directly to the provisions of the Constitution, there are many things that can better be regarded as causes, such as the immaturity of political parties, inexperience with democratic processes, and deficiencies in popular morality. One cannot expect that such shortcomings can be resolved necessarily by means of textual

revisions. If there is maturity in the people's democratic attitudes and activities, then that can be related to the rectification of the deficiencies of the text.

Because of the above considerations we cannot agree with the opinion which on the basis of a theoretical fastidiousness points out the shortcomings of the provisions of the present Constitution and holds that revision of the text is necessary in order to attain unity of interpretation.

In addition to the above view, Commissioner Takayanagi addressed the problem of the approach of the Supreme Court to interpretation and the related problem of the nature of the Constitution itself as that bears on the issue of its interpretation.

The problem of the attitude toward the interpretation of the Constitution must be considered from the central point of what the attitude of the Supreme Court should be under our system of judicial review. For example, it is natural that the interpretation of the Constitution should initially be in accord both with theory and with its text. However, many of its sections from their very nature were enacted in general and summary form. Consequently, it is to be expected that there may be a divergence of interpretation. In these cases there is nothing to be done but for the Court to decide on the basis of its free discretion which interpretation is correct. An example of this is the determination of the boundaries between the public welfare and fundamental human rights.

Also even though initially something might be perfectly clear under a theoretical or textual interpretation, it might happen that such an interpretation would run contrary to political common sense. An example of this is paragraph 2 of Article 9. In such cases the focal point of constitutional interpretation is whether the Supreme Court should be bound by textual and theoretical interpretation or whether its interpretation should be brought into accord with political common sense by means of other legal techniques.

Observation of the experience of judicial review in other countries on this problem of constitutional interpretation shows that the courts have not resorted solely to textual and theoretical interpretation but have exerted every effort to achieve interpretations in accord with political common sense. They have given paramount position to the so-called teleological or sociological interpretation which takes as its proper basis for interpretation a sufficient study of the social facts related to the case and which places primary importance on such facts in arriving at a common-sensical interpretation. By means of this method of sociological interpretation, an interpretation in accord with political common sense becomes possible and the system of judicial review can be harmoniously carried out, and moreover, this type of interpretation by the Supreme Court can become respected by all the people. Also in regard to judicial review in Japan, this approach is proper and at the same time also serves as the rationale for the avoidance of frequent constitutional revision.

From this point of view that opinion which holds that constitutional revision is necessary in order to achieve unity of constitutional interpretation where there is a division of academic opinion is incorrect. . . . When we debate whether or not the present Constitution should be revised, we must consider the special character of its style, that is to say, the manner of writing which was adopted in it. For example, in the nineteenth century, continental European constitutions set forth clearly and concisely to the necessary extent an outline of the structure of government, a chapter on rights, and also took a line of thought sufficient for those ends. The Meiji Constitution conformed to this classical pattern. However, in the twentieth-century constitutions a tendency developed under which there were written into the constitutions, not only in the preamble but also in the body of the text, certain provisions of an ideological or programmatic nature, not having the binding force of law, as a set of aims for the reconstruction of the nation, especially in the direction of greater socialization. The Constitution of Japan, above all, is of this type.

For example, its style is not one which emphasizes necessary logical perfection and legal technique as a strictly legal document; rather, it resorts to rhetorical expressions and follows a style in which important matters are written out repetitively without regard for duplication. It can also be stated that this Constitution, rather than being directed toward judges and other legalists, was written with the intention of appealing to politicians and the people. If we regard it in this light, its style is all the more a special mark of this Constitution and should not be regarded as a deficiency. For example, if one looks at it from the viewpoint emphasizing legislative drafting techniques of the former classical constitutions, its technique is indeed clumsy and thereby produces disputes in interpretation and accordingly revision can be seen as necessary in order to make the meaning perfectly clear. However, this judgment is erroneous. Rather, those who are involved in the interpretation and application of this Constitution should bear in mind the above special character of its style and it is necessary for them to apply this to their interpretation and application.

Commissioner Rōyama raised the issue of the desirable form of debate on constitutional issues in organs of government other than the courts.

Concerning problems which lie outside the power of judicial review, there is nothing to do but to rely on the National Diet. Nevertheless, in reality constitutional interpretation in the Diet cannot win the confidence of the people. The reason for this is that the political parties bring up the Constitution only when it is to their own advantage and use it as a weapon of political warfare. In like manner the cabinet also cannot be thought to pay sufficient respect to constitutional issues and to face constitutional interpretation with a judicious attitude.

Also, among not only the Diet, the cabinet, and the political parties, but also in the political activities of various groups of people and various organizations, constitutional controversy tends to be carried out with strict adherence to a specific ideology. For example, both revisionists and antirevisionists in respect to Article 9 base their arguments on a narrow, one-sided interpretation and on a predetermined specific foreign or defense policy. As a result, problems arise from the fact that confrontations over foreign policy and such are brought without resolution into the application and interpretation of the Constitution. If this situation is left as it is, even if the Constitution is revised, the problem will probably not be resolved. Before trying to solve the problem by means of revision, I think that there is much room for action in improving the state of constitutional interpretation and application.

General Summary

The confrontation of views on the interpretation and application of the Constitution is inseparable from a similar confrontation regarding the interpretation of all constitutions. We have seen, for example, that some believe there are number of deficiencies in the present Constitution and that it has already become impossible to dispose of them through interpretation and application and that, accordingly, revision is necessary. This view stands in turn on the view that the interpretation [of the text] of all constitutions must be carried out strictly and that it is impermissible to go beyond it.

The opposing view holds that it is unnecessary to revise the present Constitution and, even recognizing that there are a variety of problems involving it, they should be dealt with through interpretation and application. This, in turn, is based on the view that in such situations flexible interpretations are necessary for all constitutions, and that the area for interpretation and application should be as broad as possible. The opposition between these two views of interpretation and application has been discussed as a confrontation between a strict textual and theoretical interpretation and a sociological and teleological interpretation.

However, this problem was not treated simply as a theoretical one involving only an attitude toward and a methodology of interpretation; it was usually discussed in connection with the issue of revision. Consequently, the opposition of views on this problem appeared concretely as a problem of the various articles of the Constitution. We now turn to an examination of opinions on important constitutional issues.

3. The Preamble and Chapters of the Constitution

THE COMMISSION CONSIDERED an extremely large number of problems relating to the Constitution and covering the preamble and all the chapters. Not all commissioners expressed opinions on all problems, and there were a number of problems on which only a small number of commissioners had opinions. In this chapter we shall describe the opinions of a large number of commissioners on a very large number of problems and we shall record the important points on which there were differences of opinion. We shall set forth the various views, classified according to type, with particular reference to two approaches, proposed ideal solutions and the maintenance of the present Constitution as it is.

In addition to the specific problems in the preamble and chapters, commissioners raised others such as states of emergency, political parties, elections, and popular referenda. These will be found under separate headings. In the description of the various opinions we shall present them, as in Chapter 2, so that agreement and differences are clear as to the basic positions, attitudes, and arguments of the commissioners.

SECTION A.
THE PREAMBLE

The problem of the preamble arose from the basic character of the Constitution and its fundamental principles and the opposing views on these issues were revealed in the approaches to the writing and the phrasing of the preamble on the one hand and its content on the other. Opinions relating to the preamble were also related to the views on the two questions already dealt with as basic constitutional problems: "What kind of constitution should Japan's be?" and "How should the process of enactment be evaluated?"

Language and Style

*The view that the writing and the expressions in the preamble are not suitable
for a constitution of Japan and accordingly require revision.*

The unsuitability of writing and expression referred to here means
that the style is bad with flavors of both foreignness and translation
which are difficult to put into proper Japanese; that the sources are
foreign, exclusively American; and that the preamble is diffuse, employ-
ing many unclear technical terms. This was the view of almost all the
commissioners who pointed out these shortcomings and urged that correct sentences and expressions, superior in style and tone with a conciseness appropriate to a constitution of Japan should be used. They demanded that the above shortcomings of the preamble be recognized
even by those who opposed revision.

Commissioner Ushioda supported the above view strongly, stating:
"The constitution of any country should be written in the best language
and the best style of that country. If it has been created by the people of
the country, it will naturally turn out that way. The present preamble is
unmistakably a translation which cannot stand up as Japanese . . . it is
completely out of touch with the tone of the Japanese language. Nor is it
in accord with the Japanese mode of expression and, read aloud, the
prose is no source of pleasure. It is a matter of the first priority that the
original English text be completely discarded and the preamble be rewritten into Japanese."

He also spoke strongly on the issue of the flavor of translation: "It is
necessary to end the situation in which the preamble appears to be made
up of extracts, quotations, mixtures, and distortions of words and such
from the preamble of the Constitution of the United States and the
sayings of American presidents. Japan is not a country that became
independent of American colonialism; historically, its independence is
far older than America's. For a country like Japan to have the preamble
of its Constitution consist of a stringing together of the words of Americans and of phrases from [Allied] wartime slogans is both extremely
undignified and destructive of self-respect."

Commissioner Kojima put forth a variation of the same themes, arguing that the preamble contains expressions bringing to mind the condition of a people crushed by defeat, containing both "an apology for
defeat in war and a set of instructions or admonitions from the victorious
nations."

A majority of the commissioners urged that in general the preamble
should be rewritten into correct Japanese. But, in addition, a number of
opinions urged the inclusion of such stylistic details as "powerful sen-

tences," "lofty and elegant phrases," "sentences that the people can always love to sing," and "language which at a single reading would sound on the heartstrings of the people."

The view that the problem of the wording and expression of the preamble is certainly not fundamental and accordingly revision is unnecessary.

Two different approaches were included under this view. The first insisted that the problem of style is secondary and that the content is of primary importance. Therefore, it was argued, the content must be maintained unchanged and, hence, changes in wording might have the effect of altering the content.

The second approach was that the basis for judging what might be correct Japanese is by no means clear, and an opinion that something might not be in good Japanese may be only a subjective judgment or a purely individual preference. Commissioner Takayanagi spoke thus on this issue: "Today when international cultural exchange is flourishing, a nation's vocabulary and style of writing are constantly changing through foreign influence. Already the younger generation does not have a sense of translation in respect to the preamble. Supposing that the style is changed in accordance with the feelings of people today, it might turn out that the Japanese of the next generation might feel that the style is old-fashioned and lacking in familiarity."

Commissioner Sakanishi Shiho spoke strongly on the issue of style. "The view that the writing in the preamble is not in the Japanese style is strong, but what we call the Japanese language is now in a period of transition and what might be proper Japanese cannot be determined. Moreover, if we regard it as impermissible for the preamble not to be in correct Japanese style, then we would necessarily have to conclude that the democracy and the ideal of fundamental human rights which characterize the Constitution are also no good because they are also ultimately the product of thought developed in foreign countries."

The Content

The view that the content of the preamble is not suitable for a constitution of Japan and requires revision.

This view is inseparably connected with the fundamental question, "What kind of constitution should Japan's be?" It was argued that the content of the preamble does not conform with what would be ideal in a Japanese constitution. For example, the preambles of all constitutions should deal with such matters as their ideals, their basic spirit and principles, and the attitudes and determination of their drafters, but the preamble of Japan's Constitution does not deal with these matters satisfactorily. Those who supported this view also argued that the preamble should be revised because it is similarly unsatisfactory in regard to the other two fundamental issues: its conformity to both the universal principles of mankind and to Japanese history and tradition; and its nature as an effective, realistic constitution in accord with world trends.

Of course, this view also involved the opinion that the Constitution is not based on the freely expressed will of the Japanese people. It was argued that this is reflected both in the style and writing as shown in the strongly apologetic tone and the solemn pledge by a defeated nation toward the victors. In respect to content the preamble, it was argued, indicates that the Japanese people enacted a constitution which does not accord with the actual facts.

Commissioner Kamikawa argued this position strongly:

> The content of the preamble is completely fictitious and counterfeit and does not conform with the facts. Notwithstanding the fact that this Constitution was brought into being under an occupation, a situation where the sovereign will of the Japanese people could not exist, the preamble is written as if the Constitution had been written by the sovereign Japanese people. Once again, this Constitution must be brought into conformity with the facts. That is, today, if the Constitution is to be truly one of an independent Japanese people, this preamble should be completely rewritten and we should proclaim the aim of enacting our own free constitution, not one enacted under an Allied occupation.

Although the adherents of this view did not reject the universal principles of mankind, such as democracy and pacifism, as stated in the preamble, they said that they were emphasized at the expense of the special characteristics of Japanese history and tradition. For example, the Joint Declaration urged that the Constitution of Japan must contain a vision both of the universal principles of mankind and of a distinctive Japan. It also set forth that the vision of Japan must be constructed on the "joint consciousness of a group society with the emperor at the center and the social structure of a racial collectivity which arose from that consciousness," both of which are a part of the flesh and blood of the Japanese people and are rooted in Japanese history and tradition.

It was also argued that the preamble falls short of indicating clearly that Japan's Constitution should be effective and realistic and in accord with world trends and should therefore be revised. What the upholders of this view meant by "in accord with world trends" involved the realization of the welfare state and a positive, constructive contribution to world peace. The present preamble, it was argued, only urges the people to enjoy the prosperity which is brought about by an irresponsible free-dom and, in respect to pacifism, only idealistically to support the idea itself. Therefore, a new preamble should strongly assert along with rights and freedoms the social duties and responsibilities necessary for the construction of a contemporary welfare state and, in addition, strongly proclaim the intent to carry out a responsibility to contribute positively to the realization of world peace.

The view that the content of the preamble accurately expresses the ideals and aspirations of the Japanese people and accordingly its revision is unnecessary.

Among those who were against revision of the Constitution in gen-eral were only a few who touched on the content of the preamble. These commissioners felt that the principles of popular sovereignty, pacifism, and fundamental human rights must be maintained, and because they are emphasized in the preamble, there was no particular need to discuss it.

Commissioner Rōyama expressed the following view:

> The present preamble strongly and appropriately expresses the introspec-tive thoughts of the Japanese people on both the Pacific War and the Meiji Constitution, their determination to rise from defeat toward reconstruction and their aspiration to establish an international role for themselves. The preambles of all constitutions must proclaim high ideals and goals for the future. The criticism that the present preamble pursues ideals too far and is too far removed from reality arises from a misunderstanding of the nature of preambles. The goals in the preamble for the realization of peace and democ-racy have still not been achieved, but that makes it even more necessary to strengthen the determination expressed in those goals and this is certainly not in error.

"General Rules" or "Basic Principles"

A few of the commissioners expressed the view that in addition to a preamble there should be chapters in the text of the Constitution relat-ing to "general rules" or "basic principles." It was argued that these rules or principles should be designed to realize the abstract concepts of the preamble. In this view the preamble should include mainly items which could be described as spiritual or proclamatory and the chapters on rules or basic principles should state in legal terms concrete principles. Specific items mentioned in this regard included: the basic character of the Japanese nation; the principles of democracy and of popular sovereignty; principles involved in fundamental human rights, social solidarity and the welfare state; and pacifism. The Joint Declaration recommended a possible chapter entitled "Basic National Policy," which would contain a vision of the Japan of the future and the basis of a policy to realize that vision.

Those opposed to this suggestion simply felt that such a chapter or chapters would be unnecessary.

General Summary

The various views relating to the problem of the preamble can be summarized briefly as follows:

1. All supported the view that there should be a preamble. However, as just described, a few felt that chapters dealing with general rules or basic principles should be added to the Constitution.

2. A majority of the commissioners believed that the preamble is not suitable for a Constitution of Japan and called for a considerable change in it. But on the problem of how the preamble should be revised the views of the commissioners were inseparably related to their views on the kind of constitution Japan should have.

3. Those against revision of the preamble maintained that the principles and spirit set forth in its content should be preserved unchanged.

SECTION B.
THE EMPEROR

The principal problems dealt with regarding Chapter 1 on the emperor were the relationship between the emperor system and popular sovereignty and democracy, his position as a symbol, and the functions attached to his position. These were the fundamental problems related to the basis of the emperor system, but other questions were also raised such as succession to the throne and the finances of the imperial household.

The problem of the relationship between the emperor, popular sovereignty, and democracy was related to the fundamental question involved in the investigation of the Constitution, namely, "What kind of constitution should Japan's be?" The answer, it will be recalled, was that such a constitution should reconcile universal principles of mankind and Japanese history and tradition. The two issues were brought together in the form of a question: Does the emperor as a symbol under popular sovereignty, as set forth in the Constitution, reflect a harmony between the universal principles of mankind and Japanese history and tradition?

The Emperor System and Popular Sovereignty

The relationship between the emperor system and popular sovereignty was dealt with particularly in regard to the ideal form of the emperor system. The Constitution proclaims the principle of popular sovereignty and states that the emperor is a symbol. This means that his symbolic position is based on the general will of the people. Arising from this were two basic questions: How should we consider the relationship between the principle of popular sovereignty and the emperor system? and, Should the emperor system as set forth in the present Constitution be regarded as correct in view of what its ideal form might be?

The view that from their very natures the emperor system and popular sovereignty are incompatible and that accordingly it is necessary to bring about a fundamental change in the present Constitution where the emperor is placed under popular sovereignty.

This view was put forward by Commissioner Ōishi and ex-Commissioner Tomita. While they argued strongly against the principle of popular sovereignty, they also maintained that Japan could be a democracy without it. But their main concern was with the preservation of the emperor system as they understood it. The essence of their position on the emperor system and popular sovereignty is revealed in the following passage attributed to both men:

> The most fundamental question in the constitutions of all countries is that of the spiritual foundation of the unity of the people, that is to say, what kind of a constitutional system is required for the establishment of the national polity?
>
> From time immemorial the emperor has possessed legal authority arising from his being the center of the unity of the people and from this the people of Japan were unified. This is what some centuries of history have taught us and is attested to by the fact that the end of the war was made possible by an imperial decision. The basic meaning of the fact that the Meiji Constitution provided that the emperor was the sole possessor of sovereign power was not that it was concerned with the degree to which the emperor could utilize concrete political power, but with his legal authority as the center of the unity of the people as indicated above. Therein lies the essence of Japan's immemorial emperor system; this is a unique feature in which Japan can take pride before the whole world.
>
> On the other hand, popular sovereignty is the principle under which the legal authority for the unification of the people is placed in the people themselves and thus is opposed to the basic essence of Japan's historical emperor system. It is both a principle and a term which are completely out of touch with Japanese history and the beliefs of the Japanese people. The adoption of this principle of popular sovereignty in the present Constitution was completely against the will of the Japanese people; it was the result of the pressure and coercion of the occupation. Thus, this term, popular sovereignty, has thrown Japan's historical emperor system into confusion and has caused a loss of power to both the nation and the government. Accordingly, the phrase, popular sovereignty, must be expunged.

This view at the same time strongly asserted that the terms "popular sovereignty" and "democracy" should not be confused. For example, they argued that democracy in Japan is not democracy under popular sovereignty, but must be democracy under the historical emperor system. Commissioner Ōishi set forth this view as follows:

There is no contradiction between the possession of legal authority by the emperor as the center of the unity of the people and what is termed democratic government. The reason is that the emperor system involves the problem of the unity of the people and democratic government is a problem of the form of the exercise of national authority. Namely, on the premise that the people are unified in a single body, then democracy is the execution of government on the basis of the will of the people so unified. The belief that there is no democracy if there is no popular sovereignty ignores the fact that if there can be democracy under a system in which a monarch is sovereign there can also be democracy under popular sovereignty. Thus, democracy in Japan is under the historical emperor system, that is to say, a national polity in which legal authority resides in the emperor as the center of the unity of the people or, in other words, Japan's must be a democracy under which the emperor is the sole possessor of the authority to rule.

There is absolutely no scientific basis for the assertion that the historical emperor system was necessarily a cause of war or that there is necessarily the danger that it will be put to evil use. In brief, if it is said that Japan must be a democratic nation, there is absolutely no positive reason why there must be changes in the historical emperor system or why the principle of popular sovereignty must be adopted.

On the latter point, ex-Commissioner Tomita added: "Today in our country the belief is widespread that the theory of monarchy, that is, the emperor system, is opposed to democracy. However, it is an error to treat monarchy or the emperor system as nothing but antidemocratic. Japan has always been a nation in which the monarch and the people have been one, and in this form of government uniting the monarch and the people we have realized democracy under the emperor system."

The two men also asserted that since the western concepts of monarchy and popular sovereignty never existed historically in Japan, it follows that the use in the present Constitution of the concept of popular sovereignty is inappropriate. Because western political history is one of struggle between monarch and people it is appropriate to use "popular sovereignty" or "sovereignty resides in the people" as technical terms revealing the history in which sovereignty, once in the hands of the monarch, has been transferred to the people. But "popular sovereignty" is strange both to Japanese history and to the thinking of the people in Japan, where there has been no such struggle. Thus, the concept appears in the Constitution solely as a result of the pressure and coercion of the Allied powers.

The view that since the emperor system and popular sovereignty can be reconciled there is no need to alter the basic form of the emperor system under popular sovereignty as in the present Constitution.

This view was held by all commissioners with the exception of Ōishi and Tomita, whose views have just been described. However, there were some differences over the grounds for the argument that the two concepts can be reconciled. Going beyond the issue, there were also some differences in this group over the continuation of the term and over the emperor's functions.

The common argument here can be summarized as follows: historically and traditionally, the emperor has always been the spiritual center of the Japanese people, even though he possessed no political power. However, the present Constitution has brought the emperor system and popular sovereignty into harmony by recognizing the emperor as the symbol of the unity of the Japanese people and likewise without political power.

Commissioner Kōri expressed the following view:

The principle of popular sovereignty has already been quietly incorporated into our national sentiment and it is desirable that it should be strongly supported. Also in Japanese history the emperor has always been at the center of the race both spiritually and ethically, and for that very reason he has been well sustained by both the affection of the people and the dignity of the imperial household. This has always been without regard to whether the emperor has possessed any real political power. The present system of the emperor as symbol is supported by the people's trust and reverence for the emperor, and I believe that this situation is stable. This is all the more reason why the Constitution should be furnished with a content of this nature for the sake of and for an increase in the well-being of the people and the democratic development of the nation through the harmonization of popular sovereignty and the emperor as a symbol.

Commissioner Aichi presented a slightly different view:

It is the sincere desire of the people of this country that the history and tradition of the emperor system be maintained forever. At the same time democracy has become a part of the creed of our people. Thus, in this situation it is well to call what is termed democracy "popular sovereignty" simply as a matter of common sense. In the relationship between the emperor and popular sovereignty, it is understood that the emperor is a part of the people and exists with them. If we consider that the present Constitution places the sovereignty of our country in the people and that it has put the emperor in a position as the symbol of the unity of the people on the basis of the general will of the people, it can be said that in this respect both popular sentiment and the long tradition of our country in regard to the emperor are respected, and at the same time a harmony has been created so that it will be possible to achieve the realization of the principle of popular sovereignty.

As a variation of the above views relating to the reconciliation of the emperor system and popular sovereignty, a few held that while they are reconciled under the present Constitution, they could not be under the Meiji Constitution. For example, Commissioner, Mano stated: "If we would strengthen the authority of the emperor to the same point as under the Meiji Constitution, then there might be a contradiction with popular sovereignty. But if we take the position that the present situation should be continued as it is, then there cannot be the slightest contradiction between the emperor system and popular sovereignty."

Another opinion understood the relationship between the emperor system and popular sovereignty as a problem of the concept of the monarchical system or of its historical development. Commissioner Rōyama stated this position clearly:

The intrinsic nature of a monarchy lies basically in the fact that the monarch is the symbol of popular unity. However, the history of the monarchical system is certainly not a simple one. The intrinsic nature referred to above was the product of the experience of mankind through a long history. For example, the monarchical system characterized by the possession of substantial authority and by a relationship to the structure of power gradually disappeared, and history also teaches us that when the symbolic nature of the monarch becomes clear then the inherent nature of the monarchical system is also made manifest. In this sense the experience with the failure and the weak points of the German system of constitutional monarchy and, accordingly, the emperor system under the Meiji Constitution are also lessons of history. The emperor system under the present Constitution embodies that history in that it both follows the direction of the evolution of the monarchical system and is embellished by the history of the emperor system in Japan. Unless there is the premise of popular sovereignty, and no matter what actual powers should be granted to the emperor, it is only through the system of the emperor as a symbol that the future tranquility of the emperor system itself can be guaranteed.

At present, it may be possible that the meaning of the emperor as a symbol may not yet be fully understood. However, I do not think that the ancient Japanese emperor system has been denied by his symbolic position or that the relationship between the people and the emperor has been dissipated. Rather, I believe that as the meaning of the emperor as a symbol becomes clearer and clearer so will the reconciliation between the emperor system and popular sovereignty be realized.

Commissioner Takayanagi pointed out that popular sovereignty has become a worldwide concept, existing both under republican and monarchical systems. He pointed out that "through the political good sense of the English people, the monarchy has been solemnly preserved against a background of substantial popular sovereignty." He added: "It can also be observed that today the idea of the emperor system based on popular sovereignty has become established among our people. In this situation to present the theory that the emperor system and popular sovereignty cannot stand together and to revive old debates over concepts are both profitless and harmful. We should learn from the political wisdom of the English people who settle problems by relying on facts without placing too much emphasis on theory which has frequently led to revolution."

The Joint Declaration adhered to the same line of thought. It pointed out that to discuss the emperor system under a theory that involved a choice between monarchy or democracy was based on a confusion of eras. Also the question of the relationship between monarchy or the emperor system and democracy is in reality a meaningless one because it has already been demonstrated worldwide that democracy and monarchy can exist side by side.

The Position of the Emperor

The position of the emperor was discussed as the question of whether it is appropriate that the present Constitution stipulate that the emperor's position be that of a symbol, that is, the "symbol of the state" or "of the unity of the Japanese people." This problem was also posed in the form of two questions: Should the term "symbol" be retained as it is? and, Should it be changed to "head of state" or a similar term? Furthermore, this problem was related to the question of what the system of the emperor as a symbol should ideally be under popular sovereignty.

As might be expected from their views on the emperor system and popular sovereignty, Commissioner Ōishi and ex-Commissioner Tomita were very much opposed to the current constitutional provision that the emperor is a symbol. Their opposition was not so much to the term itself as to the fact that its use means that the emperor is not provided with the legal authority which makes him the center of the unity of the people, leaving him to be, in fact, only a symbol. They argued that there is no need for the word, "symbol," and that there must be a provision relating to the basic character of the emperor system and the Japanese nation, namely (in Ōishi's words) "the nation of Japan is a democratic country in which a line of emperors unbroken for ages eternal constitutes the center of the unity of the people."

In contrast, the view of the great majority of the commissioners was that "symbol" is appropriate and does not require revision. They, of course, also held that the present Constitution sets forth the basic and ideal form of the emperor system. However, some commissioners while supporting the general position of the Constitution on the emperor system felt that the word "symbol" is inappropriate.

The view that the provision relating to "symbol" requires revision in order to clarify the position of the emperor as head of state.

In this view the position which asserted that the word "symbol" is in general inappropriate to express the constitutional position of the emperor was frequently put forward with the following principal reasons: (1) both the word and the concept "symbol" are unclear and difficult to understand; (2) the word "symbol" has no constitutional precedent for expressing something such as monarch or president; (3) the word "symbol" is foreign, not Japanese, and is inappropriate to express the special position of the emperor; (4) "symbol" is both unscientific and unclear as a word to express the emperor's psychological, spiritual, and historical characteristics and to set forth his legal position; and (5) the concept "symbol" signifies the separateness of the symbol and what it symbolizes, but since in both history and tradition the emperor and the Japanese people have been as one with each other, to prescribe that he is a symbol is harmful to the feeling of unity.

Those who held this view urged that the emperor should be in the position of head of state and that "symbol" is inappropriate to express that position. Even though the phrase "head of state" might not be used, it would still be necessary to include a stipulation that the emperor is actually in that position. Those who argued for the inclusion of the term "head of state" were limited to a total of four. They set forth the following arguments:

"From the standpoint of both Japanese history and the beliefs of the people it is natural that the emperor be in the position of the head of the nation, thus representing it." (ex-Commissioner Shimojō Yasumaro)

"It is necessary to state clearly in writing that the emperor exists at the center of the Japanese people and, moreover, that he is in the most revered position in Japan." (Commissioner Kimura)

"Since to call the emperor a symbol also means that he is representative of the nation, I find it impossible to understand why it is not clearly recorded that he is head of state." (Commissioner Shiikuma)

"We must drop the unclear word 'symbol' and start afresh with the idea that the emperor is head of state." (ex-Commissioner Miura Kunio)

Those supporting this view also strongly asserted that even if the emperor's position is changed to that of head of state, this should not make him into the sole possessor of the power of government nor should the intent be to go back to the Meiji Constitution.

In opposition to the above view there were some who held that although the term "symbol" should be changed, the term "head of state" should not be adopted. Those of this opinion held that although the emperor should in fact be head of state, the term itself should not be used. The following were their reasons for opposing it: (1) it is unclear; (2) it is also foreign and not Japanese; and (3) to change to the term "head of state" is not that significant and there is the concern that to use it might be construed to mean that the emperor is the possessor of power in substantial matters of state and that would not contribute to the stability of the emperor system.

In general, the basis of the above reasoning was the view that the use of the term "head of state" should be avoided, but there was a diversity of opinion regarding a substitute. A number of commissioners supported the following phrasing: "The emperor represents the Japanese nation in respect to foreign countries." This was based on the view that a head of state is the possessor of the general right of representation of a nation in its international relations and this phrasing simply makes clear that the emperor has that function.

Another view held that only the term "emperor" should be used as in the present Constitution, but that his position should be clarified by the adoption of the following provision: "The emperor occupies the position of primacy in the Japanese nation and represents it." A variation on this approach was set forth by Commissioner Hirose who held that the emperor's position should be elevated and broadened by a provision such as the following: "The nation of Japan is a democracy which has the emperor as the center of the unity of the people."

Commissioner Yagi joined those who held that the emperor should be stipulated as "the center of the unity of the Japanese people" and that he "represents the Japanese nation in respect to foreign countries," and he added that there should be some stipulation in the preamble to the effect that the Japanese people should respect the emperor and his family as the nation's basic family.

A minority of the commissioners set forth opinions relating to the question of whether there should be a constitutional stipulation expressing the dignity of the person of the emperor which is connected to the opinion supporting the elevating and broadening of the emperor's position. On this issue Commissioners Aichi and Ōnishi presented the following points; because the emperor is recognized as a symbol and because his position as the center of the unity of the people is also recognized, he should be granted treatment appropriate to those special positions; to maintain his dignity he should be accorded protection different from that of the people in general; since there are difficult problems of constitutional interpretation in regard to these matters, there should be a stipulation to the effect that "the dignity of the emperor cannot be impaired"; and there should be a clear constitutional basis for the crime of *lèse majesty*.

The view that "symbol" correctly expresses the character and position of the emperor, and accordingly it is not necessary to change it.

This view was adopted by most of the commissioners who took the position that the ideal form of the emperor system in the present Constitution correctly harmonizes democracy and the traditional form of the emperor system. They believed that "symbol" expresses the fundamental special character and the core of the ideal form of the system.

The following two arguments were frequently offered to support retaining unchanged the term "symbol." First, the word sounded odd at the beginning but with the passage of time the understanding of the people has gradually broadened and it is now generally believed that it has become fixed in popular sentiment. Second, the word is appropriate for the expression of the feeling of intimacy between the emperor and the people. The ties between the hearts of the people and the emperor as a symbol should be recognized as a plus, not a minus, for the democratic government of our country.

Of course, those who held this view were also opposed to the adoption of such terms as "head of state," "position of primacy," and "the center of the unity of the people." One objection to "head of state" was that under the present Constitution the interpretation is possible that he actually occupies that position and, as a consequence, foreign countries understand his position in the country's international relations.

One of the strongest statements in support of the continuation of the emperor as symbol is the following by Commissioner Mano: "The system of the emperor as a symbol in the present Constitution is the most appropriate one. I absolutely cannot agree with the 'head of state' argument or the accompanying one that the emperor's powers should be strengthened. Placing the emperor in a nonpolitical position makes possible the long continuation of the emperor system. To place him again in a position of political power or even to inch in that direction are matters which we who have experienced the evils of the manipulation of the emperor system in the past must oppose as a matter of course."

Perhaps the opinion expressed in the Joint Declaration can be regarded as that of the majority of the commissioners. It argues that the monarch is not today at the peak of the structure of government as the center of power and that it has become the common sense view that he should be regarded as head of state. Accordingly, even though it might be desirable to make him explicitly the head of state, it should not happen that such a step might become the source of antipathy toward the emperor system.

Commissioners Mano, Ushioda, and Takayanagi opposed the insertion of provisions relating either to the dignity of the emperor or the crime of *lèse majesty*. They argued that there would be a natural circumspection about any discussion that might tend to injure the dignity of the emperor as a symbol and that this problem should be left to education and the power of public opinion. They also pointed out that laws relating to *lèse majesty* had been abused and utilized to suppress the freedom of expression.

The view that expressions such as "symbol" and "head of state" should not be used to show the position of the emperor.

Only Commissioners Ushioda and Yuzawa Michio put forth this view. Briefly, they argued that both the existence and the essence of the emperor system have a vastness and originality that cannot be shown by any words or expressions such as "symbol" or "head of state." They said that it is both impossible and unnecessary to stipulate in legal texts the essential nature and characteristics of the emperor and that to attempt to do so might give rise to the illusion that the essence of the emperor does not go beyond what is expressed by such terms and that his intrinsic nature might thereby be limited and impoverished. However, Ushioda stated that if some phrase had to be used to describe the emperor's position, then his position and functions should not be separated but some such formula as the following should be used: "The emperor is in the position of primacy and carries out acts associated with such a position."

The Functions of the Emperor

The question of what the emperor's functions should be is related to the question of his position as shown in the following five views that emerged from the discussion of both position and functions:

1. If the emperor is placed in a position of legal authority as the center of the unity of the people, then the functions accompanying that position should not be limited and he should be given specific ones relating to his position concerning the unity of the people.

2. If he is placed in the position of head of state or in a position possessing that character, he should be given functions appropriate to the position.

3. If the emperor is to remain a symbol and if he is not made head of

state or placed in the position of one, then it is still necessary to make his functions clear and the demands in respect to such functions are in agreement with those who state that he should be head of state.

4. If there is no need to use terms such as "symbol" or "head of state," it is still necessary to change the stipulations relating to the emperor's functions.

5. If the emperor is to continue as a symbol, then the scope of acts relating to matters of state as determined in the present Constitution should continue as it is.

In addition to the views indicated above, we discuss in this section whether or not the scope in acts of matters of state as currently set forth is appropriate, whether the phrase "acts in matters of state," is appropriate, and the issue of whether the emperor should also be granted a coordinating function in respect to [the branches of] government.

The view that the scope of acts in matters of state as determined in the present Constitution is not appropriate and accordingly should be changed.

Most of those who supported this view demanded only that the emperor be provided with functions which are recognized as being usual for rulers in constitutional monarchies. They did not recognize substantial functions for the emperor, but only formal ones, thus supporting the principles of the present Constitution, but they were strong in their demand that such functions be provided. Their position was generally that such functions be within the framework of both international and domestic law.

In respect to his functions under international law, it was argued that under the present Constitution it is unclear as to whether the emperor does represent the nation internationally and that his functions in this area should include the issuance in his name of such documents as the ratification of treaties, the credentials of ambassadors and the commission of full powers, and the signing of such documents.

In relation to his functions under domestic law, it was argued that both amnesty and the bestowal of honors should be direct functions of the emperor himself without the provision of attestation in regard to amnesty as in the present Constitution. As a matter of fact, the frequently held view was that in both international relations and matters of domestic law the system of attestation in the present Constitution should be abolished. Also in domestic matters the opinion was expressed that the functions of the emperor should include additional ones such as the promulgation of the budget, the exercise of the right of self-defense, and the proclamation of states of emergency.

Only Commissioners Ushioda and Nakasone argued that the emperor's functions in matters of domestic law should be reduced. Ushioda believed that the following should be eliminated from the constitutional functions of the emperor: the appointment of the prime minister and the chief justice of the Supreme Court, the attestation of the appointment of ministers of state and other public officials, the convocation of the Diet, and the dissolution of the House of Representatives. He argued that the ruler's right to appoint was simply a relic of the European struggle for power between monarch and people, that attestation of appointments simply adds dignity to the officeholders so attested, and that to give purely formal recognition to the functions of the emperor in matters of state would be harmful to his political neutrality.

Nakasone declared that the emperor should possess the power of appointment of a prime minister elected by the people, but beyond that he urged that he should be freed of functions involving power and from involvement in difficult procedural issues related to the interaction among the organs of state. He also felt it would be desirable to enable the emperor to take positive action in such fields as the support of peace, the promotion and protection of the arts and learning, and the development of international good will.

Others argued that such phrases as "acts relating to matters of state" or "acts in matters of state" should be changed. The reason offered was that there is no need for such phrases in order to distinguish them from "functions relating to governmental administration." Moreover, the phrases are superfluous because even without them it is possible to discern those matters stipulated in the Constitution to which the acts of the emperor are limited. It was also pointed out that it is both contradictory and illogical to say that the emperor does not have powers in matters of state when such matters as the appointment of the prime minister and the dissolution of the House of Representatives are by their nature important political matters.

Only Commissioners Ōishi and Miura argued that the emperor should be given a coordinative function, that is to say, the capacity to take action to control situations in which unusual political confusion develops which cannot be settled by either the Diet or the cabinet. Ōishi's argument on this point was as follows:

> Under the present Constitution, the emperor's functions are limited to those matters set forth in Articles 6 and 7, and as a result he is unable to play his role in the unity of the people. Consequently, in addition to making it clear in the text of the Constitution that the emperor has legal authority as the center of the unity of the people, the following should be added to his functions: "the execution of acts appropriate to his position in the unity of the people." By this means it would not only be made clear that the emperor can proffer questions and recommendations to the cabinet and hear reports from it, but also there would be a constitutional basis for such matters, now in dispute, as the

presentation of imperial rescripts on the occasion of the convocation of the Diet and the review of the Self-Defense Forces. In addition, it would also make possible control of the situation through the issuing of imperial rescripts on occasions of unusual national or political confusion. Such functions would be above political faction and would be carried out exclusively by the emperor who has at heart only the stability of the nation and its people.

The view that the scope of affairs in matters of state as functions of the emperor is appropriate, and accordingly should not be changed.

This view was closely related to the one that held that his position as symbol should not be changed. In other words, if his symbolic position is not changed, then there is no reason to change his functions as stated in the Constitution. Commissioner Hosokawa stated the problem thus: "The legal position of the emperor as symbol has presented absolutely no difficulty. The opinion that holds that this position should be changed would also bestow on the emperor functions relating to the administration of government, but this would be dangerous. The present system which gives the emperor a symbolic position and functions appropriate to such a position is in itself the most suitable for the maintenance of the emperor system."

As has already been pointed out, holders of this view maintain that there is no need to provide a function which would make clear that the emperor is the representative of the state in international relations. Similarly they were opposed to providing the emperor with an adjudicative or coordinating function, pointing out that he might no longer be the object of respect and affection by the people which would lead to the destruction of the foundation of the emperor system. It was also argued that such a position would be incompatible with popular sovereignty.

Commissioner Rōyama opposed an adjudicative function for the emperor:

> There is no arrangement in the present Constitution for resolving a deadlock arising from a conflict among the various organs of state. However, if such a conflict should arise, the organs of state themselves should resolve the problem by resorting to such methods as dissolution of the Diet, a general election, or, perhaps, a national referendum. In addition, under the Constitution these organs of state bear a collective responsibility to work out a solution; it should not be done by the emperor. To grant the emperor authority such as the power of adjudication flowing from the possession of sovereignty would be incompatible with popular sovereignty.

Succession to the Throne

Only a small number of commissioners expressed views on the problem of succession to the throne which was dealt with primarily under the headings of a system of empresses and abdication. However, there were conflicting views on these issues.

The view that a system of empresses and abdication should be established, and accordingly revision is necessary.
Those supporting a system of empresses put forth the following as reasons:
1. In view of the fact that there is precedent for empresses in Japanese history and in foreign countries there is no reason why empresses should not be recognized.
2. It is not impossible that the unusual situation would arise in which there would be no male qualified to succeed to the throne.
3. Empresses should be recognized because of the principle of the equality of the sexes.
4. Because the authority of the emperor is limited to formalistic and ritualistic acts, it cannot be said that a woman cannot be qualified to become emperor. In addition, the Imperial House Law provides that a woman can become regent.

In addition, it was argued that because matters relating to qualifications for succession to the throne are of grave importance the system of empresses should be provided for in the Constitution, not left simply to a possible provision in the Imperial House Law.

Those supporting constitutional recognition of abdication put forth the following arguments:
1. Precedents for abdication exist in Japanese history and abdication is recognized in many foreign countries.
2. In the event that an emperor wishes to abdicate, his decision should, of course, be carefully reviewed, but in accordance with the spirit of respect for fundamental human rights, his will should be respected.
3. It is natural that the emperor be without responsibility in the legal sense, but he cannot evade either moral or political responsibility and it is not impossible that a situation would arise in which it would be necessary that the true relations between him and his subjects must be made clear and the responsibility assumed.

The view was also expressed that at a minimum abdication should be recognized in the Imperial House Law, but that abdication at the discretion of the emperor should not be recognized. It should be limited to such very grave situations as incurable illness, either physical or mental. Commissioner Ōnishi argued that to recognize abdication at the free will of the emperor in order to make clear a moral or political responsibility would violate the principle of a hereditary monarchy.

Commissioner Ōishi argued that abdication must be provided for constitutionally (not simply in the Imperial House Law) because the Constitution currently provides for a regency in the event that the emperor is incapacitated and that this can be interpreted to mean that abdication is not recognized.

The view that there is no need to deal constitutionally with empresses and abdication.

Those against a constitutional system of empresses argued that such a system could be established under Imperial House Law and that now is not the time to set up such a system. Similar arguments were advanced against a constitutional provision relating to abdication.

The Finances of the Imperial Household

Only a very small number of commissioners were concerned with the finances of the imperial household as expressed in Articles 8 and 88 of the Constitution. The commissioners who held that Articles 8 and 88 are not suitable and should therefore be revised argued that they simply reflect the view of the occupation that the former imperial household was similar to the *zaibatsu* in its financial role and that the section of Article 88 to the effect that imperial household property belongs to the state is clearly excessive and interim and should be regarded as already having served its purpose. In addition, it was stated that the second paragraph in Article 88 to the effect that the expenses of the imperial household should be appropriated by the Diet in the budget should be eliminated as superfluous because in its absence the appropriation for such expenses would be covered by the general provisions relating to the approval of the budget.

Those against revision of Articles 8 and 88 simply stated that they should be retained as is because even though Article 8 is not altogether commonsensical it has been applied intelligently through the Imperial Household Finances Law and because it is very clear indeed that the section relating to imperial household property in Article 88 was a transitional provision.

General Summary

The various views relating to the chapter on the emperor can be summarized, in general, as follows.

Almost all commissioners held that the emperor system and popular sovereignty are in harmony and that, accordingly, the ideal form of the emperor system as set forth in the present Constitution should be supported. The view that the emperor system should be abolished was absolutely nonexistent.

In spite of the support of the emperor system in the present Constitution there was a variety of views relating to the position and functions of the emperor as a symbol. On this issue there were two opposing fundamental positions. The first was that in addition to changing the term "symbol" the emperor should be given a clear position as head of state and provided with functions appropriate to that new position. The second, in contrast, was that the emperor's position as a symbol and his functions in matters of state which are in accord with his symbolic position should be maintained as they are now.

On the issue of whether the emperor should be a symbol or the head of state, a number of views were expressed in the commission. These can be summarized as follows:

1. The view that the emperor as "the legal authority of the unity of the people" should not be limited as to function; that his governing or controlling function in states of emergency should be recognized; and that, in addition, the phrase "popular sovereignty" should be stricken from the Constitution was held by only an extremely small minority of the commissioners.

2. The view that the position of the emperor should be clarified by the use of a phrase such as "head of state" or "primacy in the state" and, in addition, his functions should be enlarged and rounded out, both domestically and internationally, to conform with the normal scope of those of constitutional monarchs was also the view of an extremely small minority.

3. The view that the position of the emperor as symbol should be retained unchanged, avoiding phrases such as "head of state" or "primacy in the state," but in order to clarify the point that in his functions the emperor is in truth the head of state, those functions should be broadened to the scope of those normally enjoyed by constitutional monarchs was the opinion of a fairly large number of commissioners.

4. The view, conforming largely to the third view above, but holding that the emperor is in a position generally representative of the nation in its external relations and accordingly only his functions relating to external relations should be altered was held by the largest number of commissioners.

5. The view that there is no need for such terms as "symbol" or "head of state" to show the emperor's position and that his functions should be reduced beyond what they are at present was also the view of only an extremely small minority.

6. The view that the emperor's position as a symbol and his functions should be retained just as they are was held by a fairly large number of commissioners.

SECTION C.
THE RENUNCIATION OF WAR

Concerning Article 9, on the renunciation of war, the central and fundamental problem was the kind of a system of self-defense Japan should have. The problems debated on this question were: (1) how should Article 9, particularly the second paragraph, be revised?; and (2) in the event that revision is regarded as necessary, what should be the basic direction and the concrete content of such revision? A large number of opinions were expressed on these questions, and many of them dealt with such issues as the current state and future trends of world politics and the present and future stages in the development of a structure of international peace.

To sum up, the debates relating to Article 9 were addressed to three problems: the ideal self-defense system for Japan; the evaluation of both the interpretation and application of Article 9; and the concrete content of revisions if revision is held to be necessary. Opinions were also expressed on the manner in which revision of Article 9 should be handled.

The Ideal System for Japan's Self-Defense

The view that the self-defense of Japan rests on the doctrine of national sovereignty, is based on the principle of independent defense which in turn is based on the right of self-defense, and, in conformity with the contemporary realities of international politics, must depend on the United Nations or another system of collective security, and accordingly it is necessary to revise Article 9.

In essence, this view held that Japan must contribute positively both to its own security and to world peace by participating in the United Nations and other systems of collective self-defense, and when Article 9 is observed from this standpoint it is contrary to an ideal system of self-defense and requires revision. Further, this view strongly asserted that Article 9 which establishes the principles of the renunciation of war and the nonmaintenance of war potential is the expression of the doctrine of reliance on other nations for defense, is out of accord with the current realities of international society and its politics, leans too far toward both conceptualism and idealism, and is, in fact, only a fantasy.

Those commissioners who held this view believed that the principle of independent self-defense based on the concept of national sovereignty and what was referred to as positive participation in the United Nations or another system of collective security are indissolubly tied together. Also they treated the right of self-defense and the principle of the independent defense of the sovereign nation as the premises for positive participation in systems of collective security. Following are two examples of this view.

Commissioner Kogure stated:

Article 9 is to be honored as an earnest prayer and as a matter of soul-searching by a peace-loving people. However, as an individual possesses the right of self-defense so does the country, as a sovereign nation, naturally possess the right of self-defense to protect its peace and independence against illegal infringement from abroad. The possession of the right of self-defense for that purpose predates the existence of the Constitution. For a sovereign nation to lose the right and the capacity for its self-defense is for it to lose its independence.

Commissioner Kamikawa stated:

The present structure of international peace is based on the idea that the security of a nation can be guaranteed only by means of a system of regional or worldwide collective security. But the necessary precondition at present is that each nation must possess its own system of security based on the inherent right of self-defense enjoyed by all nations. To attempt to achieve security through the renunciation of the will and the capacity for self-defense is out of the question. If a country's capacity for self-defense is not supported by the will and the cooperation of all the people, then truly it will be impossible to achieve power worthy of the name. If a people generally lacks the consciousness of the necessity and the mission of the nation's power of self-defense, then it cannot realize the true power of independent self-defense. Herein lies the reason why Article 9 must be revised.

The opinion of an extremely large number of commissioners who upheld the principle of independent self-defense was that the preamble and Article 9 take "the attitude of complete reliance on others" in respect to Japan's defense and that they are thus unrealistic. Commissioner Kimura's opinion is typical:

The preamble and Article 9 state that we should assume the attitude of complete reliance on others in matters of defense. This is utterly disgraceful. Viewing the realities of the current world situation, it is very clear that it is impossible to rely on the faith and justice of nations. Some argue that our country has taken the lead in disarmament and for that reason Article 9 should not be revised, but this argument represents an idealism that completely disregards the realities of international politics. In essence, the revision of Article 9 is a necessary reflection of reality, and we must clearly specify the maintenance of a defense army.

All the commissioners who were in favor of the revision of Article 9 held that it is necessary so that Japan's defense can be carried out by positive participation in the United Nations or a similar organization so that the country not only can contribute to the maintenance of its own peace and security but also to the establishment of world peace. It was also argued that since a cornerstone of Japan's foreign policy is cooperation with the United Nations then it is natural that positive participation in all United Nations activities toward the maintenance of world peace is necessary.

Commissioner Hirose stated this position well:

> The pacifism in the present Constitution is an unusually high ideal, but it is overly idealistic and not in accord with political realities. Japan's pacifism lies in defending itself and at the same time cherishing world peace or, in other words, defending pacifism simultaneously from the standpoint of our own independence and of international cooperation. Moreover, this is in agreement with the present state of the world.
>
> Thus, this pacifism viewed from the standpoint of international cooperation means complete cooperation for the strengthening of the international structure of peace, that is, the substantial strengthening of the United Nations today. Because if world peace cannot truly be maintained by the United Nations, it cannot be realized. Japan under the concept of international security must advance toward positive cooperation with the United Nations, even if it might mean agreeing to limitations on sovereignty provided it is done on a footing of equality with other nations. Also Japan must cooperate positively in the establishment of an international peace army which will be the ultimate stage of arms reduction. However, the existence of Article 9 renders impossible such activity on the part of our country. Accordingly, I believe that the revision of Article 9 is natural from the standpoint of international solidarity.

Commissioner Kamikawa presented an even broader view of the relationship between Article 9 and the development of a peaceful international situation:

> If today is the age of the cold war, the guarantee of national security becomes extremely difficult. The primary special characteristic of this age is that the peace of any one country has become inseparable from world peace. As a result, the dominant idea is that apart from regional systems of collective security, it is impossible to guarantee the security of a single nation. Thus, this system is a transitional one, leading to the completion of a universal system of collective security. At this stage the necessary precondition is that each nation must have its own system of security based on the inherent right of self-defense.
>
> The United Nations is based on the above idea; accordingly, if we argue that the United Nations is a core of our foreign policy, then we must assume the responsibility of cooperating in the collective arrangements made by the United Nations.
>
> Also arms are the means for waging all international conflicts. Consequently, it is meaningless to say that arms will disappear while there are still international conflicts. Thus, a complete reduction of arms cannot be realized until the present United Nations develops into a federation which possesses

the power of compulsory jurisdiction over armed conflicts, but that is still in the distant future.

In essence, the stage of development of international society and international law lags behind the development of domestic order and domestic law in civilized countries and the realization of a universal system of security still lies in the future. Until that realization, we must rely on emergent regional systems of collective security and we are still at the point where the complete abolition of arms is impossible. If the present Article 9 is simply an ideal and if it represents an unrealizable policy, then as a constitutional provision it is meaningless.

In a number of cases those of this opinion also held that the ideals of the establishment of a world federation or a world state and the achievement of complete disarmament will be attained, but at the present stage where those ideals are still unrealized, it is necessary to revise Article 9. For example, Commissioners Takada and Kamikawa expressed the opinion that it can be shown that there will be no change in the spirit of pacifism if there is a clear statement of the above ideals in a revised Article 9.

In response to the contention that the maintenance of a self-defense army is meaningless in the present age of nuclear warfare, Commissioners Ōishi, Kimura, and Uemura argued that the possession of a self-defense army is an absolute necessity in order to provide against local or limited wars and internal insurrection and disturbances.

The view that Article 9 should not be regarded as being opposed to the concept of the sovereign nation or not in accord with the realities of contemporary international politics and that there is no need to revise it since its ideals should be supported and regarded as in accord with reality.

This view is not opposed to the revisionist view which supports the principle of independent defense and the necessity for participation in the United Nations or a similar system of collective security, but it does place high value on the significance of the preamble and Article 9 and holds that the ideal of pacifism which is proclaimed therein must be supported to the end. This view asserts that a revision of Article 9 should not discard the ideals therein and that a Japanese system of self-defense should be formed which would support the ideals of Article 9 and would seek out a policy in conformity with the realities of international politics. This view argues that the emphasis should be placed on the present trend toward a world peace structure, not on the principle of the sovereign nation from which flow the right of self-defense and the necessity for a self-defense army. Therefore, it rejects the revision of the principles of Article 9 based on the concept of the sovereign nation.

Commissioner Mano argued the point as follows:

264   PART FOUR. THE OPINIONS OF THE COMMISSIONERS

I think that today the time has come when the past theory of the sovereign nation and the thinking embodied in the balance of power which is based on that theory must both be altered because of progressive developments in the world situation. I have no objection to the fact that a sovereign nation possesses the right of self-defense, but to argue that it is natural to possess a self-defense army because one possesses the right of self-defense is a long leap in logic. The reason is that it is impossible to differentiate between self-defense and offensive action. Today under the name of self-defense to adopt the thinking that every other country is an enemy in disguise and to act on that assumption by providing for defense could bring about the destruction of the entire human race.

Article 9 may be idealistic, but in the age of nuclear warfare the traditional balance of power cannot be a means of solving the problem of preserving world peace. Today the state of the world, no matter how many ups and downs there may be, is advancing toward a worldwide system of common guarantees and in this system Article 9 should not be revised on the basis of the traditional system of the sovereign nation.

Commissioner Takayanagi's view was roughly parallel:

At the present stage of international organization it is only to be expected that every country cannot renounce the essential right of self-defense and it can be said that therein lies the limitation of international law. However, for one example, to say that the testing of nuclear weapons is a defense measure based on the right of self-defense is not to protect the security and welfare of humanity. Nevertheless, in the future the thought that all countries must go toward the renunciation of war is required and Article 9 points the way in that direction. From the point of view of the thinking which serves as the basis for current international law, Article 9 does have a utopian aspect, but it also includes a warning not only to Japan but to all the world that if the renunciation of war is not made universal the human race will be destroyed.

From the standpoint of current international law it may be correct that the right of self-defense exists regardless of the written text of the Constitution, but I think that we should not disregard the idealistic aspect of Article 9.

Other commissioners expressed the view that the movement in the direction of complete general disarmament has begun and that therefore any revision of Article 9 should be approached with extreme care. Commissioner Rōyama strongly advocated this view:

Today we must seek standards of judgment in respect to whether Article 9 should be revised in view of the real state of world affairs and Japan's expectations in following the international road as a part of that situation. At this point it is necessary first of all to examine the problem of complete disarmament. The reason is that Article 9 is a unilateral declaration of complete disarmament by Japan standing in the vanguard of all the nations of the world. Thus, the fate of Article 9 has a very important relationship to the development of disarmament throughout the world. . . .

Today, at long last, it is clear that the track toward disarmament is being tentatively laid out. It can now be said that the significance of the renunciation of war contained in Article 9 has reached the point where it is being recognized worldwide for considerations both military and strategic. In this situation we must give very careful consideration to any revision which might contain the danger of undermining that very great significance.

He concluded his argument by pointing out that Article 9 opens the road leading to both the guarantee of Japan's security and the achievement of world peace.

Evaluations of the Interpretation and Application of Article 9

The view that there are doubts about the interpretation of Article 9, particularly on whether it recognizes the existence of the Self-Defense Forces, the possession of the right of self-defense, and collective security arrangements; that this situation has created certain problems and abuses; and that, accordingly, it is necessary to revise Article 9.

Almost all commissioners of this view held that it is possible to interpret Article 9 to render constitutional the existence of the right of self-defense, the maintenance of the Self-Defense Forces and participation in collective security arrangements. For example, the Diet enacted the Self-Defense Forces Law; the cabinet has carried it out; and the Supreme Court in its *Sunakawa* decision has held the Japanese–American security treaty to be constitutional. Thus, the legislative, executive, and judicial branches have all followed the interpretation that Article 9 does not bar measures related to self-defense. However, because the provisions of Article 9 are not completely clear and because of the ideal of pacifism in the preamble, disputes over interpretation and related political disputes have arisen, thus leading to certain problems and abuses in the application of Article 9 and these in turn have created obstructions to the realization of the ideal defense system for Japan. Therefore, the holders of this view argue that revision of Article 9 is necessary.

Two commissioners held the view that Article 9 prohibits the maintenance of any power of self-defense of any kind whatsoever. Hence, the Self-Defense Forces are unconstitutional and therefore Article 9 should be revised. On this view Commissioner Kamikawa said:

Considering Article 9, particularly its second paragraph, it is clear that basically it represents the application of the American policy of complete disarmament for Japan. In order to camouflage that policy flowery language was used to decorate the preamble and Article 9. Consequently, the interpretation that it is possible to possess military potential for self-defense under Article 9 as it stands is both a distortion of Article 9 itself and an evasion of its legal meaning. Of course, the interpretations adopted by the National Diet and the government are unwarrantable and the Supreme Court's interpretation in the *Sunakawa* decision is both murky and evasive of the issue. As long as Article 9 stands as it is, this kind of interpretation is inevitable. Consequently, if a self-defense army is ever to be possible under the Constitution, the natural conclusion is that Article 9 must somehow be revised. To say that Article 9 does not require revision is simply a distortion of that article.

Commissioner Yagi put the case in slightly stronger language:

There is the opinion that because the Self-Defense Forces have been recognized as constitutional by the cabinet, the Diet, and the Supreme Court there is no particular need to revise Article 9. But it cannot be stated that the SDF are constitutional. The Supreme Court did not positively affirm the constitutionality of the SDF. The government and the Diet enacted the SDF Law simply on the basis of a political judgment. . . . Thus, there is nothing to be said except that the SDF are clearly unconstitutional in the light of the second paragraph of Article 9. The so-called defenders of the Constitution say that since the SDF are unconstitutional they should either be abolished or reduced. My opinion is similar as to reasons. However, I say that since the SDF are unconstitutional, Article 9 should be revised or, more precisely, abolished.

In addition to the theoretical disputes surrounding Article 9, some concrete obstacles arising from it to the complete and realistic development of an ideal system of self-defense were also mentioned. The three principal problems raised were: (1) the destructive impact of the argument that the SDF are unconstitutional on the morale of SDF members; (2) the fact that the assertion that Article 9 establishes disarmament creates dissension in public opinion, which can be used for political ends, can lead to confusion in foreign policy, and create political instability; and (3) the lack of confidence created among the people by the above phenomena toward the Constitution, the Diet, the government, and the Supreme Court.

Commissioner Kimura attributed the failure of the SDF to recruit up to the authorized limit and the difficulty of attracting superior recruits to the argument that the SDF are unconstitutional.

The view that even though there are various problems relating to the interpretation and application of Article 9, a self-defense system has been adopted for the moment, and even if Article 9 should be revised the expectation would be not a solution of the problem but the creation of many new ones, accordingly Article 9 should not be revised.

Those adhering to this view held that the enactment and enforcement of the SDF Law, the conclusion of the Japanese-American security treaty, and the Supreme Court decision in the *Sunakawa* case have all indicated that the problem of Japan's defense has been well handled under Article 9 as it exists. They also maintain that the problem of the ideal system of self-defense for Japan has been dealt with while the ideals of Article 9 have been maintained. Consequently, they fear that any revision of Article 9 to accommodate the requirements of defense might lead to a loss of the ideals therein.

Commissioner Masaki expressed the following opinion on the issue of the establishment of a self-defense system under Article 9:

> When the existence of our country is at stake no one would stand idly by. As criminal law recognizes that the individual possesses the right of appropriate self-defense, so it is a principle of international law that the nation possesses the same right. Article 9 is generally regarded as having been based on that same reasonable premise. That Japan's current system of self-defense has developed to its present stage is the result of the people's having accepted the above interpretation of Article 9. Consequently, there is no necessity to attempt to make Article 9 clearer. In addition, if revision is attempted, it is likely to arouse opposition and that, I think, would have the opposite effect of obstructing the development of constitutional consciousness among the people. Rather than to revise the second paragraph of Article 9 it is far more urgent, while maintaining the present situation well into the future, to promote education which will lead the people to embrace the beliefs appropriate to themselves and their love of country.

The following three opinions set forth the difficulties, even dangers, that might be created by an attempt to revise Article 9.

Commissioner Rōyama:

> Even though the right of self-defense, the maintenance of self-defense potential and participation in systems of collective security are recognized at the moment under Article 9, the arrangement is still only tentative. In addition, there are many related points, such as the limits on the power of self-defense and the form of participation in collective self-defense systems, which are still under dispute.
>
> In a state of such confusion it might at first glance appear to be valid to cut the ground from under such disputes through the elimination or modification of Article 9, especially its second paragraph. But that would be an extremely dangerous undertaking because, if strict limits are not maintained on the power of the self-defense army and on the methods by which it can be exercised, there is the danger that the peaceful ideals of the present Constitution might be renounced. In addition, once the provisions relating to the prohibition of armaments are stricken, there is no guarantee that, through some subsequent development in the international situation, we shall not see a revival of militaristic control. This is a danger in our country in which the establishment of democracy is not yet complete. Such a move would also be against the wishes of the people. Hence, I cannot agree to the revision of Article 9.

Commissioner Yabe:

There is the opinion that because the argument of the unconstitutionality of the SDF is still supported and public opinion is divided, we must seek unity of opinion through constitutional revision. But the division that would probably be produced by an attempt to revise Article 9 would be far more deadly. I think that rather than to attempt anything that would invite such a deadly division, the best policy would be to count on the good sense of the people, striving for the easing of the current division by having the past interpretations of the National Diet, the government, and the Supreme Court gradually be accepted as established theory.

Commissioner Ushioda set forth the following points as reasons for his hesitation to support a revision of Article 9:

1. Because of the difficulty of limiting war potential, once the right of self-defense is constitutionally provided for, will it not be difficult to prevent its expansion?

2. It might be considered that Article 9 would play a restraining role in respect to the oppressive effect that an unlimited increase in armaments, once war potential is permitted, would have on the lives of the people. This benefit would have a greater value than the possible elimination of the shortcomings of Article 9.

3. Would not the initiation of rearmament invite extreme international distrust of Japan, particularly in the countries of Southeast Asia?

4. It is argued that the unconstitutionality of the SDF is destructive of the morale of those forces and has reduced the number of volunteers, but these are not the direct result of the unconstitutionality argument. These difficulties will not be remedied by revisions of Article 9, but by the improvement of the people's attitude toward the SDF.

The opinion was also expressed that the present circumstances surrounding the interpretation of Article 9 constitute a good example of the necessity for elasticity in the interpretation and application of constitutions. The positions of the National Diet, the cabinet, and the Supreme Court were pointed out as being characteristic of elastic interpretation.

Commissioner Takayanagi advanced the argument that Article 9 is in essence a political declaration and therefore should be subjected to sociological, not theoretical and textual, interpretation:

Past constitutional disputes surrounding the SDF have been carried out following the methodology of textual and theoretical interpretation. However, considering it from a purely academic point of view, Article 9 must be interpreted to be a political declaration.

That is to say, in respect to constitutions, rather than textual interpretation, sociological interpretation occupies the supreme position. The realities of contemporary international society, as social facts related to Article 9, cannot be ignored. Therefore, the interpretation that Article 9 can be regarded as stipulating unilateral complete disarmament appears to be correct as a textual interpretation, but it stands in contradiction to the good sense of international politics. However, on the other hand, in an age of nuclear weapons the correct ideal is for every country in the world to adopt the attitude of the second paragraph of Article 9 and to rely on a world peace organization for its security. Article 9 must be thought of as a constitutional norm which sets forth an ideal which, as indicated above, cannot immediately be realized; in this sense it is a political declaration.

Under this interpretation of Article 9 as a political declaration, regardless of the wording of the second paragraph, the right of self-defense is completely reserved and also the maintenance of a self-defense army is possible. Consequently, the problem of defense is not a question of constitutional interpretation and must be discussed as a problem of policy. Thus, in the age of nuclear weapons Article 9 is unparalleled as a manifestation of a world ideal and to revise it to justify the possession of a self-defense army would hazard the loss of its idealistic aspect.

From the above point of view, the revision of Article 9 in view of present conditions would not only be unnecessary but could also be considered to be an unwise political move. As long as the Supreme Court does not hand down a decision of unconstitutionality, no matter what the split in academic opinion might be, there is, in actual fact, no need to revise Article 9. Also, if at present such revision is undertaken, domestic confrontation will be intensified. Even if we suppose that revision does come about, would not the actual effect be nothing more than a simple written affirmation of the present situation? But it would be more likely to have undesirable repercussions both domestically and internationally. What is necessary today in respect to the realization of the ideals of Article 9 is that the people examine concrete ideas, not concepts. Thus, in this way the correct interpretations of Article 9 will be spontaneously determined.

Concrete Proposals for Revision

Some revisionist commissioners submitted detailed proposals in the form of drafts for revision. The matters presented in these proposals included: provisions relating to the principle of defense, a clause on international peace, the establishment of a self-defense army, its organization and activities, democratic control over it, and the duty of defending the nation.

With respect to the principle of defense and to a clause on international peace, additional provisions were presented relating to the principle of pacifism, the prohibition of aggressive war, the peaceful resolution of international disputes, international cooperation, participation in organizations for international peace, and limitations on sovereignty. Some urged that such provisions be placed in the preamble or in a section entitled "General Provisions."

In regard to the existence of the right of self-defense and the maintenance of a self-defense army, most opinions related to the army and there was virtually no demand that the right of self-defense be recognized directly in a written provision. As to the maintenance of a defense army, there were a number of opinions that there should be stipulations relating to such matters as that the mission of such an army be defense against aggression in order to protect the independence and security of the nation and the welfare of the people. Commissioners Takada and Kamikawa urged that the self-defense army should be maintained only "until the realization of the general and complete abolition of arms" or "during a transition period until war is eliminated throughout the world."

On the organization and control of the self-defense army, the following stipulations were urged: the assignment of the power of supreme command to the cabinet; the establishment by law of the organization and strength of the army; the participation of the National Diet in the mobilization of the army and important personnel matters relating to it; and the placing of the army under strict civilian control. Commissioner Uetake proposed that as a part of civilian control it would be necessary to establish a National Security Council as a constitutional body, an important reason for this step being the prevention of the conversion of the army into a private army of a political party.

With respect to the duty of the people to defend the country, it was the opinion of many that this should be stipulated in law as necessity might require, not set forth in the Constitution in the form of a duty to perform military service or of a conscription system.

The Problem of the Revision of Article 9

On the handling of the problem of the revision of Article 9, or more precisely, how the problem could be handled without revision, two proposals were set forth: to refer the matter of the interpretation of Article 9 to a national referendum; and to establish a special organ in the Diet for careful deliberation of all problems of defense, including Article 9. However, almost all commissioners opposed these proposals.

Commissioner Hosokawa believed that the resolution of the dispute over the interpretation of Article 9 should not be handled by constitutional amendment, because public opinion would be influenced by the manner in which a draft revision would be presented. He recommended that a law be passed permitting a national referendum in which the people would be called to choose between a Liberal Democratic Party interpretation and a Japan Socialist Party interpretation.

Commissioner Nakasone also called for a national referendum on whether the following four items might be permissible under Article 9: the mobilization of the SDF, the dispatch of troops overseas, a conscription system, and nuclear equipment. Such a referendum, he thought, would avoid the increase in political friction that a revision of Article 9 would cause.

Opponents of the national referendum claimed that it would be unconstitutional because it would bypass the amendment procedure; that it would also create difficulties; that Article 9 should not be separated from other issues requiring revision; that the proposal revealed a lack of confidence in parliamentary government; and that it would not really solve the conflict between the wording of the Constitution and its interpretation.

Commissioner Rōyama called for the creation of a joint committee in the Diet with fourteen members from the House of Representatives and ten from the House of Councilors, supported by a substantial staff of specialists, which would deliberate on important matters relating to the country's defense system. It would be the central policy-making body on defense matters and would assume responsibility therefor. This device, he hoped, would eventually end the split in public opinion on defense matters, something which he feared could not be done by constitutional revision. He was supported by Commissioner Takayanagi, who felt that the proposal was headed in the right direction.

However, the proposal for such a committee was attacked as being "extremely naive and overly simplistic," as avoiding the highly important issue of the revision of the nation's fundamental law, and as being unconstitutional in the absence of a constitutional base.

General Summary

The general tendency of the various views on Article 9 can be summarized as follows.

It was the unanimous view of the commissioners that the ideal of pacifism as set forth in the present Constitution should be supported as a matter of course. Also on the ideal system of defense for Japan, there was no difference in views over the fact that Japan should contribute not only to its own defense but also to world peace by participating both in the United Nations and in other systems of collective security while preparing its own defense based on the ideal of pacifism.

Under Article 9 as it stands, the system of defense, including the SDF, entry into the United Nations, and the security treaty with the United States, is both acceptable and not unconstitutional. Almost all commissioners were in agreement on this matter also. Commissioners who shared this view and who believed the SDF to be unconstitutional did not demand their abolition, but asserted that they should be made constitutional through the revision of Article 9. Thus, on the point of the acceptability of the existing defense system, all of the commissioners were in agreement and there was no demand that it should be opposed or denied because of unconstitutionality.

Views on the above points were in agreement, but were split on the issue of the revision of Article 9. Commissioners supporting its revision were in the majority. The opposition of views on revision was based on conflicting opinions relating to the following points:

1. Even though pacifism as an ideal is correct, at the present stage of development of international politics and the structure of international peace, must it be regarded as ideological, idealistic, and unrealistic? The revisionists answered in the affirmative. The antirevisionists held that in view of the currently developing movement toward complete disarmament the principle of the nonmaintenance of war potential in Article 9 has now been given a new and realistic meaning.

2. How should the concepts of the sovereign nation and of the right of self-defense be regarded? The revisionists placed a high value on these concepts and asserted that Japan's defense system today is ultimately based on them. The antirevisionists held that they are today in the process of change and asserted that for one country to use them as reasons for its defense would be harmful to the achievement of peace.

3. How should we regard the fact that Article 9 may present obstacles to Japan's defense system? The revisionist view held that there were doubtful points in the interpretation of Article 9 and that these had created various problems and abuses regarding the defense system. The antirevisionists replied, in opposition, that a defense system has already been created and that Article 9 had presented no real obstacle.

4. What would the effects of a revision of Article 9 be? The revisionists argued that the revision of Article 9 would provide the possibility for a unification of public opinion behind both a defense system and defense itself. In opposition, the antirevisionists held that defense problems would not be solved by a revision of Article 9 and that consideration should be given to the undesirable effects, both domestic and foreign, that would accompany it.

SECTION D.
THE RIGHTS AND DUTIES OF THE PEOPLE

Concerning Chapter 3 of the Constitution, "The Rights and Duties of the People," the fundamental questions deliberated by the commission were: In the provisions relating to rights and duties should anything new be added or should anything be eliminated? and Is there any need to establish clear stipulations respecting limitations on fundamental human rights? Of course, opinion varied widely on these questions.

A fundamental point of discussion which underlay both questions was the ideal form of human rights today. Another primary focus of discussion was whether problems relating to fundamental human rights should be solved by revision or by flexible interpretation and application of the Constitution. The major topics of discussion included the doctrine of the public welfare, the nature of the duties of the people, and human rights before the law. Lesser topics included: the freedom of religion, the basic principles of education, the family and the home, and the rights of labor.

The presentation of the opposing views on the problem of fundamental human rights will proceed from a discussion of the fundamental points mentioned above to an examination of the views on specific topics.

The Ideal Form of Contemporary Human Rights

The view that the present is not the age of the liberal state which overemphasizes respect for individual rights and freedoms, but the age of the welfare state which has as its aim the well being of the entire people, and accordingly Chapter 3 needs to be revised to conform to the contemporary age.

This view was held by the majority of the commissioners who were of the opinion that the rights, freedoms and duties prescribed in Chapter 3 require revision and that limitations on rights and freedoms should be made clear therein. It was also held that Chapter 3 places too much emphasis on respect for individual rights and freedoms and makes light of duties. Likewise, proponents of this view held that Chapter 3 views the state and the individual as antagonists, an attitude which reflects the thinking of the eighteenth- and nineteenth-century liberal state, but is out of step with the thinking of the twentieth-century welfare state.

The Joint Declaration, the voice of a majority of all commissioners, expressed this view as follows:

> Eighteenth-century-style democratic constitutions arose out of the struggle against the absolutist power and autocracy of the time and went toward minimizing state power and maximizing the rights and freedoms of the individual. This was only to be expected as a part of the process of the creation of democracy and of providing it with its essential content.
>
> However, today democratic thought and the place and role of constitutions based on it have had to change in accordance with changes in the form of what is regarded as a desirable human society. That is to say, the nation and state power itself have come to the point where they are structured democratically. State power in itself is not antagonistic to individual rights and freedoms, rather, it is in a position to become their most powerful guarantor. Con-

sequently, in contemporary democracy it must be considered that state power makes manifest to the maximum degree the rights and freedoms of the individual members of the nation. Accordingly, contemporary democratic constitutions in respect to the relationship between state power and the individual do not stop voluntarily at a negative, passive, and defensive position, but must direct themselves on a positive and cooperative course.

From the above perspective, it is clear that we shall be left behind in the rapid flux of contemporary society, if emphasis is not placed on the social duties of the people, their solidarity, and their cooperation, as well as on the guarantee of fundamental human rights. Rights and freedoms do not simply mean freedom from power as in past ages, but possess a positive significance in respect to power and its utilization and must be brought into being with the aim of constructing the welfare state through the maintenance of social order and the advancement of public welfare. This is the ideal form of freedom and human rights today and in the future and can be considered as the desirable form of the modernization of the social state, the welfare state of the new age.

Viewing Chapter 3 of the Constitution from this fundamental position, it must be said that its human rights provisions with the individual as the focus have an air of being far behind the times. Thus, we think that before dealing with the problems presented by each individual provision relating to human rights, it is necessary first of all to point out this fundamental issue.

The view that the significance of respect for fundamental human rights should not be lost even in contemporary constitutions, that there is nothing contradictory between the principles of the welfare state and of respect for the rights and freedoms of the individual, and that if the goal of the positive realization of individual rights and freedoms is maintained, there is no need to revise Chapter 3.

Essentially, this view is opposed to the first on the grounds that it is incorrect to hold that the liberal state has fallen behind the times either in general or in respect to Japan and that even under Chapter 3 as it stands the requirements of the contemporary welfare state can be met. Those holding this view were also opposed to adding new rights and duties or developing more fully the present ones or to setting forth clear limitations on rights and freedoms.

On this issue Commissioner Takayanagi presented the following opinion in defense of the position of the present Constitution on rights and freedoms:

> In the nineteenth century the extension of the freedoms and activities of the individual was a contribution to the welfare of all, and noninterference from the state was strongly asserted in constitutions, arising from the view that for the state arbitrarily to interfere with the individual did not contribute to the welfare of all. But at present, principally as a result of changes in the economic environment, it has come to pass that simple noninterference by the state will not substantially guarantee the human rights and freedoms of the individual; and, thus, it is emphasized that in certain areas the state has positive respon-

sibilities. This is also based on the universal concept of individualism that the state exists for the individual and not the individual for the state. This universal concept of individualism and its opposite, the theory of fascism or totalitarianism, are fundamentally different in nature.

The Constitution of Japan strongly states that the state has not only passive responsibilities, but positive responsibilities in certain necessary areas and in this point possesses a strong twentieth-century character.

The present Constitution, even though it may pose obstacles to the establishment of communism, poses almost none to the establishment of the welfare state as in America, Britain, and France. If statesmen have a strong desire to work for the establishment of such a state, it is possible through the enactment of ordinary laws and it is sufficient if there is a general [constitutional] provision to that effect. By contrast, no matter how detailed provisions appropriate for a welfare state are set forth in a constitution, if the statesmen are lacking in enthusiasm to realize such a state, the provisions will end as ideological dead letters.

Evaluations of the Application, Interpretation, and Processes of Chapter 3

The view that in the processes of Chapter 3 there are a number of inappropriate points and for that reason a number of obstructions and abuses have been produced and consequently revision is necessary.

This view holds that a number of imperfect points have surfaced in Chapter 3 because of the law-making technique involved in its drafting and that it is necessary to eliminate them so that there will be no room for the creation of problems in interpretation and application. As examples of deficiency in law-making technique, it was pointed out that there are a number of technical terms, such as "every person," "all the people," "have the right to . . . " and "the right to . . . is guaranteed," which are jumbled together and lack uniformity. In addition, there are duplications in provisions and the provisions relating to limitations on fundamental human rights by the public welfare are especially unclear. Also it was pointed out that in several places the provisions relating to the duties of the people and the responsibilities of the state are not worded clearly.

Also, it was frequently pointed out that only the demand for rights, such as freedoms of discussion and assembly and the rights of workers to organize and bargain collectively, is set forth, that the abuse of rights is flagrant, and that public morality and the social order are harmed as a result. These are problems of the processes of the Constitution, but they also raise questions about the manner in which the Constitution should be interpreted and applied.

Also with respect to law-making technique, the view was expressed that constitutional provisions should be concise, but that in Chapter 3 there are a number of overlapping provisions and that this should be remedied. Commissioner Inaba stated the following on this point: "In regard to the importance of the people's fundamental rights and their character which prevents their being taken away even by state power, Articles 11, 12, 13, and Article 97, where it deals with the supreme law, all state that fundamental rights cannot be taken away even by state power. . . . A constitution must to the greatest extent possible avoid this kind of duplication. It would be well to group all these together in a single article."

On the problem of conciseness, there were several demands that a number of provisions relating to detailed matters which should be entrusted to law might well be removed. The various provisions relating to criminal procedure were frequently singled out as examples of this problem.

The link between fundamental human rights and the public welfare was offered as another example of faulty law-making technique. The phrase, "the public welfare," it was said, is vague and its content unclear, a highly undesirable situation when it is recognized as a limitation on rights and freedoms. It was also pointed out that Articles 12 and 13 present the public welfare as a basic provision applying a general limitation on rights and freedoms, while Articles 22, 29, and others apply it to specific matters.

In the application of the provisions of Chapter 3 it was also maintained that there are striking evils, such as the emphasis solely on rights, the abuse of rights, and a disregard for law. Commissioner Hirose, for example, had the following to say:

> The excesses expressed in such phrases as "respect for human rights, contempt for duties," and "respect for the individual, contempt for the nation" give rise to evils which cannot be permitted to take their course. For example, under the name of freedom of expression, mass demonstrations such as those at the time of the riots over the security treaty [1960] are carried out and acts of violence are committed in the name of the fundamental rights of labor, as in the great strike at the Miike mine of the Mitsui Company. As a result, we have reached the point where the nation's power to maintain law and order is shaken and the legal order is being destroyed.

It was also maintained that because such a duty as that of observing the law is not clearly set forth in the Constitution, abuses such as the above are produced. The conclusion was that it is necessary to increase the provisions relating to duties.

The view that the processes of Chapter 3 are appropriate and the problems of interpretation and application are not matters that can be resolved simply by constitutional provisions and that consequently revision is unnecessary.

This view conforms with the thinking that finds fault with the law-making technique displayed in Chapter 3 and agrees with the view that importance should be placed on theoretical clarity and exactness. But it also holds that constitutional provisions preferably should be flexible and that the present Constitution is based on that idea. For this reason the Constitution can be made to conform to actual situations and requirements without the need for revision. Therefore, in this view there is no immediate necessity for constitutional revision because there are disputes over interpretation.

In view of the above, commissioners adhering to this position believed that efforts should be expended on flexible interpretation and application, particularly by means of court decisions, rather than on the enactment of strict new provisions. This view also held that social solidarity and the discharge of the social responsibilities of the individual can be realized through a proper interpretation of the public welfare. Consequently, it was held that the phrase "the public welfare" is constitutionally appropriate and that for the most part the courts have handed down appropriate interpretations of the term. Commissioners Mano and Takayanagi both addressed this problem.

Commissioner Mano stated: "That the Constitution should be interpreted by means of the concept of social solidarity is shown by the use of the phrase 'the public welfare.' In cases dealing with specific concrete problems involving the public welfare, the Supreme Court ultimately makes the decisions. In this sense the phrase is gradually made concrete on a case-by-case basis through the accumulation of precedent. . . . Accordingly, it is possible that, in general, it is sufficient to have only the limitation of 'the public welfare.'"

Commissioner Takayanagi stated: "To set down detailed constitutional provisions relating to limitations on fundamental human rights is to limit the scope of the exercise of free discretion through the deep wisdom of the Supreme Court and is simultaneously to render permanent through the Constitution the thinking of a certain specific generation. The essence of the Constitution of Japan is that it should be flexible, that it should not be frequently amended, and that limitations on fundamental human rights should be determined by the courts in accordance with changes in the times. This sort of legislative policy or process is appropriate and, in addition, Supreme Court decisions can be considered to be generally in accord with common sense." He also believed that a situation where the people clamor only for their rights and view lightly their duties and responsibilities is a serious one, but the solution must wait on "the improvement of constitutional education and the power of sound public opinion."

The Public Welfare as a Limitation on Fundamental Human Rights

The view that the provision relating to the public welfare as a limitation on fundamental human rights is inadequate and that it is necessary to change it to make clear both the basis and the boundaries of such limitation.

The view that the provisions of the present Constitution relating to restrictions on fundamental human rights are inadequate was based on the following two arguments.

First, these provisions place too much emphasis on respect for fundamental human rights and do not make clear that they must be subject to some restrictions both because of the need to realize the contemporary welfare state and because of individual responsibility to the society as a whole. It was further asserted, on the above basis, that it is necessary to prevent improperly broad interpretation and application of the ambiguous phrase, "the public welfare," by making clear both the limits of and the basis for restrictions on the rights and freedoms of the people while at the same time responding to the requirements of the contemporary welfare state by changing to a wording which will make concrete the content of the public welfare.

Second, there is the problem of law-making technique, already referred to. For example, the Constitution in Articles 12 and 13 sets forth the public welfare as a general limitation on fundamental human rights, but it also recognizes specific restrictions by the public welfare on the freedoms to choose an occupation and to change residence in Article 22 and on the right of property in Article 29 and this produces doubts in interpretation. In this situation it has been possible to argue that it is improper to impose any restriction whatsoever on those rights and freedoms which are not specifically limited by the public welfare. On this basis some commissioners argued that it is necessary not only to retain the provisions relating to general restrictions for the public welfare, but also to add provisions placing specific restrictions in the name of the public welfare on each right and freedom.

On the problem of general restriction the most frequent opinion was that wording much more concrete or positive than "the public welfare" should be used. Thus, in addition to suggesting such phrases as "public order," "public morality," "public security," or "fundamental democratic order," it was frequently asserted that it should be made clear that restrictions should be recognized where they are necessary in order to achieve the objectives of the welfare state.

Commissioner Kamikawa commented as follows on this issue:

> It can be considered that "the public welfare" implies such objectives as public order. But because it also has a far broader meaning it would be well to

set it forth in writing both carefully and concretely. Therefore, it should be stated that limitations on the exercise of human rights are permissible in the following situations: (1) when the fundamental rights of others may be disregarded or impaired; (2) when the public welfare itself might be harmed; (3) when the aim is to destroy the basic democratic order; (4) when it is recognized as necessary in order to attain the objectives of the welfare state; and (5) when it is necessary to guard against the perils of an emergency. Point (1) above is generally in accord with the present Article 15; (3) is designed to circumvent dictatorial political movements; and (4) applies to those situations where limitation on individual freedoms, especially the right of property, is inescapable in order to realize the social welfare state.

Commissioner Ōnishi's view was representative of those who urged that there should be both general and specific limitations on human rights. He stated: "It is necessary to make changes which will show both general limitations on human rights by the doctrine of the public welfare and specific ones on each human right. By this means it will be possible to prevent crimes and misdemeanors arising from the abuse of human rights. For example, freedom of assembly would be guaranteed to the extent that it would not impair public order, safety and peace, good morals, and public health. Similarly, the freedom to choose an occupation would be guaranteed to the extent that it would not impair respect for the individual, public interest or safety, good morals, and public health."

The opposing view was that it is unnecessary to enact specific restrictions on each type of right or freedom. Those of this view held that if general provisions are suitably provided then specific ones will not be needed. However, it was also argued from this point of view that any such restrictions should be concise and consequently the limitations stated in Articles 22 and 29 should be dropped.

The view that the provisions relating to the public welfare as a limitation on fundamental human rights are adequate and that therefore there is no need to change them.

Proponents of this view held that there would be no real gain if the constitutional limitations were made more specific, and that it would be more appropriate to have the concrete content of the public welfare be determined primarily by the accumulation of legal precedents.

Commissioner Yabe presented this view in the following statement:

Freedoms relating to the internal life of the individual such as the freedoms of thought and conscience cannot, I believe, be limited even in the name of the public welfare, but in respect to other kinds of rights and freedoms, limitation in the name of the public welfare is clearly necessary. However, even though an attempt is made to use slightly more concrete terms in the articles of the

Constitution, a certain degree of abstractness would still be inescapable and as a consequence there is no need to change the phrase "the public welfare." There is no way to make the concept more concrete except through laws. In cases where disputes arise in respect to such laws, the flexible approach is to entrust them to the courts. There is no way to eliminate the abuse of rights except to endeavor to raise the consciousness of citizens through the accumulation of case law.

Provisions on Duties

The view that the present Constitution overemphasizes rights and slights duties and consequently there must be more provisions relating to duties.

This view held that the position of Chapter 3 can be shown by the phrase "up with rights, down with duties." It sets forth only three duties—to pay taxes, to provide education, and to work—obviously making its treatment of duties both extremely incomplete and brief. Consequently, it is necessary to strengthen those public duties that are based on the principle of social solidarity. To do so will mean that this chapter will be brought into accord with the tendencies of the contemporary welfare state and that it will provide a legal basis for the demand for the fostering of the concept of the nation and of respect for the social order.

It was suggested that such new duties as the following might be inserted into the Constitution: to respect and observe the law (including the Constitution), to be loyal and faithful to the country, and to defend the homeland. The justification frequently put forward was that these duties are natural, but in the current situation the evil of contempt for them is striking. Among those advocating the duty to defend the nation, some felt that only that duty was constitutionally necessary and that the duty of military service, that is, a system of conscription, should be left to determination by law if the need arose.

The view that the present Constitution should not be regarded as overemphasizing rights and underemphasizing duties and that an increase in provisions relating to duties would harm the guarantee of human rights.

Commissioner Takayanagi was one of the strongest proponents of this view. His opinion was as follows:

It is argued that the present Constitution is out of balance because it emphasizes only the rights of the people and has only a few provisions on duties. However, the reason it does is that it places great emphasis on the spirit of the "rule of law" which is indeed its strong point. Provisions concerning fundamental human rights in all constitutions have as their principal aim the prevention of the abuse of political power by those in authority and not simply the establishment of norms for the protection of the general populace. This is the thought behind liberal democratic constitutions and ours shares it.

That to respect duly enacted laws as a duty of the people has no basis in the Constitution is appropriate; it exists prior to a constitution. Accordingly, an increase in the number of duties in the Constitution is not really required. In addition, the enumeration of a number of duties in a constitution will greatly dilute the force of the provisions relating to fundamental human rights and, even more, will weaken the principle of the rule of law which is a necessary condition for the success of liberal democracy.

Holders of this view were particularly critical of the proposal to include the duty of loyalty to the country. The reasons given included: that it might adversely affect the guarantee of human rights and weaken democracy, that it might be interpreted to include the duty of military service, and that the patriotism that such a provision is designed to foster can be strengthened only through education.

Human Rights before the Law

The view that the provisions relating to the guarantee of human rights before the law are too detailed, are ambiguous on a number of points, and therefore require revision to be put into good working order.

On this matter Commissioners Ōishi, Kojima, and Chiba maintained that what is necessary is that the constitutional guarantee should be limited to a general statement and the detailed provisions be entrusted to the Code of Criminal Procedure or other law.

A number of commissioners dealt with ambiguous issues relating to rights before the law. The issues are listed here without attribution:

1. "Procedure established by law" in Article 31 should be changed to "procedures of just and proper law" to make clear that both procedure and substantive conditions should be determined by law and not simply procedure in the narrow sense, as the present provision implies.

2. Article 33 should be revised to make possible emergency arrest as well as arrest while a crime is in progress.

3. "Judicial officer" in Articles 33 and 35 should be changed to "judge."

4. The latter part of Article 34 should be clarified so that it can become the basis of a habeas corpus law.

5. "Cruel punishment" in Article 36 should be changed to "punishment inflicting pain by inhumane methods." It was also suggested that provisions be enacted prohibiting excessive bail and the complete confiscation of property as methods of punishment.

6. "Testimony against himself" in Article 38 is unclear. Does the right of silence implied here include the right not to disclose even one's name and place of residence?

7. In respect to "his own confession" in Article 38 it should be made clear that this does not include confession made in open court so that such a confession might be the basis of a verdict of guilty even in the absence of corroborative evidence.

The view that the provisions relating to the guarantee of human rights before the law in the present Constitution are adequate and therefore require no revision.

The general case for this view was well presented by Commissioner Masaki: "Regarding the actual situation in which there was no adequate guarantee of human rights prior to the enactment of this Constitution, it is necessary to retain the present constitutional guarantees in order to protect those rights. In addition, if in the ten years and more since the enactment of the Constitution, the Japanese people had become adequately skilled in the application of the provisions guaranteeing these rights, then it might be acceptable to leave all these matters to the provisions of the Code of Criminal Procedure. If investigative officers have not yet acquired skill in handling this problem, then it is better to have provisions relating to it set forth clearly in the Constitution."

Commissioner Mano took the position that even though there may be a number of ambiguous points in these provisions, the accumulation of court precedents will take care of them in time and so there is no need for revision.

On the question of the abuse of the right of silence it was stated that this could be taken care of, not by constitutional revision, but by suitable revisions of the Code of Criminal Procedure. It was also held that it would be dangerous to make possible a verdict of guilty on the sole basis of confession in open court.

No one supported the complete abolition of capital punishment. Commissioner Ōnishi supported prohibition of the death penalty for women, minors, and those convicted of purely political offenses. Commissioner Sakanishi, a woman, opposed discrimination between the sexes on this issue. Commissioner Mano declared that the problem should not be dealt with in the Constitution, but by law in accordance with the spirit of the times. Commissioner Mizuno argued that it would be premature to abolish capital punishment "because our country has not yet seen the effective stabilization of order and our general level of culture has not yet attained a sufficiently high plane." Commissioner Masaki felt that the solution might lie in an improvement of the thinking of judges who might impose the death penalty. Commissioner

Kamikawa approached the problem from a different angle: "Because man is not by nature a moral creature, if the warning of punishment is lacking, there is the danger that crimes will be committed. When, as in our country today, the inhuman act of murder is so widespread as to be a common everyday occurrence, to revise the Constitution so as to abolish capital punishment would contain the danger of promoting that evil."

Other Important Issues relating to Chapter 3

THE FREEDOM OF RELIGION. There was no discussion of the freedom of religion as a general principle. However, there was an opposition of views regarding Article 20, especially the provisions relating to the prohibition of the granting of privileges to religious organizations by the state and to the state's refraining from religious education or any other religious activity. Of particular concern was the application of these points to the Ise Grand Shrine and Yasukuni Shrine.

The following views reveal support for the revision of Article 20. A general guarantee of freedom of religion as a fundamental human right is sufficient; to make clear, as Article 20 does, other matters leads only to social confusion. Certain religious matters are of particular importance to Japan, therefore it is necessary to change the prohibition of government activity in religious affairs. Article 20 is an expression of occupation policy, aimed particularly at Shintō, and therefore the separation of church and state should be expunged.

The opposition simply held that no revision is necessary. However, on the matter of Ise Grand Shrine and Yasukuni Shrine, one opinion held that the problem could be solved if they were treated on a basis different from that of other religious organizations.

THE BASIC PRINCIPLES OF EDUCATION. There were numerous opinions to the effect that, because of the importance of education, the provisions of Article 26 are insufficient and that, consequently, a set of basic principles of education should be clearly set forth in the Constitution.

There were two basic opinions on this issue. The first was that there should be in the Constitution a statement of basic educational policy which should deal with the content, the mission, and the ideal form of education. This opinion was based on the fact that there is at present nothing which could take the place of the Imperial Rescript on Education of the past [1890] and that therefore there are no authoritative standards for education. It was also argued that certain evils have developed, such as the impairment of political neutrality in education, which must be dealt with. For example, Commissioner Hirose stated that there should be a clear statement of the basic principles of education in the Constitution: "In concrete terms this would mean clearly setting forth the responsibilities of the state in such matters as the equality of opportunity for education, the clarification of the mission and the ideal form of education, the proper carrying out of education in the schools on the basis of the standard of the democratic nation with the emperor at the center of the unity of the people, and the guarantee of political neutrality in the educational operations of the schools."

The second view was that there should be a provision guaranteeing the realization of the equality of educational opportunity. The latter view was based on the aim of the attainment of the contemporary welfare state. The aim of this view was to implant the idea of the collective base of social solidarity of the welfare state. One opinion stated that the basic principle should be that education should be carried out "with full consideration of the complex development of the individual personality, respect for human rights, and the cultivation of awareness of the solidarity of society." Along this same line another opinion urged that there should be a constitutional provision to the effect that "young people, as a part of their social education, should practice group living as determined by law and should receive physical, mental, and moral education."

The opposing view held that it is unnecessary to provide in the Constitution for basic principles of education. One argument by Commissioner Takayanagi maintained that long-term matters, such as basic education policy, which would extend into future generations should not be rendered permanent by means of constitutional stipulations, but should be left to law, such as the present Basic Education Law, which could be changed as the times change.

THE FAMILY AND THE HOME. The revisionist view on the family and the home was that Article 24 with its emphasis on respect for the individual and the essential equality of the sexes in family matters is inappropriate to the communal life of the family and the preservation of the home and as a consequence it should be replaced. Specific issues raised included the following: overemphasis on respect for the individual and equality of the sexes in Article 24; contempt for the family concepts of cooperation, fellow-feeling, and respect and affection particularly between parents and children and husband and wife; the disappearance of the tradition of the ancient Japanese family system; and the creation of a variety of social problems.

It was also argued that as a reflection of the fact that the home is the basic unit of society, the nation bears the responsibility to protect and defend the family. It was also stated that this responsibility arises from the need to realize the contemporary welfare state.

An important socio-economic issue that was dealt with in respect to the family was the atomization of farmland flowing from the principle of equal inheritance.

The three following views deal with the issue of the enactment of constitutional provisions relating to the communal life of the family and the protection of the home.

Commissioner Hirose:

> In addition to respect for the individual and equality of the sexes, two more principles—harmonious union and continuous development—should be added to Article 24, and these four principles should be clearly set forth as constituting the internal order of the family. These should be the guiding principles for such things as the Civil Code and social security legislation. Because the family as a natural communal unit is the foundation of both the household and the nation, the state has the responsibility to protect it, as well as the individual, in all matters such as welfare administration, financial policy, and farm policy. Therefore, the responsibility of the state to protect the family as the cooperative body for living which is the foundation of both marriage and blood relationships must be stipulated in the Constitution.

Commissioner Kamikawa: "Article 24 must be regarded as an attempt to convert the ancient Japanese family system into a western-style system. This obliterates the *Gemeinschaft* character of the family in which love and sacrifice come into play. Accordingly, it must be made clear that the home is the natural and basic collective unit of society and that it has the right to receive protection from both society and the state."

Commissioner Yagi: "It is necessary to make clear that the home is the unit of the social structure, that the Japanese people have traditionally looked up to the imperial family as the main family of the nation, and that through this the emperor exists as the object of veneration of the Japanese people. However, these matters are unrelated to the structure of government, and they do not partake of the character of law; also because they are *Gemeinschaft* phenomena I think I would like to see them dealt with not in the main text but in the preamble of the Constitution."

The opposing view held revision of Article 24 to be unnecessary, primarily because its basic principles are appropriate for the determination of the modern family and the ideal form of the home. Commissioner Nakagawa stated the case for opposition strongly:

> The traditional family system was based on the principle of succession from ancestors to posterity in the male line, was held together by the power of the father as the head of the family and by feudal authoritarianism, and prevented the democratization of family life. It must be stated that the present Constitution, in addition to such matters as respect for the individual and equality before the law in Articles 13 and 14, also established respect for the individual

and the equality of the sexes in family life. This was a matter of great significance in respect to both the modernization of the traditional Japanese family system and the ideal form of modern democratic society.

It is correct to preach about cooperation, respect, affection, and fellowship for the happiness of the entire family, but these are moral problems and it is best to leave them to morality, education, and social policy; they should not be brought into the world of law. If the attempt is made to do so, they will be adjudicated according to the values of the old traditional family system and the ideal form of modern family life will be lost.

Another problem debated was that the system of equal inheritance based on Article 24 has produced the atomization of farmland, a very important social and agricultural problem. It was argued that to prevent this it is necessary to reserve for each farm family a specified area of farmland as family property and to recognize its nontransferability. On this problem Commissioner Chiba declared: "In order to prevent the atomization of farmland through equal inheritance, it is necessary to recognize in the Constitution the independent inheritance of farmland by the eldest son or other competent person and also limitations on the conveyance and attachment of farmland."

Those opposed to revision as a means of solving this problem recognized the necessity for preventing atomization, but argued that the problem should be handled by measures for the protection of agriculture, such as special laws for loans to farm families.

THE RIGHTS OF LABOR. The opinion was frequently expressed that because the three rights of labor (to organize, to bargain, and to act collectively) are recognized unconditionally and without limitation, even by the public welfare, various abuses have resulted, particularly political activity by labor unions and excesses in strike activity. The conclusion was that limits on these rights should be clearly set forth. Commissioners Kamikawa, Hirose, and Ōnishi, for example, argued jointly that the three rights of labor should be guaranteed but only for the specific objectives of the maintenance and improvement of conditions of work. They also argued that public officials, because they differ from workers in general in both status and the character of their duties, should be clearly limited in their enjoyment of these three rights. Two commissioners also held that the Constitution should contain provisions relating to such matters as minimum wages, equal wages for men and women, and annual paid vacations.

Commissioner Takayanagi argued against any constitutional limitation on the grounds that the Supreme Court in its rulings had already dealt with the principal problems that the proponents of limitation had raised. It has already ruled on such matters as the exercise of the rights

of labor in accordance with the public welfare and with due consideration for other fundamental human rights, including the right of property, and the subjection of the labor rights of public officials to greater
limitations from the standpoint of the public welfare. He also pointed
out that any prohibition of political strikes would be opposed by labor
for fear that it would be extended to cover all strikes on the pretense that
they might be political and that this opposition would create even greater
labor disturbances.

BASIC ECONOMIC AND SOCIAL PRINCIPLES. Those who supported the
inclusion in the Constitution of basic economic and social principles did
so because they felt it to be necessary to clarify the principles of the
contemporary welfare state. They argued that the Constitution is behind
the times on this important issue and that it should make clear that the
legislative and executive branches bear the responsibility for promoting
the realization of the welfare state and that the people are equally responsible for cooperating in its realization.

There was not only a demand for the inclusion of new sections in the
Constitution, possibly under the headings of "General Rules" or "Basic
Principles," dealing with such matters as the principle of social solidarity
or the basic principles for the construction of the social state, but also the
presentation of a wide range of concrete provisions dealing with social
and economic problems not specifically covered in the present Constitution. These included such items as cooperation between capital and
labor, the protection of agriculture and of small and medium business
enterprises, the promotion of foreign trade, the protection and encouragement of science and technology, protection of copyright, the protection of cultural assets, assistance for young people, and a minimum wage
system.

Those who opposed the inclusion in the Constitution of basic social
and economic principles argued that both principles and specific problems could be dealt with by appropriate legislation and, in the words of
Commissioner Yabe, "to set forth in the Constitution in excessive detail
certain social and economic principles would be to place restraints on
dynamic social and political developments."

THE RIGHTS OF PROPERTY AND OF MANAGEMENT. In regard to the
provisions of Article 29 relating to the protection of the right of property, there were a number of demands that, from the necessity to make
clear the principles of the contemporary welfare state, the right of property of the individual should not be absolute and, hence, it must be made
even clearer in Article 29 that the right of property, particularly because
of its public nature, carries a responsibility.

It was also argued that there should be provision in the Constitution

288 PART FOUR. THE OPINIONS OF THE COMMISSIONERS

for the right of management. The reason advanced was that small and medium enterprises in particular are frequently ill-equipped to respond to the demands of labor and that to balance off the three rights of labor it is necessary to grant the right of management to those who manage.

On the right of property those who opposed any change in Article 29 argued that, although its language might appear to be a little old-fashioned, no problems had arisen from its application. Further, it was felt that any future problem could be handled through legislation.

Those against the inclusion of a right of management in general opposed it on the grounds that the content of the right is unclear and that, furthermore, it seems to be covered by the right of property in Article 29.

General Summary

The general outline of the views relating to Chapter 3 on the rights and duties of the people can be stated in summary form as follows.

The central confrontation of views on Chapter 3 revolved around two closely related questions: whether it is sufficient to have only the present "public welfare" as a limitation on fundamental human rights or whether it is necessary to add certain supplements or adjustments relating to rights and duties. Behind this opposition of views was the pervading issue, that we have already seen in a number of cases, namely, whether the Constitution must be revised through the enactment of new provisions or whether it should remain unchanged because problems can be dealt with through interpretation and application which can be left to legislation and judicial decisions.

In addition, the confrontation was also revealed in the form of ideology or principle. The majority view argued: that the present Constitution is based on the eighteenth- and nineteenth-century principle of the independent nation; that it is behind the times in that it is not in accord with the principles of the twentieth-century welfare state; that for this reason it is necessary to clarify the social responsibilities of the people; and that revision of this chapter is necessary in order to make clear the limitations on rights and freedoms, thus correcting the excesses of emphasis on individual rights and freedoms.

In rebuttal, the minority antirevisionist view maintained the following: that the principles of the contemporary welfare state have been adopted to a considerable degree by the present Constitution; that it is not impossible under the present Constitution to realize those principles completely; and that the principles are not incompatible with the principle of respect for individual rights and freedoms. Finally, this view argued that the principle of individual rights has been produced through the actual preservation and perfection of individual rights and freedoms and that, accordingly, the call for a strengthening of limitations on such rights and freedoms on the basis of the principles of the welfare state is not proper.

SECTION E.
THE NATIONAL DIET

The position of the National Diet and its organization were the two fundamental issues that commanded the attention of the commissioners. Consequently, many opinions were expressed on these two matters and a striking confrontation of views was evident. There was also an opposition of views on a number of minor matters relating to the Diet such as the status and terms of office of members, the system of sessions, the order of business, and other operational items.

A particular point of contention was whether the Constitution, as in Article 41, should continue to specify that the Diet is "the highest organ of state power." However, closely related to that problem was the issue of what the basic structure of government as determined in the Constitution should be because such a structure would determine the position of the Diet in respect to the other organs of government. It is to that problem that we shall first turn.

The Ideal Fundamental Structure of Government

The view that because there are problems relating to such basic principles as popular sovereignty, the separation of powers and the parliamentary cabinet system as determined in the present Constitution, it is necessary to revise them fundamentally.

This view was held by only a minority of the commissioners. It appeared in three different forms. The first was set forth by Commissioner Ōishi and ex-Commissioner Tomita, who argued, as has already been described, that popular sovereignty be eliminated from the Constitution and that the emperor be placed in a position of legal authority as the center of the unity of the people. In their view the Diet would be continued as an organ representative of the people and would be responsible for the supervision of the national administration. It is obvious that under such a system the position of the Diet would be fundamentally different from what it is under the present Constitution.

The second position was argued by Commissioners Nakasone and Inaba. They advocated the idea of an elective prime ministership which would involve both the abolition of the parliamentary cabinet system and the clarification of the separation of powers. They would retain and even expand the idea of popular sovereignty as the prime minister would be elected directly by the people. They believed that their proposal would make even clearer the separation of the executive and legislative powers. This proposal would also obviously result in a completely different position for the Diet.

The third proposal, put forward only by Commissioner Takayanagi, did not involve the Diet directly. He suggested, simply for purposes of discussion, the creation of a fourth power of government, namely, the electoral power. This tentative proposal called for the constitutional creation of an election commission which would, in the name of the people, assume control over legislation relating to elections, thus insuring that the Diet members, as selfishly interested parties, would not control electoral matters. However, the effect of this proposal on the Diet would be indirect rather than direct and would involve only a single small area of legislation.

The view that there is no need to change such basic principles as popular sovereignty, the separation of powers, and the parliamentary cabinet system in the structure of government as determined in the present Constitution.

Almost all commissioners were of this view. They supported the principles mentioned above and proposed revisions simply to make them more concrete. The Joint Declaration set forth this view clearly. In general it argued that the present Constitution has as its basic spirit the traditional liberal democracy in the Western European style which, of course, emphasizes political principles such as the above-mentioned popular sovereignty, the separation of powers, and the parliamentary cabinet system.

The Joint Declaration saw the following as the special characteristics of the basic structure of government in the present Constitution: (1) the emperor as symbol based on popular sovereignty; (2) the system in which the Diet with the House of Representatives supreme under the separation of powers possesses the legislative power; and (3) the parliamentary cabinet system based on a cooperative relationship in which the Diet and the cabinet are closely tied together. "These three special characteristics are bound together as one," the Declaration said, "and can be considered to have become as blood and bone in the form of a Japanese-style democracy deeply rooted in the political traditions of our country, and thus we would like to see them supported and developed. Accordingly, any constitution which might endanger these characteristics must be opposed."

Commissioner Hirose supported the three basic principles under discussion here but called for a reorganization of the structure of government which would realize what he referred to as "the cooperation and the independence of the three powers." He said: "The basic structure of the Japanese government is that the emperor as an organ of the state occupies the supreme position and possesses the authority determined by the Constitution in matters of government. Below this the National Diet, the cabinet, and the courts exercise the legislative, executive, and judicial powers. The independence and the cooperation of the three powers are thus regarded as the basic principles of governance." He asserted that the present government conforms to this basic picture, but that "cooperation and independence of the three powers" should be treated as fundamental principles.

The Position of the National Diet

The view that because the provision of Article 41 that the National Diet is "the highest organ of state power" is inappropriate from the standpoint of both the ideal structure of government and the separation of powers and because in actual operation various abuses have been created, this provision must be changed.

Article 41 provides that the Diet shall be "the highest organ of state power" and "the sole law-making organ of the State." However, virtually all commission discussion centered on the "highest organ" provision. The commissioners in general simply accepted the law-making role of the Diet as flowing naturally from its legislative power. Only two opposing opinions were expressed on this problem.

Commissioner Kamikawa asserted that in all countries that have adopted parliamentarianism it is natural that "laws in the formal sense" be enacted by the legislature but that "laws in the substantial sense" are not monopolies of legislatures. He pointed out that the Constitution itself recognizes forms of national laws enacted by organs other than the Diet such as cabinet orders, rules of the Supreme Court, and ordinances. Accordingly, he argued, the provision "sole law-making organ" is improper and should be revised.

In reply Commissioner Takayanagi argued that since the Constitution itself provides for exceptions such as those pointed out by Kamikawa it should not be regarded as contradictory. He said that the only dubious point is whether the Constitution has the intent of prohibiting delegated legislation which is indispensable to the modern state. He declared that it is possible to interpret the Constitution as not prohibiting delegated legislation, that it is presently being carried out, and that there have been no improprieties. He concluded that it is not necessary to change the "sole law-making" provision.

The discussion centered on the provision in Article 41 that the Diet is "the highest organ of state power." The view holding that this provision should be changed maintained: (1) that it is contradictory to both the ideal basic structure of government and to the principles of the separation of powers and of the parliamentary cabinet; and (2) that it has resulted in various undesirable phenomena in politics.

We have already observed the three views of Commissioner Ōishi, Commissioners Nakasone and Inaba, and Commissioner Hirose in the position of the Diet within an ideal structure of government. Here we shall add only a few general observations from these three views relating directly to the position of the Diet. In respect to the "highest organ" provision, Ōishi argued simply that the phrase should be eliminated and the Diet should enjoy only its natural function as a law-making organ and also should supervise national administration as the organ representing the people.

Nakasone and Inaba insisted, as was indicated earlier, that the parliamentary cabinet system had to be abolished and the election of the prime minister adopted in order to achieve a true separation of powers. Their argument ran as follows: the present system of parliamentary cabinets has degenerated into government by collusion between the Diet and the cabinet, and the Diet's role as the highest organ has brought about distortions in the structure of the state. Therefore, in addition to the direct election both of Diet members and of the prime minister there should also be established a constitutional court of judges who would be subject to review by the people. By these means the three powers would be separated to a maximum degree and the mutual checks and balances among them would be strengthened. If all this were to be done, the character of the Diet as the highest organ of state power would simply dissolve of itself.

The Hirose view, as has already been pointed out, of "the independence and cooperation of the three powers" would naturally result in a change of the Diet's position. Hirose argued that as an organ of the state the emperor would be the head of state and thus it would be inappropriate to refer to the Diet as the highest organ of the state. But he concluded that the Diet should be designated as "a basic organ of state power" both because it is the foundation of national administration and because it is directly representative of the people.

Except for the above rather special positions, most of the commissioners who called for a revision of the "highest organ" provision argued that it is in contradiction to the principle of the separation of powers and that it signifies "Diet absolutism" or "Diet omnipotence." More specifically, the following two arguments were put forth as reasons for revision. First, the thinking that regards the Diet as the highest organ might be proper for a system of centralized power as in the Soviet Union or other communist countries, but it is improper for a structure of government of liberal democratic countries which have the separation of powers as a basic principle. Second, the concept opposes the legislature to the government [cabinet] and even though this was proper for the eighteenth-century age of liberalism and democracy when it was necessary to weaken the power of government through the legislature, it is not proper for the present age of mass democracy in which the government and the legislature must not willfully oppose each other but must stand together cooperatively on the same foundation, namely, the people. On this point Commissioner Ōnishi asserted that since World War I constitutional systems centered on legislatures failed as democracies and fell into dictatorial government, a lesson that should be heeded.

Commissioner Ushioda spoke as follows against the "highest organ" provision:

> . . . it is meaningless to give unchanged to the people the despotic authority which has been wrested from a minority; there must be the simultaneous establishment of constitutional government. But a provision to the effect that the Diet is "the highest organ of state power" is opposed to the principle of constitutional democratic government. In order to defend freedom and human rights all despotic and absolutist power must be disavowed. We who have tasted the bitter experience of the deification and absolutization of the emperor in the past must not be led astray once more by the deification and absolutization of the people. Constitutional government is where no organ of the state or any part of one possesses absolute supreme power and where each exercises and protects its share of authority. But for the Constitution to recognize the highest authority of only a single and specified organ known as the National Diet must be termed a suicidal action by the Constitution itself.

Another view maintained that the "highest organ" provision expresses a highly important political principle, namely, that the Diet should be the central organ of national administration because it directly represents the people. Moreover, the constitutional position of the National Diet is of great importance because of the extremely low position of the Imperial Diet under the Meiji Constitution. However, this view argued strongly that this provision is undesirable because, while it might be proper for a Soviet constitution, it is contrary to the principle of the separation of powers. In addition, it contradicts other provisions of the Constitution. For example, the Diet is not the highest organ because the Constitution bestows the power of judicial review on the courts in respect to Diet-enacted laws and the government also has the constitutional right to dissolve the House of Representatives.

Others pointed out that the "highest organ" provision is without concrete content and is therefore without efficacy. Thus, it was argued, a provision that does nothing more than to point out a simple position unaccompanied by any specific concrete powers is not only unnecessary but could be actually harmful if broadly interpreted.

A number of commissioners also pointed out that this provision has led to undesirable phenomena in the operation of the nation's legislative system and in its parliamentary and partisan politics. Such phenomena are excesses or abuses of authority by the Diet which have arisen from the fact that the phrase "highest organ" gives the impression of meaning the absolute position, the omnipotence, and the supremacy of the Diet. The following were frequently mentioned as examples of abuses and excesses: (1) upward revisions of the budget and members' bills accompanying it; (2) abuses of the power of the two houses to investigate national affairs; (3) the attitude strongly held by many that the cabinet is simply a branch of the Diet; (4) the frequency with which the Diet meddles in details of administration; (5) the fostering of arrogance and the feeling of superiority in Diet members and the loss of moral sense and a sense of self-control by Diet members and the consequent loss of efficiency in the consideration of national affairs and the breeding of waste of government funds; (6) some correction by the Diet of bureaucratic government but at the price of needless interference with the administrative power; (7) the spread of the idea of legislative omnipotence from the Diet to the prefectual assemblies; and (8) the tendency to look down on the executive branch while taking shelter under Diet authority, for example, in the form of needless restrictions on cabinet ministers and ministry officials in the committees of both houses.

These abuses were also pointed out by commissioners who were Diet members. However, a counterargument was raised to the effect that the source of abuses was not in the provisions of the present Constitution but in the misconduct of political parties and Diet members.

The view that the provision that the National Diet is "the highest organ of state power" is of considerable significance, that it involves no theoretical contradictions, that the various abuses are a separate problem, and accordingly there is no need to revise this provision.

Commissioner Rōyama voiced strong support of this provision:

That the Constitution treats the National Diet as "the highest organ of state power" is related to the denial of powers of government to the emperor. Also it sets the National Diet apart from judicial and administrative organs as that organ where the people act through their duly elected representatives. It must be understood that the intent was to provide the Diet with the highest function in the determination of the will of the people. If the ultimate power of decision on the will of the people is not granted to the Diet, it is necessary to grant to the emperor to a certain extent the power of government or of control. If one stands in the position of being unable to accept a return to such an emperor system, then he must also oppose any change in the present provision. The phrase "highest organ of state power" is abstract and possesses diverse meanings, but I believe that by its very existence it makes clear where the locus of sovereignty lies.

Commissioner Furui believed that the phrase is debatable in terms of legal theory but that "in the political concept expressed therein there are a number of great and deeply significant points such as the declaration of the great principle of popular sovereignty, the rejection of bureaucratism, and the significance of human rights and their firm guarantee." Commissioner Takayanagi defended the phrase on the following grounds: (1) that it does not express the principle of centralization of power as in some communist constitutions; (2) that its real meaning lies in its shift from executive supremacy of the Meiji Constitution; and (3) that the power of the Diet is not without limitations set forth in the Constitution itself, and consequently such limitations are not inconsistent with the Diet's role as "highest organ."

Commissioner Mano presented what was probably the most reasoned defense of the "highest organ" provision:

> Among the organs of the three powers of government the Diet is the only one formed by direct election by the people. We must think that the National Diet was determined to be "the highest organ of state power" in order to express clearly the idea of popular sovereignty elsewhere than in Article 1. This is clear if we examine the circumstances of the enactment of the Constitution. It is necessary to keep this provision for the future cultivation of democracy in our country.
>
> In regard to the power of judicial review there are a number of opinions which hold it to be in contradiction to calling the Diet the "highest organ." But the Constitution did not establish only the separation of powers; it simultaneously set up checks and balances. The power of judicial review is nothing other than a part of the system of checks and balances. Therefore, this "highest organ" provision must be interpreted to be naturally in harmony with judicial review; it cannot be interpreted to be in direct contradiction of it.
>
> Also it is an error to think of "highest organ" as if it were directly the power to order, to direct, and to supervise. The relationship is this: not until there is a Diet can there be a cabinet; not until there is a cabinet can the courts exist. This arises from popular sovereignty. In summary, the Constitution on the basis of the principle of popular sovereignty provides a position one level higher for the Diet which consists of members elected directly by the people. There isn't the slightest contradiction with the Constitution as a whole.

Those who believe that actual abuses in government are an issue separate from the "highest organ" provision argued that the phrase itself has a strong resonance and that the abuses arise from the political parties and the Diet members themselves. Thus, the abuses cannot justify a change in this key provision.

The Structure of the Diet: The House of Councilors System

In the discussion of the structure of the Diet the question was raised as to whether the bicameral system should be continued. However, this was a minor issue. The principal problem was the House of Councilors, particularly in regard to its organization.

Only Commissioner Inaba supported the adoption of a unicameral system. He argued that the present bicameral system means the duplication of activities, such as members' questions and ministers' answers, in the two houses and also that a unicameral system would be a bold solution to many of the problems confronting the present House of Councilors. Commissioner Ushioda raised a series of doubts about the bicameral system without advocating unicameralism. The basic thrust of his position was his doubt that the second or upper house has the virtues that its supporters claim. However, he also felt that there is no guarantee of the success of a unicameral system.

All the other commissioners supported the bicameral system. In general, they found its raison d'être in the following points.

1. To have some difference in the character of the two houses is desirable, but even if they are almost identical, the bicameral system would still be useful. To achieve serious deliberation on problems, it is necessary to have both houses consider matters.

2. Since it is impossible to develop appropriate means to check the abuses of the House of Representatives, the bicameral system must continue to be accepted.

3. In view of the English debate over the abolition of the House of Lords, a proposal for the abolition of the House of Councilors would have no real chance of success and would not be worth the effort.

4. It would not be meaningless even if the two houses were identical. Even on the same problem it would still be meaningful to have two separate considerations at different points in time.

5. To continue the bicameral system is meaningful with the power of decision residing in the House of Representatives and the role of critic in the House of Councilors.

While the commissioners almost unanimously supported the continuation of the bicameral situation, more specifically the retention of the House of Councilors, they discussed at some length the problem of whether the upper house should be made nonpartisan. Opinions fell into four general groups on this issue.

One group maintained that the House of Councilors should be made neutral. They anticipated that the political character of the upper house could be mitigated by the addition of a small number of nonelected members. Some commissioners doubted the efficacy of such a step. Another group advocated not only the addition of nonelected members, but also a constitutional provision guaranteeing the neutrality of the House of Councilors. To achieve this goal it was suggested that councilors be removed from party rolls and that they be prohibited from serving either as cabinet ministers or parliamentary vice-ministers.

Two other groups supported the continuation of the partisan nature of the upper house. For example, Commissioner Yagi pointed out that the system of direct election naturally resulted in the upper house's being partisan, but he did support a cooling-off period so that both houses could give serious consideration to legislation coming before them. Finally, another group, while supporting the bicameral system, urged that consideration be given to remedying the situation that would occur if the two houses are controlled by different political parties.

The view that the House of Councilors differs in organization from the House of Representatives and that consequently the electoral system for the upper house as provided for in the present Constitution should be changed.

The greater part of the commissioners who supported the continuation of the bicameral system, especially the House of Councilors, were critical of the constitutional provisions relating to it. They argued against both direct election of councilors and local and national constituencies set forth in the Law for the Election of Public Officials which is based on Article 43. Opinions varied widely on how the electoral system should be changed.

One extreme opinion was that all councilors should be nonelected. They should be persons of learning and experience appointed by the cabinet. It was also felt that approval of the House of Representatives for such appointees should be required.

A more widely held opinion was that only a part of the House of Councilors should be made up of nonelected members. A majority of those who supported a revision of the organization of the upper house held this opinion, but there was certainly no agreement among them as to how the nonelected members should be selected. The following illustrate the range of suggestions:

1. Those having experience as prime minister or as speaker of either house or long-time service as members of either house should be made lifetime members of the House of Councilors.

2. Some kind of a body should select upper house candidates from among skilled veteran politicians; the people should vote on these candidates and those elected should be appointed by the cabinet.

3. A system of either indirect election or of recommendation and appointment should be adopted.

4. Two types of members should be created: the first, to be elected at large from the entire country by electors who are members of the *todōfuken* assemblies from among those who are currently cabinet ministers or members of either house and those who have had such experience; and the second, to be elected in the House of Representatives from among nominees selected by a Committee for the Selection of Candidates for the House of Councilors. The committee would consist of the prime minister, the speakers of both houses, the chief justice of the Supreme Court, and representatives of various groups appointed by the House of Representatives. Numbers of the two types would be equal, but the total number would be less than the current membership of the upper house.

5. The prefectures should be abolished and a system of regions should be created instead. A total of 150 members should be elected from the regions as election districts. In addition, fifty members should be selected by resolution in both houses from among those who have had more than twenty years of service in the two houses and from among persons of learning and experience.

6. A group of members should be added who would be selected by some kind of a selection agency. This would preserve the principle of election, but insure that the two houses would differ in character. There should be no functional representation, but methods should be devised to insure the selection of candidates with experience or with certain specializations.

7. The small election district should be established for the House of Representatives and the national constituency of the House of Councilors should be abolished. For the upper house there should be a combination of a bloc system of elections and the democratic election of a minimum of twenty nominated members.

8. The upper house membership should be limited to about a hundred and it should consist of one member elected from each *todōfuken* unit [a total of forty-eight at the time] and a group of nominated members coming from the three branches of government and representatives of the public.

Finally, a third recommended method was that the members of the House of Councilors should be selected by the House of Representatives. Commissioner Ushioda recommended the adoption of the Norwegian constitutional device of a single election for both houses with one-quarter of the successful candidates being selected by the parliament for the upper house and the remaining three-quarters constituting the lower house. Commissioner Ōnishi recommended the following method: a Committee for the Selection of Candidates for the House of

Councilors would be established which would then determine a number of candidates about double the number of seats and from this number the House of Representatives would elect members of the House of Councilors in numbers proportional to the number of seats held by each party in the lower house.

Some members touched on the problem of the number of seats in the upper house. Some proposals favored about 150 and others about 100, the latter number because it approximates the size of the British House of Lords and of the United States Senate.

The view that the system of elections for the House of Councilors established in the present Constitution should be maintained.

Those holding this view were particularly opposed to the suggestions that there be nonelected members. In addition, while recognizing the existence of problems relating to the organization of the House of Coun cilors, they did not think that any of the proposals were correct alternatives to the present system and therefore could not discern any positive reason for changing it. Of course, they also recognized the special importance of the electoral system in a democratic system of government. A few commissioners who supported the election system in general also felt that there should be some changes in it. For example, ex-Commissioner Hitotsumatsu Sadayoshi called for the abolition of the national constituency and its replacement with the bloc system of representation. On the other hand, Commissioner Yagi supported the retention of the national constituency, but the abolition of the local [prefectural] constituencies.

The problem of whether the powers of the House of Councilors should continue as they are is linked to the problem of the supremacy of the House of Representatives. A wide variety of opinions, listed below, was expressed on these related issues:

1. The opinion that the powers of the House of Councilors should remain as they are

2. The opinion that the supremacy of the House of Representatives should be strengthened, if a group of nonelected members is added to the House of Councilors

3. The opinion that the powers of the two houses should be equal

4. The opinion that the powers of the House of Councilors should be strengthened in regard to deliberations on personnel matters which must have the approval of the Diet

5. The opinion that the supremacy of the House of Representatives should be weakened in certain areas, if the House of Councilors is made into a nonpartisan and neutral body

6. The opinion that the powers of the upper house should be

strengthened by such means as the prior consideration in that house of such matters as personnel, the settlement of accounts, and foreign affairs

7. The opinion that the House of Councilors should be granted certain new powers if it is to be a nonpartisan and neutral body.

The Status and Terms of Office of Diet Members

In regard to the status and terms of office of Diet members, it was proposed that there be a provision to the effect that they "are representatives of all the people and are not bound by commitments" (as seen in various continental European constitutions of the nineteenth century and later). It was suggested that this might replace "members representative of all the people" in the present Article 43.

Some of those supporting this view were also for the revision of the organization of the House of Councilors by such means as the addition of nonelected members. One group advocated a constitutional provision to the effect that in the execution of their duties, members of both houses should act as if bound only by their consciences in order to achieve the benefit of the people as a whole and not simply the demands of one segment of the people or the electorate.

In opposition, it was argued both that the present provision in Article 43 covers the proposed change and that "not bound by commitments" would create many disputes particularly in relation to the ties between members and their parties.

There were a number of proposals concerning changes in the terms of office for Diet members. Commissioner Furui advocated a shortening of the term of representatives to three years, arguing that it would serve to stabilize the lower house because a shortening of the term would reduce the likelihood of dissolution. On the other hand, Commissioner Ōnishi urged the extension of the term of representatives to five years, arguing that this would tend to inhibit dissolution and thereby contribute to the stability of cabinets and that the longer term would enable members to worry less about reelection and to devote more time to Diet business.

Commissioner Ide asserted that the six-year term for councilors is too long because it permits them to become too relaxed. Commissioner Furui also advocated the shortening of the six-year term to four years. Another view was that there seems to be no good reason to maintain the difference in the length of terms of the members of the two houses.

Commissioner Ōnishi argued for a provision that would call for the dissolution of the House of Councilors as well as of the House of Representatives and that would provide that if either were dissolved the other would be also so that elections for both could be held simultaneously. His view was supported by Commissioner Kamikawa.

Other commissioners upheld the terms of office as currently provided for in the Constitution.

The pros and cons of three other questions were discussed by the commissioners in regard to other problems involving Diet members. Is it necessary to lay down provisions relating to an upper limit of the number of Diet members and to the filling of vacancies? Should there be a provision relating to the undesirability of concurrently being a Diet member and a cabinet minister? Should the provisions relating to the freedom from apprehension, lack of responsibility for statements and votes and the right to an annual salary be retained unchanged in the Constitution?

Activities of the Diet

On the question of sessions one opinion proposed that a system of two ordinary sessions per year be adopted. It was argued that this system would have the following benefits: an improvement in efficiency, the stabilization of the cabinet, and the prevention of abuses of the current system of extraordinary sessions. Proponents of this view were against year-round sessions because they would further reduce the efficiency of the Diet.

Though many commissioners supported the current system of sessions, recommendations for changes in some minor details were made. Commissioner Ushioda argued that the fact that the Diet must await an imperial convocation before meeting both impairs the autonomy of the Diet and is not in accord with democratic government. Along the same line Commissioner Ide wondered if it might not be well to empower the speakers of the two houses to convoke the Diet.

Commissioner Kamikawa recommended a change in the quorum provision of the Constitution to read that a vote approving a measure would be "a majority of the total membership," instead of "a majority of those present."

Several commissioners also proposed the adoption of the system of joint sessions of the two houses both to correct some of the weak points of the bicameral system and to adopt the strong points of the unicameral system.

The current committee system also came in for a good deal of discussion. However, the question was dealt with not as one directly involving constitutional provisions, but rather as one requiring considerable study and planning for improvement because so many of the activities and functions of the Diet depend on the operation of the standing committee system. It was pointed out that one source of problems in the operations of the Diet is the fact that the Constitution has adopted the British system of parliamentary cabinets in respect to relations between the Diet and the cabinet, and the American committee system in its internal organization.

Some commissioners discovered the following abuses in the current committee system: (1) members of standing committees become specialists in only those matters of concern to the committees to which they are assigned and tend to be interested only in those areas; (2) the standing committees become frozen and fall into sectionalism, because standing committees are established to match the various ministries, they appear to be representatives of those ministries and are prevented from grasping national affairs as a whole; and (3) because committees are central to the consideration of bills, the ministers and other top people in the ministries are tied down in these committee deliberations and the efficiency of administration is lowered. Ministry officials are adversely affected even when the Diet is not in session because committee meetings continue.

Remedies for the above and other difficulties were also suggested as follows: (1) standing committees should be limited in number to such matters as the budget, accounts, and discipline, and special committees should be established for the consideration of bills as they may be needed; and (2) the House of Representatives should adopt the British-style system of the plenary session, and the House of Councilors the American-style committee system.

General Summary

The various views relating to the National Diet, as expressed in the commission's deliberations, can be summarized in general as follows:

1. Virtually all commissioners supported such basic principles relating to the organs of government as determined in the present Constitution as popular sovereignty, the separation of powers, and the parliamentary cabinet system. However, a minority of commissioners set forth the following proposals: that the provisions relating to popular sovereignty be eliminated; that the parliamentary cabinet system be abolished and the system of popularly elected prime ministers be adopted; and that consideration be given to a revision of the principles of the separation of powers and the representative system and to the adoption of the principle of the rights of the electorate.

2. On the position of the National Diet, the main question dealt with

was whether it is necessary to change the "highest organ of state power" provision in Article 41. A majority held that this provision should be eliminated. The confrontation of views on this issue can be summarized as follows: (a) The view supporting the elimination of the "highest organ" clause argued that it is in contradiction of the basic principle of the separation of powers and other provisions resting on it, particularly the right of judicial review, and that it also runs counter to the present trend toward the strengthening and stabilization of executive power. The opposition view held that the provision should not be eliminated because the Constitution recognizes both the separation of powers and checks and balances and, hence, there is no contradiction between the "highest organ" provision and checks and balances. Furthermore, the provision is possessed of great significance in the sense that it negates the position of the Imperial Diet under the Meiji Constitution. (b) Those favoring elimination of this provision also argued that it gives the impression of the absolute omnipotence of the Diet, thus giving rise to such evils as the Diet's abuse of its powers. The opposition view held that any evils arise from the attitudes of the political parties and of Diet members, not from this provision.

3. On the organization of the Diet virtually all commissioners upheld the present bicameral system. However, a majority of the commissioners held that the organization of the House of Councilors should be changed in order to make possible a differentiation between the two houses. Many suggestions for change were made including the frequent one that provision should be made for nonelected councilors. On this point it was frequently urged that the upper house should be made neutral or placed on a nonpartisan basis.

4. Many opinions were expressed on the activities of the Diet, particularly on the necessity to improve the committee system, which is central to Diet operations.

SECTION F.
THE CABINET

The principal problems addressed in regard to the cabinet were: whether the parliamentary cabinet system should be continued or whether it should be abolished and the system of the elective prime minister be adopted; the organization and powers of the cabinet; and the status and powers of the prime minister. The parliamentary cabinet system and the system of the elective prime minister were the basic and comprehensive issues. If one takes the position that the parliamentary cabinet system be abolished and the elective prime minister system adopted, such problems as the organization and powers of the cabinet and the status and powers of the prime minister would also undergo fundamental change. Consequently, those combined issues will be addressed first.

The Parliamentary Cabinet System and the Election of the Prime Minister

The view that the parliamentary cabinet system should be abolished and the system of the elected prime minister be adopted.

This view was advanced by only two commissioners, Nakasone and Inaba. It was supported wholly or in part by only four others, ex-Commissioners Tanaka Isaji and Sugiwara and Commissioners Shiikuma and Chiba. All the other commissioners were opposed to this view and held that the basic principle of the parliamentary cabinet system as established in the present Constitution should be supported.

Commissioner Nakasone developed an elaborate new structure of government based on the system of the elective prime minister. The following is a brief summary of its principal points. Political parties winning a specified number of votes in the immediately prior general election would nominate candidates for prime minister and vice prime minister. The paired candidates would run in a national election to be held at the same time as the general election for the House of Representatives. The two candidates receiving the highest number of votes would be elected and appointed by the emperor for a term of four years. Victorious candidates could be reelected, but a third term would be prohibited. The voters would have the right of recall. The prime minister would present bills, the budget, and treaties to the Diet. He would have the power of veto over Diet-enacted legislation, including the budget in whole or in part, and would also appoint cabinet ministers who could not simultaneously be Diet members. The Diet would continue to be bicameral. Bills and the budget would come into existence only after a vote by the House of Representatives. The House of Councilors would have the right of decision on treaties, the right of consent to prime ministerial appointments to important policy-making positions, and the right of appointment of Supreme Court justices. The Diet would also have the power of impeachment of the prime minister and the vice prime minister.

Commissioner Nakasone advanced the following principal arguments in support of his scheme:

1. To expand the principle of popular sovereignty by means of the direct popular election of the prime minister and to entrust "the freedom to make the government" to the hands of all the people is to make

possible a powerful democracy. Today when the fate of all the world, of all humanity, depends on the efforts of supreme political leaders, the more important issue is not freedom from governmental power but the people's direct possession of the power to make the government that holds their fate in its hands. In Japan today the development of science, technology, and mass communications, the improvement of the education and the knowledge of the people, and the high level of political interest all make possible the shift to a direct popular election of the chief governmental leader and away from the [present] indirect form.

2. The very real shortcomings of Japanese government today, such as the instability of the executive power, the factionalism of the political parties, and the estrangement of the people from government, originate in the parliamentary cabinet system. The eradication of these shortcomings will be possible only when that system is supplanted by the system of the elective prime minister. Nakasone argued that because the prime minister is selected from the Diet which is a nest of factions it has become an arena for struggles over political power and the prime ministership. In addition, because the prime minister stands on a balance of factions, his position is tenuous and he can neither plan nor carry out long-range projects. Therefore, the elective prime minister system will lead to the elimination of the evils of factional politics and of the instability of the executive power.

3. In today's Japan there is still lacking a new political authority to take the place of the past authority of the emperor. Any such new political authority must find its base among the people. The elective prime minister system will create a firm fixed point in the prime ministership for this new political authority. The system will make it possible to restore the feeling of oneness between the state and the people by giving all the people the direct right to choose the supreme political leader. It will also become possible to eliminate both the lack of political interest among the people and their estrangement from government and to create a firm fixed point for government itself.

4. To criticize the system of the elective prime minister as containing the danger of a shift to dictatorship or as being in contradiction of the emperor system is improper. Past examples of the emergence of dictatorships under systems of the popular referendum grew from special conditions at particular stages of the histories of the societies involved and of the development of democratic processes. Under the proposed system, the emperor would remain in both the spiritual and historical senses the symbol of the unity of the people, while the prime minister would become the center of the functional unity of the people. Also under the new system, because the emperor would appoint the prime minister who would have been elected by the people, the emperor would

be in the position of confirming the verdict of all the people, not, as under the present system, a verdict of a Diet which does not have the full confidence of the people.

The view that the parliamentary cabinet system should be supported and the elective prime minister system opposed.

As was pointed out above, a great many commissioners were opposed to the system of the elective prime minister. A number of reasons were put forth to support this opposition. Rather than to itemize the large number of specific reasons, the broad headings under which they fell are given below.

1. (The opinion that in Japan the conditions which would make possible an American-style presidential system are lacking) This opinion, of course, saw the elective prime minister system as resembling the American presidential system. One argument pointed out that the American federal system with its basis of political parties in local areas provides the political and social conditions necessary for the presidential system. Another argument was that the political level of the Japanese people lags behind that of the American people.

2. (The view that the strengths and weaknesses of both the parliamentary cabinet and the presidential systems should be thoroughly studied) Commissioner Ōnishi emphasized that the problem was not simply the election of a prime minister, but of a system of government based on such an election and that it is the system that should be carefully studied. Commissioner Takayanagi was concerned by the example of the de Gaulle Constitution in France which was designed to remedy the weaknesses of the cabinet under the Third and Fourth republics. He argued that the Constitution had resulted in a weakening of the National Assembly, a decay of the principle of the rule of law, and the appearance of a presidential dictatorship. He was therefore opposed to the introduction of a presidential system into Japan.

3. (The opinion that the elective prime minister system would not bring with it the authority of the unity of the people and would also be in contradiction to the emperor system) Commissioner Ōishi argued strongly against the elective prime minister system based on the premise of the emperor as symbol because it would contain the inherent danger of the destruction of the substance of the unity of the people as viewed from Japan's long history. Commissioner Kamikawa argued that the proposed system would result in a mix of the monarchical and the republican which would be incompatible with the emperor system.

4. (The opinion that the source of the political abuses in our country is not in the parliamentary cabinet system but in other matters such as the political parties and the electoral system and therefore, it is necessary

to remedy those abuses at the source rather than to adopt the presidential system) The widely held view was that if the necessary changes were made in the electoral system, the character of the political parties, and the attitudes of politicians, then the parliamentary cabinet system would be successful, but that if they remained unchanged, then the elective prime minister system would not work. It was also pointed out that the separation of the cabinet from the Diet would render the government even more inactive and incapable with more governmental instability as the result.

5. (The opinion that it is necessary to achieve stability for executive power, but the presidential system should not be adopted for that reason and we must be warned of its dangers) This opinion recognized the necessity for the stabilization and strengthening of the executive power in this age of mass democracy to replace the conventional idea of the omnipotence of the Diet. However, it emphasized the importance of the continued recognition of Diet control and the stabilization of the cabinet built on the trust of the Diet. It was argued that if the elective system is adopted while control in the hands of the Diet is strengthened, then a head of government without direct connection with the Diet would drift away from it and become powerless. On the other hand, if control of the Diet is weakened under such a system, there would be a drift toward dictatorship.

6. (The opinion that the key to the success of democratic government lies in the sound development of party government, but the elective prime minister system would not contribute to it) This view argued that because under the proposed system, cabinet ministers would no longer be Diet members, a single party would not be the foundation of the cabinet and thus the union between the cabinet and the Diet would disappear, a tendency toward conflict between the elected prime minister and the Diet would be created, and it would truly become impossible for political parties to carry out their functions.

It was also argued that the remedy for current political abuses is to bring about under the parliamentary cabinet system the exchange of political power between the two great popular parties, the Liberal Democrats, and the Socialists. The fundamental source of both the evils of factionalism and the abuses in Diet operations is the underdevelopment of these two political parties.

7. (The opinion that under the proposed system there is the danger of electing an unqualified person, thus leading to the possibility of the prime minister's becoming a dictator) The argument here was that the individual popularity of prime ministerial candidates would possess great political weight. The hero-worship element would be strong with the inherent danger of the creation of a dictator.

8. (The opinion that the system would bring with it discord between the executive and legislative branches and would not be equipped with appropriate means for settling situations leading to collisions between the two branches) Here major emphasis was placed on the American experience where the president and the majority in the Congress have been of different political parties.

9. (The opinion that considering as a whole the present state of politics in our country, this is not the time for the adoption of the system of an elective prime minister) Commissioner Furui put the argument as follows: "In our country the history of liberalism and democratic government is short and their foundations are weak. Moreover, the idea of prewar nationalism still remains strongly rooted. Meanwhile, the strengthening and broadening of the power of the state in order to socialize state functions have been advancing in accord with the times. In such an environment it is clear that if the system of the elective prime minister is adopted, it will bring with it the bureaucratization of politics and administration and there would be the fear that the development of democratic government would be hindered."

Commissioner Mizuno, while conceding that the idea has the attraction of novelty, held that the time is not yet right for it for the following reasons: (1) the parliamentary cabinet system still has widespread and strong support; (2) the elective prime minister system is viewed as having certain built-in dangers; and (3) there is insufficient general appreciation of either the theory behind it or its possible advantages and disadvantages.

The Cabinet and Executive Power

The view that the provision of Article 65 that "executive power shall be vested in the cabinet" is inappropriate and needs to be revised.

Commissioner Hirose urged that this provision be changed to read: "The cabinet is the organ related to the formulation and promotion of national policy and is in charge of the executive power." He argued that this change would make clear the important mission inherent in the nature of the cabinet, preserve the strategy and coordination necessary for national policy, and clarify the role of the cabinet as the national organ responsible for handling complex issues of foreign relations and complicated problems of domestic policy.

In respect to executive commissions there was also the opinion that a different designation should be used for them. Examples would be the National Personnel Authority, the Fair Trade Commission, and the National Public Safety Commission. Commissioner Kamikawa pointed out that there are various academic theories concerning their character, but in terms of function they are independent to a certain degree of the cabinet. Thus, it is meaningless to say that all executive power is vested in the cabinet.

The view that this provision is sufficient as it stands and it is unnecessary to revise it.

One approach to this issue was Commissioner Rōyama's. In strictly legal terms there may be doubt that "formulation and promotion of national policy" can be directly determined to be functions of the cabinet, but for it to be so recognized, the problem is one of the actual functions and capacities of the cabinet, not a matter of a constitutional provision. In addition, Commissioner Tagami pointed out that the relationship between executive commissions and the cabinet can be disposed of simply as a problem of constitutional interpretation. Commissioner Takayanagi concurred with this view, pointing out that the executive commission as developed in Great Britain and America is based on the realistic requirements of the contemporary state and that in Japan its constitutionality has been recognized.

The Organization of the Cabinet:
The Status and Powers of the Prime Minister

THE STATUS OF THE PRIME MINISTER. Much of the discussion on the status of the prime minister revolved around his right to appoint and dismiss cabinet ministers. Those favoring the elimination of this right argued that: (1) there is a contradiction between it and the idea of the cabinet's collective responsibility; (2) it encourages needless cabinet reorganization; and (3) it is one source of the evils of factionalism [because the prime minister can use the right of appointment to reward members of his faction with cabinet ministerships].

In opposition it was argued that this right is a valuable means for preserving the unity of the cabinet by making it possible to prevent the collapse of cabinets because of internal disunity, a common phenomenon under the Meiji Constitution.

THE DESIGNATION OF THE PRIME MINISTER. On the method of designation of the prime minister, there was a division of opinion between those who felt that the present system should remain unchanged and those who felt that there should be limits both on those with the right to designate the prime minister and on those to be designated.

The opinion that the House of Representatives should have the right of designation and designates should be limited to its members.

This opinion held that the right to designate the prime minister should be limited to the House of Representatives as a part of the process of making the House of Councilors into a nonpartisan body. Commissioner Hirose urged that designees be limited to members of the lower house. Commissioner Kamikawa concurred, pointing out that this would strengthen the lower house without reference to making the upper house nonpartisan.

The opinion that the House of Representatives should have the right of designation and the scope of the designates should remain as it is.

Commissioner Onishi argued that the right of designation should be limited to the House of Representatives because it is unreasonable to have the House of Councilors participate since the upper house does not have the right to vote nonconfidence in the cabinet. He also asserted that it would be improper because it would draw the upper house into political struggle.

The opinion that as the House of Representatives should have the right of designation, the scope of designates should not be limited.

This opinion, also expressed by Commissioner Ōnishi, was based on the view that the House of Councilors should be composed of nonelected men of learning and experience and that designates should not be limited to Diet members. In addition, the current stipulation that more than half of the cabinet ministers should be Diet members should be abolished. However, this did not mean that Diet members could not be cabinet ministers, but simply that if they were so appointed they would have to resign their seats.

The opinion that the method of designation of the prime minister should be retained as it is.

Those holding this opinion perceived no particular difficulties in the present system. In addition, it was pointed out that the prime minister is in actual fact the president of the majority party, and in the event of a coalition cabinet the usual procedure would be for the parties to agree among themselves on a prime minister designate; thus designation by the Diet is nothing more than a system for confirming the man who has already been chosen off the floor of the Diet. It was also asserted that it would be improper to exclude the democratically elected House of Councilors from the designation process.

Relations between the Cabinet and the Diet

THE INDIVIDUAL RESPONSIBILITY OF CABINET MINISTERS. The only opinion expressed on the individual responsibility of cabinet ministers was that it is not necessary to have a constitutional provision. While there was no real opposition to such a provision, it was pointed out that under the present system if a cabinet minister is charged with maladministration of matters under his jurisdiction, the prime minister is free either to defend the minister under the principle of collective responsibility or to dismiss him.

THE CABINET'S RESPONSIBILITY TO THE DIET AND TO THE HOUSE OF REPRESENTATIVES. Whether the present provision that the cabinet is responsible to the Diet should be changed to responsibility to the House of Representatives was the issue here. However, it was pointed out that only the lower house is empowered to vote nonconfidence in the cabinet and that therefore the cabinet responsibility is in reality only to the lower house, not to the Diet as a whole. Consequently, there is no need to limit responsibility only to the lower house.

PASSAGE OF NONCONFIDENCE RESOLUTIONS BY THE HOUSE OF REPRE-SENTATIVES. Proposed limitations on the right of the House of Representatives to pass nonconfidence resolutions included: (1) a change in the vote from a majority of those present to a majority of the entire membership; (2) a statement of the precise number of Diet members required to introduce a nonconfidence motion; and (3) the adoption of a specified cooling-off period before a vote on a nonconfidence motion. It was argued by Commissioners Ōnishi and Kamikawa that it is easy to organize a nonconfidence vote and that there are many matters which might thus lead to a weakening of the cabinet and instability in the government. Those opposing any limitation mustered the following reasons: (1) to limit the number necessary to introduce a nonconfidence motion would place undue restrictions on minority parties, bar the expression of popular will, and close a safety-valve of democratic government; (2) a mandatory cooling-off period would cause difficulties if a nonconfidence motion were introduced in the closing days of a session; and (3) in our country there has been no abuse of nonconfidence resolutions that would lead to cabinet instability.

THE DISSOLUTION OF THE HOUSE OF REPRESENTATIVES. The question concerning the dissolution of the House of Representatives was whether it should be made clear that in addition to the occasions when a nonconfidence resolution is passed, the cabinet might decide to dissolve the lower house for other reasons. The only real opinion expressed on this problem was that there is no special necessity for a constitutional provision. However, it was recognized that the ability of the cabinet to dissolve the Diet freely is a necessary condition for the parliamentary cabinet system and so if it was decided that there should be a constitutional clarification of this point there would be no objection.

THE CABINET'S RIGHT TO PRESENT BILLS. Several commissioners felt that while Article 72 specifies that a duty of the prime minister is to present bills, it is not clear that "bills" includes drafts of laws. It is also necessary to eliminate doubts regarding the interpretation of the cabinet's right to present bills which is not listed as a cabinet function in Article 73.

THE CABINET'S POWER OF VETO OVER BILLS PASSED BY THE DIET. Commissioner Ōnishi urged that provision should be made for both the veto power for the cabinet and a method by which reconsideration might be requested by the cabinet within a fixed period after the receipt of a law passed by the Diet. This would enable the cabinet to veto measures passed as a result of the power of pressure groups and not in the best interests of the country as a whole.

The opposing view on the power of the veto was that it is necessary under the American presidential system, but not under Japan's parliamentary cabinet system.

THE SCOPE OF TREATIES REQUIRING DIET APPROVAL. Commissioners Kamikawa, Ōnishi, and Uetake argued as follows for a limitation on the scope of treaties requiring Diet approval. "The present Constitution holds that all treaties are to be approved by the Diet. Currently there are many treaties dealing with economic and other technical matters; to have each one approved by the Diet is excessively complicated. However, the American usage of the executive agreement should not be a model. Consequently, the scope of treaties requiring Diet approval should be limited to treaties involving important political affairs such as those relating to collective international organizations, treaties involving important economic matters such as treaties of commerce, treaties imposing charges on the national treasury, and treaties involving the rights and duties of the people."

Commissioner Takayanagi opposed this suggestion. He held that Diet approval of all treaties is an ideal embodiment of the principle of the democratization of foreign policy; that it is difficult to attempt to draw a dividing line between those treaties which might require Diet approval and those which might not; and that under the present provisions the government acts "with common sense in accordance with reality."

DELEGATED LEGISLATION. In connection with the provision of Article 73, item 6 that the issuing of cabinet orders is a cabinet function the question of whether it is necessary to establish a clear constitutional provision relating to delegated legislation was brought up.

Arguing that Article 73 is unclear on this point, Commissioner Ōnishi supported a separate provision relating to authorized and delegated legislation:

> For example, the Diet can delegate to the cabinet by law for a set period the authority to issue cabinet orders which prescribe certain legal matters. In these

cases the content, scope, and objective of the delegation must be designated in appropriate legislation. Where the law concerned clearly specifies it, there should be a provision to the effect that the cabinet can delegate through an order this authority to another government agency. Since the legislative power beyond question lies in the Diet, even when delegated legislation is approved for the cabinet, it is necessary that the Diet place strict limitations on it. To recognize delegated legislation for the cabinet would also be effective in dealing with states of emergency.

Commissioner Takayanagi was in opposition basically because the problem of delegated legislation is being handled without inconvenience under the Constitution as it stands. He also pointed out that it is possible for the Diet to pass legislation under the present Constitution granting full powers to the executive branch to deal with states of emergency. However, he asserted that because such legislation would be accompanied by the danger of dictatorship a strict time limit should be imposed in such legislation.

The Civil Service System

Article 73, item 4, provides that a function of the cabinet is "to administer the civil service." Two problems were raised in regard to this provision: the meaning of the term "civil servant," and the necessity for a constitutional organ to guarantee the status of civil servants.

THE SCOPE OF THE TERM "PUBLIC OFFICIAL." It was pointed out that in Article 15 the term "public official" is used, and in Article 73 the term "civil service" is used, thus making the meaning of "civil service" unclear. On this point Commissioner Hirose suggested that it should be made clear that public officials are "those who are charged with the exercise of state power based on the trust of the people." By this means, he said, not only would what is termed simple labor be excluded from the ranks of the public officials, but all of the latter would be servants of the entire community and the execution of their duties would have to be based on that spirit.

However, this view was opposed on the grounds that "public officials" in Article 15 has a broad meaning, and "civil service" in Article 73 a narrow one and that therefore no clarification is needed.

A CONSTITUTIONAL ORGAN TO GUARANTEE THE STATUS OF CIVIL SERVANTS. Both the problems involved in this issue and the opposing views on it can best be set forth by quoting two opposed opinions. Commissioners Hirose and Ōnishi stated:

Because . . . the status and treatment of public officials must be guaranteed constitutionally, a personnel authority possessing independent status should be established by the Constitution. Its organization and competence would be determined by law, but its members would be appointed by the cabinet with the consent of a nonpartisan House of Councilors. The fundamental rights of public officials as workers should be guaranteed within the limits of the law with the aim of the maintenance and improvement of their standards of labor, but it must be made clear that their rights can be subjected to special limitations, unlike those of ordinary workers. Because the basic rights of public officials as workers should be limited in this fashion, it is necessary to establish through the constitutional personnel authority guarantees of treatment and status.

Commissioner Rōyama stated:

I am opposed to the opinion that it is necessary to elevate a body such as the present National Personnel Authority to the level of a constitutional organ.

Today's civil service system is divided into two areas of different character: personnel administration and personnel superintendence. The first involves the guarantee of the rights and the benefits of public officials such as impartial evaluation and advice on the revision of pay scales and should be the responsibility of an organ independent of the cabinet. The area of superintendence involves such matters as the classified civil service system, the improvement of efficiency, training and promotion, but there is no absolute necessity that this should be done by an independent agency. . . .

Viewing the experience of the National Personnel Authority, I think that it would be well to transfer the field of personnel superintendence to a cabinet organ which would deal with it as a cabinet responsibility and to give the NPA control over the rights and benefits of public officials. However, I do not think that there is any need to elevate it to a constitutional organ for that purpose. To elevate its position only formally would not have any effect.

General Summary

The question of whether the system of the elective prime minister should be adopted was considered. Only a small minority advocated this system; the majority supported the current parliamentary cabinet system. The advocates started from the basic premise that an analysis of the causes of Japan's contemporary political problems must be the first step in handling the problems of contemporary democracy in our country. Consequently, they proposed a concrete scheme calling for a sweeping reorganization of the governmental structure within which the system of an elective prime minister would be placed. Opponents generally took the position that although the proposed system was worth serious consideration, the time is not yet right for it.

Another fundamental question was that of the relations between the Diet and the cabinet. The issue here was whether it is necessary to broaden and strengthen the authority of the cabinet in order to moderate its subordinate position created by the role of the Diet as "the highest organ of state power." Specific questions included possible abuse of the nonconfidence resolution by the Diet, cabinet veto power over Diet-passed legislation, and a limitation on the scope of treaties requiring Diet approval.

A number of additional specific issues were dealt with, most of them involving technical matters or dubious points of interpretation. Generally there was no disagreement over the substance of such matters. Mainly, differences of opinion were simply over the necessity for revision to take care of the problems.

SECTION G.
THE JUDICIARY

The fundamental question in respect to Chapter 6, "The Judiciary," and overspreading the entire field was whether judicial supremacy as adopted in the present Constitution, that is, the principle of the broadening and strengthening of the judiciary, should be preserved. Under that broad question the following were some of the specific concrete issues: the problem of the hierarchical structure of the courts, namely, whether all judicial power should be unified under the Supreme Court; the possible creation of special courts; the system of constitutional review; and the popular review of Supreme Court justices. Lesser questions dealt with the rule-making power of the courts, judicial administration, and open trials. There was also some discussion of such problems as the improvement of the organization of the courts which were not directly related to the constitutional role of the judiciary.

The Broadening and Strengthening of the Judicial Power

In the simplest terms, the fundamental principle of the broadening and strengthening of the judicial power means that the judicial courts, with the Supreme Court at the apex, have been given the constitutional power of jurisdiction over all judicial cases, not only civil and criminal but administrative as well. No special courts, such as administrative courts, are permitted under the Constitution. The scope of the judicial power has been broadened by placing the final judgment in judicial review in the Supreme Court and by giving it the rule-making power and the power of appointment of lower court judges. In addition, the judicial branch has also been strengthened vis-à-vis the legislative and executive branches through the power of judicial review. Finally, there was an increase in the powers of the Supreme Court in the area of judicial administration. All this was frequently referred to as the broadening and strengthening of the independence of the judicial branch.

Almost all the commissioners took the position that the above role of the judiciary is a strong point of the present Constitution and should be preserved. Two basic reasons were presented to support this position. First, this broadened and strengthened judicial power must be preserved in order to protect the fundamental human rights of the people. Second, the judicial system under our present Constitution is proper as the means for providing an unchanging structure for the maintenance of the principles of constitutional government and for elevating the dignity of the law. This is possible through the provision of unity to the proper interpretation of the law by means of a single hierarchy of courts with the Supreme Court at the summit.

In addition, Commissioner Takayanagi particularly emphasized the rule of law and held that that principle is indispensable to the success of parliamentary democracy. Hence, he argued, the policy of broadening and strengthening the judicial power, as adopted in the present Constitution, is necessary to make the principle of the rule of law effective and therefore the policy must be preserved.

In spite of the broad support for the basic principle there was also the frequently expressed opinion that various provisions of the Constitution relating to the judiciary should be revised both to correct problems revealed in the actual operations of the judiciary and to clarify the relationship between the judicial power and the legislative and executive powers. Those advocating revision were primarily concerned with easing the Supreme Court's distress because of the excessive burden of cases and consequent delay of justice, with creating special courts to deal with administrative, labor, and military cases and with the clarification of the power of judicial review.

Several of the commissioners felt that one source of the difficulties of the current judicial system is that an essentially American judicial system was incorporated into the Constitution and that it did not fit neatly into a Japan that possessed a completely different history, tradition, and system in judicial matters.

The Establishment of Special Courts

The view that the present Constitution's complete prohibition on the establishment of special tribunals is not proper and that it is necessary to revise Article 76, paragraph 2, to enable the establishment of military, administrative, and other special courts.

This view held that Article 76, paragraph 2, not only makes the establishment of special tribunals impossible, but also prevents administrative organs from conducting trials or hearings of final judgment. The complete prohibition of special tribunals, especially administrative courts, is far too strict, and this prohibitory provision should be eliminated or mitigated.

1. The opinion based principally on the necessity for the establishment of military courts is tied closely with the view that revision of Article 9 is necessary for the establishment and consolidation of a self-defense system and for the creation of a self-defense army. The proposal was to establish constitutionally military courts as special tribunals. The arguments for military courts were, first, that trials for crimes of military men should be conducted by independent military courts standing outside the structure of ordinary judicial courts because of the special nature of armed forces and their duties and, second, that such trials should not be conducted according to ordinary criminal procedure.

2. In a number of instances those advocating the establishment of military courts also called for the constitutional establishment of administrative courts having jurisdiction over administrative matters and falling outside the judicial structure headed by the Supreme Court.

Commissioner Ōishi put the argument as follows:

> Speaking from the premise of the separation of powers, the judicial power should be limited to the power to adjudicate civil and criminal cases as under the old Constitution. Trials of administrative matters should be set apart from the judicial courts; administrative courts composed of persons with knowledge and experience in administrative matters should be established; and disposition of administrative cases should be entrusted to them. Because knowledge of administrative matters is an indispensable prerequisite in administrative trials, to assign such trials to ordinary judicial courts is to go beyond the capacities of judges. The burden on the judges is one source for the delay of trials. To state that the executive power must submit, if the judicial power holds illegality in administrative matters, is to destroy the separation of powers. Because administrative discretion and maneuverability must be respected, matters to be judged in administrative trials must be defined in law.

Commissioner Kamikawa proposed that the phrase "special tribunals" be changed to "extraordinary tribunals." He argued that extraordinary tribunals (or, alternatively, "emergency tribunals") are those created on an exceptional and temporary basis on occasions of special necessity and that such courts should be prohibited. However, he asserted, special courts are established to hold trials of persons in special categories or to deal with special matters and are outside the structure of ordinary courts. Military, administrative, and constitutional courts are regarded as special courts in this sense.

The view that the present prohibition on special tribunals is proper and that special courts should not be established.

This view was based on the assumption that the prohibition of special tribunals and the unification of the court system under the Supreme Court are appropriate for the establishment and strengthening of both constitutional government and the rule of law and for the guarantee of the fundamental human rights of the people. Proponents of this view also argued that the necessity for special courts had not been established and, even if it were, there would be no justification for setting them up outside the general structure of the courts.

Commissioner Mano, for example, argued against the establishment of any special courts, be they administrative, labor, election, or tax. The general reasons he set forth were as follows:

1. The principal reasons put forward for the establishment of administrative courts are that they would be more efficient and that their judges would be possessed of special knowledge and experience in administrative matters. However, efficiency can be achieved and judges with special qualifications be obtained without setting up special courts. The objectives could be achieved if special branches were established within the existing court structure where special problems could be handled by specialists in the appropriate fields. He also pointed out that on the basis of the experience of administrative courts under the Meiji Constitution it did not necessarily follow that new administrative courts would advance judicial efficiency.

2. To establish independent special tribunals nationwide would be difficult from the standpoint both of personnel and of facilities.

3. If the proposed special courts were to be regarded as judicial courts, then confusion would ensue because there would be several different systems of judicial courts. If they were not to be so regarded, in judgments made by the highest court in each category, it would not be clear where the final binding force would reside. If final binding force were recognized in these courts, then the people could not bring action in the judicial courts in such suits. This would take away the fundamental right of access to the courts as provided for in Article 32, a highly improper situation.

The opinion opposing the establishment of military courts as special tribunals.

Commissioners who were opposed to a revision of Article 9 to create a self-defense system were naturally also opposed to the establishment of military courts. Commissioners Aichi and Kamikawa who supported both a revision of Article 9 and the establishment of military courts believed, however, that it would be sufficient if such courts were set up as courts of first instance within the court structure under the Supreme Court.

The opinion opposing the establishment of administrative courts as special tribunals.

Those holding this opinion set forth the following principal reasons: abuses were numerous in the administrative courts under the Meiji Constitution; and assuming there is a need for courts to handle administrative trials, then it would be sufficient to establish them either as lower courts in the present judicial structure or as special sections within existing courts. Those of this view also held that special study and training would be adequate to provide the necessary capability for judges to handle trials in administrative matters.

Commissioner Takayanagi pointed out that the old administrative courts were not truly independent because they were a part of the executive branch and tended to act at the convenience of the government. He also declared that the hearing officers knowledgeable in the affairs of administration did not dispose of cases more efficiently than judges of the ordinary courts; indeed, the delay of suits in administrative courts was notorious.

Commissioner Rōyama pointed out that there has been an increase in administrative cases because of the tendency toward a national society and the welfare state, and in the number of cases of a professional or technical nature, and suggested that the situation might be handled by introducing judicial procedures into administrative organs or committees or by providing them with quasi-judicial powers. However, he stated that in any case the way must remain open for possible appeal to the regular judicial courts.

The Power of Judicial Review

The central questions in respect to the power of judicial review were: Should the system be preserved as it is? Or is it necessary to create a constitutional court or to give the Supreme Court the characteristics of one? A large number of opinions were expressed on these two questions, and they raised the following series of questions: Should the system of judicial review of laws be abolished? Should the constitutional review of abstract cases be recognized? Should the power of judicial review be limited only to the Supreme Court? and Should the power of judicial review of treaties be recognized?

THE JUDICIAL REVIEW OF LAWS. Commissioner Ōishi was the only one who advocated the abolition of the power of judicial review. His opinion on this matter can be summarized as follows. On the basis of the separation of powers for the courts to declare a law passed as constitutional by the legislative branch to be unconstitutional is an infringement on the legislative power by the judicial power. The right of judicial review is also undemocratic in that it can lead to the negation of a law passed by the representatives of the people. The determination of unconstitutionality should be by a popular referendum, not by the courts. Originally, the right of judicial review was designed to protect the freedom of the individual, but today the exercise of that right would interfere with the positive fostering of the life of the people because it stresses restraint on the actions of the state. Finally, according to the text of the Constitution, the right of judicial review extends to all actions of the state, including matters of a high political character such as treaties and the dissolution of the House of Representatives. This will lead to the politicization of justice, a development to be feared.

Commissioner Kamikawa did not support the abolition of the right of judicial review, but did point out that if it continued then Article 41 ("the highest organ of state power" provision) would have to be revised because of the contradiction between judicial review and legislative supremacy.

In opposition to the abolition of the right of judicial review it was maintained that in general the good sense of the Diet would operate but there is no guarantee that no laws will be made in contravention of the guarantee of fundamental human rights. To cover such cases reliance on the good sense of the Diet or on popular criticism expressed through elections is not enough; judicial review should be retained. In response to Ōishi's arguments it was pointed out that under the system of separation of powers in our Constitution there are built-in limitations on the judicial power, and therefore it is proper to recognize the right of the courts to deliberate even on matters with a high political content. The right of judicial review is a part of the system under which the authority of each power of government is checked by the others, thus enabling the national government to operate harmoniously as a whole. Finally, it was argued that to advance the efficiency of the contemporary welfare state is no justification for the abolition of the right of judicial review.

It was also argued that there is no direct contradiction between judicial review and legislative supremacy that cannot be resolved through constitutional application and interpretation.

A CONSTITUTIONAL COURT. What was discussed as a constitutional court was one possessing the right of jurisdiction over abstract constitutional issues. Thus, it would differ from the Supreme Court which has the character of a regular judicial court which determines constitutionality in actions involving concrete cases. Most of the opinions expressed on this matter were against it.

Commissioner Inaba stated the case for a constitutional court: "The power of judicial review of the Supreme Court based on Article 81 is insufficient. A constitutional court should be established so that clear and rapid resolutions of constitutional disputes can be achieved. The following benefits would ensue: (1) the strengthening of democracy and the raising of the level of the guarantee of fundamental human rights and freedoms; (2) the advantage of rapidly controlling political struggles and divisions of public opinion arising from conflicting interpretations of constitutional issues; and (3) control over the excesses of the majority party because the government, the Diet, and the majority party would all have to respect the judgment of a constitutional court."

Those who objected to the creation of a constitutional court presented the following principal arguments: political battles being fought in the Diet would be carried into the courts; political issues would end by being treated as legal issues; and the separation of powers would be violated by the establishment of an organ which would be strikingly superior to the others.

Commissioner Mizuno presented the following opposing view. "To establish a constitutional court or to give the Supreme Court the characteristics of one would result in such concerns as the following: (1) the drawing of such a court into the confusion of political conflict; (2) the impairment of the positions of independence and impartiality of judges; (3) uneasiness over possible hindrance to just and fair judgments because of the generally conservative tendencies of the judges of such courts; (4) the creation of an impression of coercive control over Diet legislation by the court; and (5) the possibility of a disruption of the principle of the separation of powers."

In addition, Commissioner Takayanagi presented the view that a constitutional court, as the term was being used, is unnecessary, but there might be some merit in a system in which there would be a supreme court which would specialize in ordinary civil and criminal cases and a constitutional court specializing in [concrete] constitutional cases. However, he indicated a preference for strengthening the character of the present Supreme Court as a constitutional court by methods similar to those used in respect to the United States Supreme Court, such as to improve the appeals system or to leave final judgments in ordinary civil and criminal cases to lower courts.

Those who opposed the establishment of a constitutional court and the adoption of a system of abstract judicial review were also against giving the present Supreme Court the character of a constitutional court.

THE RIGHT OF ABSTRACT CONSTITUTIONAL REVIEW. The precedents of the Supreme Court hold that judicial review under the present Constitution extends only to concrete legal conflicts, not to abstract cases. Apart from opinions supporting the establishment of a constitutional court, no commissioner expressed the opinion that the right of abstract constitutional review be granted to the judicial courts.

However, there was a conflict of opinion over how the current situation might be recognized. One opinion held that there should be a specific constitutional provision denying the right in order that there could be no doubt on the issue. Another view was that since the Supreme Court has already ruled that it does not possess the right of abstract judicial review, nothing more need be done. Commissioner Mano commented as follows: "The special feature of constitutional interpretation by the courts is that it is carried out, not abstractly, but in relation to concrete cases arising from political and social life and from a concrete and realistic point of view. This process is possessed of great worth. If abstract review is recognized, there will the danger that the constitutional interpretations of the courts will become abstract without foundation in reality."

JUDICIAL REVIEW IN THE SUPREME COURT AND THE LOWER COURTS. Opinions were split on the issue of judicial review, one group holding that the Supreme Court alone should have the right, the other that it be shared with other courts.

Commissioner Ōnishi expressed the view that only the Supreme Court should be granted judicial review because the actual practice in our country is that where lower courts decide issues of constitutionality or unconstitutionality, their decisions are usually appealed to the Supreme Court. Therefore, the right should be granted exclusively to the Supreme Court in order to speed up trials, to increase the authority of the Supreme Court, and to prevent the impairment of the prestige of the lower courts through the frequent reversal of their decisions.

Commissioners Takayanagi and Mano argued against Supreme Court exclusivity. First, if the Supreme Court is regarded as being simultaneously a court of first instance and the court of last resort on constitutional issues then its judgments will be purely conceptual without the backing of the determination of facts. Second, they argued, it is important that the Supreme Court hand down a decision on constitutionality only after the problem has been examined in a lower court trial in which the relevant facts have been brought out and after a thorough public discussion of the lower court decision has occurred. They also maintained that the current process can result in the cultivation of the constitutional consciousness of the people.

THE JUDICIAL REVIEW OF TREATIES. The case against judicial review of treaties was well stated by Commissioners Mizuno and Kojima: "Treaties should not be the object of judicial review because they are created by agreement with other countries and it is improper for the courts of one country to make a judgment on their validity or invalidity. In addition, the review of treaties frequently could involve political questions and acts of state as well as questions of international good faith."

Opinion was split on the question of whether there should be a clear constitutional provision excluding treaties from the right of judicial review. The discussion also touched on the issue of the relationship in terms of effective force between the Constitution as the supreme law and treaties, but this problem is considered below as an issue relating to Chapter 10, "The Supreme Law."

A SYSTEM OF REVIEW BEFORE THE FACT. Two proposals were put forward regarding review before the fact, that is, a review by the courts or some other governmental organ as a part of the process of the enactment of law or treaty and before promulgation. Commissioner Ōnishi proposed that the Supreme Court be given such a function. Commissioner Hirose suggested that a Commission for the Review of Constitutional Problems, as a special organ charged with the duty of reviewing bills and treaties for constitutionality as a part of the deliberative process, be established in the Diet. However, these proposals were opposed by other commissioners.

The Appointment and Popular Review of Supreme Court Justices

The commissioners also examined whether it is necessary to change the present system of appointment of Supreme Court justices, that is, by cabinet appointment, and whether it is necessary to change the system of popular review. These questions were usually linked to each other.

THE APPOINTMENT OF SUPREME COURT JUSTICES. One group of commissioners held that the present method of appointment of Supreme Court justices is not proper and that it should be supplemented with a committee system. One subgroup held that it would be sufficient to establish by law an advisory committee on appointments, while a second subgroup argued that a screening committee or a selection committee should be established by the Constitution.

Those who supported an advisory committee asserted that the selection of qualified appointees should not be left only to the cabinet. It was pointed out that such a committee was set up at the time the Supreme Court was first appointed, but because there was concern that it might make unclear the responsibility of the cabinet it was dropped. It was also stated that such a committee might help to insure impartiality in this important personnel matter. It was also asserted that an appropriate advisory organ might serve to close the gap between public opinion and the justices.

Those supporting the creation of a screening or selection committee asserted that such a committee should be completely independent of the government and that it would eliminate political or partisan considerations from the appointment process. Such a committee, it was argued, would also eliminate the necessity for the popular review of the justices.

Because he asserted that under the parliamentary cabinet system it is improper to have the cabinet alone responsible for the personnel matters of justices, Commissioner Hirose proposed an elaborate scheme for their appointment. A nonpartisan House of Councilors would nominate the chief justice who would be appointed by the emperor. Grand Bench justices would also be appointed by the emperor after nomination by the cabinet with the consent of the House of Councilors from a list of nominees prepared by a selection committee. Petty Bench justices would fall into two groups: imperial appointees and nonimperial appointees. The former would go through the same process as for Grand Bench justices; the latter would be nominated by the judicial assembly of the Supreme Court and appointed by the cabinet.

Those opposed to this view maintained that it is not necessary to revise the Constitution in order to alter the current process of selection. For example, if it is deemed necessary to control the possible abuse of the cabinet's power of appointment by partisan political considerations through the device of an advisory committee, such a committee can be created by law.

THE POPULAR REVIEW OF SUPREME COURT JUSTICES. The majority of the commissioners were of the view that the current system of popular review of justices is improper and should be abolished. They set forth a long list of reasons for their view:

1. Popular review is meaningless because the people cannot make a judgment of the fitness of justices because of a lack of knowledge of their characters, knowledge, and opinions.

2. Justices may sometimes be swayed by public opinion, and this might lead to an eventual loss of independence of mind.

3. The system may be abused, thus leading to an impairment of the independence of the justices.

4. It costs a considerable amount of money.

5. It is said that the system may constitute a bond between the people and the justices, but because the voting is only a formality it is doubtful that such a bond can exist and, moreover, it might not even be desirable.

6. Such a system might even give people a false impression of the significance of elections and voting.

7. A system of recall is not effective in large areas and is unreasonable on the national level.

8. If justices were elected, then dismissal by referendum would be reasonable, but it is unreasonable to use a national referendum only for purposes of dismissal.

9. There are defects and abuses in the system. For example, if a voter has not made up his mind and records nothing on his ballot, it is unreasonable to interpret that as a vote not approving the dismissal of a justice. It is doubtful that any reasonable system of voting can be worked out.

10. There is the opinion that this system is an expression of popular sovereignty and should be continued, but it is too simpleminded to think that democracy can be achieved through a purely logical realization of the principle of popular sovereignty. The system is excessively formalistic and conceptualistic and goes too far toward the idealistic.

A number of substitute proposals were made, including the sufficiency of the current system of impeachment; a review every eight years by a nonpartisan House of Councilors; a term limited to a period of seven or ten years; and the creation of a committee for review of qualifications, consisting of properly qualified individuals, which would be empowered to decide on dismissals.

Only a minority supported the maintenance of the system of popular review. However, reasoned support for the system was presented as follows:

1. The system is consistent with the fact that the election of both the legislative branch (directly) and of the executive branch (indirectly) depends ultimately on the will of the people.

2. The justices are appointed, and the fact that the system of popular review was adopted in regard to their dismissal silently exerts great pressure for the protection of the propriety of appointments and is therefore of considerable significance.

3. What is involved is not the ability of the people to judge the general fitness of the justices, but rather the expression of judgment in specific instances where dismissal is under consideration for reasons involving, for example, matters of morality.

4. Experience has shown that since the first occasion no considerable outlay of funds has been required.

5. The system strengthens the people's knowledge of and familiarity with the judiciary and therefore contributes to the judicial education of the people.

6. Experience has shown that no intelligent justice who has handed

down a decision in defiance of public opinion has been dismissed as a result of popular review and that no justice has been led to fear popular review or has lost his attitude of unrestrained freedom of conscience.

Other Problems Relating to the Judiciary

COMPOSITION OF THE SUPREME COURT. Two questions arose concerning the composition of the Supreme Court: Should the number of Supreme Court justices be determined by the Constitution? Should it be stipulated in the Constitution that the Supreme Court can handle cases and make judgments in the Grand Bench and the petty benches?

Commissioners Ōnishi and Kamikawa argued that the number of Supreme Court justices should be stipulated in the Constitution in order to prevent either the government or the Diet from increasing the number of justices more or less at will. Those in opposition argued that the number of justices has been treated as a problem that could be changed in accordance with the requirements of the times and that to date there has been neither misgiving nor danger that the government or the Diet would act arbitrarily on this matter. While conceding that the composition of the Supreme Court might be changed in order to speed up legal proceedings, they said that this could be done by changes in the law, not in the Constitution.

Those supporting constitutional recognition of the division of the Supreme Court into the Grand Bench and the petty benches argued that it should be done in order to prevent the delay of justice by providing a necessary number of petty benches and enabling them to handle appeals in the second instance.

In opposition it was argued that the necessary reforms could be achieved through revision of laws, not the Constitution. It was also asserted that the problem of the delay of justice in the Supreme Court was broader than the issue of the petty benches.

THE RULE-MAKING POWER. On the issue of the rule–making power, Commissioners Ōishi, Hirose, Kamikawa, and Ōnishi argued that in order to clarify the relationship between the Supreme Court's rule-making power and the Diet's power of legislation, it is necessary to qualify the rule-making power with the phrase "within the limits of law." The basis of this argument was that the Diet is the sole law-making organ and that legal procedures should be determined by laws enacted by the Diet. Commissioner Tagami declared that there should be a constitutional provision to the effect that such fundamental matters as legal procedures can be determined by law and that rules cannot be in conflict with laws.

On the other hand, Commissioners Mano, Sakanishi, and Mizuno asserted that no constitutional revision is required to clarify the relationship between rules and laws. Their arguments were: (1) that the relationship should not be debated on the grounds of the purely mechanical application of such concepts as the Diet's position as the sole law-making organ or the separation of powers; (2) that Supreme Court precedents on the matter are the basis of the current handling of the problem; and (3) that the Supreme Court has never made any decisions holding that rules are superior to laws.

THE POWER OF JUDICIAL ADMINISTRATION. The point was raised that the Constitution is not clear that the power of judicial administration is assigned to the Supreme Court. However, the only opinion expressed was that there is no need to clarify this in the Constitution. Commissioners Mizuno and Takayanagi strongly asserted the opinion that to transfer administrative matters relating to the judiciary from the courts to the executive branch should absolutely not be done in order to preserve the independence of the judicial power.

However, Commissioner Aichi raised the point as to whether the scope of judicial administration carried out by the Supreme Court under the present Constitution is too broad. He said: "At present, personnel matters of secretaries, salaries, building and repairs, the Public Prosecutors' Review Committee, and the training of students for careers in law and justice all fall under judicial administration as carried out by the Supreme Court, but judicial administration by the courts should be limited to matters which are more directly or more closely related to the exercise of the judicial power. . . ."

THE PRINCIPLE OF PUBLIC TRIAL. Article 82 reads in part as follows: "Where a court unanimously determines publicity to be dangerous to public order or morals, a trial may be conducted privately, but trials of political offenses, offenses involving the press, or cases where the rights of the people as guaranteed in Chapter 3 of this Constitution are in question shall always be conducted publicly." There was one opinion that this proviso should be eliminated and another that "unanimously" should be changed to "a majority of the court" in order to facilitate the approval of closed trials.

Those supporting elimination of this provision argued that it is excessive to insist on public trials even in the matters enumerated. It was also argued that nonpublic trials might be justified in cases where secrecy in foreign relations is a consideration and also in military cases if a self-defense army is sanctioned in the future.

Commissioners Mano and Mizuno argued that strict limitations on secret trials would contribute to the democratization and fairness of trials, would increase the people's confidence in trials, and would give content to the guarantee of human rights. It was also argued that the provision should be retained because no evils had appeared under it and because history has demonstrated that secret trials of political crimes have been prejudicial to the accused.

General Summary

A very large number of problems relating to the judiciary were dealt with, but the central issue was the basic principle adopted in the Constitution, namely, that the judicial power should be broadened and strengthened. Almost all commissioners held that this principle should be preserved.

The most frequently treated problem related to the basic principle was the right of judicial review. One opinion, while supporting the basic principle, held that judicial review raised the position of the courts excessively in respect to the Diet. But the majority view was that the present system of judicial review should not be changed. A very small minority supported the establishment of a constitutional court or the bestowal on the present Supreme Court of the character of such a court.

The most striking division of opinion occurred on the issue of the method of appointment of Supreme Court justices and the system of popular review which might lead to dismissal. Of particular concern was whether the present system would function effectively to obtain persons qualified for appointment as Supreme Court justices. On this point it was frequently argued that to obtain such persons and to guarantee their independence on the bench, an advisory committee on appointments should be established and the system of popular review abolished. Related to this concern was the aim of preventing the injection of political and partisan motives into both appointments and popular review.

Those opposed to constitutional revision as an approach to these two problems argued that an advisory committee system could be established by law and that the important thing about the system of popular review is that it maintains the ideal form of judicial power as based on the principle of popular sovereignty while preserving a harmony between the Supreme Court and public opinion. In fact, the opposition of views on what the courts and the judicial power should be under popular sovereignty underlay the discussion of the propriety of both the system of judicial review and the system of the popular review of Supreme Court justices.

Section H.
Finances

Article 83 reads: "The power to administer national finances shall be exercised as the Diet shall determine." Consequently, the basic problem dealt with in relation to finances was whether the system centered on the Diet, thus further strengthening its position, is proper. This question went beyond finances and was also related to the issue of the Diet as the "highest organ," particularly in regard to its relationship with the cabinet.

In addition to the above basic problem, other concrete problems, as issues of the Diet's power to decide the budget, such as the following were dealt with: the system of emergency financial measures; the related problems of the Diet's power to increase budget appropriations and of members' bills accompanying the budget; the problem of continuing expenditures; situations where the budget has not been enacted; and limitations on the expenditure and use of public funds. The number of opinions expressed on these questions was not particularly large.

A Diet-based Financial System

The view that the financial system determined by the present Constitution is overly biased in favor of the Diet, that there is a need to adjust the authority of the cabinet and the Diet in financial matters, and that amendment is necessary to that end.

This view included the following points. It is natural under the ideal form of democracy and parliamentary government that the basic principle be adopted that the Diet is at the core of the financial system. However, even while preserving this basic principle, it is necessary to emphasize the responsibilities and the authority of the government (cabinet) for the management of the complicated financial affairs of the contemporary society. Thus, from this point of view the Constitution is overly biased in favor of the Diet, the authority of the Diet and the cabinet in these matters should be adjusted, and it is necessary to act in order to make possible coordination of finances, measures for financial soundness and flexibility, and the prevention of abuses in state expenditures. From this point of view such items as the following were demanded: limitations on the right of the Diet to increase budgetary items, and systems involving discretionary and continuing expenditures and emergency financial measures.

As indicated above, the question of the Diet as the highest organ was also involved in the issue of finances. For example, in pursuit of his ideal of the "independence and cooperation of the three powers," Commissioner Hirose had the following to say on the financial system: "The essential nature of the national budget which is the nucleus of the financial system makes it indivisibly one with administration which is the responsibility of the cabinet. In the light of this fact, the system favoring the National Diet over the cabinet in respect to the budget must be regarded as inadequate. Therefore, I think that the authority of the cabinet in relation to the budget must be strengthened and the Constitution should be revised so that we may expect a comprehensive and sound budget and measures for the taking of such financial steps as the occasion may demand."

Commissioner Aichi, while recognizing that the management of the nation's finances should be controlled by the sovereign people, pointed out the extreme complexity of the budget, the position of the cabinet as its drafter, the need to prevent increases of and abuses in expenditures through Diet action, and urged constitutional revision of financial provisions as a remedy.

The view that even though it is necessary to improve the relationship between the Diet and the cabinet in financial management, it is not necessary to revise the Constitution to achieve that goal.

The view here was that the necessary improvement could be achieved by revision of the Finance Law or by interpretation of the present provisions of the Constitution. On this issue Commissioner Rōyama had the following to say:

> . . . a number of abuses have developed, such as the negotiations between the government party and the various ministries in the process of budget-drafting in the cabinet. In order to correct them, it is necessary to establish the leadership of the prime minister in the process of budget drafting, particularly in the cabinet conferences on the budget. To that end it is necessary to bring about a scientific and logical change in the Finance Ministry's methods of budget revision. For example, such measures as the creation of an Office of the Budget in the cabinet and a Cabinet Ministers' Budget Committee with the finance minister as chairman should be considered. But I think that any such changes should be made before any constitutional amendment.

Commissioner Takayanagi pointed out that under Article 83 the power of the Diet over the budget is not unlimited. Consequently, he said, it is possible to adjust the relationship between the cabinet and the Diet through the Finance Law and other legislation and in actual operations.

Emergency Financial Measures

This problem was linked to the general issue that the Constitution contains no provisions relating to states of emergency. On the one hand, it was urged that a revision is necessary to make it possible for the cabinet to take appropriate steps, such as discretionary expenditures, to deal with financial emergencies. On the other hand, it was argued that no such revision is needed.

A majority of the commissioners took the position that some constitutional provisions for dealing with financial emergencies is necessary. Within this group, however, were some who held that strict limitations should be placed on the cabinet's authority to take emergency financial measures, such as the careful definition of situations in which the power could be exercised and a requirement of ex post facto approval by the Diet.

Commissioners Tagami and Takayanagi argued that no special constitutional provisions were needed to enable the cabinet to deal either with general emergencies or with financial emergencies. They asserted that the situation could be anticipated by the passage of appropriate legislation.

Nonpassage of the Budget

A majority of the commissioners believed that the Constitution is deficient in not providing for measures to be taken in case the budget is not approved. They believed that the system of the interim budget as provided for in the present Finance Law is inconvenient. A number of proposals were made to remedy this deficiency.

Commissioner Ōishi: "At a minimum it should be provided that the management of finances, within the limits of the budget of the previous year, would not be suspended."

Commissioner Yoshimura: "The system of interim budgets as recognized in the Finance Law should be established by the Constitution."

Commissioner Ōnishi: "Both the principle of carrying out the budget of the previous year and interim budgets are improper. What is needed is an arrangement along the following lines: When the budget for the coming year has not been approved by the end of the current fiscal year, the cabinet is empowered to make all expenditures necessary to achieve the following objectives or to continue assistance for their achievement: (1) to maintain facilities established by law and to execute acts provided for by law; (2) to fulfill responsibilities related to state obligations under law; and (3) to continue construction, procurement, and other operations, the expenses for which have already been approved in the previous year's budget."

Commissioners Hirose and Aichi: "In this situation it is desirable . . . to create a constitutional system of discretionary expenditures entrusted to the cabinet. That is to say, within limits established by law, the cabinet would be empowered to make expenditures on its own responsibility of only the following types: (1) those necessary for the execution of laws; (2) those necessary for matters involving the responsibilities of the cabinet as established by law; and (3) those relating to special matters as determined by law. In addition, the ex post facto approval by the Diet of such expenditures would be required."

Those opposed to a constitutional provision to deal with situations involving the nonpassage of the budget by the Diet simply argued that it should be done by means not involving changes in the Constitution.

The System of Continuing Expenditures

Four commissioners argued for a constitutional provision recognizing the system of continuing expenditures both because of the intrinsic importance of such a system and because such expenditures actually exist although they must be regarded as exceptions to the principle of the annual approval of the budget.

Those opposed to this view argued that Article 85 goes no farther than to require the approval of the Diet for the expenditure of state funds, and Article 86 simply calls for the Diet to consider and decide on an annual budget. Therefore, Diet-approved continuing expenditures are constitutional under Article 85. Furthermore, they are also recognized under the present Finance Law. Consequently, there is no need for a constitutional recognition of continuing expenditures.

Diet Increases in the Budget and Members' Bills

There was a considerable number of opinions on limitations on Diet increases in the budget and on members' bills accompanying it which held that abuses arose from them resulting in waste of state funds, the loss of cabinet responsibility in the formulation and execution of the budget, and financial confusion. Naturally, those of this opinion favored constitutional limitations on both increases and members' bills.

The principal remedy proposed was the granting of the right of dissent to the cabinet in regard to such upward revisions. It was argued that this right would be a powerful supplement to the right to present the budget. The right of dissent is the other face of the right of cabinet consent to such increases. Commissioner Kamikawa's recommendation was one of the more specific: "Upward revisions of the budget by the Diet must be limited. A provision reading as follows should be adopted: 'When the Diet revises the budget presented by the cabinet, increasing the amount of the expenditures or adding new titles and items, the consent of the cabinet must be obtained. However, when a majority of more than two-thirds of the total membership of each house agrees, this limitation does not apply.'"

Only a very small minority shared the following opinion of Commissioner Ōnishi: "The veto power or the right of dissent by the cabinet are means of correcting the excesses of upward revision of the budget by the Diet and of members' bills. But it would be most desirable to prohibit them completely."

Those opposing argued that these two problems could be dealt with either by reasonable interpretations of the legal principles of the budget itself which contain built-in limitations on upward revisions or by establishing limitations by law, thus eliminating the necessity for constitutional revision.

The Expenditure and Use of Public Funds or Other Public Assets

Article 89 limits the appropriation and expenditure of public money or other property for the use, benefit, or maintenance of any religion or any charitable, educational, or benevolent enterprises not under the control of a public authority. It was the opinion of a majority of the commissioners that this provision is unreasonable and not in accord with present circumstances in our country and should be either abolished or revised. Usually opinions on this problem were split into two groups: the first dealing with religious institutions or associations, and the second with educational, charitable, or benevolent enterprises. Some argued that if the intent of Article 89 is to warn against the waste of public moneys, then it is unreasonable to single out only religious and other types of organizations involved in this article.

Those holding that a limitation on the expenditure of public moneys for religious organizations is improper linked Article 89 with both the separation of church and state and the abolition of Shintō as a state religion and argued that it was designed primarily to eliminate public financial patronage for Shintō shrines, particularly Ise Grand Shrine and Yasukuni Shrine. Of course, they believed this policy to be improper.

It was argued that the Ise and Yasukuni shrines are not simply for individual worship, but possess an intrinsically national character on which it would be natural to expend public money. It was further pointed out that it is permissible for public money to be given to private religious schools with the aim of assisting their general educational programs and that this is in contradiction to the situation relating to the Ise and Yasukuni shrines.

One opinion held that the provisions relating to educational, charitable, and benevolent enterprises in Article 89 should be eliminated and that it should deal only with religious organizations. Commissioners Ōnishi and Uemura suggested the elimination of the phrase dealing with nonreligious organizations and the insertion of the following provisions: "However, there shall be no hindrance to making special provision in law regarding mausolea of the imperial family or of the war dead." Commissioners Hirose and Yamasaki asserted that the principle of the separation of church and state should be stated clearly and separately in relation to the freedom of religion, not to finances.

A majority of the commissioners felt that the limitation on the expenditure of public funds on educational, charitable, and benevolent enterprises is improper, because in the planning and complete development of such enterprises it is necessary for the state to lend positive financial assistance.

Those opposing the above view held that Article 89 need not be revised because any real problems can be handled through actual operations. For example, Commissioner Takayanagi argued as follows:

> This provision, together with Article 20, establishes the principles of freedom of religion and of the separation of church and state. In order to make the religious freedom of the individual complete, the separation of church and state is necessary. In this sense, the principles of this provision must be preserved.
>
> However, the application of these principles should be a matter of common sense, not of textual interpretation; any action should be regarded as constitutional to the extent that it does not involve either the expenditure of public money or the granting of privileges to specific religious sects. One opinion holds that this article should be revised so that public money can be expended on the Ise and Yasukuni shrines, but if the aim is to revive state Shintō by this means, then it is in violation of the principle of the separation of church and state. However, if it is made clear that the intent is not to grant special privileges to Shintō, it is not unconstitutional to maintain Ise Shrine as an important cultural asset, providing strict limitations are placed on such maintenance.

In regard to Yasukuni Shrine, Commissioner Inaba suggested that a solution might be to treat it as a special nonreligious memorial hall, thus avoiding the treatment it was accorded under the old Constitution.

In regard to assistance to nonreligious organizations, Commissioner Tagami pointed out that the intent of this provision is to prevent government control and restraint of such organizations through financial assistance. Therefore, he saw no reason to revise this provision since the problem can be dealt with through flexible application of a textual interpretation of the phrase "under the control of." Such a procedure would both satisfy his interpretation of Article 89 and take care of the fact that the article is not in accord with current situations in Japan.

Other Problems relating to Finance

One opinion held that the provision in Article 88, "all Imperial Household property shall belong to the State," should be eliminated, but another held that it need not be.

Several opinions asserted that it was necessary to clarify the provisions relating to final accounts and the Board of Audit. On this issue Commissioners Kamikawa and Ōnishi stated: "Final accounts should be accorded the same importance as the budget. But in the present Constitution nothing more is said than that they should be submitted to the Diet, leaving unclear whether the consent of the Diet is required. This matter is in contravention of the principle of the central role of the Diet in the financial system." Commissioners Hirose and Ōishi stated that the Constitution should clearly specify that the Board of Audit is independent of the cabinet.

Commissioner Kamikawa stated that the provision of Article 91 that the cabinet shall report at least annually to the Diet and the people on the national finances should be eliminated from the Constitution and instead stipulated in the Finance Law.

Commissioner Hirose urged that consideration be given to the establishment of constitutional provisions relating to an economic council and to economic planning. In rebuttal, Commissioner Uemura held that constitutional establishment of an economic council would be doubtful because of the existing economic responsibilities of the cabinet and the Diet and that even though it is recognized that economic planning should be based on the budget, it is doubtful that the procedure should be made constitutional.

General Summary

As has already been emphasized, a majority of the commission believed that the establishment of the Diet as the center of the system of finances was at one with the structure of government established by the present Constitution in which the National Diet is "the highest organ of state power." Consequently, those who felt that the tendency toward the supremacy of the Diet over the cabinet has gone too far and that the relationship between them should be brought into balance also believed that the same thing is true in the financial system and called for a change. The above consideration underlay the fairly large number of specific problems relating to the financial system that came under discussion.

In general, those opposed to the above view shared the same concerns about the financial system, but came to the conclusion that what is required to remedy the situation is not constitutional revision, but changes in the actual administration of finances and in the Finance Law and other legislation.

SECTION I.
LOCAL SELF-GOVERNMENT

The principal problems relating to local self-government included: the ideal form of contemporary local self-government; the relationship between the state and local public entities; the varieties, organization, and powers of local public entities; and methods of election of their heads. The basic problem was what the ideal form of local self-government should be. All other problems were tied to it in one way or another.

The Ideal Form of Contemporary Local Self-Government

The view that because local self-government today should not be biased toward the freedom and independence of local public entities from the state and because it is necessary that there be cooperation between the state and local public entities in order to realize the welfare state, it is necessary that the provisions regarding local self-government in the present Constitution be changed.

This view recognized that local self-government is the foundation of democratic government and regarded as natural the necessity for providing for its expansion, but nevertheless it also held that the ideal form of local self-government should not call needlessly for the local decentralization of power, that is, the independence and autonomy of local public entities from the state, but in order to realize the welfare state both national government and local self-government must be based on an organic and cooperative relationship. From this point of view, the present provisions relating to local self-government are deficient.

Some specific shortcomings of the present Constitution in this area were also pointed out. They included the lack of a provision relating to the nature of the basic relationship between the state and local public entities, the tendency implied in the phrase "principle of local self-government" to stress only the independence and autonomy of local public entities from the state, and doubts concerning the possibility under present interpretations for the establishment of the wide-area system in response to the requirements of wide-area administration. It was also stated that because some constitutional provisions certainly are not appropriate to the actual operation of local self-government at present, confusions and abuses have arisen which have obstructed efficient and coordinated national administration and have prevented the harmonious development of local self-government itself.

The following long quotation from the Joint Declaration clearly states the issues involved in this point of view:

> The ultimate point at issue in local self-government is how to achieve harmony and coexistence between what must be termed the basic principle of local self-government, namely, the decentralization of power and the local autonomy of the residents on the one hand, and economy in expenditures and the improvement of administrative efficiency which flow from the requirements of the contemporary welfare state on the other hand. Consequently, the problem is not simply to pay lip-service to the concept of local self-government, but from the broad and elevated viewpoint of the development and stabilization of the life of the people to consider both the reality and the form, and the limits thereon, of local self-government on the basis of the concrete relation between the above issues. At present the centralization of power is criticized as being both arbitrary and antidemocratic. In addition, the attitude of following the decentralization of power as if it were a golden rule because it is democratic cannot escape the criticism of being either childish or anachronistic.

> In simpler terms it is a question of the relationship between national administration and local self-government. The two are joined organically. Local public entities have no existence completely independent of the state; just as the existence of the state is a prerequisite so is the existence of national administration a prerequisite for local government. Thus, we must not forget that what is termed "the principle of local self-government" means that national and local government are democratic and that they stand together in efficient harmony. Decentralization must be regarded from this point of view.

> Because decentralization is based on differences in the social conditions of various areas, as those conditions change so must there be changes in decentralization. If local social conditions are equalized, if special local characteristics are lost, and if local areas through the development of transportation and communication are converted into wide areas, then the broadening of local administration and the centralization of power are inescapable. It is necessary to provide an elasticity so that an adaptation to historical and social change can be achieved.

To give concrete constitutional form to the organic relationship between national administration and local self-government, Commissioner Kōri suggested two additions to the local self-government provisions. The first would be: "The exercise of the power of administration in local areas must be carried out with respect for local self-government." This, he declared, would make respect for the principle of local self-government compatible with the realization of a democratic and efficient harmony between the state and the local area in a situation in which the latter is not independent of the former. The second would be: "The state and local public entities must cooperate and strive for the advancement of the welfare of the people." This would make clear that the central concern of both national and local government should be the popular welfare, not simply their compatibility or incompatibility or the maintenance of a strict distinction between their affairs.

The following long comment by ex-Commissioner Ota Masataka stresses both the theoretical difficulties arising from the ambiguity of the phrase "the principle of local self-government" and a number of specific problems which have resulted:

Because the meaning of what is termed "the principle of local self-government" is extremely unclear, considerable confusion has arisen in both theory and in the actual practice of local government.

For example, on the theoretical side the following points, among others, are most unclear. (1) Does local self-government as recognized in the present Constitution mean self-government by organizations or by residents? (2) Are the powers constitutionally possessed by local public entities inherent, bestowed by the Constitution, or approved by affirmation? (3) Do what are termed local public entities include both prefectures and cities, towns, and villages? Or only cities, towns, and villages? And assuming that the former is the case, what is the relationship among the four categories? Accordingly, in respect to the question of what the principle of local self-government is, it might be possible to arrive at an interpretation through the establishment of some basis for thinking.

Next, the theoretical problems are also reflected in the actual operations of local self-government and have produced the following situations.

1. Regarding the administration of local self-government as a whole, there is too great a gap between the goals of the present Constitution which are to strengthen the independence and autonomy of local public entities and to stabilize the foundation of the democratization of the national administration and the actual state of the administration of local self-government. That is to say, the scope of the affairs that are entrusted to the independent management of local public entities is growing progressively smaller and, at the least, being tied down to the concept of local self-government in the old sense of the self-government of organizations has got to the point of preventing the smooth execution of local administration.

2. The following evils in the administration of local self-government have come to be recognized:

a. On items not under the control of government orders the autonomy of local public entities is given full play and this is particularly striking in areas outside ordinary business matters.

b. As a result of a lack of overall control over the relationship between the prefectures and the cities, towns, and villages there is a regrettable lack of close liaison between those units in the execution of administrative matters.

c. The relationship between the heads of local public entities and their assemblies is based on the American presidential system, but because the system of checks and balances is based on measures such as dissolution and reconsideration, methods which are not readily available to an elective governor, there are frequent cases of the needless involvement of the assembly in the executive power.

d. The lack of integration of the administrative arms of the state means that the prefectures are flooded with uncoordinated and mutually contradictory measures from the state with a resulting multiplication of confusion.

e. The poverty of local resources invites the direct administration of assistance from the national treasury, increases the dependence of local public entities on the national treasury, provides more frequent opportunities for interference by government offices in the administration of local public entities, and heightens the degree of confusion therein.

f. The system of election for the heads of local public entities invites actions by the heads with an eye toward election and hinders impartiality in administration.

g. Provisions relating to supervision and direction by the state of local public entities are extremely weak, depending on individual ordinances and not recognizing in any coordinated fashion the rights to give advice and to require action.

h. In the face of unified action on the part of such labor unions as the Japan Teachers' Union, the local public entities as represented by their heads, for example, are likely to be disunited and thus made to dance to the tune of the opposition.

In view of the above points, I think that it is necessary to set forth clearly in the Constitution the concrete meaning of the principle of local government. I also think it necessary that the relationships between the state and the prefectures, cities, towns, and villages and between the prefectures and the cities, towns, and villages be made clear constitutionally and especially the power of the state to supervise the prefectures, cities, towns and villages should be both determined and strengthened by the Constitution.

The view that recognizes the necessity for conformity with the trends in contemporary local self-government, but that does not see the need to revise the Constitution because the problem can be managed by the elastic interpretation and application of the present provisions.

This view placed a high value on the significance of the present chapter relating to local self-government and also recognized that it is the tendency of local self-government not simply to strengthen decentralization of power but also to harmonize it with central authority. But because local self-government must be in accordance with the requirements of the times, it is proper to recognize in an elastic manner the broadening of the areas to be entrusted to both legislation and administration and so the provisions of the present Constitution are all most appropriate since it is possible through their elastic application to dispose of actual problems.

Commissioner Takayanagi stated the position of the proponents of this view as follows:

The enactment of a special chapter on local self-government in the present Constitution was based on the view that because there is the danger in a unitary country of a shift to the authoritarian state through the excessive concentration of power, it is necessary as a preventative measure to strengthen local self-government.

However, in a highly industrialized society such as ours at present, to freeze in the Constitution the authority relationships among the units of local self-government and the relationship between them and the state is improper, particularly for economic reasons. From this point of view, that the Constitution has not provided anything in detail on these points, but relies on law to cover them, must be considered one of its strong points.

Therefore, problems such as whether the present major units of local self-government should be abolished and so-called wide areas or regions be established or whether the present units should be retained and a cooperative organization be developed for them are not constitutional issues. They can be resolved somehow by means of law.

Commissioner Tagami argued that "to the degree that an entity possesses a public character so does its relationship with the state become closer and it must be accepted that it be under the supervision of the state through law." But he asserted that the problems could be dealt with by law without the necessity for constitutional revision.

Commissioner Rōyama recognized the necessity for the establishment of wide-area administration, but believed that it could be done by law. But he also declared that to try to create wide-area administration only by constitutional amendment "would probably give rise to both confusion and opposition in both administrative policy and the formulation of plans."

Local Autonomy and Types of Local Public Entities

"THE PRINCIPLE OF LOCAL AUTONOMY." The issue here was whether the phrase "the principle of local autonomy" in Article 92 should be changed. One group held that it should because it is not sufficient to indicate the ideal form of contemporary local self-government. Another group held that, while being abstract, it still reveals the importance of local autonomy and is adaptable to elastic interpretation. In view of the fact that it is difficult to come up with a good substitute, the phrase should remain, but some provision clarifying the relationship between the state and local public entities should be added. A third group held that the phrase should remain unchanged. The view was also expressed that it was more important to define the scope and types of local public entities than to deal with the principle.

THE SCOPE AND TYPE OF LOCAL PUBLIC ENTITIES. *The view that it is necessary to enact provisions making clear the scope and type of local public entities for the sake of the reform of the todōfuken system or the establishment of the wide-area system.*

It was argued that Articles 92 and 93 provide only for "local public entities" and so it should be stipulated constitutionally that such entities include both the *todōfuken* and cities, towns, and villages as in the present Local Autonomy Law. It was also asserted that the present ambiguity raised questions about the constitutionality of proposals to create the wide-area system, to abolish the *todōfuken*, and to abolish the elective system for the governors of the *todōfuken*.

Commissioner Ōishi made the simple suggestion that "types" be added to the phrase "organization and operations of local public entities." That would permit beyond any doubt the creation, alteration, or abolition of local public entities by law.

There were many opinions which argued both for wide-area administrative regions replacing the *todōfuken* system and for the simultaneous shift of local autonomy to the cities, towns, and villages where it could be greatly expanded. The following views of ex-Commissioner Ota constitute a good statement of this position.

> In view of the actual state of development of industry, the economy, society, culture, and transportation and of the necessity for broad and coordinated management, because the present area of the prefectures is excessively confined, they should be conveniently rearranged and a provincial or wide-area system laid out. For example, the very recent social and economic development of our country has broadened the economic and social spheres of the residents of local public entities, demanded a rectification of regional discrimination, and brought on the necessity for coordinated development. However, the result has been to create administrative confusion between prefectures and cities, towns, and villages or between prefecture and prefecture or among cities, towns, and villages and, in addition, the ineffective expenditure of funds. Also the actual state of affairs is one in which matters which should be handled over a broad area are confined within a sense of "a narrow autonomy" and there is no progress. I suggest that under these circumstances we should have serious second thoughts about what the present prefectural system should be like and about the two-layer system of prefectures and cities, towns, and villages.
>
> In addition, for the following variety of reasons, the present prefectural system has become a barrier to administrative development.
>
> 1. Through a speeding up of the consolidation of cities, towns, and villages their scale and administrative and financial capabilities have tended toward gradual expansion and strengthening and the prefectures have strengthened their character as organizations which should carry out only supplementary

administrative functions for the cities, towns, and villages. These facts suggest the strengthening of cities, towns, and villages as the basic local public entities and the reorganization of the prefectures.

2. Since traffic and river administration, planning for disasters and coordinated development all require execution from an integrated point of view transcending the former narrow limits, this also requires consideration from the standpoint of both the nation and of the will of the residents of the area.

3. Economic development calls for a broadening of the scale of enterprises and, naturally, if the administration of industry is not also broadened, its effectiveness cannot be raised.

Because of the above points I believe that it is impossible to discover an appropriate solution without the abolition of the present prefectural system and the creation of a regional or provincial system. Thus, in order to make the above suggestion for a regional system into a reality it is necessary to make constitutionally clear that what are termed local public entities are only cities, towns and villages.

The view that revision in order to make clear the scope and varieties of local public entities is unnecessary.

Those holding this view felt that it is a strong point of Article 92 that it has no provision concerning the scope and types of local public entities and relies on elastic legislation and operation. Also it was felt that what is preferable to constitutional revision is the speedy development of cooperative relations both between the state and local public entities and among public entities themselves. In supporting this view, Commissioner Kōri pointed out that the establishment of the so-called regional system might not be the solution to the problem of wide-area administration and that a constitutional establishment of the regional system might not solve all problems.

The Selection of Heads of Local Public Entities

The view that since Article 93 which provides for a uniform system for the election of heads is not proper, it is necessary to revise it.

This view held that the present uniform method of selection is not appropriate and should be replaced by a system under which the method of selection would be determined by the size of the local public entity involved. It was also asserted that the most democratic method for the selection of the head should also be considered in relation to the type of organization involved. The following suggestions were made on the method of selection.

Commissioner Hirose: "Heads of basic local public entities, as defined by law, should be elected directly by the residents or appointed by the assembly, as determined by relevant local ordinances. However, for the area of the national capital, the problem should be handled by a special regulation under law."

Commissioner Ide: "A system of indirect election should be considered."

Commissioner Yoshimura: "For cities with populations under 200,000, the council and manager system should be adopted; for towns and villages it should be possible to adopt the committee system; the governors of *todōfuken*, the mayors of cities with populations over 200,000, members of assemblies, councils, and committees should be elected directly by the residents. But mayors of cities with populations under 200,000 and the mayors of towns and villages should be elected by councils or committees from among their own members."

Commissioner Furui: "The principle of direct election should be adopted, but it should be made possible to approve special exceptions through laws or ordinances in accordance with the size of the entity and to prevent uniformity of control over local public entities."

The view that the system of direct election established in Article 93 should not be changed.

Here most of the views held that the system should be preserved, because of the principle of local autonomy, particularly the right of self-government of local residents. However, Commissioner Nakasone, advocating his elective prime minister system, argued that under it the heads of all organs of government should be directly elected.

The Functions of Local Public Entities

Commissioner Ōnishi asserted that in order to reconcile local autonomy and the tendency toward the centralization of power, the phrase "under the direction of the state" should be added to Article 94 and the following provision inserted: "The state must devise means to achieve throughout the country a balance in the standard of living at the level of the residents of the best of the local public entities." He believed that it was necessary to promote in the Constitution such matters as local grants-in-aid and tax refunds.

Commissioner Hirose believed that Article 94 should be changed to make clear the relationship between matters of law and matters of ordinances and to make possible the establishment of penal provisions relating to the violation of ordinances.

Of course, there was also the view that it is not necessary to add any constitutional provisions relating to the functions of local public entities.

Special Local Laws

There were a number of opinions held in respect to Article 95 which requires a vote of the residents of the local public entity in the event that a special [national] law might be applied to a single locality so that it could be either abolished or revised.

Commissioners Hirose and Kamikawa held that this provision amounted to a recognition of the right of a specific local public entity to control the will of the National Diet in clear contradiction to the highest organ of state power provision. Commissioner Ōnishi believed that the provision is superfluous because, if, for example, a vote of the residents might be required when prefectures are to be reorganized or a wide-area system be established, it is possible for there to be an expression of will in the assembly of the local public entity or for a reflection of the local will in the National Diet. Nothing important has happened to date under this provision, but since there may be important issues in the future then the scope of the applicability of this provision should be clearly set forth, according to Commissioner Kōri.

In opposition, Commissioner Takayanagi pointed out that the intent of Article 95 is that no special law shall be enacted in disregard of the will of the local public entity to which it will be applied and that this intent is reasonable. It has been thought that the consent of the local assembly is sufficient without appealing to the vote of the residents, but even so there is no need for a revision of the system at present.

General Summary

The basic issue discussed here was the ideal form of contemporary local self-government which involved the problem of the basic relationship between the state and local public entities which in turn involved the issue of the centralization of authority and its possible decentralization. On this basic question it was strongly asserted that there should be no futile demands for decentralization of power, but that an organic, cooperative relationship between the state and local public entities be constructed. One conclusion was that the present provisions of the Constitution lean too far toward the decentralization of power. As described, a number of commissioners demanded changes in the present provisions dealing with local self-government. A central concern here was the possible establishment of the wide-area system of administration.

In general, those supporting the present constitutional provisions on local government agreed in substance on the ideal form of contemporary local self-government and on the necessity for adjusting the balance between the centralization of power and local self-government. The first group held that it is necessary to specify clearly in the Constitution some guidelines for the reform of local government, while the second group held that such reform is possible by such means as legislation or actual operations and that constitutional revision is not absolutely necessary. The second view also held that in order to cope flexibly with the development of local self-government it is desirable to stay within the present provisions of the Constitution.

SECTION J.
AMENDMENT

The view that held that revision of Chapter 9, "Amendments," was necessary did so for the following reasons: that the provisions of Article 96 contain many unclear points, that there are a number of doubts regarding its interpretation, and that the process of amendment contained therein is too strict.

One problem relating to amendment was whether, as can be seen in a few foreign constitutions, there should be stipulations placing clear limits on amendments such as, for example, those which would make impossible amendments directed at the principle of popular sovereignty or at the emperor system. On this issue those supporting and those opposing such limits did so on purely theoretical grounds. However, both sides opposed a stipulation in the present Constitution clearly specifying either limitations or no limitations on amendment. For example, it was the unanimous view of all commissioners that there was no need to enact any provision relating to limits on amendment. Consequently, on this matter we shall stop with the few words above.

The Interpretation of Article 96

The view that revision is necessary in order to eliminate doubts in interpretation arising from numerous unclear points in Article 96.

The following points were frequently raised by those of this view.

1. That because the meaning of "initiated" in the phrase "amendments to this Constitution shall be initiated by the Diet" is unclear, the interpretation is doubtful. Does it mean that only Diet members have the right to present drafts of constitutional amendments? Or does the cabinet also have that right?

2. That because the meaning of "concurring" in the phrase "through a concurring vote of two-thirds or more of all the members of each house" is unclear, the interpretation is doubtful. Does it mean that the two-thirds vote is a condition to be applied at the time a member submits a bill for constitutional amendment or a condition at the time each house passes a draft amendment?

3. That because the meaning of "an integral part of this Constitution" in the phrase "shall . . . be . . . promulgated as an integral part of this Constitution" is unclear, there are doubts concerning the form of amendment.

The solutions presented for the above three problems were simple. First, it should be made clear that the cabinet also possesses the right of initiation of amendments. Second, the conditions for the presentation of draft amendments should be stipulated, and the word "pass" or "approve" should be used in respect to the decisions of the two houses. Third, the phrase "an integral part of this Constitution" should be deleted.

Commissioner Yagi stated that at least part of the difficulty regarding "initiated" and "as an integral part" arose from the problem of translation of the MacArthur draft. He also urged that the phrase "at a special referendum or at such election as the Diet shall specify" should be changed to simply "a national referendum" with any details to be handled by a law concerning such a referendum.

Commissioner Ōnishi recommended that the cabinet be given the right to initiate amendments, that Diet members be enabled to present draft amendments when two-fifths or more of the total membership of both houses approves, and that the word "initiate" not be used when the Diet presents a draft amendment to the people for their approval.

The view that because it is possible to clarify the unclear points in Article 96 by either legislation or interpretation, revision is unnecessary.

Commissioner Rōyama, supporting this view, argued that although the Constitution does not clearly set forth the cabinet's right to initiate amendments it should not be taken to mean that it denies such a right and that the issue should be clarified by means of a law relating to the procedure of amendment. He also pointed out that under the present parliamentary cabinet system the cabinet can initiate an amendment in the Diet through the majority party which it represents. Commissioner Takayanagi also pointed out that the cabinet can present a draft amendment through an individual cabinet member [who is a Diet member].

The Amendment Process as Set Forth in Article 96

The view that because the conditions for the process of amendment as determined in Article 96 are too strict, it is necessary to modify them by means of revision.

The basis for this view was that the amendment process for any constitution should not be too strict. Today, both international and domestic situations develop with great rapidity and political activity is also in an age of rapid change. In these circumstances the stability of the Constitution as the basic law must be preserved, while at the same time the amendment procedure should provide the Constitution with a pliability and an elasticity which will make possible both the management of and adaptability to the various situations flowing from the contemporary scene. From this point of view Article 96 is far too strict.

The Joint Declaration presented a reasoned justification for this view. In situations where the procedure for constitutional amendment is too strict and amendment is "either extremely difficult or next to impossible," a difficult problem is created when an unanticipated situation, threatening to the nation and its people, develops. Either the need to deal with the situation is placed above the Constitution or the Constitution is honored. In the former situation the action taken might be judged to be unconstitutional, a situation in which the value and the dignity of the Constitution have been impaired. Indeed, the constitutional order would have been destroyed, strictly speaking. In the latter situation the Constitution may have been preserved, but the existence of the nation and the people would have been brought to the verge of destruction. And that would mean that the possibility for the destruction of the foundation of the Constitution itself had been created.

In conclusion the Joint Declaration stated:

> In any event in a situation where constitutional amendment is extremely difficult or next to impossible, it is certain that a great gap will be created between the text of the Constitution and the requirements of reality as reflected in the objective situation accompanying changes in the times. It is possible to cover the situation to a certain extent through flexible interpretations and applications, but there are specific limits on that. When the demands of the real situation go beyond the maximum limits set by the Constitution, then the way will be open to the violation, the revision, or the abolition of the Constitution or to the destruction of the basic society.
>
> Accordingly, to close the door too narrowly on constitutional amendment can lead to the death of the Constitution. When the Constitution of Japan is regarded from this basic point of view, the procedures for amendment in Chapter 9 are too strict, and amendment is, in fact, extremely difficult or next to impossible. Therefore, this chapter must be simplified and modified.

Commissioner Kamikawa described the amendment procedure as being among the strictest in the world for the reason that it "possesses the character of a law of occupation control enacted by the Allied nations." Naturally, he urged modification of the procedure.

The two provisions singled out as contributing most to the strictness of the amendment procedure were (1) the two-thirds majority of the total membership of each house required for the initiation of amendment, and (2) the final approval by a majority of the people voting in a national referendum. Some argued that since the requirement for Diet passage is so high, all amendments should not necessarily have to be voted on by the electorate; others, that if all amendments had to be popularly approved, then the requirement for Diet passage should be lowered.

Commissioner Ōnishi recommended that the two-thirds majority be reduced to three-fifths. He also stated that the national referendum should not be used in the following two cases: when a draft amendment is passed by a majority of three-fifths or more in each house, and when an amendment is approved by a majority of three-fifths or more of those present at a joint session of the Diet which would be called after the House of Representatives has approved an amendment by a three-fifths or better majority of its total membership, but the House of Councilors has approved it by a simple majority of its total membership. However, a national referendum would be held in a situation where each house approved a proposed amendment by only a simple majority of the total membership. To prevent a nonrepresentative vote in the national referendum caused by a high abstention rate, the number of valid votes would have to reach at least 30 percent of the total number of eligible voters.

Commissioner Hirose advocated a system under which a national referendum would not take place when both houses approved an amendment by a two-thirds vote, but would when one house passed it by a simple majority and the other house after having passed it by a two-thirds majority requested a national referendum.

A minority of those favoring revision held that if the national referendum is retained, it would be sufficient to hold one if both houses passed a proposed amendment by simple majorities. However, the Joint Declaration opposed this on the grounds that it would result in frequent Diet initiatives for amendments for it would take no more to approve one than it would take for an ordinary law.

The view that there is no need to modify the amendment procedure.
This view held that the procedures of Article 96 might be strict, but not overly so and that to modify them would lead to the fear that the stability of government would be impaired. The following two views present the arguments against revision.

Commissioners Tagami, Kōri, and Ushioda:

> The amendment procedure set forth in Article 96 is fairly strict and it may be appropriate to modify it in the future, for example, by making the national referendum unnecessary. . . . [C]onstitutional stability is not a matter of

whether or not the amendment procedure is strict; fundamentally, it depends on the stability of the government itself and on whether the people are sufficiently endowed with the capacity to sustain democratic government. Consequently, if in the future our government becomes stable, and if our people become sufficiently endowed with the capacity for democratic government, it will be desirable to simplify constitutional amendment, placing trust in the people. However, at the present stage we believe it is necessary to stand in the way of the danger of extreme change by having amendment procedures as strict as those at present.

Commissioner Takayanagi:

If the amendment process is simple, then there is the danger that the majority party for its own partisan reasons may arbitrarily alter the Constitution. In addition, if it is made difficult, then amendment required by social and political change becomes impossible. The problem is which of the above should be emphasized. However, where amendment procedures are difficult, as in the case of the present Constitution and of the American Constitution, changes consonant with social, economic, and political conditions can be brought about in the meaning and the content of the Constitution by means of administrative practices and court precedents without resorting to amendment. . . .

Thus differences in the ease or difficulty of amendment do not necessarily coincide with differences in the stability and flexibility of constitutions. If rigid constitutions such as the present one can experience satisfactory application and interpretation, they will be in effective accord with social, political, and economic change.

Commissioner Mano spoke against revision of the amendment procedure offering the following reasons: from the standpoint of other constitutions, the two-thirds majority provision is not overly strict; the national referendum in all cases is proper in view of such matters as the principle of popular sovereignty, confidence in the people, and dependence on popular discussion in cases of constitutional amendment; and the requirement of a minimum vote in the national referendum is unnecessary because it is inconceivable that any proposed amendment would fail to bring out large numbers of voters.

General Summary

The majority opinion of the commissioners was that there are many unclear points in the provisions of Article 96 and thus revision is necessary in order to remove doubts in interpretation. The opposition view was that revision is unnecessary because the unclear provisions can be handled by legislation or interpretation. This confrontation of views went back ultimately to the problems of attitudes toward and the methods of constitutional interpretation.

Also there was the issue of whether the requirements of a two-thirds vote in both houses for affirmation and of the national referendum are too strict. The majority of the commissioners regarded them as being so, making amendment "either extremely difficult or next to impossible," thus creating the danger of the encouragement of constitutional change through violence. In opposition, it was argued that constitutional stability depends not on amendment procedures, but on government stability and the people's trust in the Constitution. Thus, in situations where amendment is difficult it is necessary to proceed in accordance with actual circumstances by means of such devices as judicial precedents and administrative practices.

SECTION K.
THE SUPREME LAW

The principal issue dealt with in respect to Chapter 10, "The Supreme Law" was its raison d'être. One view held that Articles 97, 98, and 99 are all unnecessary or should be transferred to other chapters, thus eliminating this chapter completely. However, another view placed a high value on its raison d'être and insisted that it should be maintained as it is. Still another view argued that this chapter has made clear the principle of the rule of law which should be emphasized.

Regarding Chapter 10, on the Supreme Law

The view that does not recognize a special raison d'être for the chapter on the Supreme Law, that it has resulted in a variety of evils and should therefore be eliminated.

The following four arguments were advanced by the proponents of this view:

1. Article 97 does nothing more than to state a rationale for respect for fundamental human rights, sets forth matters so natural as to require no special provision and repeats matters with the same intent as Article 11.

2. Article 99 does nothing more than state the natural fact that the Constitution should be upheld and respected.

3. Articles 97 and 99 are not only superfluous as indicated above, but are actually harmful. Article 97 produces the evil of a prejudice in favor of rights; Article 99 by not placing on the people the responsibility for upholding and respecting the Constitution, invites their disregard for it.

4. Article 98, paragraph 1, does nothing more than to establish the natural fact that the Constitution is superior to laws and so forth. In

addition, its second paragraph should be transferred to a separate chapter relating to international peace.

A number of commissioners also expressed the view that this chapter on the supreme law was mistakenly inserted during the process of enactment in order to establish the supremacy of federal [national] law as in the United States Constitution.

The remainder of this section consists of a summary of the views of the individual commissioners who were not in favor of the continuation of Chapter 10 as it is.

On Article 97 Commissioners Inaba, Kamikawa, Ōishi, and Ōnishi expressed the view that it simply repeats the proclamation of the importance of fundamental human rights, as it appears in Articles 11, 12, and 13; consequently, the intent of all four articles should be expressed in a single article to appear in the chapter on the rights and duties of the people. Commissioner Kamikawa added that Article 97 simply recapitulates the history of the acquisition of fundamental human rights, an empty exercise for a Japan that has not had the experience of a political struggle or revolution for the acquisition of those rights. Commissioner Hirose was one of those who argued that Article 97 places excessive emphasis on human rights, pointing out that since it touches in no way on limitations on those rights, it has come to be recognized by some as an unconditional guarantee.

In regard to Article 98, Commissioner Kamikawa argued that its first paragraph is simply a direct translation of Article 6, paragraph 2 of the Constitution of the United States, asserting that the supremacy of federal law is necessary in the United States, but meaningless in a unitary country like Japan. In addition, he stated: "The second paragraph relating to treaties and international law is needed, but it should be shifted to an article relating to the observance of treaties and established law as a part of a chapter dealing with a basic principle concerning peace and security." Commissioner Hirose pointed out that paragraph 1 might be interpreted to support the argument that the courts possess the right of abstract constitutional review and that paragraph 2 might possibly be interpreted to mean that treaties are superior to the Constitution. He recommended elimination of Article 98 as a solution to these problems of interpretation.

Respecting Article 99 Commissioner Hirose stated that it reflects the earlier thinking that the essence of a constitution was to restrict the authority of those in power at a time when constitutions were created in struggles against despotic monarchs. Today when that battle has been won constitutions must be binding on government and people alike. In addition, the Constitution should emphasize that the people have a responsibility to obey the law, as natural as that might seem to be to some.

Commissioner Kamikawa pointed out that the original basis of Article 99 was to provide for an oath of office to be taken on the occasion of the enthronement of the emperor and of the appointment of public officials, but the original aim became lost and the present wording was approved. This accounts for the failure to mention a responsibility of the people to uphold the law. He argued, therefore, for the institution of the custom of an oath of office pledging support and defense of the Constitution to replace Article 99 and the insertion somewhere else of the people's responsibility to respect the law.

On the problem of the principle of the rule of law, Commissioner Hirose supported the principle in general, but thought that "the principle of the observance of duties as a corollary premise to the protection of rights should be clearly set forth in the Constitution." The chapter must be amended, he said, since its articles "encourage various evils in actual politics such as overemphasis on rights and the disregard of duties."

The view that the chapter on the supreme law has an important raison d'être and should therefore be preserved.

The general reasons for the support of the three articles of this chapter can be summarized as follows:

1. Even though Article 97 duplicates Article 11 and others, it is necessary for the awakening of the consciousness of the people to the importance of fundamental human rights.

2. Article 99 is necessary for it heightens the awareness of respect for human rights in public officials who are assigned to wield the power of the state.

3. Article 98 is necessary both because it reveals a basis for the system of constitutional review of Article 81 and because it makes clear the validity of treaties in domestic law.

4. This chapter should be preserved because of its great significance in setting forth the principle of the rule of law.

5. Even though the upholders of the traditional legal technique in the drafting of laws argue that Article 97 is superfluous because it duplicates Article 11, this article should not be evaluated simply from the standpoint of legal technique.

On Article 97 Commissioner Mano had the following to say:

Article 97 proclaims the importance of fundamental human rights and it is necessary that the people be brought to an awareness of that importance. The opinion that because it duplicates Article 11 and others it is unnecessary is an opinion that follows German-style legal technique. . . . In addition, it cannot be thought that the existence of this provision in itself is productive of great evils. Even though it can be said that there is abuse of human rights based on an excessive consciousness of them on the part of some people, there is also, on the other hand, an infringement of human rights based on an insufficient consciousness of them on the part of public officials. Therefore, to emphasize only the abuse of human rights and to try to restrain them would mean only to weaken respect for them and to encourage the evil of their infringement.

In respect to the treaties provision of Article 98, Commissioners Mano, Mizuno, Tagami, and Yamasaki argued that even though it raises the question of whether it extends the right of judicial review to treaties, that problem can be resolved, not by revision, but by the interpretation or actual application of the provision.

Arguing in support of the first paragraph of Article 98, Commissioner Ōishi declared: ". . . to keep a provision stating that the Constitution is the supreme law is necessary in the sense that it makes clear that Japan has adopted the principle of written law. That is to say, to make clear that the Constitution of Japan, which is a written charter, is the supreme law is highly important because it also makes clear that what is supreme as the national will is the Constitution of Japan as a written code and that customary law, precedents, the fundamental norms of natural law and other matters are not superior to the Constitution."

On Article 99 Commissioner Takayanagi wrote that constitutions are written in respect to those who govern and that consequently they should provide for the duty of respecting and upholding the constitution by those who wield power and deal not at all with responsibility of the people in this regard. "Thus, it is natural that the people should obey the Constitution, but to write this into the Constitution would have the effect of weakening the rule of law, that is, the principle that those who rule are bound by law." Commissioner Mizuno declared that the duty of the people to obey the Constitution should not be based on constitutional provisions, but on such things as social education.

Those supporting this chapter emphasized its significance as a statement of the basic principle of the rule of law and that there should be no amendment which would weaken this principle. Commissioner Takayanagi, the strongest proponent of the rule of law, wrote as follows:

> Even though the present Constitution does not use the term "rule of law" it has very powerfully adopted the principle. Along with parliamentary government the rule of law is one of the special features of the Constitution. . . .
>
> The principle of the rule of law is made manifest in Chapter 10. Article 97 sets forth the history of the principle; Article 98 provides as a means of realizing the principle along with Article 81 the American method of judicial review; and Article 99 strongly sets forth the idea of a government completely under law.
>
> The core of the rule of law lies in the respect for the guarantee of fundamental human rights in government and all constitutions are laws having as their rationale the defense of fundamental human rights. Accordingly, if the

354 PART FOUR. THE OPINIONS OF THE COMMISSIONERS

rule of law is professed, it amounts to the assertion of the rights of the people. Because law is the defense of rights and freedoms, the defense of law is simultaneously the defense of rights and freedoms. Therefore, the opinion that holds that the present Constitution overemphasizes rights and disregards duties is not based on a correct understanding of the rule of law. . . . [B]ecause under the present conditions in our country it is indispensable that the people become well-versed in the principle of the rule of law which can bring about the success of liberal democracy, this chapter should not be revised.

The Constitution, Treaties, and International Law

Those stating that the relationship between the Constitution on the one hand and treaties and international law on the other is unclear offered the following opinions.

Commissioner Ōnishi stated that in order to make clear that the Constitution is superior to treaties, Article 81 [judicial review] should clearly list treaties and they should also be included in Article 98, paragraph 1. Commissioners Hirose and Kamikawa both recommended a separate chapter setting forth general provisions or principles regarding international peace and respect for international law.

However, Commissioners Kamikawa and Takayanagi argued against a constitutional provision clarifying the relationship under discussion. Commissioner Kamikawa recognized the considerable theoretical difficulty of attempting to determine whether the Constitution or treaties should be regarded as superior. His views were that the question should be debated in political, not theoretical, terms; and that there need be no constitutional provisions regarding the relationship between the Constitution and treaties or judicial review of treaties.

Commissioner Takayanagi expressed the following opinion:

> At the present stage of development of international society it is proper that in terms of domestic law the theory be that the Constitution is superior to treaties. Also to hold an international treaty to be unconstitutional is an important step involving international good faith and should not be taken lightly. It is the course of wisdom to go as far as possible toward not holding treaties to be unconstitutional by such means as interpreting domestic law so that treaties would not be held unconstitutional and in cases where it is unavoidable adopting the theory of the act of state and leaving the matter to the decision of the executive branch. However, it would be going too far to say that all treaties should not become the objects of judicial review.

General Summary

The view of the majority was that all three articles of Chapter 10 are either unnecessary or should be shifted to other chapters and that, consequently, this chapter in its entirety is without justification and should be eliminated. Those holding this view asserted that the principles set forth in this chapter, such as respect for fundamental human rights, the respect for and defense of the Constitution, and the supremacy of the Constitution in the corpus of national law are, of course, important, but since they are also natural, it is unnecessary to go so far as to establish this chapter which has brought with it such evils as the absolute view of human rights.

Those opposed to the above view argued that the chapter should be continued as it is because it has sufficient reason for being, the principles contained in it should be strongly supported in our country today, and it should not be the target of criticism that it has brought certain abuses in its wake.

Another strong reason brought forward in support of this chapter is that it sets forth the principle of the rule of law. However, those advocating change or elimination of this chapter argued that while the adoption of the rule of law is good, this chapter has features which go too far toward overemphasis on rights and disregard of duties and lacks the concept of the observance of duties which is a premise of the rule of law.

The other principal point of discussion was the clarification of the effective relationship between the Constitution and treaties and international law, an issue on which there was, once again, a confrontation of opinion.

SECTION L.
STATES OF EMERGENCY

The question confronting the commission on states of emergency was as follows: "In order to deal with crises or states of emergency is it necessary to enact special provisions relating to the organs of government and the rights and freedoms of the people?" All commissioners were in agreement that some measures were necessary for the handling of extraordinary situations such as crises or states of emergency, but opinions differed on whether a constitutional provision should be enacted to cover the situation. Among those who favored a constitutional stipulation, one group supported only a concise, basic statement, leaving the details to law, but another felt that the constitutional provision should be fairly detailed in order to prevent abuse of emergency procedures.

The Constitution and States of Emergency

"States of emergency" as discussed here included such matters as war, insurrection, large-scale violence, great panics, economic chaos, natural disasters, and widespread epidemics of contagious diseases. The present Constitution has no provisions relating to states of emergency. All commissioners agreed that in spite of that lack, consideration has been given to the occurrence of states of emergency and the necessity for taking appropriate emergency measures to deal with them. However, the majority view was that the Constitution should, of necessity, have an existing provision to provide a means for coping with states of emergency.

The view that it is necessary to set up a constitutional provision regarding states of emergency in order to provide a clear basis for measures to deal with them and to prevent abuses by limiting such measures to the necessary minimum.

Many commissioners believed that the Constitution's failure to devote sufficient consideration to measures to be taken in emergency situations is its single greatest deficiency. They pointed out that a state of emergency is an abnormal and irregular situation, but measures to deal with one should not be practical ones lying outside the Constitution nor should they be regarded as exercises of national emergency powers lying beyond the Constitution and taken without regard for it. On the other hand, to employ methods provided for in the Constitution and to carry them out in accordance with the Constitution would be based on the principles of a written constitution and of constitutional government itself. The only constitutional provision relating to emergencies empowers the cabinet to convoke the House of Councilors in times of national emergencies (Article 54).

It was also pointed out that to deal with states of emergency it would be necessary to adopt measures which would place exceptional restrictions on the rights and freedoms of the people. The only basis for such restrictions in the present Constitution is the doctrine of the public welfare. Commissioners Yabe and Kōri maintained that such a wide interpretation of the public welfare is dangerous and so it is necessary to establish a clear constitutional provision confining emergency measures to the necessary minimum in order to prevent abuse of rights and freedoms.

Commissioners Inaba and Hirose argued that if there is no constitutional basis for emergency measures, then opposition to them will develop on the ground that they are either unconstitutional or dictatorial and control over the emergency will become impossible and chaos compounded.

Those holding this view were also critical of the position that the public welfare could be used as a basis for emergency measures providing that such measures be made subject to subsequent review by the Supreme Court. Commissioner Aichi declared: "I cannot agree with the

thinking that without setting up any kind of a provision we should toler-
ate even unconstitutional actions in the event something happens and
expect at some later day to make the best of the situation by means of a
Supreme Court decision." Commissioner Ōishi declared that the lack of
an emergency provision in the Constitution is based on the premise that
there is a national emergency power lying outside the Constitution and
that to recognize the exercise of such power means the destruction of the
Constitution. Commissioner Kamikawa argued strongly against ex post
facto review by the Supreme Court, asserting that it would be impossible
for the court to make a decision in such matters that would not harm its
position.

The view that it is possible under the present Constitution to take necessary steps
to deal with a state of emergency, that a clear constitutional provision on this
matter might be subject to abuse, and that consequently no constitutional provision
is needed.

Some holding this view asserted that the basis for emergency procedures in the absence of a constitutional provision might be either unwritten principle (Commissioner Takayanagi) or the law of necessity (Commissioner Mano). Commissioners Ushioda and Mizuno placed their reliance on the public welfare provisions of the Constitution. In addition,
Commissioners Mano and Furui argued that the solution was to enact
laws relating to states of emergency which would authorize the government to take necessary steps by means of cabinet orders. On the other
hand, Commissioner Rōyama argued that attempts either to amend the
Constitution or to enact laws to deal with states of emergency would be
inadvisable because they would cause political confrontation and confusion among the people.

Commissioner Takayanagi declared that those who supported an
emergency provision believed that "a constitution should be a complete
code providing for every eventuality." He added: "However, the Constitution of Japan is based on the premises of parliamentary democracy
and the principle of the rule of law . . . and in this kind of constitution
to list provisions relating in detail to states of emergency would be undesirable because it would dilute fundamental rights and thereby the principle of the rule of law. Moreover, on the occasion of a state of
emergency those who govern and who adopt emergency measures must
have a strong awareness that they must restore with the greatest possible
speed not a part of the constitutional order, but its entirety."

Provisions Relating to States of Emergency

The majority view on items which should be provided for in relation to
states of emergency was that in order to prevent the abuse of authority

under emergency measures, the Constitution should contain rather detailed provisions regarding them.

The Joint Declaration set forth a detailed list of provisions for dealing with states of emergency: a limitation on states of emergency by a listing of situations in which they can be proclaimed; a limitation on the area to be covered, either regional or national; limitations or suspensions of fundamental human rights in accordance with the type of emergency (military, economic, disaster, etc.) involved; Diet approval of a proposed proclamation of emergency; a clear time limit; and continuation of the Diet during an emergency.

General Summary

All commissioners were agreed that there is a need for measures to deal with states of emergency, but opinion was divided on whether there should be a constitutional provision dealing with them. The majority view supported constitutional provisions for the following reasons:

1. Under a written Constitution it is impermissible not to have a clearly stated provision relating to measures for dealing with states of emergency.

2. In the event that there is no constitutional basis for emergency measures, then to take such measures becomes impossible as a matter of practical politics.

3. If the Constitution determines that measures can be taken in states of emergency, then it is possible to prevent the danger of the abuse of power in such situations.

The minority view in opposition to a constitutional provision was based on the following reasons:

1. Even under the present Constitution, it is possible to take measures to deal with a state of emergency.

2. To clarify the state of emergency in the Constitution would be to create the danger of the abuse of power.

3. An attempt to establish constitutional provisions relating to states of emergency would create needless political confusion.

Proponents of a constitutional provision also argued both that a lack of one would make it impossible for either the cabinet or the Diet to deal with a state of emergency and that if such measures were taken they would have to be regarded as either unconstitutional or extraconstitutional, which would be destructive of the Constitution.

Those opposed to this view argued that the principle of necessity would justify any appropriate action taken to handle a state of emergency and that the problem is not that of unconstitutionality or illegality of such an action. It was further pointed out that if the issue of constitutionality arises, then the basis for emergency action could be found in the public welfare by means of a flexible interpretation of the Constitution.

Basically, the confrontation on this issue revolved around these two questions: Is the problem of the state of emergency to be regarded as strictly one falling within a written Constitution? Or should it be regarded as lying outside a written Constitution?

Section M.
Political Parties

In the present Constitution there is no provision at all dealing with political parties. Consequently, the central issue was whether the Constitution should have a new provision on political parties. Because parties lie at the very foundation of the system of government, there was the view that a statement of such matters as the ideal form and the character of political parties should appear in the Constitution which would contribute in turn to the healthy development of parliamentary government and of the parties themselves. The opposing view, while recognizing the importance of parties, held that no constitutional provision was required. The commissioners were about evenly split between these two views.

Constitutional Provisions on Political Parties

The view that as a reflection of the importance of the position and role of political parties in parliamentary democracy, provisions relating to them should be inserted into the Constitution.

The demands that there should be constitutional provisions relating to political parties stood on the following arguments: the position and role of political parties in contemporary parliamentary democracies have reached a stage where they cannot be ignored; the character and activities of political parties have become the keys to deciding the success or failure of democratic and parliamentary government; the Constitution neglects these facts and takes a negative and uninterested attitude that treats the parties as lying outside it; and, therefore, it is both impossible and impermissible not to have constitutional provisions relating to parties.

Supporting this view, Commissioner Hirose made the following points: the political party is responsible for government today; it controls the fate of the people, the nation, and the Constitution; political parties and the Constitution stand in an inseparable relationship with each other; and the problem of the political parties is the problem of the fate of the Constitution itself. Commissioner Hosokawa asserted that it is insufficient to argue that the freedom of association is an adequate guarantee of the position of political parties, not only because they are the framework of politics itself but also because they are fundamentally different from labor unions and other forms of organization. While supporting this position, Commissioners Kōri and Yabe declared that the Constitution should go no further than to set forth a basic position relating to the ideal form of political parties under parliamentary or democratic government; more detailed provisions might result in a hampering of their essential functions.

Those opposing this view warned against improper limitations on the formation or activity of political parties by either the Constitution or law.

Specific Stipulations on Political Parties

On matters to be stipulated in respect to political parties, in many cases the position was set forth that even though there should be constitutional provisions relating to parties, in general what should appear were basic matters held to the necessary minimum. For example, the Joint Declaration suggested two possible basic provisions: "All the people, in order to participate in the formation of the political will, shall be able freely to organize political parties. The objectives, activities, and organization of political parties must conform to the principles of democracy." Or: "The establishment of political parties shall be free, but their activities and internal order must conform to democratic principles." Either, it was asserted, would avoid two difficulties in respect to the constitutional recognition of political parties: the barring of certain types of parties; and the imposition of detailed restrictions which would take away the freedom and autonomy of the parties. Within such a framework it would be possible to enact a political parties law to handle details in accordance with the will of both the people and the parties themselves.

Commissioner Yabe, while agreeing with the general tenor of the Joint Declaration opinion, suggested the addition of another provision: "The funds of political parties shall be a matter of public record."

The above position, favoring a minimum basic statement, was held by a majority of the commission. However, Commissioner Hirose recommended a detailed set of provisions. His intent was to create a structure which would be strongly opposed to political parties representing only certain classes and to antidemocratic parties. His suggestions included a statement to the effect that activities "which are designed to make only a section of the people into the base of the sovereignty of the nation of Japan shall be regarded as opposed to the principles of democracy" and called for a prohibition of the sponsorship of candidates in a national election and of election campaigns by any political organization the internal order and activities of which are "not in accord with the principles of democracy."

The Present State of Political Parties and a Political Parties Law

The view supporting a constitutional provision relating to parties in almost all cases touched on the present condition of political parties in Japan. The argument was that to eliminate the shortcomings and evils of today's parties and to encourage the development of healthy party government, two things are required: to provide a constitutional basis for a political parties law; and to provide a stimulus for the parties themselves. Both would have the effect of pointing out the ideal form for parties and of promoting a consciousness of the importance of parties.

From a completely different standpoint, Commissioner Yagi spoke for a constitutional provision on parties because under the Meiji Constitution parties were always under the strict control of the government and were also subjected to political oppression. Free party politics became operative only under the present Constitution and actually then only after the end of the occupation. Under these circumstances not to deal with parties in the Constitution is hardly a contribution to the development of party politics.

Commissioner Yabe urged that a constitutional provision would provide the basis for a political parties law which would make possible democratic control over the internal order of the parties. In addition, he believed that a party law should cover such matters as the election of a party president and the method of officially nominating candidates for the Diet which is currently left to the parties as a completely private matter. While regarding a parties law as a means for improving the parties, he also recognized the importance of raising the political level of the people and of encouraging the efforts of the parties themselves to that end.

Commissioner Kōri believed that it would be extremely difficult to formulate an effective parties law because of the necessity of allowing a considerable degree of latitude for the very different parties to determine their own internal orders. It is also of great importance to attempt to determine the kind of law that would both eliminate present evils of the parties and be effective in their future development.

The view that recognized the importance of the role and position of parties under parliamentary democracy, but held that it is unnecessary to have a constitutional provision concerning them.

A common element in the view here is that parties by nature stand outside both the Constitution and laws and that only in such a position can they fully discharge their functions. Commissioner Ushioda was against any law which would bind parties tightly because it would destroy their original aim. He asserted that he was against a prohibition of antidemocratic political parties which would not also be applied to other types of antidemocratic organizations and individuals.

Commissioner Takayanagi asserted that both the guarantee of the freedom of association and the possibility of control over parties by means of the public welfare doctrine were sufficient to cover the activities of parties. Commissioner Rōyama pointed out that any situation in which a law would provide what an antidemocratic party was and what antidemocratic activity might be and in which the Supreme Court would be enabled to determine the constitutionality of such a law would be a very difficult situation indeed. He said: ". . . when a political party is controlled by the Constitution or by legislative means, respect for parties is lost and the danger is that the opposite effect of preventing their free and healthy development will be produced. The evils of political parties in Japan today, for example, the phenomenon of factionalism, are rooted in such matters as the structure of Japanese society and the political awareness of the Japanese people. This is not something that can be solved by simple legal measures."

Those against a constitutional provision relating to parties opposed even a general one which might not be any more than a clear statement of the ideal form of a democratic political party. Such a provision, it was argued, would be so general as to be meaningless and, in addition, might easily be applied to limit the free activity of parties. Commissioner Furui argued as follows: "Political parties must be allowed to develop naturally. It is the people who criticize and direct political parties or encourage them; no organ of state should participate in this activity. If provisions are established to control or regulate parties, they are dangerous and should be denounced. . . . Even trifling procedural provisions may become the means for the oppression of political parties in certain times and places. . . ."

Those against a constitutional provision were also against a political parties law. Although there is room for improvement in the parties, a parties law is not necessarily the means to bring it about. Strict enforcement (or improvement) of such laws as the election law and the law for the regulation of political funds should be sufficient to achieve their objective of raising the level of politics. Improvements in elections and raising the political consciousness of the people would also lead to a bettering of the parties. In addition, controls over parties either by the Constitution or a specific law would endanger their development.

Commissioner Yoshimura declared that the greatest evils in Japan's party system today are factional strife and the confrontation between the government and the opposition parties. The causes of factionalism are the massive cost of elections and the frequent and capricious reorganizations of the cabinet, neither of which can be taken care of by either the Constitution or a law. The normalization of conduct in the Diet [the reference is to the conduct of the opposition parties toward the cabinet] can be determined by whether the parties possess enthusiasm, good faith, and common sense. Neither the Constitution nor law can be a solution.

General Summary

All commissioners were agreed on the importance of political parties as the foundation and moving force of the political structure. However, there was an almost even split between those who favored and those who opposed a constitutional provision relating to parties.

Those who favored such a provision presented the following arguments:

1. The Constitution should take a positive attitude toward the parties by means of a provision recognizing their important position.

2. A constitutional provision should deal with the ideal form of the political party. It should provide that the character and the internal order of parties must stand on the principle of democracy and should also be the basis for a political parties law.

3. Both a constitutional provision and a political parties law are necessary for the development of party government by eliminating the evils of Japan's present parties and nurturing sound party government.

The opposition was based on the following arguments:

1. Political parties should be regarded as being beyond the control of the Constitution. By nature they undergo a natural development and should be able to function without any control by national law.

2. A provision respecting the ideal form and character of a political party would be meaningless because it would state only an abstract and general principle. If detail is entered into, the danger of negating party politics would be created.

3. The development of sound party politics is not a problem of the Constitution or a political parties law.

SECTION N.
ELECTIONS

The problem here was not the overall question of the election system itself, but whether it is necessary to establish a special constitutional organ designed to guarantee fair elections. What was involved was not elections of all public officials, but only the election of Diet members. The phrase "to guarantee fair elections" referred not to the fair conduct of elections, but rather to the enactment of a fair election law, that is, one guaranteeing fairness in all aspects of the election procedure.

Commissioners Hirose, Ōnishi, Nakasone, and Takayanagi all presented concrete plans for a constitutional organ for elections. The first three proposals were for constitutional amendments, but the Takayanagi plan (which was presented with three different variations) was only a suggestion for possible future study. All these plans called for the creation of a constitutional organ independent of both the cabinet and the Diet which would have the responsibility of guaranteeing free elections in the sense described above. However, all four of these plans received little support from other commissioners, apart from the feeling that they were worth future study.

A Constitutional Organ to Guarantee Free Elections

The view that a special constitutional organ should be established to guarantee free elections, especially through the enactment of an appropriate election law.
Here fell the four proposals referred to above. The basic position held in common by all four was that, in order to recognize the principle of popular sovereignty and the parliamentary democracy based on it, free elections are the most important basic condition and they especially require a fair election law. However, it was argued, to achieve that end it is necessary to create an independent constitutional organ possessing special constitutional powers. The reason for the last point is that it is impossible to draft and enact a special election law by following the constitutional procedures for ordinary laws.

Commissioner Hirose summarized the situation as follows: ". . . [N]either Diet members nor the political parties nor the cabinet because of their positions are qualified to pass legislation relating to elections. Just as under the principle that judges do not judge themselves, so in respect to an election law, it is necessary that it be drafted by impartial third parties, removed from the position of Diet members or party politicians whose interests are at stake. The present Council on the

Election System is designed to that end, but before its reports relating to revisions of the Election Law are presented to the Diet, they are subjected to devastating changes by the cabinet and the political parties. Therefore, it is necessary that there be created a constitutional organ possessing special powers relating to the study, the drafting and the enactment of an election law."

As indicated above, the four proposals shared a basic position. However, they differed in the details of the creation, organization, and operation of the constitutional election organ that they were to create. Here only two items from the four plans will be mentioned, primarily because of their novelty.

Commissioner Takayanagi argued that since Montesquieu's day a fourth power, the electoral power, had been added to the traditional three, executive, legislative, and judicial. This has arisen from the fact that political parties have been in charge of democratic government because the majority party comes into control of both the executive and legislative branches, which, in a sense have thus become one. He argued farther that the National Diet cannot possess the competence to enact a fair election law and the cabinet which is formed by the majority party cannot administer a fair election law impartially. His solution was to create a constitutional election commission independent of the three branches of government which would be tied directly to the electoral power by being elected by a national referendum and be completely isolated from the parties. Its responsibilities would be to draft a bill relating to fair elections which would be voted on in a national referendum and then to administer and conduct elections carried out under the law so enacted.

The Ōnishi proposal called for three, not one, constitutional election bodies. The first would be a Commission on the Determination of Election Districts which would determine the boundaries of election districts on the basis of a constitutionally determined number of Diet members and of constituents to be represented by each member. The second would be an Election Court, appointed by the Supreme Court from among candidates possessing the qualifications of Supreme Court justices, which would be responsible for advisory opinions to the Diet when it is deliberating on election laws and regulations relating to such matters as election campaigning, penal provisions, and the conduct and administration of elections. The Diet could override an Election Court opinion only by a vote of two-thirds or more. Finally, there would be a Commission for Election Administration, similar to the present one with the same title, but established under the Constitution instead of under the Law for the Election of Public Officials. No one supported this scheme.

*The view that recognized the necessity for the guarantee of free elections and
especially for the enactment of an appropriate election law, but held that it is
unnecessary to establish a constitutional organ for that purpose.*

This view rested on several different positions, which are discussed
below.

1. The way to achieve fair elections is not by means of a change in the
constitutionally established system. After pointing out that fair elections
cannot be expected only by means of constitutional provisions or election
laws, especially in a country like Japan where the tradition of liberal
democratic government is still weak, Commissioner Kamikawa went on
to say: "The character of Japanese politics lies in the fact that political
parties are private, not public. Both party reform and election reform
are fundamental. Therefore, the simple establishment of a constitutional
body designed to guarantee free elections will not achieve these reforms.
Rather, I think the fundamental problem lies in such matters as the
nurturing of the political consciousness of the people, the development
of political education and the reform of the traditions of the past."

2. The method of selection of commission members and the national
referendum on the election law to be drafted by the commission are both
undesirable.

This view was directed at the provisions, described above, of the
Takayanagi plan. Commissioner Kamikawa was particularly critical of
these points. He declared that there was no guarantee that the nomination procedure (involving a committee consisting of the prime minister,
the speakers of both houses, the chief justice of the Supreme Court, and
representatives from the academic world and the press) would be impartial and without partisan political feelings; that the people would find it
difficult to judge the qualifications of nominees and would end by relying on partisan considerations; and that votes in the national referendum on the election law would be simple yes or no votes without due
consideration being given the content.

3. It is going too far to confer the power of legislation on the election
commission, but if it is to be granted the authority only to conduct and
supervise elections, it need not be a constitutional body.

This was also directed against the Takayanagi proposal. Commissioner Rōyama was the principal proponent of this argument.

Finally, the Takayanagi concept of the electoral power was supported
by no other commissioner. Commissioner Ōishi was critical of the concept because, he said, it undermines the whole idea of parliamentary
government, both because it eliminates partisanship which is the essence
of democratic government and because it removes an important element
of the legislative power from the hands of the Diet. Commissioner
Kamikawa pointed out the contradiction between an election commis-

sion possessed of legislative power, no matter how restricted, and the provision in Article 41 that the Diet is the sole law-making organ of the state.

General Summary

The central issue was whether it is necessary to establish a special constitutional body in a position independent of both the Diet and the cabinet in order to guarantee the enactment of a fair election law. The view favoring such a body was based on the following two positions: that the enactment of a fair election law is the most important condition for the realization of both the principle of popular sovereignty and parliamentary democracy; and that the present situation in our country is that the enactment of an election law would be determined on an extremely partisan basis.

All commissioners were agreed on the necessity for the guarantee of the enactment of a fair election law. However, the opposition of views came over whether it is necessary to establish a special constitutional body to that end. An extremely small number of commissioners expressed positive support of this idea. A number of opinions opposed it. The majority thought it should be given further consideration without expressing positive agreement.

SECTION O.
NATIONAL REFERENDA

In the present Constitution there are two types of national referenda: one for constitutional amendments, and the other the popular review of Supreme Court justices. The problem under discussion here was whether the system should be extended to special issues. The question involved was whether the principle of direct democracy should be extended beyond the two issues recognized in the present Constitution. The current national referenda can be regarded as exceptions to the principles of parliamentary government and the parliamentary cabinet system. Only a minority of the commissioners supported the system of national referenda on special issues.

Referenda on Special Issues

The view that there should be a system of national referenda on special issues in order that the will of the people can be directly expressed and so that parliamentary government can be completely realized.

This view, in essence, is that under the representative system of parliamentary government the will of the people can be expressed only in the form of the election of Diet members. In addition, the exercise of the right of suffrage should be expanded into a system of national referenda so that the will of the people can be directly expressed. The reasons for this view are as follows.

1. The election ballot is insufficient as an expression of the people's opinions on special issues. The opinion here was that under the present system of representative government the vote in Diet elections is frequently colored by the charm and personality of the candidates as individuals rather than by considerations of policy. Commissioner Nakasone pointed out that a national referendum, taken before a Diet vote, to seek the views of the people at large before a law or a treaty is passed by the Diet could then become the basis for political parties to decide their positions and thus would be a meaningful device to prevent confusion and conflict in national affairs.

2. The expansion of a system of national referenda would be a manifestation of new political conditions and the foundation of a constitution based on popular sovereignty. This position was Commissioner Nakasone's and flowed from his advocacy of the elective prime minister. It will be recalled that his proposal was based on the view that the election of the nation's highest leader must be under the direct control of the people in this age when their fate may depend on the slightest actions of their leaders. The system of the direct election of the prime minister would be reinforced by a direct national referendum when there is a conflict of views between the cabinet and the Diet on an important question. Such a question would be submitted to a referendum after consultation between the prime minister and the Diet. It was also asserted that although it is frequently said that national referenda might be a potential source of dictatorship, the fact of the matter is that dictatorship would spring from special sources and conditions, not simply from a national referendum.

3. The system would enable the people to play a moderating role in government and is a necessary condition for the full achievement of a system of representative government. The referendum would provide the sovereign people with a moderating role in situations where the cabinet and the Diet had reached a deadlock or where considerable social unrest might be produced because of a division in public opinion.

Commissioner Yabe pointed out that when there is a sharp confrontation between the cabinet and the Diet dissolution of the lower house is available for use, but since that calls for a national election it might not be easy to resort to it. Also in general elections there are situations in which the will of the people is not clearly reflected in matters of policy. However, he also wondered whether a constitutional amendment might not be required since it might be possible to interpret the requirement for a national referendum on constitutional amendments to apply also to referenda and suggested that the matter might be dealt with by law.

Commissioner Rōyama was in essential agreement with Yabe and suggested that a referendum might be authorized on the basis of a petition demanding one submitted by the people. He also asserted that there need not be a conflict with the "sole law-making organ" provision, provided that the Diet took the national referendum to be only a form of consultation with the will of the people. Commissioner Rōyama also made some specific suggestions. He believed that referenda should be limited primarily to important laws and treaties with the further limitation that they be used only where a constitutional issue is involved or where important policy issues were not debated in elections. On constitutional issues the point would not be a resolution of the point in dispute, but the expression of opinion on related political issues. He also suggested that the House of Councilors might be the appropriate organ to initiate submission of a matter to a national referendum since both cabinet and lower house might be too deeply involved in the issue in question. He also raised the difficulty of the question of determining the conditions for the initiation of a referendum.

The view that the system of the national referendum should not be instituted constitutionally because it is against the principle of democracy, because it has certain shortcomings, and because it is preferable to strive for the nurturing of parliamentary government and the parliamentary cabinet system.

This view was put forward for the following reasons:

1. Systems such as national referenda which are called manifestations of direct democracy are not at all democratic. Commissioner Ushioda was a strong advocate of this position. He argued that the essence of democracy lies in the process of the effort toward discussion and persuasion as the means to attain the unanimous will of all. The simple "yes" or "no" vote of the national referendum bypasses the above process and is not democratic. He said: "The situation is not that of the small ancient city-state; in the contemporary nation-state the effort to attain unanimity can be carried out only by having a small number of representatives discuss and deliberate. The national referendum which calls only for a 'yes' or 'no' conclusion by the majority of the people who are unable to discuss and deliberate on their own cannot be called democracy." He added that the argument that the increase in the knowledge of the masses of the people in this day of mass communication makes it possible for the people to express their conclusions on the matter involved in a

referendum does not hold water because the people do not participate directly and are only "idle spectators." He also doubted the argument that a national referendum can carry out a moderating influence.

2. There are many shortcomings and abuses in national referenda and it is preferable to rely on the nurturing and perfecting of indirect democracy and the parliamentary cabinet system.

The principal arguments for this view were the following:

1. Government is extremely complex and requires a high degree of judgment and consequently direct democracy in a large, extremely populous country is difficult to achieve, according to Commissioner Hirose. Therefore, he declared, efforts should be poured into the perfection of the system of indirect democracy, and "we should not adopt a system of direct democracy going beyond what we have."

2. It is inappropriate to address important problems with a method which calls for a simple "yes" or "no" as the referendum does, according to Commissioner Kamikawa.

3. Commissioner Kamikawa also pointed out the following possible evils: manipulation of the vote by the government, which would administer referenda; influences on the vote by momentary political circumstances; the dependency of the fate of the nation on the emotions and moods of the people; and the possibility of the creation of a dictatorship through the referendum.

4. It is doubtful that the great mass of the people possesses sufficient understanding and judgment in matters such as politics, law, finance, and foreign policy. Under a representative system not all Diet members are perfect, but it is an incontestable fact that the knowledge and experience of Diet members is greater than that of the people in general. (Commissioner Yagi)

Finally, Commissioner Ōnishi perceived the following evils if a system of direct democracy is adopted at the present time: a feeling of disdain toward parliamentary politics which should now be developed; greater and greater disorder and confusion in government if a set number of Diet members or of voters is given the right to initiate referenda; and the danger of a decline into mob government, that is, government not by the people, but by their base emotions.

General Summary

The great majority of commissioners opposed the opinion that there should be a constitutional system of national referenda on special questions. They believed that it is necessary to work instead for the nurture and perfection of representative government and the parliamentary cabinet system on which the present Constitution is based. They also emphasized the various evils that might be produced by the system such as the ease of falling into dictatorial government.

The minority argued that it was necessary to establish a system for resolving collisions between the cabinet and the Diet which would involve a direct appeal to the will of the people. This, it was argued, would also contribute to the perfecting of parliamentary government.

Ultimately, the conflict in views over the national referendum system can be traced to differences in the evaluation of the system of direct democracy.

4. The Need for Constitutional Revision

THE VARIOUS VIEWS on the fundamental problems of the Constitution of Japan and the important questions concerning each chapter have been set forth in Chapters 2 and 3. These views were naturally related to the question of whether the provisions of the Constitution should be kept as they are or whether revision is necessary. Each commissioner's opinion on the above fundamental problems and important questions was inseparable from the issue of the necessity for constitutional revision.

Views on the necessity for constitutional revision fall into two broad groups: those supporting it and those opposing it. The revisionist opinion was in the majority, and the antirevisionist opinion in the minority. This classification of opinions is based on the conclusions held by each commissioner. The revisionists were not in agreement on all points and the same was true of antirevisionists. In both groups there were numerous differences both in basic thinking and in reasons offered for and against revision; and on certain problems both groups shared common opinions. Even where there was agreement on the necessity for revision, there were differences on whether it should be broad, covering many sections, or narrow, limited to only one. However, the specific content of views in favor of revision (the majority) and views opposed to revision cannot be classified with absolute clarity and simplicity into two opposing groups on all points. In this chapter, we shall set forth the views for and against revision, attempting to clarify them, and with particular reference to the reasons for this opposition and for the differences that existed within each of the two basic positions.

GENERAL TRENDS IN THE OPPOSING VIEWS

As it is used here, "revision" refers to the general alteration of the express language of the preamble and all chapters of the Constitution.

On the whole, the two views on revision differed simply on whether it is necessary to undertake such a modification of both the text and the form of the Constitution. The view holding it to be necessary supported revision as here defined, while the opposing view, not infrequent in the commission, argued that the objective of revision could be achieved by means of the interpretation and application of the Constitution as it stands. Some commissioners, while opposing the view that interpretation and application would be sufficient, were also against general revision but in actual fact agreed with the demands of the revisionists on specific constitutional points. However, in this regard, "revision" as here used must be regarded as a general revision of the text, as pointed out above. However, this results in a confusion in the distinction between the two basic views, because some of those opposing general revision (and thus to be classified as antirevisionist) also supported amendment of certain specific points (and thus to be regarded as revisionist). Although the revisionist view was in the majority, it was also not uniform; it can be split into many groupings on a variety of grounds.

THE SCALE OF REVISION. In regard to the scale of revision there were also two divisions: one supporting a broad scale and the other a narrow one. The former held that many changes were required covering the entire Constitution and thus resulting in a broad rewriting of the present document. In opposition, the other view was that revision of only certain specific sections was necessary. The majority of those favoring revision also called for broad-scale revision; thus, it can be said that this was the "argument for complete revision," while the other view could be termed the "argument for partial revision." However, the argument for complete revision held that such basic constitutional principles as popular sovereignty, democracy, pacifism, and respect for fundamental human rights should be maintained and many holding this view also asserted that the present Constitution should not be completely changed.

BASIC POSITIONS ON REVISION. Even though some revisionists called for the enactment of a new and independent constitution, no one went so far as to demand that the present one be abolished or revoked and a completely new one enacted through the operation of the so-called constituent power. Those supporting a new and independent constitution called for revision to be carried out in both form and procedure according to the amendment process as determined by the present Constitution. Even so what these revisionists wished is in fact a new and independent constitution.

TIME AND METHOD OF REVISION. Even among the revisionists there was absolutely no uniformity in regard to the time and method of revision. Although there was agreement on the point that revision requires careful consideration, there was a confrontation between two views on the timing. The first was that the time has already come to set out on a course toward revision and a passive attitude should not be adopted on the grounds that caution is necessary. The other view was that caution is required and that there should be no haste in deciding on a time for revision both because it requires careful consideration and because it should not be embarked on until after a careful and penetrating review of both the foreign and domestic situations. There was also the view that the time for revision should be left to the political decision of the Diet and the cabinet and should not concern the commission itself. But there was the opposing position that the commission's consideration of the necessity for revision should also include the time for revision.

As to the method of revision there was also a confrontation of views. One held that there should be a complete and comprehensive revision of the Constitution in all respects. The other was that there should be an order of priority established among the points requiring revision and that the revision should be made by stages.

In regard to time and method of revision it was the majority opinion among the revisionists that today is already the time to start on the course toward revision, that such a course should speedily be established and the necessary initial steps be taken, and that all points requiring revision should be dealt with at the same time. The minority view in general held that today is not necessarily the time to embark on revision, because all points put forth by the majority as requiring revision do not necessarily call for it. Their reasons varied as to why revision is unnecessary, but also they did not maintain that the present Constitution is completely without its shortcomings.

REASONS FOR THE OPPOSING VIEWS ON REVISION

Out of what did the confrontation of views on the necessity for revision arise? The sources of difference among the members of the commission lay in their basic thinking in relation to the three fundamental problems that the commission confronted in its reexamination of the Constitution, namely: (1) its ideal form; (2) the evaluation of the process of enactment; and (3) the basic attitudes toward its application and interpretation.

On the ideal form of the Constitution of Japan it was evident that the commissioners were all agreed that it should be freely enacted by the Japanese people, in accord with Japan's history and tradition as well as the principle of universal human rights, and realistic, effective, and in harmony with world trends. But what separated the revisionist view from the antirevisionist view was not necessarily disagreement over the concrete content of such words and phrases as "independent," "principle of universal human rights," "Japan's history and tradition," "world trends," and "realistic and effective"; rather, it was based on differing views of possible defects and shortcomings in Japan's Constitution as measured against the ideal form described above. The majority revisionist view arose from the feeling that there are such shortcomings and defects, and the opposing view that there are not. But not all those who recognized such shortcomings and defects could be classified as revisionists for some believed that they could be dealt with through legislation, court decisions, and the operation of government itself without constitutional revision.

Among the revisionists the assertion was frequently made that the texts of all constitutions should precisely and adequately set forth both their ideals and the means to achieve them in an unmistakable fashion and that the present Constitution is defective in this regard. In opposition, it was maintained that in general the ideals of a Constitution cannot be realized simply by means of textual provisions, but rather the point of emphasis should be on what was termed a "living constitution" and thus the discussion of the ideal form of the Constitution should avoid excessive concentration on textual provisions. This latter view further argued that it is probable that the history and tradition of Japan would naturally be woven into such a living constitution and, equally importantly, the ideals of the present Constitution would actually be realized if it really is a living Constitution and that revision is not needed.

It was the majority opinion in the commission that the present Constitution was not enacted on the basis of the freely expressed will of the Japanese people. This led directly in many cases to the view that revision is necessary for this reason as well as because of problems relating to the content of the Constitution. On the other hand, the minority view against revision stemmed in part from the point that the absence of the popular will in the process of enactment was not necessarily improper under the circumstances at the time. A special point bearing on the timing of revision among those opposing revision was that those of the generation which bears both direct and indirect responsibility for the lost war under the old Constitution are particularly unsuited to discuss revision of the present Constitution. Therefore, it was argued, the decision on the need for revision should be left to the coming generation.

In regard to the evaluation of the interpretation and application of the present Constitution, it was the majority view in the commission that revision is needed, because there are necessary limitations on the application and interpretation of all constitutions, and because the stage has been reached where it is no longer possible to deal with the shortcomings and defects of the present Constitution by means of application and interpretation alone. The opposition view that revision is not needed

held that even though there are limitations on the application and interpretation of all constitutions, at the same time their scope should be
recognized as being as broad as possible and that, consequently, the
variety of problems apparent in the present Constitution can be solved
through elastic interpretation and application.

There was also the revisionist view in this connection that as a matter
of both legal methodology and constitutional process the texts of all
constitutions in theory should be precisely set forth so that there is no
room for doubts in interpretation. Consequently, since the wording of
the present Constitution has led to numerous disputes in both interpretation and academic theory, and since this is an obvious defect, revision is
necessary in order to close off the areas producing such disputes as
much as possible.

In opposition it was argued that the thinking is improper which holds
that revision is necessary in order to unify both academic theory and
interpretation and to eliminate disputes on the technical legal grounds
that constitutional processes must be strictly honored. All constitutions
no matter how perfectly drafted in theory are nothing more than blue-
prints or plans, and consequently the function of application and interpretation is to make it possible for the documents to operate as "living
constitutions." It was further argued that when a constitution's actual
operation is offered as a reason for the need for revision, that view is
improper which holds that points which can be decided by means of
interpretation, legislation, and court decision should be dealt with by
means of constitutional revision. Behind the confrontation between
these two views there is a difference in fundamental thinking in regard
to constitutions, namely, whether they should be regarded as static or
dynamic instruments.

Here too the opposition of views was not a simple and well-defined
one. The source of this difficulty was that the conflict was not produced
over general and abstract questions as might be gathered from the above
account, but over concrete problems of the application and interpretation of specific constitutional provisions. For example, some revisionists
held that certain problems could be dealt with by application and interpretation and thus did not require revision.

There were also fundamental differences in thinking on the problem
of the timing of revision. For example, the attitude was expressed that
even as of today it cannot be said that the people's understanding and
awareness of the Constitution have been sufficiently nurtured and firmly
established, and as a result to undertake revision under such conditions
would have to be regarded as not necessarily being based on the true will
of the people. Thus, a decision on revision should be left to the future

when the development and the establishment of the people's understanding and consciousness of the Constitution can be counted on.

On the question of timing it was also argued that constitutional revision should be decided on purely theoretical grounds, removed from political considerations such as the possibility of foreign and domestic consequences of an attempt at revision. Some felt that such consequences, though to be expected, should not be feared. But some revisionists held what was called the "cautious revision opinion," namely, that the time and method of revision should be treated with care because of the possible foreign and domestic consequences, thus ending in a position close to that of those who held that revision is unnecessary.

In general, antirevisionist commissioners opposed each specific argument of the revisionists, primarily on the grounds that they approved of the actual state of the application of the Constitution, that is to say, the administrative actions, the court decisions, and the legislation in existence. As an example, in regard to the various provisions of Chapter 3 relating to the rights and duties of the people, they opposed the revisionist claim that revision is necessary in order to make clear certain limitations on fundamental human rights. At the same time they approved existing legislation limiting fundamental human rights in the name of the public welfare as being constitutionally justified.

Thus, many antirevisionist commissioners approved the actual state of the functioning of the present Constitution, since the actions already undertaken by the Diet, the cabinet, and the courts are permissible within the limits of application and interpretation of the Constitution as it stands. This view differs from the antirevisionist position expressed outside the commission that attacks some existing legislation and other acts involving the application of the Constitution as being unconstitutional. Also some commissioners holding the above view did not clearly express an opinion as to whether, for example, the Self-Defense Forces Law should be recognized as falling within the limits of the application and interpretation of the present Constitution.

VIEWS ON PROBLEMS OF REVISION

[In the original the material contained in this section appears in Section B and Section C of this chapter. Section B is devoted to the view that revision is necessary; Section C to the view that it is unnecessary. Each of these sections has two subsections: a major one devoted to the views of the majority, and a minor one devoted to "special opinions." Both sections have the same headings and subheadings. To shorten the text of the translation these sections have been combined into one. The headings and subheadings are the same as those in the original, but all the opinions have been combined under each heading and subheading. Although the substance is identical, the reorganization means that the text of the translation does not parallel the text of the original.]

In this section the wide variety of views on the necessity for the revision of the Constitution is described. They are divided into four categories: the majority view that revision is necessary; a number of special individual views of commissioners in the revisionist camp; the minority view holding that revision is unnecessary; and a small number of special individual opinions within the minority view.

Problems Relating to Basic Thinking on the Constitution

EVALUATION OF THE PROCESS OF ENACTMENT OF THE PRESENT CONSTITUTION. One majority view on the evaluation of the process of enactment of the present Constitution can be summarized as follows. The present Constitution was not enacted on the basis of the freely expressed will of the Japanese people; the enactment was an expression of Allied occupation policy for Japan; General Headquarters presented to the Japanese government a draft which was in reality an order; the draft of the Japanese government's version was based on GHQ's and the revisions made in the Diet were all under the direction and supervision of GHQ. In addition, even in those situations where the wishes of the Japanese side were adopted, it happened only to the extent that they were in agreement with occupation policy, that is to say, within the limits of GHQ's basic policy.

A second view was that the present Constitution should be revised if only because the process of enactment prevented the free expression of the will of the Japanese people. Also, because there are a number of defects and shortcomings in its content, revision is necessary from the standpoint of both content and enactment.

The minority view simply held that the opinion that the process of enactment of the present Constitution was not based on the directly expressed will of the Japanese people is incorrect. In reality the enactment was carried out as a responsibility based on the acceptance of the Potsdam Declaration which resulted from the lost war. Although it is admitted that the Constitution was enacted under the occupation and within the ambit of occupation policy and that the wishes of the Japanese side were accepted only to the extent that they were in agreement with the basic policy of GHQ, both the international and domestic situations at the time were complicated, and the conclusion should not be reached that the enactment took place only under compulsion from GHQ or the Allied powers. In addition, it should be accepted as a fact that the will of the Japanese government and people was reflected in the Constitution in no small degree. This minority view therefore held that the necessity for the revision of the Constitution should be decided not on the basis of the process of enactment, but on the basis of its content and actual functioning.

However, there were several special variations on the majority view. One held that it cannot be said that the Constitution was necessarily not enacted on the basis of the freely expressed will of the people. At the time of enactment the Constitution was not far removed from the will of the people and in this regard it is necessary to evaluate both the free efforts and the desires of the Japanese people. Another view held that the various elements in the process of enactment were extremely complicated and it is impossible to make a simple and incisive judgment as to whether it was or was not based on the free will of the people.

In addition, there was a special minority opinion which held that revision of the Constitution is unnecessary because of the welcome nature of its content, even though it be admitted that it cannot be termed as having been enacted on the basis of the freely expressed will of the people.

THE IDEAL CONSTITUTION FOR JAPAN. Japan's constitution, in the majority view, should be one which has been freely enacted by the Japanese people; is in accord with the history, tradition, individuality, and national character of Japan as well as the universal principle of fundamental human rights; and is realistic, effective, and in harmony with world trends. In addition, all constitutions should provide, both adequately and precisely enough to leave no room for doubt, for an approach to their ideals and the realization thereof. If the present Constitution is viewed from the above standpoint, the following conclusions must be reached: its rationale does not accord with the ideal of what Japan's constitution should be; it is visionary in nature and is not only lacking in sufficient indications of the means for its realization, but its processes are both illogical and ambiguous; and there are many doubtful points of interpretation.

The minority view accepted the above three characteristics of an ideal constitution for Japan. However, it held that the present Constitution does not fall so far short of the ideal that there are shortcomings and defects that absolutely must be revised now. Another minority view held that it is impossible to arrive at agreement on the definition of such phrases as "principle of universal human rights," "Japanese history and tradition," "world trends," and "realistic and effective," as set forth by the revisionists in their demands for the revision of the preamble and various chapters of the Constitution. A third view was that emphasis should not be placed on how the ideal of a constitution should be embodied in the instrument but rather on the "living constitution" and the problem of what legislation and social conditions can give birth to constitutional ideals. Thus, the thinking of the revisionists who believe it necessary to revise the Constitution completely in order to make it an ideal one is not correct. The present Constitution should be considered on the basis of whether in actual fact its operation has created difficulties which must somehow be eliminated.

Some revisionists did not accept the views on the ideal constitution as set forth in the majority view above. One held that a constitution should not be thought of as simply a written document and it should not be discussed only in light of whether or not what are called its ideals have or have not been written into it. Another view was that although the text of the constitution should naturally be the foundation, the accumulation of authoritative interpretations, legislation, judicial precedent, and its actual application form a living constitutional order, resulting in a situation where it is not absolutely necessary that there be strict adherence to the provisions of the text of the constitution. Another view asserted that the necessity for a uniquely Japanese constitution should not be emphasized to the point where it might lead to a diminishing of the principle of universal human rights, thus leading to a collapse into the so-called reverse course away from democracy; rather, that universal principles should be used as to add flavor to the special Japanese characteristics and individuality in the constitution.

THE APPLICATION AND INTERPRETATION OF THE PRESENT CONSTITUTION. A majority view held that in the application and interpretation of all written constitutions there are specific limits and to recognize too broadly the scope of such application and interpretation will lead to the negation of the Constitution. A second view was that the present Constitution has a number of shortcomings which have already gone beyond the point where they can be dealt with by interpretation and application; therefore, elimination of these shortcomings through revision is necessary.

In opposition, the minority held that although there are various problems relating to the present Constitution, they should be handled through its application and interpretation and since this is already being done by legislation, court precedents, and administrative action there is no reason for revision. It was also argued that since there should be elastic interpretation of all constitutions, the scope of both application and interpretation should be recognized as being as broad as possible. Another view was that what are cited as evils in the present Constitution should not be regarded as having necessarily been produced by its imperfections and shortcomings and in addition it does not necessarily follow that these evils will be immediately remedied by revision.

A special view among those who held that the application and interpretation of the present Constitution indicate no necessity for revision was that the special nature of the present Constitution is in its style which is not in accord with the classical constitutional methodology which sets great store on logical rigidity. Therefore, interpretation should be approached flexibly in accord with that special character.

Within the majority view there was also the opinion that held that contradictions, lack of clarity, and imperfections in the Constitution can be handled to a suitable degree by means of application and interpretation, especially by means of Supreme Court decisions, although there are natural limitations on interpretations of this kind. However, it should be recognized that the three branches of the government do possess certain special authority in respect to constitutional interpretation and therefore it is impossible to agree with the revisionist view that calls for a broad revision of the text in order to eliminate doubts in interpretation by means of logical exactitude. But if through actual observation it is determined that there are irregular points, then it is appropriate to eliminate them by revision.

Another view in this category was that what can be taken care of under the actual application of the Constitution should be excluded from the scope of revision, while at the same time the written Constitution should not be allowed to become a dead letter through the accumulation of interpretations in judicial precedents, administrative practice, and Diet legislation.

Revision of the Preamble and the Various Chapters

THE PREAMBLE. The preamble in one majority view should be completely revised because it is inappropriate for a Constitution of Japan in respect to style, wording, content, and sources. Another view was that the style and wording should be changed to correct Japanese prose which would be both concise and high in style. The content must be changed to include not only the ideals and the determination of an independent Japanese people, but also a magnificent proclamation of an independent position which would contribute positively to the realization of both international peace and the defense of our own country, discarding especially a pacifism which is ineffectually dependent on a foreign country.

There was also the special revisionist opinion that in addition to fundamental changes in the preamble a chapter on "General Principles" or "General Provisions" should be added and the spirit of the preamble should be written into the text in accord with such general principles.

A minority view admitted the imperfections of the style and wording, but held that these did not constitute an absolute reason for its revision.

Another view was that the principles and the spirit expressed in the preamble must be preserved and the content must not be changed under the guise of alterations in the style and wording.

THE EMPEROR. Among the revisionists a majority view held that the ideal form of the emperor system must be in accord with popular sovereignty and, therefore, the emperor system as established in the present Constitution on the basis of popular sovereignty must be preserved. Also it was asserted that the position of the emperor as a "symbol" under the present Constitution is appropriate, but it is also necessary to set forth his position clearly as "the head of state" in terms of his functions. Therefore, the provisions relating to the emperor's role in affairs of state should be completed by a reference to his role in foreign relations where, as "head of state," he would represent the state in general matters in its foreign relations.

The minority antirevisionist view was in agreement with the first view regarding the ideal emperor system indicated above. However, the fear was expressed that if the emperor did enjoy the functions and the position of a formal head of state there might be the possibility of a reversion to the emperor system as it was under the old Constitution and that should not be. It was further pointed out that in his capacity as "symbol" the emperor has in actual fact represented the people of Japan in their external relations and that consequently the idea that he must be explicitly termed the "head of state" through constitutional revision is unacceptable.

However, there were a number of special opinions relating to the position of the emperor which differed from the majority view of the revisionists. One view held that the emperor system provides the spiritual foundation of the nation, thereby giving fruit to the unity of the people. The present Constitution has adopted the principle of popular sovereignty and has made the emperor a mere "symbol," denying his legal authority as the center of the unity of the people of Japan. Therefore, not only should the phrase "popular sovereignty" be eliminated, but the emperor should be placed in a position of legal authority arising from the unity of the people and should be provided with a mediating function permitting him to resolve possible conflicts among the organs of state.

It was also argued that popular sovereignty by its very nature is incompatible with the emperor system and that Japan's democracy must be a democracy under a sovereign emperor. Therefore, it is necessary to change the idea, as adopted by the present Constitution, of an emperor system based on the sovereignty of the people.

Another view held that it is acceptable to retain the emperor's position as a symbol, but both his domestic and foreign functions must be broadened to make clear that he is actually the head of state. Others held both that his foreign and domestic functions should be broadened and that he should explicitly be made the head of state. Another argument was that although it is acceptable to retain the emperor as a symbol, his functions in affairs of state should be further reduced while he is given a more active role in nonpolitical cultural and social affairs. A final view was that no term such as symbol or head of state should be applied to the emperor, and his functions in national affairs should be reduced even more than are his present acts in matters of state.

THE RENUNCIATION OF WAR. Naturally, there was a wide variety of opinions regarding the possible revision of Article 9. They are summarized below.

The views approving the revision of Article 9 were as follows:

1. The ideal of pacifism must be supported as a matter of course and it absolutely must be preserved.

2. As an ideal, pacifism in itself is proper, but Article 9, particularly the nonmaintenance of war potential, is unrealistic, idealistic, and visionary at the present stage both of international politics and of the structure of international peace.

3. Japan's self-defense structure today must be based on the concept of the right of self-defense possessed by all independent countries.

4. Article 9 raises difficulties in respect to Japan's self-defense. That is to say, because of doubts about the interpretation of Article 9, certain problems and abuses have developed.

5. It is necessary to revise Article 9 and to clarify the issue of the maintenance of a self-defense army both in terms of national defense itself and in terms of cooperation with international peace-keeping organizations, particularly the United Nations and other systems of collective security. Civilian supremacy must be maintained as well as democratic control over the self-defense army. If such a revision is carried out, it will be possible to unify national opinion in respect to Japan's defense and basic policy in foreign affairs.

Special opinions favoring revision of Article 9 were as follows:

1. It is argued that the Self-Defense Forces are not unconstitutional but they must be regarded as clearly being so. Consequently, Article 9 must be amended to make the SDF constitutional.

2. Since constitutional provisions should not go beyond statements of general principle, there should be only a provision permitting the maintenance of an army for self-defense, and such matters as its organization and functions and the system of civilian control should be provided for only by law.

3. Since the ideals of Article 9 must be highly valued, that article should be maintained even today just as it is. Because it is difficult today

to realize those ideals, necessary concrete measures must be devised to guarantee Japan's security. Accordingly, while Article 9 should be continued unchanged, another part should be added to it relating to "measures to guarantee the security of the nation," thus providing a constitutional basis for the existing defense structure.

Views holding revision of Article 9 to be unnecessary were as follows:

1. The ideal of pacifism as set forth in the present Constitution must, of course, be preserved. In addition, the defense of Japan while providing for the national security must be directed toward the ideal of pacifism and at the same time must contribute to both national security and to world peace by participation in systems of collective self-defense such as the United Nations and others.

2. Under Article 9 as it presently exists, the defense system already adopted, including the Self-Defense Forces, participation in the United Nations, and the Japanese-American security treaty, is not unconstitutional.

3. Article 9, particularly its second paragraph, should not be regarded as unrealistic, visionary, and idealistic, but the principle of the renunciation of war potential should be regarded as possessing a new and realistic meaning, particularly in view of the movement today toward the achievement of complete disarmament.

4. Today the concept of the right of self-defense residing in individual nations is undergoing change, and for one country to offer it as the reason for its defense possesses the danger of harm to the general achievement of peace.

5. Even under the present Article 9, a defense structure has already been created without being confronted with insurmountable obstacles.

6. It cannot be said that through a revision of Article 9 a unification of national policy on defense and the defense structure will be realized. On the other hand, the undesirable effects, both foreign and domestic, that will accompany attempts at such revision must be taken into account.

A special opinion on the renunciation of war was also given. It is possible to interpret Article 9 as being a political declaration or the statement of a constitutional standard setting forth an ideal impossible of immediate realization at the present stage of international society. Under this view it has still been possible to maintain a self-defense army, notwithstanding the wording of the second paragraph of Article 9. Even though the establishment of a self-defense army and other matters cannot be approved under a strict interpretation of Article 9, revision should not for that reason be considered necessary. In other words, the problem of our national defense is not a constitutional one; it must be debated as one of national policy.

THE RIGHTS AND DUTIES OF THE PEOPLE. Some who favored the revision of Chapter 3 argued that it is prejudiced in favor of the rights and freedoms of the people and against their duties and responsibilities, stating that therein the evil of making light of the social order and the welfare of all the people is strikingly made manifest. Also the thinking favoring freedom runs counter to the principles of the contemporary welfare state, which stands on the concept of social solidarity.

Another view was that the concept of "the public welfare" which is set forth in the present Constitution as a limitation on the fundamental human rights of the people is a vague one. On the one hand, there is the fear that fundamental human rights might be improperly limited by law in the name of the public welfare; and on the other hand, proper laws establishing limitations on fundamental human rights under the public welfare doctrine might be held to be unconstitutional, thus leading to possible abuses of those rights. Therefore, a provision should be added clarifying the degree to which fundamental human rights may be limited.

It was also argued that the provisions relating to rights and duties should be supplemented and fully completed in order to bring them into accord with the principles of the contemporary welfare state. Expanding on this view was another which held that since the present title of Chapter 3 is based on the old concepts of "rights and duties" it should be changed to "The Welfare and Obligations of the People" in order more clearly to indicate the new concepts of the contemporary welfare state.

Among those who felt there is no necessity to revise Chapter 3 were some who argued that any problem arising out of the possible conflict between fundamental human rights and the public welfare or out of the development of the concepts of the welfare state can be taken care of by the application and interpretation of the Constitution and should consequently be left to legislation and court precedents.

It was also argued that the present Constitution should not be regarded as being behind the times because it is not directly in accord with the principles of the contemporary welfare state, the requirements of which can be met under the Constitution as it stands. It was further declared that what is asserted to be a basic principle of the welfare state, namely, that the responsibility for the guarantee in actual fact of the rights and freedoms of the people is placed on the state, has already been adopted in Article 25 of the present Constitution. Thus, a preferable course of action is to emphasize Article 25 rather than to strengthen limitations on the rights and freedoms of the people in the name of the principles of the contemporary welfare state.

THE NATIONAL DIET. The majority of commissioners, even those who believed that the provisions relating to the National Diet should be revised, also held that such basic principles as popular sovereignty, the representative system, the separation of powers, and the parliamentary cabinet system should be preserved. However, it was also asserted that the provision of Article 41 which states that "the National Diet is the highest organ of state power" runs counter both to the principle of the separation of powers and the present trend toward the strengthening and stabilization of the executive branch. In addition, this provision gives the impression of the absolute omnipotence of the Diet, thereby leading to possible abuse of power by the legislative branch. For these reasons this provision should be changed.

In addition, it was argued that although the bicameral system should be preserved, it is necessary to change the structure of the House of Councilors by some means such as the addition of nonelected members in order to differentiate it in character from the House of Representatives.

Among the opinions favoring revision of the provisions relating to the Diet was the special opinion that the present parliamentary cabinet system should be abolished and replaced by the system of an elective prime minister. In regard to the structure of the Diet, another view was that it will be impossible to preserve a difference in character between the two houses if both are to be composed of popularly elected members. Therefore, a start should be made toward a unicameral system. It was also asserted that perhaps the House of Representatives should be organized under the party system while the House of Councilors should be made nonpartisan, with the latter undergoing a broad change in both structure and functions. This same view also advocated the granting of special and exclusive powers to the House of Councilors relating to important matters of state requiring particular impartiality.

Some of those believing revision of the Diet provisions to be unnecessary held that the Diet should continue to be "the highest organ of state power." This view was based on the attitude that the present Constitution recognizes the separation of powers and checks and balances and thus, viewing the Constitution as a whole, there is no contradiction between Article 41 and other provisions such as those relating to judicial review. It was also pointed out that the "highest organ of state power" provision eliminates the subordinate position of the Imperial Diet under the Meiji Constitution.

It was also held that although Article 41 gives rise to the impression of the absolute omnipotence of the Diet and thus may lead to such evils as the abuse of power, those evils arise from problems of the political parties and the attitudes of Diet members; this provision is not the cause. The argument was also put forth that the bicameral system should be preserved. However, the achievement of the goal of giving the House of Councilors a character different from that of the House of Representatives can be realized through a revision of the Election Law while preserving the elective nature of the upper house.

THE CABINET. The majority of those supporting revision of the cabinet provisions felt that the parliamentary cabinet system must be preserved and the system of an elective prime minister must be rejected. However, to preserve the parliamentary cabinet system it is necessary to correct the excessively subordinate position of the cabinet in relation to the Diet, and to strengthen its authority in order to strive for a stabilization of its position, while revising the "highest organ of state power" provision.

Of course, the view supporting the system of an elective prime minister included the idea of developing a powerful executive branch based on a foundation of popular support.

Those holding revision of the cabinet provisions to be unnecessary argued that the present system should be continued without changing the position of the Diet as the highest organ of state power, and without strengthening the authority of the cabinet (and thus weakening the Diet). Likewise, the system of an elective prime minister should not be considered because Japan is lacking in the conditions under which the election of the prime minister should be carried out, and accordingly the system would not only be ineffective in eliminating problems of Japanese politics, but also would be dangerous.

THE JUDICIARY. Most of those supporting revision in the judiciary asserted that the basic principle adopted in the present Constitution of broadening and strengthening the judicial power must be preserved. It was also argued that the present system of judicial review should not be changed; that a constitutional court should not be established; and that the Supreme Court should not be given the character of a constitutional court. This group concentrated on the method of appointment of Supreme Court justices and the revision of the system of popular review of their appointment and dismissal. The argument was that the present systems of appointment and popular review are not adequate for preventing the intervention of political and party considerations. Therefore, a consultative commission on appointments should be established and the system of popular review of Supreme Court justices should be abolished. The emphasis in this view was on the necessity for the selection of well-qualified justices for the Supreme Court.

However, among those favoring revision of the provisions relating to the judiciary the following special opinions were expressed. Military and administrative courts, as special tribunals lying outside the system of regular judicial courts, should be established. A constitutional court should be created or the Supreme Court given the character of a constitutional court. The system of judicial review of laws should be abolished. Abstract judicial review of laws should be carried out by the

National Diet itself as a part of the legislative process and to that end a committee for the review of constitutional problems should be set up in the Diet.

Those holding revision of the judiciary provisions to be unnecessary naturally supported the basic constitutional approach of broadening and strengthening the judicial power. However, it was also felt that there is no need to strengthen the system of judicial review beyond what it is at present. The view was also expressed that a consultative commission on Supreme Court appointments could be established by law without constitutional revision. The system of popular review of Supreme Court justices was also supported as being an element of the ideal form of judicial power as based on the principle of popular sovereignty and also as a means to insure a concurrence between the Court and public opinion.

FINANCES. The majority view favoring revision of the section on finances pointed out that particular emphasis should be placed on the responsibilities and powers of the government, particularly the executive branch, in handling the complicated finances of the contemporary nation and that the present financial system, which favors the Diet, should be changed to achieve both an integrated handling of finances and the prevention of abuses.

Therefore, it was argued, provisions must be enacted relating to such matters as the handling of financial emergencies, continuing expenditures, measures to be taken when the budget is not approved, Diet amendments increasing the budget, and limitations on members' bills accompanying the budget.

It was also argued that the provisions of Article 89 relating to restrictions on the expenditure of public funds on religious organizations and charitable, educational, and benevolent enterprises have no reasonable basis, and since they are also not appropriate to the present circumstances of our country they should be either abolished or revised.

Those holding that revision of the financial provisions is unnecessary, in opposition to the revisionist view, held that since the basic structure of government under the present Constitution, which makes the Diet the highest organ of state power, should not be changed, it follows that the present provisions relating to finances should also not be changed. Also while it was agreed that the present functions which favor the Diet should be changed in order to achieve comprehensive management of finances and to prevent waste in national expenditures, this problem can be dealt with through administrative operations, the Finance Law, and other legislation without resort to constitutional revision.

In respect to Article 89 it was held that since it has in actual practice been applied without the development of abuses, there is no particular need for revision.

LOCAL SELF-GOVERNMENT. The majority favoring revision argued that the present constitutional provisions relating to local self-government are inclined too far toward decentralization of power which should not be idly advocated at present. Local self-government, rather, should be based on an organic, cooperative relationship between the state and local public entities. What is particularly necessary is the enactment of provisions which will clearly define the types of local public entities and the method of election of their heads. Such provisions would make possible the reform of the present prefectural system, the establishment of a regional system in conformity with the requirements of wide-area administration, and, in addition, a clear definition of the ideal relationship between the state and local public entities. Through such revision it will be possible to state plainly in the Constitution the guidelines for the reform of local self-government.

Those holding revision to be unnecessary, while recognizing the existence of problems such as those pointed out above, asserted that reforms are possible through legislation and actual administrative measures without necessarily resorting to constitutional revision.

AMENDMENT. Supporters of revision of the amendment procedure argued that there are many unclear points in Article 96, which should be revised in order to eliminate doubts in interpretation. The amendment procedure outlined in Article 96 is too strict and should be modified. To support this point they argued that since amendment is so difficult, almost impossible, there is a possible danger of the encouragement of a resort to violence in order to achieve constitutional change.

Those who felt that amendment is unnecessary argued that the unclear points in Article 96 can be dealt with by legislation or interpretation. While admitting that the amendment process is strict, they also argued that there is no need to change it. However, it should not be thought that the only way to achieve constitutional stability is through a strict process of amendment; rather, reliance should be placed on general political stability and the faith of the people in the Constitution. If amendment is difficult, then administrative actions and court precedents must be the means to handle the actual state of affairs under the Constitution.

THE SUPREME LAW. The majority of the revisionists held that the three articles of Chapter 10, on the supreme law, are all either unnecessary or should be shifted to other chapters. Accordingly, they held that this chapter in its entirety is without justification and should be eliminated. However, a minority view held that paragraph 1 of Article 98 should be retained because of its importance as an indication that Japan has adopted the principle of a written constitution—in other words, that it does not recognize natural law, fundamental norms, and the law of reason which lie outside a written constitution.

Those holding revision to be unnecessary argued that this chapter was created for a particular purpose, thus that it has a special significance and must be highly valued. The basic reason for its retention is that in order that fundamental human rights be respected it is a necessary requirement that the various organs of state involved in the application of the Constitution must respect it so that in turn the fundamental human rights of the people will also be respected. Elimination of this chapter might result in a diminution of respect for fundamental human rights.

STATES OF EMERGENCY. The supporters of revision held that the fact that the present Constitution has no provision for dealing with states of emergency is a grave deficiency. It was further argued that it is impermissible under a written constitution not to have an express provision relating to states of emergency, because even though it can be argued that it is possible both legally and theoretically for the state to take the necessary measures even in the absence of a specific constitutional provision, such measures are impossible as a matter of practical politics without such a provision. Constitutional provisions will also prevent the abuse of power during states of emergency. Accordingly, constitutional provisions should be enacted, establishing a basis for measures to be taken in states of emergency and setting up the general principles to be followed.

The opposing view was that while it is necessary to have measures for dealing with states of emergency, they need not be provided for in the Constitution. In situations where there is a real necessity for dealing with a state of emergency it is recognized as an unwritten principle that the executive or legislative branch is empowered to take the necessary action regardless of whether there is a provision in a written constitution. If a constitutional justification is necessary, it can be found in an elastic interpretation of the Constitution, particularly in regard to the public welfare. In addition, an express provision in the Constitution, instead of limiting the abuse of authority, might actually encourage it because it might be used as a justification for the proclamation of a state of emergency. The anxiety was also expressed that any attempt to enact such a constitutional provision might create dangerous and unnecessary political turmoil.

POLITICAL PARTIES. Those supporting a constitutional provision relating to political parties advanced a number of arguments. First, because political parties are the foundation of the political system, the Constitution should deal expressly with them. A constitutional statement on the ideal form for political parties wo today's parties and in nurturing soun provisions should be supplemented by a eliminating the evils of by some that the Constitution should se nment. Constitutional parties and their internal organization shoul rty law. It was added democracy. t the character of the principles of

Those opposing a constitutional provision relat. argued that parties should be regarded as lying outsic. litical parties Constitution; they by their very nature develop naturally ntrol of the of performing their functions free of restriction by natre capable addition, healthy party government cannot be achieved only th law. In enactment of general and abstract principles relating to the for th the character of parties. In addition, detailed stipulations relating to part. nd might even inhibit party politics. Finally, the development of healthy party government is not a problem of the Constitution or of a political party law; contemporary problems of the parties cannot be solved by either.

ELECTIONS. Both sides agreed that as desirable as the enactment of a fair election law might be for the realization of the principles of both popular sovereignty and parliamentary democracy, it is not necessary to establish a constitutional body to that end. One suggestion was that a law be enacted creating a drafting body for such a law independent to a certain extent of both the cabinet and the Diet, that it be given the responsibility for drafting such a law, and that special procedures be set up to guarantee respect for the deliberative process in the Diet's consideration of the bill.

NATIONAL REFERENDA. Both sides agreed that there should be no constitutional provision establishing national referenda on specific issues. However, among those holding that revision is unnecessary a reason for not having such referenda was that there should be no exceptions to the present constitutional principles of the parliamentary cabinet system and the representative system. It was also urged that the two systems be nurtured and perfected as a means for preventing the possible use of referenda in order to establish dictatorial government.

Time for Revision

It was the majority view that it is necessary to revise the Constitution at the earliest possible time both because of important problems involved in the process of enactment and because of a large number of shortcomings and defects in its content. It would also be a natural step for the Japanese people to whom independence has been restored and for a now completely sovereign nation. Naturally they were opposed to the argument

for revision, but that in view of its impor-
that the time is n/ made aware of the necessity for revision and
tance the people/ g those supporting revision in general there were
urged to haste/ at today is not the time. One view here held that
However, e/ home and abroad are too unstable at present and a
those who a/ ch to revision is necessary at a time when the country is
conditions ch/ ed in a genuine confrontation on the Constitution. Revi-
cautious ed/ wait until an overwhelming majority of the Diet is in step on
already wait/ and until a draft can be prepared that can win the consent of a
sion sland/ ajority of the people. Until such an environment can be created,
the i/ ation is necessary and we must not act in such a way that a forced
gre/ revision under present circumstances will be followed by another revision after a shift in political power.

Another opinion was that the commission should not be involved in determining the time of revision, for the actual question of revision is a great and politically decisive one that should be decided by the Diet and the cabinet and ultimately by the general will of the people. It was also said that constitutional revision must be carried out through the joint action of the major political parties and only when the parties reach general agreement on points involving fundamental political confrontation and therefore the issue should be left to a future generation. In other words, constitutional revision should be carried out in stages when common agreement has been reached among the major parties on such issues as the system of an elective prime minister which could serve as the first step in reaching common agreement.

In addition, it was argued that the core of the problem of revision is Article 9 with all other issues being secondary, because those who fear revision of Article 9 are opposed to revision in general. Therefore, if it is possible to bring an end to the dispute over Article 9, then the time may have arrived for revision of other provisions.

Those holding revision to be unnecessary argued that because constitutions are fundamental national laws, revision should be carried out only when there are absolute obstalces to constitutional action. A flexible attitude toward constitutional interpretation will solve most problems. The present Constitution has functioned so far without absolute obstacles having appeared and thus revision is not necessary.

Another view was that today the people's understanding and awareness of the present Constitution have not yet been either sufficiently developed or firmly established and that the thinking of the period of the old Constitution still has strong roots. Thus if revision is undertaken today it will not only not be based on the independent decision of the people, but will also involve the danger of a retrogression to the thinking of the old Constitution. Revision must be left to the next generation for the decision on the necessity for it should wait until that time in the future when the cultivation and the establishment of the people's awareness of the Constitution is an observable reality.

Finally, it was argued that in realistic terms if constitutional revision is attempted today, there will be both the danger that great domestic political confusion will be created by the division of public opinion on the issue and the expectation that undesirable consequences will be produced on the international scene. Revision should not be carried out under such potentially unstable domestic and international conditions.

APPENDIX: *Biographical Data on Commissioners*

(These brief biographical sketches provide a few clues on the background of the commissioners. The information here may throw some light on the reasons for their opinions during the commission hearings. It should be remembered that all commissioners listed as members of the National Diet were affiliated with conservative political parties. Dates listed at the end of each entry indicate the initial appointment of members active when the commission completed its work or the period of tenure of former members.)

COMMISSIONERS FROM THE HOUSE OF REPRESENTATIVES

Aichi Kiichi: b. 1907; graduated, Tokyo University, political science, 1931; career bureaucrat in Finance Ministry including service in Great Britain and France; elected, House of Councilors, 1950; elected, House of Representatives, 1955; Minister of International Trade and Industry, 1954; Chief Cabinet Secretary, 1957; Minister of Justice, 1958; high official of Liberal Democratic Party. 29 July 1960.

Aoki Masashi: b. 1898; graduated, Tokyo University of Agriculture, 1920; journalist and newspaper official, 1923–36; served on a number of commodity control agencies during World War II; elected, House of Representatives, 1949. 23 December 1960.

Chiba Saburō: b. 1894; graduated, Tokyo University, French law, 1919; studied economics as graduate student at Princeton University (U.S.A.); businessman; governor of Miyagi prefecture immediately after World War II; elected, House of Representatives, ten times since 1925; Minister of Labor, 1954; president, Tokyo University of Agriculture, 1955; member of delegation to San Francisco peace conference, 1951. 23 December 1960.

Furui Yoshimi: b. 1903; graduated, Tokyo University, British law, 1925; career bureaucrat in Home Affairs Ministry, rising to governor of Ibaragi and Aichi prefectures and head of Police Bureau during the war years; elected, House of Representatives, 1947; Welfare Minister, 1960. 30 July 1957.

Ide Ichitarō: b. 1912; entered business, 1931; graduated, Kyoto University, agricultural economics, 1943; elected, House of Representatives, 1946; Agriculture and Forestry Minister, 1956 and 1957. 10 July 1959.

Inaba Osamu: b. 1909; graduated, Chūō University, German law, 1936; completed graduate work, Chūō University, 1940; Professor, Chūō University, 1945; elected, House of Representatives, 1949; important positions in LDP. 30 July 1957.

Kojima Tetsuzō: b. 1899; graduated, Tokyo University, French law, 1922; lawyer, including three years in legal research with New York City law firm; elected, House of Representatives, 1947; Minister of Justice, 1960. 30 July 1957.

Nakagaki Kunio: b. 1911; studied Indian philosophy at Tōyō University; elected, House of Representatives, 1947; Minister of Justice, 1962. 20 December 1963.

Nakasone Yasuhiro: b. 1918; graduated, Tokyo University, political science, 1941; entered government service, 1941, but immediately became accounting officer in Imperial Navy; after demobilization returned to government service, specializing in police administration; elected, House of Representatives, 1948; Minister of State for Science and Technology and chairman, Atomic Energy Commission, 1959; extremely active in conservative party politics. 30 July 1957.

Noda Uichi: b. 1903; graduated, Tokyo University, English law, 1927; career bureaucrat in Finance Ministry, including posts in U.S., Great Britain, France, and China; elected, House of Councilors, 1950; Minister of Construction, 1951; elected, House of Representatives, 1953. 29 July 1960.

Shiikuma Saburō: b. 1895; graduated, Chūō University, law, 1927; career bureaucrat and newspaper executive; elected, House of Representatives, 1946; Vice Speaker, House of Representatives, 1958. 22 February 1963.

Sudō Hideo: b. 1898; graduated, Tokyo University, German law, 1921; career bureaucrat until resignation, 1942; served in wartime commodity control agencies; elected, House of Representatives, 1947; Agriculture and Forestry Minister, 1948; Minister of State for Economic Stabilization and for Reparations (concurrently), 1951; Minister of State for Local Autonomy, 1960; Minister of Agriculture and Forestry, 1960. 23 October 1963.

Yamasaki Iwao: b. 1894; graduated, Tokyo University, German law, 1919; career bureaucrat in Home Affairs Ministry, rising to Minister in Higashikuni "surrender" cabinet, 1945; purged; after depurge, elected, House of Representatives, 1952; Minister of State for Local Autonomy and chairman, National Public Safety Commission (concurrently), 1960. 30 July 1957.

COMMISSIONERS FROM THE HOUSE OF COUNCILORS

Kimura Tokutarō: b. 1886; graduated, Tokyo University, English law, 1911; lawyer; Attorney General, 1946; Minister of Justice, 1946, 1948; president, Tokyo First Bar Association, 1951; Minister of State for National Security, 1952–53; elected, House of Councilors, 1953. 30 July 1957.

Kogure Budayu: b. 1893; graduated, Keio University, economics, 1917; served with Mitsui Bank and other business enterprises, including presidencies of banks and businesses; beginning in 1924, elected, House of Representatives (eight terms); elected, House of Councilors, 1956; high official, Liberal Democratic Party; Minister of Transportation, 1960. 30 July 1957.

Kōri Yūichi: b. 1902; graduated, Tokyo University, jurisprudence, 1929; bureaucrat in Ministry of Home Affairs, rising to governor of Ishikawa prefecture and to Vice Chief Secretary of the Cabinet; elected, House of Councilors, 1950; Minister of State for Local Autonomy, 1957; high official, Liberal Democratic Party. 27 January 1959.

Sakomizu Hisatsune: b. 1902; graduated, Tokyo University, law, 1926; bureaucrat in Finance Ministry, including service in U.S.; Chief Cabinet Secretary, 1945; resigned to be appointed to House of Peers, 1945; elected, House of Representatives, 1952 (two terms); elected, House of Councilors, 1956; president, Economic Planning Board, 1960; Minister of Postal Services, 1961; officer, Liberal Democratic Party. 29 October 1963.

Sasamori Junzō: b. 1886; graduated, Waseda University, politics and economics, 1910; studied in U.S. ten years, B.A., Ph.D., University of Denver; president of Aoyama Gakuin and Tokyo Junior College of Economics; elected, House of Representatives, 1946 (four terms); Minister of State for Demobilization and for Reparations, 1947; elected, House of Councilors, 1953. 31 August 1962.

Uetake Haruhiko: b. 1898; graduated, Tokyo Commercial University, 1923; taught briefly at Nihon University, then entered power company; joined railway company, 1936, and rose to presidency; elected, House of Councilors, 1947; Minister of Postal Services, 1959; filled important offices in various conservative parties. 12 March 1963.

COMMISSIONERS FROM AMONG PERSONS OF LEARNING AND EXPERIENCE

Hirose Hisada: b. 1889; graduated, Tokyo University, political science, 1914; bureaucrat, rising to governor of Mie and Saitama prefectures; Welfare Minister, 1939; chief, Cabinet Bureau of Legislation, 1940; Welfare Minister and Chief Cabinet Secretary, 1944; governor of Tokyo, 1945; elected, House of Councilors, 1953. Originally appointed as member from House of Councilors, 1958; appointed as man of learning and experience, 12 June 1959, after completion of House of Councilors term.

Hosokawa Ryūgen: b. 1900; graduated, Tokyo University, law, 1923; joined *Asahi Shimbun*, Japan's leading newspaper; served as bureau chief in New York City; became chief editor, 1944; elected, House of Representatives, 1947; noted political commentator. 30 July 1957.

Kamikawa Hikomatsu: b. 1889; graduated Tokyo University, political science, 1915; assistant professor there, 1917; studied in U.S., Great Britain, and France, 1918–22; full professor, 1923; emeritus, 1952; leading diplomatic historian. 30 July 1957.

Mano Tsuyoshi: b. 1888; graduated, Tokyo University, political science, 1914; entered legal profession and became prominent lawyer, serving both legal associations and various government committees; Supreme Court justice, 1947–58. 1 July 1958.

Masaki Akira: b. 1892; graduated, Tokyo University, German law, 1918; appointed prosecutor, 1920; rose to chief prosecutor, Hiroshima Appeals Court, survived the atomic bomb and transferred to Nagoya Appeals Court also as chief prosecutor; purged by occupation and became private lawyer. 30 July 1957.

Mizuno Tōtarō: b. 1894; graduated, Meiji University, law, 1918; became lawyer, 1920; president, Tokyo Bar Association, 1949; member, many committees dealing with legal issues. 30 July 1957.

Nakagawa Zennosuke: b. 1897; graduated, Tokyo University, law, 1921; academic career at Tōhoku University, 1921–61; authority on civil law, especially family law. 30 July 1957.

Ōishi Yoshio: b. 1903; graduated, Kyoto University, law, 1929; professor emeritus, Kyoto University; constitutional law authority. 30 July 1957.

Ōnishi Kunitoshi: b. 1899; graduated, Waseda University, political economy, 1926; professor, political science, and economics. 30 July 1957.

Rōyama Masamichi: b. 1895; graduated, Tokyo University, political science, 1920; professor, Tokyo University, 1928 until 1939 when he resigned in protest over discharge of colleague for political reasons; head of Tokyo Research Institute of Political Science and Economics; elected, House of Representatives, 1942; political commentator and author of numerous political science books; president, Ochanomizu Women's University, 1954. 30 July 1957.

Sakanishi Shiho: b. 1896; to U.S. to study, 1921; B.A., Wheaton College, 1926; Ph.D., University of Michigan; head, Japan section, Library of Congress, 1930–42; returned to Japan, 1942; literary critic; only woman on commission. 30 July 1957.

Tagami Jōji: b. 1907; graduated, Tokyo University, law, 1930; joined faculty of Tokyo University of Commerce, 1935, and became full professor, 1942; dean of the faculty of law, 1963; has published in fields of constitutional problems and administrative law. 30 July 1957.

Takada Motosaburō: b. 1894; graduated, Tokyo University, English literature, 1917; joined *Mainichi Shimbun* (newspaper) and served as bureau chief in New York and London; became chief editor, 1938; left newspaper, 1947; served in high positions in news agencies and broadcast organizations. 30 July 1957.

Takayanagi Kenzō: b. 1887; graduated, Tokyo University, law, 1912; assistant professor, Tokyo University, 1912; studied in U.S. and Europe, 1915–20; professor, Tokyo University, 1921; president, Seikei University, 1949; distinguished authority on Anglo-American law. 30 July 1957.

Uemura Kōgorō: b. 1894; graduated, Tokyo University, political science, 1918; entered government service rising to vice-director, Cabinet Planning Board, before retiring, 1940; served during war on government agencies involved in coal industry; president, Japan Air Lines. 30 July 1957.

Ushioda Kōji: b. 1901; left Keio University as political science major and entered college in U.S. in 1922; after 1925 studied in England (under Harold Laski) and Germany; assistant professor, Keio University, 1930; full professor, 1932; dean of Faculty of Law, 1946; president, Keio University, 1947–56. 30 July 1957.

Yabe Teiji: b. 1902; graduated, Tokyo University, political science, 1926; studied in U.S., Great Britain, and Germany; retired, professor, Tokyo University,

1945; president, Takushoku University, 1955; political commentator and author of books in political science. 30 July 1957.

Yagi Hidetsugu: b. 1886; graduated, Tokyo University, electrical engineering, 1909; professor and dean, Tōhoku and Osaka universities; president, Osaka University, Tokyo University of Engineering, Musashino University of Engineering; invented Yagi antenna; elected, House of Councilors, 1953; awarded Cultural Medal, 1956. 1 July 1958.

Yoshimura Tadashi: b. 1900; graduated, Waseda University, political science, 1924; graduate student, political science and public administration, Columbia University, 1929–31; traveled in Europe; lecturer, Waseda University, 1932, and full professor, 1938; also professor at Tōkai and Takushoku universities; has written on bureaucracy, local government, and contemporary politics. 30 July 1957.

FORMER COMMISSIONERS: HOUSE OF REPRESENTATIVES

Ashida Hitoshi: b. 1887; graduated, Tokyo University, law, 1912; entered diplomatic service and stationed in Russia, France, and Turkey before resignation, 1932; elected, House of Representatives, nine times after 1932; president, *Japan Times*, and lecturer, Keio University; Welfare Minister, 1945; Foreign Minister, 1947; Prime Minister and Foreign Minister, 1948; published extensively on world politics. 30 July 1957 to 20 June 1959 (deceased).

Araki Masuo: b. 1901; graduated, Kyoto University, economics, 1925; entered Transportation Ministry and served in various posts until 1944 when he transferred to Munitions and Commerce and Industry Ministries; mayor, Ōmuta City, 1946; elected, House of Representatives, 1947; Minister of Education, 1960. 1 July 1958–22 July 1960 (resigned).

Fujieda Sensuke: b. 1907; graduated, Tokyo University, English law, 1930; entered government service and specialized in prefectural administration; elected, House of Representatives, 1949; Minister of State for Defense, 1961. 1 July 1958–7 July 1959 (retired).

Fukui Morita: b. 1885; graduated, Tokyo University, German law, 1913; became lawyer, 1914; held positions in business firms, especially in textiles; attorney general, 1946; president, Tokyo First Bar Association, 1953 and of Japan Bar Association; elected, House of Representatives, 1958. 29 July 1960–24 October 1960 (House of Representatives dissolved).

Funada Naka: b. 1895; graduated, Tokyo University, English law, 1918; entered Home Affairs Ministry and served in important positions until resignation in 1939, to enter Chamber of Commerce work until 1946; elected, House of Representatives, five times in prewar period and seven in postwar period; Minister of State for Defense, 1955; speaker, House of Representatives, 1963. 30 July 1957–24 October 1960 (House of Representatives dissolved).

Hashimoto Ryōgo: b. 1906; graduated, Tokyo University, German law, 1930; entered government service specializing in finance and taxes; elected, House of Representatives, 1949; Minister of Welfare, 1951. 29 July 1960–21 November 1962 (deceased).

Kita Reikichi: b. 1885; graduated, Waseda University, philosophy, 1908; studied at Harvard; entered teaching and rose to professor, philosophy, Taishō University; also journalist, founded *Sokoku* (Fatherland), a magazine; founded Tama College of Art, 1935; purged as founder of *Sokoku*; elected House of Representatives seven times beginning in 1936. 30 July 1957–22 April 1958 (House of Representatives dissolved).

Kiyose Ichirō: b. 1884; graduated, Kyoto University, law, 1908; became lawyer; studied in England, France, and Germany; elected, House of Representatives, thirteen times since 1920; speaker and vice speaker, House of Representatives; Minister of Education, 1955; chief counsel, Tōjō Hideki, Tokyo war crimes trials. 30 July 1957–1 February 1960 (retired to become House of Representatives speaker).

Kobayashi Kanae: b. 1889; graduated, Nihon University, English law, 1911 (?); became prosecutor in Tokyo and professor, Nihon University; later graduated, Berlin University, and investigated legal and economic problems in England, France, and Germany; returned to Japan, 1927, and later became dean of Faculty of Law, Nihon University; became lawyer; elected, House of Representatives, six times after 1930; Vice Speaker, House of Representatives. 10 July 1959–24 October 1960 (House of Representatives dissolved).

Kosaka Zentarō: b. 1912; graduated, Tokyo Commercial University, 1935; entered Mitsubishi Bank; filled positions in private business; elected, House of Representatives, 1946; active in party politics; Minister of International Trade and Industry; chairman, National Public Safety Commission; Minister of State for Procurement; Foreign Minister, 1960. 30 July 1957–22 July 1960 (resigned).

Matsumoto Shunichi: b. 1897; graduated, Tokyo University, French law, 1921; career diplomat; posts in Belgium, France, and French Indochina and within Foreign Ministry; purged by occupation; ambassador, Great Britain, 1952–53; elected, House of Representatives, 1955. 30 July 1957–22 April 1958 (House of Representatives dissolved).

Miura Kunio: b. 1895; graduated, Tokyo University, German law, 1920; career bureaucrat, rising to chief, Cabinet Bureau of Legislation and Chief Cabinet Secretary; purged by occupation; elected, House of Representatives, 1942; returned, House of Representatives after de-purge; president of private railway, 1948. 23 December 1960–30 January 1963 (deceased).

Nakamura Umekichi: b. 1901; graduated, Hōsei University, law, 1922; became lawyer; also served in several ministries; elected, House of Representatives, ten times after 1936; Justice Minister, 1956 and 1957; Construction Minister, 1960. 1 July 1958–24 October 1960 (House of Representatives dissolved).

Nishimura Naomi: b. 1905; graduated, Tokyo University, law, 1929; entered government service and specialized in police administration; governor, Kochi prefecture, 1945; elected, House of Representatives, 1949; Minister of State for Defense, 1960. 10 July 1959–22 July 1960 (released to become chairman of House of Representatives standing committee).

Ozawa Saeki: b. 1898; graduated, Nihon University, law, 1923; became lawyer, 1924; served in Tokyo city assembly; elected, House of Representatives, 1947; Transportation Minister, 1948; concurrent Communications Minister, 1949; Construction Minister, 1954; Minister of State for Administrative Management and (concurrently) Hokkaido Development, 1960. 1 July 1958–30 June 1959 (released to become chairman of House of Representatives standing committee).

Takahashi Teiichi: b. 1899; passed bar examination, 1924; graduated, Nihon University, law, 1925; became prosecutor in Aomori, 1928, and other locations; resigned and entered private practice, 1945; elected, House of Representatives, 1948. 29 July 1960–24 October 1960 (House of Representatives dissolved).

Tanaka Isaji: b. 1906; graduated, Ritsumeikan University, law, 1934; became lawyer; elected, House of Representatives, ten times after 1942; purged by occupation; Minister of State for Local Autonomy, 1956; vice speaker, House of Representatives, 1963. 10 July 1959–23 October 1963 (House of Representatives dissolved).

Tomita Kenji: b. 1897; graduated, Kyoto University, political science, 1921; entered government service and specialized in police administration; governor of Nagano prefecture; Chief Cabinet Secretary, 1940 and 1941; imperial appointee, House of Peers, 1941; purged by occupation; elected, House of Representatives, 1952. 10 July 1959–17 October 1963 (released to become chairman of House of Representatives standing committee).

Ueki Kōshirō: b. 1900; graduated, Tokyo University, law, 1925; entered Finance Ministry and rose through ranks becoming head of Monopoly Bureau, 1945; elected, House of Representatives, 1952; Justice Minister, 1960; president, Sagami Women's University, 1968. 30 July 1957–30 June 1959 (released to become chairman of House of Representatives standing committee).

Yamamoto Kumekichi: b. 1893; graduated, Meiji University, law, 1919; lawyer; head of many business firms; elected, House of Representatives, five times. 30 July 1957–22 April 1958 (House of Representatives dissolved).

FORMER COMMISSIONERS: HOUSE OF COUNCILORS

Aoyanagi Hideo: b. 1897; graduated, Tokyo University, political science, 1922; joined Yasuda Bank, 1926; entered Ministry of Home Affairs, 1927, and rose through ranks; elected, governor, Aichi prefecture, 1947; elected, House of Councilors, 1953. 17 February 1961–8 August 1962 (resigned).

Hirose Hisatada: (see entry above, under "Commissioners from among Persons of Learning and Experience"). 1 July 1958–2 May 1959 (House of Councilors term completed).

Hitotsumatsu Sadayoshi: b. 1875; graduated, Meiji School of Law, 1902; began as judge but shifted to prosecutor and then entered private practice in 1920; elected, House of Representatives, 1928; Communications Minister, 1946; Welfare Minister, 1947; Construction Minister, 1948; elected, House of Councilors, 1950. 30 July 1957–7 July 1962 (House of Councilors term completed).

Ishiguro Tadaatsu: b. 1884; graduated, Tokyo University, law, 1908; entered Ministry of Commerce and Agriculture and rose through ranks, becoming Agriculture and Forestry Minister, 1940; imperial appointee, House of Peers, 1943; Agriculture and Commerce Minister, 1945; elected, House of Councilors, 1947. 17 October 1958–7 July 1959 (resigned).

Kajiwara Shigeyoshi: b. 1900; graduated, Tokyo University, German law, 1923; entered Ministry of Agriculture and Forestry and rose through ranks; elected, House of Councilors, 1953. 30 July 1957–17 October 1958 (resigned).

Murakami Giichi: b. 1885; graduated, Tokyo University, German law, 1912; entered government service in railway work; became high official in South Manchuria Railway Co., and other railway and transportation companies; Transportation Minister and imperial appointee to House of Peers, 1945; elected, House of Councilors, 1947; Transportation Minister, 1951. 30 July 1957–31 August 1962 (resigned).

Ota Masataka: b. 1886; graduated, Tokyo University, economics, 1912; held financial posts in government; became vice-president, *Hochi Shimbun* (newspaper); president of several business firms; after 1930 elected, House of Representatives, seven times; Minister of State for Local Autonomy, 1955; elected, House of Councilors, 1959. 31 August 1962–18 October 1963 (released to become chairman of House of Councilors standing committee).

Shimojō Yasumaro: b. 1885; graduated, Tokyo University, political science, 1909; after holding important government offices, imperial appointee to House of Peers, 1940; professor, Nihon University, 1944; elected, House of Councilors, 1947; Minister of Education, 1948; president, Kōriyama Women's Junior College, 1950. 27 January 1959–7 July 1962 (House of Councilors term completed).

Sugiwara Arata: b. 1899; graduated, Osaka Higher Commercial College, 1922; entered Foreign Ministry; graduated, University of Vermont (U.S.), 1925; filled diplomatic posts in Washington, Shanghai, and Nanking; served in Foreign Ministry and wartime Greater East Asia Ministry; purged by occupation and became lawyer; elected, House of Councilors, 1950; Minister of State for Defense, 1955. 17 February 1961–7 July 1962 (House of Councilors term completed).

Tachi Tetsuji: b. 1889; graduated, Tokyo University, political science, 1914; bureaucrat, rising to governor of Tottori, Ishikawa, and Toyama prefectures and of Tokyo; elected, House of Councilors, 1951. 30 July 1957–5 December 1960 (released to become chairman of House of Councilors standing committee).

Tenbō Hirohiko: b. 1907; graduated, Tokyo University, political science, 1928; bureaucrat, specializing in transportation and railroads; vice president, National Railways Corporation, 1951; elected, House of Councilors, 1956. 7 July 1959–7 July 1962 (House of Councilors term completed).

Yoshino Shinji: b. 1888; graduated, Tokyo University, German law, 1913; Minister of Commerce and Industry, 1937; vice president, Manchuria Heavy Industrial Development Company, 1938; elected, House of Councilors, 1953; Transportation Minister, 1955; president, Musashino University. 30 July 1957–1 July 1958 (resigned).

Yuzawa Michio: b. 1888; graduated, Tokyo University, economics, 1912; bureaucrat in prefectural posts, rising to governor of Miyagi, Hiroshima, and Hyogo prefectures; Minister of Home Affairs, 1942; imperial appointee, House of Peers, 1943; purged. 31 August 1962–21 February 1963 (deceased).

FORMER COMMISSIONERS: MEN OF LEARNING AND EXPERIENCE

Kanemasa Yonekichi: b. 1892; completed primary school; associated with labor movement from early years; official of prewar social mass parties; studied labor movements in China, India, and Europe before World War II; president, Japan Confederation of Labor; member, National Public Safety Commission. 30 July 1957–28 November 1963 (deceased).

Kaya Seiji: b. 1898; graduated, Tōhoku University, physics, 1923; professor, Tōhoku, Hokkaido, Tokyo Engineering, and Tokyo universities; president, Japan Science Council, 1954; president, Tokyo University, 1957–63. 30 July 1957–17 December 1957 (resigned).

Saka Chiaki: b. 1895; graduated, Tokyo University, German law, 1919; bureaucrat in Home Affairs Ministry, rising to governor of Hyogo and Gifu prefectures and Hokkaido; member, House of Peers, 1945; became lawyer, 1946. 30 July 1957–29 May 1959 (deceased).

Selected Bibliography

1. REPORTS OF THE COMMISSION ON THE CONSTITUTION

Plenary Meetings

Kempō Chōsa Kai Dai [1–131] kai Sōkai Gijiroku [Commission on the Constitution: Minutes of the [1st to 131st] plenary meeting]. 131 vols. 1st meeting, 13/14 August 1957; 131st meeting, 3 July 1964.

Committee Meetings

Kempō Seitei no Keika ni kansuru Shoiinkai Dai [1–49] kai Gijiroku [Subcommittee on the process of the enactment of the Constitution: Minutes of the [1st to 49th] meeting]. 49 vols. 1st meeting, 16 January 1958; 49th meeting, 12 September 1961.

Kempō Chōsa Kai Dai-ichi Iinkai Dai [1–49] kai Kaigi Gijiroku [Commission on the Constitution: Minutes of the [1st to 49th] meeting of the First Committee]. 49 vols. 1st meeting, 17 September 1958; 49th meeting, 13 July 1961.

Kempō Chōsa Kai Dai-ichi Iinkai Shoiinkai Dai [1–5] kai Kaigi Gijiroku [Commission on the Constitution: Minutes of the [1st to 5th] meeting of the First Committee's subcommittee]. 5 vols. 1st meeting, 2 November 1960; 5th meeting, 21 December 1960.

Kempō Chōsa Kai Dai-ni Iinkai Dai [1–42] kai Kaigi Gijiroku [Commission on the Constitution: Minutes of the [1st to 42nd] meeting of the Second Committee]. 42 vols. 1st meeting, 17 September 1958; 42nd meeting, 19 July 1961.

Kempō Chōsa Kai Dai-ni Iinkai Shoiinkai Dai [1–5] kai Kaigi Gijiroku [Commission on the Constitution: Minutes of the [1st to 5th] meeting of the Second Committee's subcommittee]. 4 vols. (minutes of two meetings combined in one volume). 1st meeting, 27 October 1960; 5th meeting, 14 December 1960.

Kempō Chōsa Kai Dai-san Iinkai Dai [1–39] kai Kaigi Gijiroku [Commission on the Constitution: Minutes of the [1st to 39th] meeting of the Third Committee]. 39 vols. 1st meeting, 17 September 1958; 39th meeting, 21 July 1961.

Kempō Chōsa Kai Dai-san Iinkai Shoiinkai Dai [1–4] kai Kaigi Gijiroku [Commission

405

on the Constitution: Minutes of the [1st to 4th] meeting of the Third Committee's subcommittee]. 4 vols. 1st meeting, 27 October 1960; 4th meeting, 14 December 1960.

Division Meetings

Kempō Chōsa Kai Rengo Bukai Dai [1–3] kai Kaigi Gijiroku [Commission on the Constitution: Minutes of the [1st to 3rd] meeting of the combined division]. 2 vols. (minutes of the second and third meetings in one volume). 1st meeting, 21 December 1961; 2nd and 3rd meetings, 16 September and 16 October 1963.

Kempō Chōsa Kai Dai-ichi Bukai Dai [1–25] kai Kaigi Gijiroku [Commission on the Constitution: Minutes of the [1st to 25th] meeting of the first division]. 25 vols. 1st meeting, 10 January 1962; 25th meeting, 25 July 1963.

Kempō Chōsa Kai Dai-ni Bukai Dai [1–23] kai Kaigi Gijiroku [Commission on the Constitution: Minutes of the [1st to 23rd] meeting of the second division]. 23 vols. 1st meeting, 18 January 1962; 23rd meeting, 3 October 1963.

Kempō Chōsa Kai Dai-san Bukai Dai [1–30] kai Kaigi Gijiroku [Commission on the Constitution: Minutes of the [1st to 30th] meeting of the third division]. 30 vols. 1st meeting, 9 January 1962; 30th meeting, 1 October 1963.

Kempō Chōsa Kai Tokubetsu Bukai Dai [1–9] kai Kaigi Gijiroku [Commission on the Constitution: Minutes of the [1st to 9th] meeting of the special division]. 9 vols. 1st meeting, 31 January 1962; 9th meeting, 29 July 1963.

Public Hearings

Kempō Chōsa Kai Dai [1–46] kai Kōchōkai Kiroku [Commission on the Constitution:Record of the [1st to 46th] public hearing]. 46 vols. 1st hearing, 1 November 1958; 46th hearing, 20 March 1961.

Kempō Chōsa Kai Dai [1–9] kai Chikubetsu Kōchōkai Kiroku [Commission on the Constitution: Record of the [1st to 9th] regional public hearing]. 9 vols. 1st hearing, 24 February 1962; 9th hearing, 11 August 1962.

Kempō Chōsa Kai Chūō Kōchōkai Kiroku [Commission on the Constitution: Record of the central public hearing]. 1 vol.: 28/29 September 1962.

Committee Reports

Kempō Seitei no Keika ni kansuru Shoiinkai Hōkokusho [Report of the subcommittee on the process of the enactment of the Constitution], 639 pp.

Kempō Unyō no Jissai ni tsuite no Dai-ichi Iinkai Hōkokusho: Kokumin no Kenri oyobi Gimu·Shihō [Report of the First Committee on the actual operation of the Constitution: Rights and duties of the people and the judiciary], 466 pp.

Kempō Unyō no Jissai ni tsuite no Dai-ni Iinkai no Hōkokusho: Kokkai·Naikaku·Zaisei· Chihō Jichi [Report of the Second Committee on the actual operation of the Constitution: National Diet, cabinet, finances, local autonomy], 408 pp.

Kempō Unyō no Jissai ni tsuite no Dai-san Iinkai Hōkokusho: Tennō·Sensō no Hōki·

Saikō Hōki [Report of the Third Committee on the actual operation of the Constitution: Emperor, renunciation of war, and the supreme law], 308 pp.

Commission Report

Kempō Chōsa Kai Hōkokusho [Report of the Commission on the Constitution], 1,161 pp.

Appended Documents

Kempō Chōsa Kai Hōkokusho Bunsho Dai [1–12] *go* [Report of the Commission on the Constitution: Appended Document No. (1 through 12)]: (1) *Kempō Chōsa Kai ni okeru Kakuïn no Iken* [Opinions of individual members of the Commission on the Constitution], 782 pp. (2) *Kempō Seitei no Keika ni kansuru Hōkokusho* [Report on the process of the enactment of the Constitution], 781 pp. (3) *Kempō Unyō no Jissai ni tsuite no Chōsa Hōkokusho: Kokumin no Kenri oyobi Gimu·Shihō* [Report on the investigation of the actual operation of the Constitution: Rights and duties of the people and the judiciary], 466 pp. (4) *Kempō Unyō no Jissai ni tsuite no Chōsa Hōkokusho: Kokkai·Naikaku·Zaisei·Chihō Jichi* [Report on the investigation of the actual operation of the Constitution: National Diet, cabinet, finances, local autonomy], 410 pp. (5) *Kempō Unyō no Jissai ni tsuite no Chōsa Hōkokusho: Tennō, Sensō no Hōki·Saikō Hōki* [Report on the investigation of the actual operation of the Constitution: Emperor, renunciation of war, and the supreme law], 308 pp. (6) *Kihonteki Mondai ni kansuru Hōkokusho* [Report on basic problems], 135 pp. (7) *Zembun·Tennō·Sensō no Hōki·Kaisei·Saikō Hōki ni kansuru Hōkokusho* [Report on the preamble, the emperor, the renunciation of war, amendment, and the supreme law], 268 pp. (8) *Kokumin no Kenri oyobi Gimu·Shihō ni kansuru Hōkokusho* [Report on the rights and duties of the people and the judiciary], 171 pp. (9) *Kokkai· Naikaku·Zaisei·Chihō Jichi ni kansuru Hōkokusho* [Report on the National Diet, the cabinet, finances, and local autonomy], 330 pp. (10) *Kempō Mukō Ron ni kansuru Hōkokusho* [Report on the invalidity of the Constitution], 71 pp. (11) *Kōchōkai ni kansuru Hōkokusho* [Report on the public hearings], 285 pp. (12) *Kaigai Chōsa ni kansuru Hōkokusho* [Report on overseas investigations], 350 pp.
Kempō Chōsa Kai Jimukyoku [Secretariat of the Commission on the Constitution]. *Kempō Unyō no Jissai ni tsuite no Chōsa Hōkokusho (Kempō Chōsa Kai Hōkokusho Fuzoku Bunsho Dai 3-go—Dai 10-go) Sakuin* [Index to the reports on the investigation of the actual operation of the Constitution: Appended Documents Nos. 3 through 10 of the Report of the Commission on the Constitution], 91 pp.

2. Works Cited

Commission on the Constitution, Secretariat of. *Comments and Observations by Foreign Scholars on Problems concerning the Constitution of Japan, 1946.* Tokyo:

1964. (No publisher indicated). 284 pp. There is also a seven-page separately printed supplement.

Henderson, Dan Fenno, ed. *The Constitution of Japan: Its First Twenty Years, 1947–67*. Seattle and London: University of Washington Press, 1968. 323 pp.

Itoh, Hiroshi, and Beer, Lawrence Ward. *The Constitutional Case Law of Japan: Selected Supreme Court Decisions, 1961–70*. Seattle and London: University of Washington Press, 1978. 283 pp.

Maki, John M., ed. *Court and Constitution in Japan: Selected Supreme Court Decisions, 1948–60*. Seattle and London: University of Washington Press, 1964. 445 pp.

———. "The Documents of Japan's Commission on the Constitution," *J. of Asian Studies* 24, no. 3 (May 1965): 475–89.

Supreme Commander for the Allied Powers, Government Section. *Political Reorientation of Japan: September 1945 to September 1948*. U.S. Government Printing Office. (n.d. but probably 1949). 1st vol. pp. i–xxxv, 1–401; 2nd vol. (Appendices), pp. 403–1300.

Takayanagi, Kenzō. "The Conceptual Background of the Constitutional Revision Debate in the Constitution Investigation Commission," *Law in Japan: An Annual* 1 (1967):1–24. (A translation by John M. Maki of Takayanagi Kenzō, "Kempō Chōsa Kai ni okeru Kempō Rongi no Shisōteki Haikei," *Jurisuto* 309 [1 November 1964]: 36–46.)

———. "Opinion on Some Constitutional Problems: The Rule of Law" in Henderson, *The Constitution of Japan*, pp. 89–114. (A translation by John M. Maki of a section of a long opinion submitted by Professor Takayanagi to the 114th plenary session of the Commission on 19 July 1963.)

———. "Some Reminiscences of Japan's Commission on the Constitution," in Henderson, *The Constitution of Japan*, pp. 71–88.

Index

Note: This book is to a large extent self-indexed. The detailed table of contents, the mechanical organization of the report so that the content of the different sections follows the order of the articles of the Constitution, and the generous use of subtitles make it possible to track down with little difficulty the problems dealt with in the text.

This brief index provides references to items not easily located either through the table of contents or through the subtitles. See also the names of individual commissioners for references to their opinions as expressed in direct or indirect quotations.